Advanced Investments

Steve L. Slezak, Ph.D.

MACK ASRAT
FEBRUARY 2018

PUBLISHED BY:

THE GREAT COURSES
Corporate Headquarters
4840 Westfields Boulevard, Suite 500
Chantilly, Virginia 20151-2299
Phone: 1-800-832-2412
Fax: 703-378-3819
www.thegreatcourses.com

Printed in the United States of America

Steve L. Slezak, Ph.D.

Associate Professor of Finance
Director of the Carl H. Lindner III Center for Insurance and Risk Management
University of Cincinnati

Professor Steve L. Slezak is an Associate Professor of Finance and the Director of the Carl H. Lindner III Center for Insurance and Risk Management in the Carl H. Lindner College of Business at the University of Cincinnati. Before joining the University of Cincinnati, he served as a faculty member in the finance departments of the Stephen M. Ross School of Business at the University of Michigan and the Kenan-Flagler Business School at The University of North Carolina at Chapel Hill. He received his Ph.D. in Economics from the University of California, San Diego.

At the University of Cincinnati, Professor Slezak's teaching focuses on investments (including portfolio management, fixed income analytics, and derivative securities), risk management, and insurance. Until recently, he was the Faculty Advisor to the Johnson Investment Counsel Student-Managed Fund. He has received a number of awards at the University of Cincinnati, including the Harold J. Grilliot Award for Exemplary Service to Undergraduate Organizations and the Michael L. Dean Excellence in Classroom Education and Learning EXCEL Graduate Teaching Award. He also received the Weatherspoon Award for Excellence in MBA Teaching while at UNC–Chapel Hill. Professor Slezak has had various administrative and leadership roles at the University of Cincinnati, including Academic Director of MBA Programs, Undergraduate Program Director of Finance, and Finance Department Head.

Professor Slezak's recent research focuses on how informational problems adversely affect managerial incentives and the effective management of risk. More specifically, his work examines optimal portfolio construction with liquidity costs and model uncertainty, managerial and investor "short-termism," corporate fraud, and the pricing of idiosyncratic risk. The results of his research have appeared in top-tier finance and economics journals, including *The Journal of Finance*, the *Journal of Financial Economics*, *The Review of Financial Studies*, the *Journal of Financial and Quantitative Analysis*, and the *Journal of Economics and Management Strategy*. ■

Table of Contents

INTRODUCTION

LECTURE GUIDES

Table of Contents

Table of Contents

Advanced Investments

Scope:

Increasingly, individual investors have access to a wide variety of investment opportunities and a rich array of information about such opportunities. Much of this information is quantitative, providing either metrics based on mathematical models from financial economics or the raw data with which investors can conduct their own analysis. This course examines the analytical aspects of investing to allow you to produce and/or translate quantitative information so that you can create an effective investment strategy.

Because the material is analytical, the course does not shy away from quantitative methods. However, the goal of the course is to create an intuitive understanding of the underpinnings, justification, and the strategic role of each analytical method. Whether you intend to manage your own investments or delegate the management of your wealth to professionals, it is critically important to have such an understanding.

Effective investing is a 5-step process. Step 1 is to define a set of investment objectives. Step 2 is to collect and analyze information on the variety of investment opportunities available in the market. Step 3 is to react to the output of step 2 to develop and implement an investment strategy that aligns with the investment objectives. Step 4 is to evaluate the effectiveness of steps 2 and 3 relative to the objectives. Step 5 is to revise steps 2 and 3 based on the feedback from step 4—and so on. That is, effective investing is a continual process of defining, analyzing, reacting, evaluating, and revising.

The goal of this course is to provide you with a systematic and quantitative approach to each of these steps.

The examination of step 1 begins with Lecture 1, which delineates the investment goals investors might have. Lecture 2 then develops a framework for investing that combines passive investing (investing in index funds designed to "be" the market) with active strategies (actively seeking to "beat" the market). This framework lets you pick how active to be, given the demands on your time and the return from active investing. Given this context, Lecture 3 examines the evidence from psychology that humans make systematic cognitive mistakes when processing and reacting to information. This lecture warns that these mistakes negatively impact the efficacy of active investment strategies. You will also learn about the efficient market hypothesis (lectures 5 and 6), which states that market prices accurately reflect information. The goal of these lectures is to examine whether active investing is profitable. The evidence is mixed.

The analysis of step 2 begins with Lecture 7, which develops time value of money concepts and formulas, the building blocks of security valuation. Using these techniques, the course examines pricing and the sources of variability in returns for stocks and bonds. For bonds, the course examines pricing (Lecture 8), why bond yields vary with time to maturity (Lecture 9), and bond risk (including interest rate risk and credit risk metrics in lectures 10 and 11). For stocks, the course examines how value is created in firms and how that value translates into stock returns and risk (lectures 12 and 13).

For step 3 (optimal reaction), lectures 15 and 16 examine how to quantify the behavior of security returns and how to combine securities in portfolios to control risk while achieving investment portfolio growth. These lectures provide a baseline portfolio approach to investing; no particular view on active versus passive investing is taken. However, these lectures highlight one of the most important concepts of the course—namely that the efficacy of any particular investment must be assessed by considering its contribution to risk and return in an optimally formed investment portfolio. Using this insight, Lecture 17 develops the capital asset pricing model (CAPM), the most commonly used equilibrium asset pricing model. The CAPM justifies the market "beta" as the appropriate measure of risk for any security; it also specifies how efficient (or fair) prices of securities should vary with beta. In doing so, the CAPM provides a useful benchmark for active portfolio management; by specifying when a security's price is "just right," it specifies when a security is mispriced. Lecture 18 examines how to exploit mispriced securities; lectures 20–23 analyze financial options and show how they can be used to speculate or hedge risks.

Step 4 in the investment process (evaluation) is considered in Lecture 19, where a variety of commonly used performance metrics are examined. Because the best metric for evaluating a portfolio depends on the portfolio's role in the investor's overall investment strategy, a variety of potential roles and the appropriate metrics for each role are considered.

Consistent with step 5 (revision), the final lecture revisits the debate about active versus passive management in the context of empirical evidence counter to CAPM; this lecture explores multi-factor models that have been developed as alternatives to CAPM. ■

Investment Decisions and Goals

Lecture 1

There are two main goals for this course. The first goal is for you to become an informed consumer of the plethora of investment information out there. The second goal is for you to be able to identify the pros and cons of a specific investment approach and then make a conscious choice based on a full understanding of the trade-off between alternatives. In order for you to be able to optimally react and make conscious choices, it is important for you to have a well-defined objective or goal in mind. This lecture will identify a set of nontrivial potential goals an investor might have.

Return Targets and Risk

- Think about an appropriate set of goals and objectives you might have as an investor. That is, what are the different aspects of investment performance you might care about? These objectives include things like the following.
  - Return targets/benchmarks and risk
  - Time horizon and desire for bequests
  - Growth versus income, liquidity
- The first item is risk and return. If risk and return were considered separately, everyone would make trivial choices: Everyone wants high return and no risk. But there are very few things you can do that will increase your average returns without increasing risk.
- The most notable thing you can do to increase return without bearing more risk is to invest with pretax dollars via a pension fund, 401(k), or individual retirement account. These accounts either let you invest with salary before it is taxed or let you deduct your investment from your taxable income. You will be taxed eventually, but always in the future. This is better than getting taxed

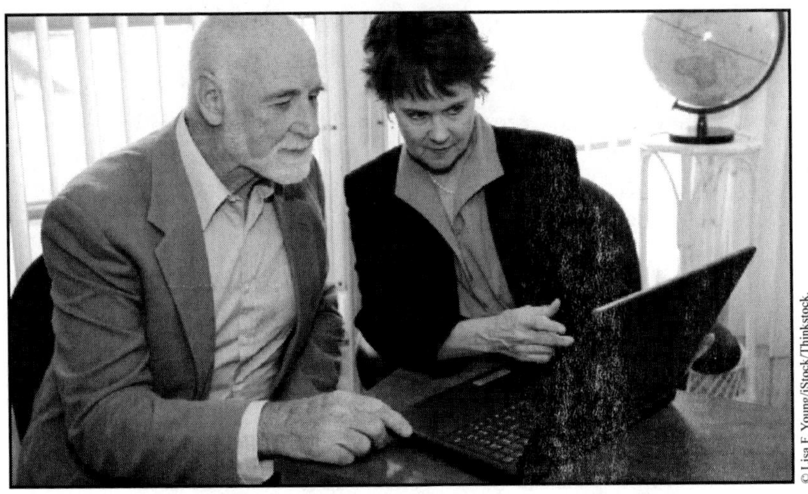
© Lisa F. Young/iStock/Thinkstock.

It is recommended that you start planning for your retirement when you are young and take an active role in managing your finances as you age.

now because you will have more of your money making money, working for you.

- Of course, there are legal limits on the amount you can invest in these ways, but you should invest as much as you can these ways. If not, you are merely increasing your taxes, with no personal benefit associated with this increased cost.

- Aside from tax strategies, most other strategies entail bearing more risk to get a higher return. As a consequence, it is important for you to reflect on your personal trade-off between risk and return. How much extra return do you have to get in order to be willing to take on a risk? Similarly, how much wealth are you willing to give up in order to shed risk? It is fairly difficult to answer these types of questions quantitatively; however, this is the kind of trade-off you will be faced with often.

- At this point, it is probably very difficult for you to quantify the trade-off between risk and return simply because it is difficult to know what risk is. The goal of this course is to give you metrics that will allow you to compare risks across securities. These metrics are also useful for quantifying the risk of a portfolio.

- There is a fairly prevalent notion that people should be less risk averse. Presumably, many entrepreneurs have risked everything to push what turned out to be the next revolutionary idea, including the Wright brothers and Steve Jobs.

- First, let's make a clear distinction between opportunities and preferences. Many of the strategies you will develop in this course are important because they provide you with a best set of opportunities within which to choose. However, within that set of best opportunities, you must decide which one of those opportunities is optimal for you. That's because what is optimal for you depends on your preferences, or how you feel about how wealth contributes to and how risk detracts from your happiness.

- Second, regarding the suggestion that everyone must take risk to succeed, there is the notion that perhaps our preferences get in the way of our opportunities—that sometimes we limit our outcomes because we underestimate what we could achieve if we just got out of our own way. Often, people systematically fail to see the full set of opportunities they could create for themselves, and because of that, they choose actions that foreclose on opportunities that would make them better off. However, the notion that you have to take risks to succeed might simply be a misguided conclusion based on bad statistics and confusion about something called conditional probability.

- A conditional probability is the probability that something will happen conditional on something else happening. With respect to risk taking and success, there are two conditional probabilities that we might calculate. One is the probability that, given that someone is successful now, they took risk in the past. The other conditional probability is the probability that, given that someone took risk in the past, they are successful now.

- If you are trying to decide whether to take risk or not, then the probability of success given risk versus the probability of success given that you don't take risk are the relevant conditional probabilities. You want to know, conditional on taking risk, how many people succeed versus fail—not, conditional on success, how many people took risk versus played it safe.

Time Horizon and Bequest Motives

- A second important dimension for an investment strategy is your time horizon. There are two aspects to this. The first has to do with the passage of time and the natural cycles of life: your age relative to retirement. While we all probably have preferences for being one age versus another, this aspect is not something you choose. The second aspect, however, is driven purely by your preferences: whether you want to consume all of your wealth eventually or whether you want to leave a legacy, or bequest.

© jerry2313/iStock/Thinkstock.

Part of your retirement plan is determining whether you want to bequest some or all of your wealth at your time of death.

- Both of these aspects matter because they affect some very basic parts of an optimal investment strategy. You view your human capital—the biggest asset you have—as part of your investment portfolio. As such, your investment strategies may be different as you get a clearer sense of what that asset is worth and how much you can alter it.

- Your goals regarding a legacy have an impact on the rate at which you should save when young and the rate at which you should consume out of savings or your investment when old. For these aspects, you should think of your investment strategy as having two dimensions: a time-series, or dynamic, dimension and a cross-sectional, or static, dimension.

- For the static dimension, you should put yourself in a particular place in your life and in a particular market condition. In each of the states, you need to consider how to allocate your wealth in that state cross-sectionally—i.e., across all of the available investments in the market.

- The dynamic part has to do with the fact that in each of these states, you may want to hold different cross-sectional portfolios. For example, you will want more risky equity when you're young and more risk-free fixed income when you're old. As a consequence, you should look ahead and make gradual adjustments from one cross-section to the next. That is, you need a dynamic transition strategy.

- Some of the changes in the "states" will be predictable, such as your age and retirement. The exact timing of other states will be much less predictable; for example, when will there be a recession? In terms of your goals and preferences, you need to figure out the extent to which you care about maintaining a given lifestyle.

Growth, Income, and Liquidity

- A third investment dimension you should come to terms with is your need for income from your investments versus your desire for growth in the value of your portfolio. For this, again you have to be careful not to mix up opportunities and preferences. You may have a definite preference—or need—for having your investments generate a steady stream of income, for example, because you are retired with no other ongoing source of income to support your monthly expenses. In contrast, if you are young and have a job that more than covers your expenses, rather than have your investments generate cash now, you may prefer that they simply grow in value over time.

- However, sometimes the growth-versus-income distinction spills over into a limit on opportunities. If you need income, then you might be tempted to only consider funds that focus on income-generating securities, such as the stocks of firms that pay high dividends. Funds that focus on growth stocks, on the other hand, invest in the equity of firms that, rather than pay dividends, reinvest their earnings back in the firm to fuel expansions and increases in the stock price.

- Thus, with the growth-versus-income objective, you typically get a difference in the types of securities considered. That is, by picking a particular objective, you may be a priori limiting the types of investment opportunities available to you.

- A better way to think about growth versus income is in terms of liquidity, which is defined in two dimensions: the time dimension and the price dimension. A liquid security is one that can be turned into cash (i.e., liquidated) very quickly, without having the price fall significantly. If, keeping the price fixed, it takes a long time to find a buyer at that price, that security is not very liquid. And, if over a short period you have to drop the price by a lot to get a buyer, then that security is also not very liquid.

- Think of the liquidity of a security as determining how costly it is to trade, with more liquid securities being cheap to trade and less liquid securities being expensive. Your desire for liquidity can be related to your objective to have your investments generate income or growth.

Time/Effort

- There is another dimension that you need to come to terms with that is not typically mentioned but is extremely important. As part of your objectives, you should view your approach to investment management not solely in terms of the growth and stability in your wealth it produces. You should also consider the cost and benefit of the time you spend managing your investments—and not doing other things, like focusing on your career, your kids or grandkids, a hobby, etc.

- Your calculus for any strategy should always consider the extra cost (in terms of time and effort, transactions costs, risk) versus the extra benefit of adopting that strategy. This principle should apply when making micro decisions, but it equally applies at the macro level, when you decide whether to manage your own investments or delegate to professionals and when you decide to adopt an active or a passive approach.

- If passive, you simply invest in a well-diversified portfolio that can be on automatic pilot. Periodically, you will have to make some adjustments, because no practically obtainable portfolio can be completely passive. In contrast, if active, you must be active on three fronts: You have to be active in collecting and analyzing information, actively respond to your analysis and trade, and continually evaluate the effectiveness of the first two.

- The key issue regarding active versus passive management is whether you can earn a high enough return on your effort and time to justify active management. Evidence will only show you the financial benefit and costs of activeness; only you can put a value on your time and attention.

Suggested Reading

Holt and Laury, "Risk Aversxion and Incentive Effects."

McGrayne, *The Theory That Would Not Die.*

· Liquidity more expensive in down mkts

1. Collect Info.
2. Act / Trade
3. Evaluate above two

Questions to Consider

1. How risk averse are you? Consider the following choices.

Table 1.1

Option A	Option B	Expected Payoff Difference (A – B)
1/10 of $2.00, 9/10 of $1.60	1/10 of $3.85, 9/10 of $0.10	$1.17
2/10 of $2.00, 8/10 of $1.60	2/10 of $3.85, 8/10 of $0.10	$0.83
3/10 of $2.00, 7/10 of $1.60	3/10 of $3.85, 7/10 of $0.10	$0.50
4/10 of $2.00, 6/10 of $1.60	4/10 of $3.85, 6/10 of $0.10	$0.16
5/10 of $2.00, 5/10 of $1.60	5/10 of $3.85, 5/10 of $0.10	-$0.18
6/10 of $2.00, 4/10 of $1.60	6/10 of $3.85, 4/10 of $0.10	-$0.51
7/10 of $2.00, 3/10 of $1.60	7/10 of $3.85, 3/10 of $0.10	-$0.85
8/10 of $2.00, 2/10 of $1.60	8/10 of $3.85, 2/10 of $0.10	-$1.18
9/10 of $2.00, 1/10 of $1.60	9/10 of $3.85, 1/10 of $0.10	-$1.52
10/10 of $2.00, 0/10 of $1.60	10/10 of $3.85, 0/10 of $0.10	-$1.85

At which point do you switch from preferring option A over option B to preferring option B over option A? If the switch occurs higher in the table, you are more risk averse than if the switch is lower in the table. Why? Does your switching point change if you multiply the dollar amounts in the table by 100? 1000? 10,000?

2. Once a person retires, he or she has more free time to spend on hobbies, family, and/or travel. If you have not yet retired, do you think you will want to spend more or less money per month when retired than when working? If you have retired, what did you expect and what actually happened relative to what you expected? Did you actually think about your spending habits prior to retirement?

Investment Decisions and Goals

Lecture 1—Transcript

Welcome to the course on advanced investments. You know, the world around us is full of messages about personal investing. Personal investing has often been at the center of public debate, for example. Following the mortgage crisis and the resulting financial crisis of 2008, much public debate focused on excessive consumer debt and a lack of financial literacy among the populous. In response, many states revised primary education curricula to include coverage of personal finance and investing.

There was also much debate about the investment implications of the Federal Reserve's quantitative easing programs following the 2008 financial crisis. These programs were designed to spur growth during the so-called "great recession" that followed the crisis by flooding the market with money to keep interest rates low. Current and future retirees, who rely on the safety and income from fixed income investments with returns that are closely tied to those of government bonds, had three major concerns.

First, with interest rates at historically low levels, the income from such investments would make it difficult to make ends meet. Second, what would happen to the value of their investments when interest rates eventually would rise? And third, what impact would the loose monetary policy have on future inflation? With the prospect of future inflation eroding the purchasing power of investments, what could investors do to protect themselves?

Less recently, there has been much debate concerning the appropriate role of the government in forcing savings for retirement and the extent to which individuals should be able to put Social Security contributions into riskier investments like stocks. The huge decline in the market in 2009 may have muted this debate, but perhaps only temporarily.

In addition to public policy debates, there are many messages about investments that come from people trying to sell something. For example, there are many books, written and published by people trying to sell books, claiming to show sure-fire strategies for getting rich. Not surprisingly, there is not much demand for books that show sure-fire strategies for losing money.

Also, there are many online brokers who are interested in selling their brokerage services that compete with each other to provide the snazziest, easy-to-use analytic tools and trade platforms in which you can invest and manage your portfolios. Since they make a commission whether you buy or sell, they just want you to trade. Perhaps with this goal in mind, the sites typically provide plenty of stimuli.

Finally there are messages from professional investment and wealth managers who want you to buy their services, all claiming that they have the expertise and unique perspective to guide you through these turbulent times and put you on a path to prosperity.

In this course, I'm not selling you get-rich schemes. I'm not selling you brokerage services, and I'm not selling you my wealth management services. I am, however, selling you what I think I can provide as a professor. As a professor, my job is not to simply provide information or to tell you what to think. Rather, I think my job as a professor is to teach you how to think for yourself.

With this in mind, I have two main goals for the course. First, I want you to be an informed consumer of the plethora of information on investments that's out there. I want you to be able to separate the wheat from the chaff and be able to know how to optimally respond when you find an actual kernel of truth.

Second, I want you to be able to identify the pros and the cons of specific investment approaches, and then be able to make a conscious choice based on a full understanding of the trade-offs between these alternatives.

In order for you to be able to optimally react and make conscious choices, it's important for you to have well-defined objectives or goals in mind. In this lecture, we will identify a set of non-trivial potential goals an investor might have. By non-trivial, I mean things that are more subtle than "I want to be reach now and forever." When it comes to wealth, it's obvious that more is better. What might be less obvious is how important liquidity is to you. How important is risk? How important is being able to leave a legacy, either to members of your family or a cause that you hold dear?

So let's think about an appropriate set of goals and objectives you might have as an investor. That is, what are the different aspects of investment performance you might care about? These objectives include things like return targets or benchmarks and risk, time horizon, and a desire for bequests. Growth versus income and liquidity. Investors may differ in the dimensions that they think are the most important. My hope is that the discussion in this lecture allows you to identify what is most important to you.

Let's go through each objective separately. The first item is risk and return. I have paired these together because, if considered alone, everyone would make a trivial choice. Everyone wants high return and no risk. There are very few things you can do that will increase your average returns without increasing risk.

The most notable thing that you can do to increase return without bearing more risk is to invest with pre-tax dollars via a pension fund, a 401(k), or an individual retirement account. These accounts either let you invest with salary before it is taxed or let you deduct your investment from your taxable income. You'll be taxed eventually, but always in the future. This is better than getting taxed now because you will have more of your money making money, or working for you. In fact, let's say that your return on your investment is R per dollar per year. You invest for T years before getting taxed, and your tax rate, let's say, is x. Then for every dollar you invest pre-tax, you will have $x(1 - x)[(1 + R)^T - 1]$ more dollars after T years—after you pay the tax then.

So, for example, if your tax rate is 25%, the annual return is 10%, and you invest for 20 years before you retire, you will have about \$5 for every dollar invested pre-tax rather than \$4 if you invest post-tax. If you invest for 30 years, then you will have \$16 rather than \$13 for each dollar invested, and if the return is 15% rather than 10%, you will have nearly \$62 rather than \$50 after 30 years. The point is that it adds up.

Of course, there are legal limits to the amount that you can invest this way, but, you should invest as much as you can this way. If not, you're merely increasing your taxes with no personal benefit associated with this increased cost. I should note, the tax rules and policy can be very complex and nuanced. If the rules are unclear to you or ambiguous in any way, given some "tax-advantaged" investment vehicle, I suggest consulting a tax expert before taking any leaps.

Aside from tax strategies, most other strategies entail bearing more risk to get a higher return. As a consequence, it is important for you to reflect on your personal trade-off between risk and return. How much extra return do you have to get in order to be willing to take a risk? Similarly, how much wealth are you willing to give up in order to shed a risk? It's fairly hard to answer these types of questions quantitatively. Yet, this is the kind of trade-off you will be faced with often.

There are some online surveys you can take that determine how much you dislike risk. These surveys typically ask a series of questions like, "Which do you prefer: a 50-50 chance at $10,000 or $2000, or a 50-50 chance at $9000 and $2500?" The surveys then assume that your preferences can be described mathematically by a specific function, which has a parameter called the coefficient of risk aversion. This coefficient is supposed to characterize your aversion to risk. Once the survey calibrates the coefficient to your answers, then the calibrated function can be used to determine your preferences over other investment alternatives.

This strikes me as kind of an odd exercise. The survey makes some assumption about the form of your preferences, then forces your answers to fit that function, and then uses the function to determine your preferences. Don't you know your preferences naturally? Rather than go through this survey process, I think it is better for you to simply reflect on a particular choice you might be facing. What choices will allow you to sleep at night, and what choices make you nervous?

At this point, it is probably very hard for you to quantify the trade-off between risk and return simply because it is very hard to know what risk is. My goal with this course is to give you metrics that will allow you to compare risk across securities. These metrics are also useful for quantifying the risk of a portfolio.

Another thing that I want to discuss with respect to the trade-off between risk and return is the fairly prevalent notion that people should be less risk-averse. How many times have you heard, "If you want to be rich, you have to take risks. Go for greatness and swing for the fences"? This presumably is the story behind many entrepreneurs who risked everything to push what turned out to be the next revolutionary idea—like the Wright brothers and manned flight, Steve Jobs and the iPod, Elon Musk and PayPal, Tesla Motors and, now, travel at 800 miles per hour in frictionless pneumatic tubes.

On this, I have two comments. First, I want to make clear the distinction between opportunities and preferences. Many of the strategies we will develop in the course are important because they provide you with the best set of opportunities within which you can choose. For example, in Lecture 15 we will discuss how to combine securities together into a variety of optimal portfolios. These portfolios are optimal in the sense that, for any level of risk, they have the highest average return; and, for any level of average return, they have the lowest possible risk.

With the techniques developed in that lecture, you'll be able to improve your opportunities to include that set of best portfolios. But, within the set of best opportunities, I cannot tell you which ones are optimal for you. That's because what is optimal for you depends upon your preferences, and how much you feel about what's the trade-off between wealth and risk, and how much risk detracts from your happiness.

The second point I want to make regarding the suggestion that everyone should probably be less risk-averse concerns the notion that sometimes your preferences get in the way of your opportunities; that sometimes we limit our outcomes because we underestimate what we could achieve if we just got out of our own way. As you will see when we discuss behavioral biases in investing, I am a bit sympathetic to this view. I do believe that often people systematically fail to see the full set of opportunities they could create for themselves and, because of that, they choose actions that foreclose on opportunities that would make them better off. However, I also think that the notion that you have to take risks to succeed might simply be a misguided conclusion based upon bad statistics and a confusion about something called conditional probability.

Let me explain further. A conditional probability is the probability that something will happen conditional on something else happening. With respect to risk-taking and success, there are two conditional probabilities that we might calculate. One is the probability that, given that somebody is successful now, that they took risks in the past. The other conditional probability is the probability that, given that somebody took risk in the past, they are successful now.

What is typically reported is the former probability—the probability that someone we know is successful took risk. We hardly ever talk about people who are not successful, mainly because we don't know who they are. They're not successful.

But which conditional probability is relevant for you? If you're trying to decide whether to take a risk or not, then the probability of success given risk versus the probability of success given that you don't take risk, those are the relevant conditional probabilities. You want to know, conditional on taking risk, how many people succeed versus fail—not, conditional on success, how many people took risk versus played it safe.

To see the difference, consider the following simple example. Let's say we have a sample of 100 people who are perfectly representative of the population as a whole. Out of the population as a whole, we've got 100 people. Let's say that out of that 100 people, there are 80 that took risk and 20 that did not, and out of the 100, 44 turned out to be successful while 56 did not.

Typically, what is reported is the frequency with which successful people took risk. That is, what is reported is the probability of risk-taking conditional on being successful. To calculate that probability, we would need to know how many out of the 44 that turned out successful took risk. Let's say that 32 out of the 44 of the successful people took risk, while 12 out of the 44 successful people played it safe. Thus, the probability of taking risk given success is simply 32 divided by 44, or 72.7%.

Most reporters condition on success because they don't interview unsuccessful people. Reporters interview successful people because they are successful, and they start to notice that many, in fact, most, in this case, took risk. That's a story. And in order to increase your chance of being successful, you have to take risk, right? Wrong.

To see that the conclusion that you should take risk is wrong in this case, let's look at the data again. What you really want to know is, what is the probability of success, given that you take risk. Remember that out of the 100 people in total, 80 took risks, and out of those 80, 32 were successful—those are the 32 same successful people that we looked at before. So, the probability of success given risk taking is 32 divided by 80, or 40%. What, then, is the probability of success given no risk taking? Well, out of the 100 in total, only 20 did not take risk, and out of those 20, 12 were successful. So, the probability of success given no risk-taking is 12 divided by 20, which is 60%.

Thus, the best policy is to play it safe. Thus, the news reports are misleading. That is, the probability of risk-taking given success does not tell you what you want to know.

Perhaps what is really being said in news reports is that people tend to measure risk wrong and avoid taking what they perceive is risk, but actually isn't. Thus, rather than saying you should take risks, the advice should be something like "Rather than just assume something is risky, you should be careful to measure the risk correctly and seize good opportunities that present themselves."

While this is not as catchy as "Go for greatness," it is good advice, and I will show you how to measure risk correctly in the course. But it's going to be up to you to decide how much risk you feel you're comfortable with.

A second important dimension for an investment strategy is your time horizon. There are two aspects to this. The first has to do with the passage of time and the natural cycles of life—your age relative to retirement. While we all probably have preferences for being one age versus another, this aspect is something that you don't get to choose. The second aspect, however, is driven purely by your preferences—whether you want to consume all of your wealth eventually, or whether you want to leave a legacy or a bequest.

Both of these aspects matter because they affect some very basic parts of an optimal investment strategy. For example, the conventional wisdom is that you should invest more heavily in riskier securities when you are young. This is not because you are less risk-averse when young, but rather because a poor outcome is likely to be less costly when you are young than when you are older.

This makes sense if you think of your overall investment portfolio as including the biggest asset you have, which is your human capital. When young, this asset typically generates a stream of salary payments that can substitute for the cash flows generated by investments. When young, you have some flexibility to alter or rebalance the human capital part of your portfolio along with other parts in reaction to market conditions. After retirement, you typically have far less flexibility. You should view your human capital as a part of your investment portfolio. As such, your investment strategies may be different as you get a clearer sense of what that asset is really worth, or how much you can alter it.

Your goals regarding a legacy have an impact on the rate at which you should save when young and the rate at which you should consume out of the savings for your investments when you're old. In Lecture 7 we will examine the set of calculations which will give you guidance on this specific matter.

For these aspects, you should think of your investment strategy as having two dimensions—a time-series, or a dynamic dimension, and a cross-sectional, or a static dimension. For the static or cross-sectional dimension, you should put yourself in a particular place in your life and in a particular market condition. For example, retired at the start of a recession, or maybe 10 years into a career with multiple opportunities for advancement based upon performance in a mild expansionary economy. Something like that. In each of these states, you need to consider how you would allocate your wealth in that state cross-sectionally, across all of the different available investments in the market at that time.

The dynamic part has to do with the fact that in each of these states you may want to hold different cross-sectional portfolios. For example, as we discussed earlier, you'll want a more risky equity portfolio when young and more risk-free fixed income investments when old. As a consequence, you should look ahead and make gradual adjustments from one cross-section to the next. That is, you need a dynamic transition strategy.

Some of the changes in the states will be predictable, such as your age and retirement. The exact timing of other states will be much less predictable. For example, when will there be a recession? When we discuss the Capital Asset Pricing Model, or CAPM, in Lecture 17, we will see how you should approach such transitions.

For now, just recognize that, in terms of your goals and preferences, you need to figure out the extent to which you care about maintaining a given lifestyle. Now, let me be clear. I don't want to focus on the lifestyle part. Rather, I want you to come to terms with the maintaining part. That is, I'm not saying you need to decide whether you want to have the lifestyles of the rich and famous or the lifestyle of a pauper. Of course, we'd prefer to be rich rather than poor. What I am asking is how important is it to you, whatever the level of your wealth, that you be able to maintain that level in the sense that there are not going to be huge variations in that level over time.

Most of us have the goal of limiting the downside once we get to a particular level. That is, most like to ratchet up, but not ratchet down. If that is your goal, there are strategies to help you achieve that goal, and we'll consider those in a subsequent lecture in the course.

A third investment dimension you need to come to terms with is your need for income from your investments versus your desire for growth in the value of your portfolio. For this, again you have to be careful not to mix up opportunities and preferences. You may have a definite preference—or need—for having your investments generate a steady stream of income, say because you are retired with no other ongoing source of income to support your monthly expenses. In contrast, if you're young and have a well-paying job that more than covers your expenses, rather than have your investments generate cash now, you may prefer that you have the investment simply grow in value over time.

But, sometimes the growth-versus-income distinction spills over into a limit on opportunities. If you need income, then you might be tempted to only consider funds that focus on income-generating securities, such as stocks of firms that pay high dividends. Funds that focus on growth stocks, on the other hand, invest in equity in firms that, rather than pay dividends, reinvest their earnings back into the firm to fuel expansion and increases in the stock price. Thus, with the growth-versus-income objective, you typically get a difference in the types of securities considered. That is, by picking a particular objective, you may be a priori limiting the types of investment opportunities available to you.

I think a better way to think about growth versus income is in terms of liquidity. Liquidity is defined in two dimensions—the time and the price dimension. A liquid security is one which can be turned into cash, i.e., liquidated, very quickly, without having the price fall significantly. If, keeping the price fixed, it takes a long time to find a buyer at that price, that security is not very liquid. And, if over a short period of time you have to drop the price a lot to get a buyer, then that security is also not very liquid. Housing is a very illiquid asset. Shares in Procter & Gamble are very liquid assets. Corporate bonds are somewhere in between.

We will examine liquidity in detail in a subsequent lecture. For now, simply think of liquidity of a security as determining how costly it is to trade, with more liquid securities being cheaper to trade and less liquid securities being more expensive.

Your desire for liquidity can be related to your objective to have your investments generate income or growth. If a security does not pay dividends, but it is very liquid, you can always generate income from that security merely by liquidating a small fraction periodically. If, however, that security is not liquid, such a strategy will be overly costly. In that case, you'll want to consider more liquid securities or securities that pay dividends.

You can think of dividends as periodic liquidity provided by the firm. The issue, then, is whether the liquidity provided by a dividend paying stock is cheaper or more expensive than that from a growth stock that can be sold quickly with little price concession. We will examine how to measure the liquidity of a security so that, if you have a need for your investments to create a steady stream of income, you can quantify the trade-off between investing in growth versus income securities.

Also, even if you don't have a need for the trade-off to generate income, you may want to think about liquidity anyway. This is true since liquidity is something that people demand when they need cash. There are some things for which people need cash that are typically related to life-cycle events, such as college education for their kids, a wedding, retirement, et cetera. These types of events mostly occur independently of market conditions.

Other reasons people need cash may be related to market conditions. The best example is when there is a recession and many people lose their jobs and need to liquidate some investments in order to replace lost wages or salary. Unless this possibility is anticipated and planned for, this can be problematic since, for most securities, liquidity is more expensive in down markets, exactly when you need it the most.

With the liquidity metrics developed in a subsequent lecture, you will be able to identify securities that are likely to have relatively good liquidity in down markets and, based upon that, hold some of these securities as a precaution. Realize, however, that because you will likely not be the only investor seeking such securities, securities that are liquid in downturns may be very expensive. The issue you have to contend with is, how important is it to you that you be able to maintain a given lifestyle in both up and down markets. If that is very important to you, then the extra expense of these securities may be worth it. While I can show you how to measure the cost, it's up to you to decide whether it is worth it.

There is one other dimension that you need to come to terms with that's not typically mentioned, but I think is extremely important. As part of your objectives, you need to view your approach to investment management not solely in terms of the growth and stability in the wealth that it produces. You should also consider the cost and the benefit of the time you spend managing your investments, and not doing other things like focusing on your career, your kids or grandkids, a hobby, something else.

Your calculus for any strategy should always consider, what is the extra cost, in terms of time and effort, transactions costs, risk, say, versus the extra benefit of adopting that strategy? This principle should apply when making micro-decisions, such as, for example, deciding whether to look more closely at REITs versus MLPs (Master Limited Partnerships). This principle equally applies at the macro level, when you decide whether to manage your own investments or delegate it to professionals, and when you decide to adopt an active or a passive strategy.

If passive, you simply invest in a well-diversified portfolio that can be put on automatic pilot. Periodically, you'll have to make some adjustments since practically obtainable portfolios that are available can't be completely passive. In contrast, if active, you must be active on three fronts. One, you have to be active in collecting and analyzing information; two, you have to actively respond to your analysis and trade; and, three, you have to continually evaluate the effectiveness of the first two. In Lecture 24, we will examine a set of performance evaluation metrics that you can use to evaluate your performance and that of the professionals that you might delegate your investment portfolio to.

The key issue regarding active versus passive management is whether you can earn a high enough return on your effort and time to justify the active management. It's a bit too soon for us to examine the evidence on this, because you need to have a much better sense of what active versus passive management entails. But realize that any evidence will only show you the financial benefit and costs of activeness. Only you can put a value on your time and your attention. My guess is that, for many of you, the time spent on investing will be intellectually stimulating, so much so that you won't view it as a cost at all. Thank you very much.

A Framework for Investing

Lecture 2

For investments, so much is driven by the aggregate behavior of many, many investors all expressing their views through a market. To the extent that the aggregate beliefs of investors can be subject to both whim and information, it is very difficult to know what current prices mean. There is a framework within which to consider investments, and you will learn the structure of that framework in this lecture. You will learn how you can layer various types of active management strategies on top of a passive market portfolio.

Step 1

- This framework lets you see exactly where you might be able to add value and how to evaluate whether you are actually adding value. This framework can also be useful for seeing where and whether a professional is adding value for you.

- Step 1 is to start with a passive portfolio, one that mirrors every security in the world. While such a portfolio will be difficult to build on your own (because it will be too expensive), many mutual fund companies (like Fidelity or Vanguard) offer index funds that are designed to mirror broad-based indexes, which themselves are like portfolios of securities selected by some criterion.

- Spend some time looking on the Internet to find either index funds or exchange-traded funds (ETFs), which are supposed to track such indexes as the S&P 500, the Russell 2000, and the MSCI. Because these funds are just supposed to track an index (that is, when the index goes up 1%, the fund increases in value by 1%, too), the managers of these funds are not actively managing the fund by trying to find securities or form positions that will outperform the index. Thus, you want to find a fund or an ETF with the lowest fees and the lowest tracking error.

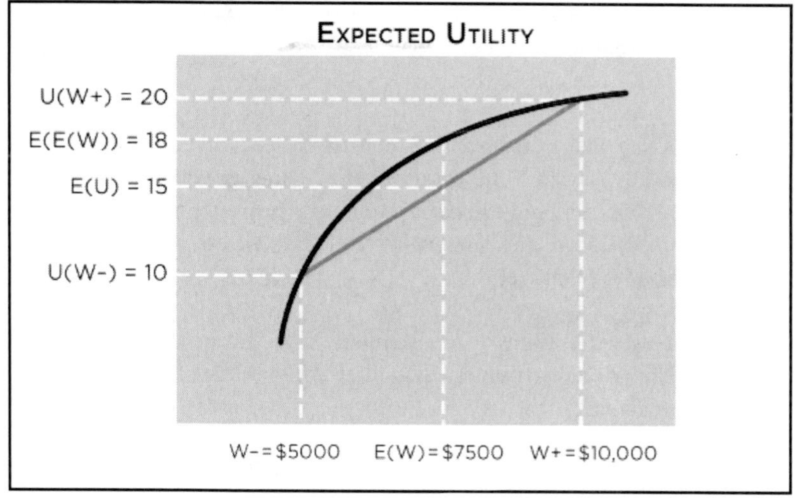

- An ETF is a closed-end fund. Think of an ETF as merely a firm that, instead of owning machines, buildings, and raw materials, owns financial securities. Thus, you can buy and sell shares in these ETF firms.

- Many specialized ETFs are formed to mirror the returns of a specific sector (such as consumer goods, financials, health care, technology, utilities, services, etc.) or an industry (such as automobiles, telecommunications, etc.) within a specific sector. In fact, they tell you exactly what they hold. Thus, because there are market prices for the securities they hold, it is fairly easy to know what the value of the ETF is—it's simply the value of the portfolio they hold.

Step 2

- Now that we have a passive portfolio that represents all of the sectors and locations across the globe, we know, at a minimum, we will be able to capture the returns on the "market." The idea is that because people typically don't like risk, they discount the prices of the securities in the market below the value that they will generate in the future, on average. Because people are risk averse and discount prices, there is a positive average return associated with investing.

- Step 1 assures you that you will get growth on your savings. In step 2, you want see if you can beat the market in some way. There are a few ways you can do that.

- Let's say that you have a bunch of ETFs for each sector. And, because we want to be passive, we're going to want to divide the money we're going to invest into amounts to invest in each sector in proportion to the amount of wealth these sectors represent in terms of total market cap.

- That is, we want to determine what fraction of the total amount of money invested in the world that is invested in the manufacturing sector, for example. We invest that fraction in a manufacturing sector ETF. And whatever fraction of the total money invested is invested in financials, we invest that fraction of our money in a financial sector ETF—and so on. If we do that, we will have a passive portfolio. We will own the market.

Beating the Market

- With this structure, there are three things that you can do to beat the market—that is, to get a bigger return than the market return. The first thing you can do is to try to "time" the market. You have all of the money you want to invest in this market portfolio of risky securities. The broadest thing you can do to beat the market is to get out of the market and into low-risk treasury bonds if you think the market is going to go down.

- Of course, this raises a bunch of questions, including which bonds to buy. But the main point is that you can beat the market by moving money in and out of treasuries. If the market is going to out-perform treasuries, then take money out of the savings account and buy stock. But if you think the market is going to fall, then take your money out of the market and put it in treasuries.

- It is likely that there are significant differences in the risks of all stock versus all treasuries, but if you can predict which market will do better, then there is no risk—you always get the higher of the two returns. If you think it is impossible to predict which market will do better, then there is a big difference in risk, and a better approach would be to hold some in treasuries and some in stock.

- For example, if you start out with 40% safe treasuries and 60% global stock, then you can try to do better by upping the 60% in stock when you think stocks are going to do well and upping the 40% on treasuries when you think stocks might tank. This is asset allocation—that is, you must decide how to allocate your investment across asset types, with stocks and bonds being the two most common types.

- Holding fixed the amount you have in stock versus treasuries, the second thing you can do is to reallocate money across sectors. This is easy to do if you have sector funds or ETFs. Just sell off some of your position in one ETF and use the proceeds to buy more of another ETF in a different sector. This makes sense if you think that the return in the sector you sell will be lower than the return in the sector you buy into. In a sense, you are timing not the "market," but across sectors.

- The third thing you can do is, while holding fixed the amount you whave in risky securities and holding fixed the amount you have within each sector, you can try to find individual securities within a sector that you think may outperform that sector. This is stock picking. The idea is that you can, by studying individual securities, find those that you think are undervalued and will go up a lot. While this stock may be in your ETF already, it will likely represent a very small fraction of the ETF.

- For some ETFs for fairly broadly defined sectors, the biggest stock held by the ETF will represent only a few percent, with many ETFs holding hundreds of securities. For some sectors defined by a few very large firms, a single firm may be 10 to 15% of the ETF.

- This way of thinking about an investment portfolio makes clear what you need to do to justify moving away from a passive "market" portfolio. In order for you to do any of the three things noted to beat the market, you have to make clear why you think stocks will do better than treasuries, why one sector or industry will do better than some other sector or industry, and why an individual stock you want to buy will do better than the sector or industry that that stock resides in as a whole. You must convince yourself.

- There are two things you need to do to convince yourself. The first is to understand the sector or industry. What allows some firms to make higher profits than others? Is that sustainable or contestable? If something is going to change in the future, what makes one firm better than another at adjusting to these changing conditions? And if the market is going to change in some way in the future, what changes favor one firm over another? It is important to have clarity on exactly what you are betting on.

- Once you know that you have a firm that will do better under one circumstance than another, then you know what you're betting on, and you can be more focused in collecting information that will help you characterize the likelihood that that firm will do better than others.

- On the other side, think about what might go wrong. Is the company you are looking at one that has an advantage now? How typical is it that such advantages are short lived—that other firms can leapfrog over them in terms of technology? Is there a risk that something big may fail? How common is such an event?

- Basically, think about what would make a particular firm experience a significant loss. If you cannot think of such a loss, then that's good. But if you can, then ask yourself, why you would buy just that firm when you could own many such firms? The chance of all of them having a catastrophic failure is much lower than any one of them having such a failure. If you can think of any sources for such failures or think that such failures are common, then you better be sure about your bet paying off before you expose yourself to such a bad outcome.

- Once you have a clear picture of what you are betting on will and won't happen, the second thing you have to do is ask yourself whether or not the market already knows and reflects what you know. A company that is run better than another is not necessarily a better investment; it is only a better investment if its superiority is not already valued by the market.

- The fourth thing you have to do once you have convinced yourself that it is not reflected by the market is to ask yourself what other things that you may not have thought about may be reflected in the market—what may keep the price low because that is where it should be.

Suggested Reading

Bernstein, *The Investor's Manifesto.*

Bogle, *Common Sense on Mutual Funds.*

———, *The Little Book of Common Sense Investing.*

Swensen, *Unconventional Success.*

Questions to Consider

1. You have a choice between buying an ETF of insurance company stocks or spending the same money on the stock of a single insurance company. Which makes you feel more comfortable: being able to know something about the single stock but having little diversification across insurance companies or having some diversification within the insurance industry but perhaps not knowing as much about each of the stocks in the ETF?

2. The passive "market" portfolio consists of all the securities traded in the world. What is your guess at the fraction of the world's portfolio that comes from securities from U.S.-based companies? What do you think is the relative size of the fraction of the U.S. security portfolio that is U.S. government debt versus U.S. corporate debt?

A Framework for Investing

Lecture 2—Transcript

Until very recently, I was the faculty advisor to the Johnson Investment Counsel Student-Managed Fund at the University of Cincinnati. The student-run fund is a small fund, with about a half a million dollars invested in stocks, bonds, and alternative investment vehicles like Real Estate Investment Trusts, or REITs, and Master Limited Partnerships, or MLPs.

In some ways, you and my student managers may be very similar. You and they have heard a bunch of stuff, from courses and off the web, about investing and are not quite sure what to think about it all. That's likely because there are so many conflicting messages. In the case of my university students, the college itself sends mixed messages. In the classroom, most finance professors preach market efficiency, which suggests passively holding a broad index fund. But the flat screen TV monitor in the lobby runs financial news programming with guests touting active management, saying things like, "There are really good buying opportunities out there in the consumer durables sector for those who are willing to get on the train before it leaves the station."

You and they may also be intimidated by both the amount of material and the material itself. Much of the material can be fairly mathematical with a heavy emphasis on statistics. Sometimes it seems like the mathematics is just there to obscure something that is really common sense. Other times, the material doesn't seem to make any kind of sense, common or otherwise.

My role as a faculty advisor to the fund is unlike the typical role played by faculty in lecture-style courses. In lecture-style courses, the professor usually tells the students what to think. With the fund, I let the students decide what they should be thinking about, what they should be doing, and how they should be doing it. Ironically, this freedom often paralyzes them, making them reluctant to make a decision at all. They're so used to thinking that there is a correct answer. They don't understand that there are no text book answers or easy-to-follow recipes for success at investing in the real world. Rather, because markets reflect the aggregate behavior of many investors, who collectively have beliefs that are equal parts whim and useful information, it is very hard to know what the market is saying, let alone predict what it might do.

Furthermore, many of my student managers are working on the fund basically in their spare time, on top of course work, exams, papers, internships, part-time jobs, and worries about who they are going to go out with on Thursday night.

So that my student managers are not overwhelmed, I needed a framework that would allow them to add value—but also a framework that would be okay if it had some benign neglect. I also felt that each student could gain confidence by being able to become an expert in a particular area, either a type of security, say, equity versus fixed income; or a sector, say, manufacturing versus consumer discretionary; or an industry, say, entertainment versus pharmaceuticals.

I think the framework I developed for them will be useful for you too, my other students. While my guess is that most of you are not worried about who you are going to go out with on Thursday night, or any other night, my guess is also that most of you have significant demands on your time also, and also need a framework that is open to varying degrees of activity and will allow you to focus on some specific areas of interest to you.

The framework is useful from a pedagogical viewpoint as well. It lets you see exactly where you might be able to add value. It also lets you see how to evaluate whether you're actually adding value. I should note here that while I've been talking about what you can do, all of the material covered in this course also applies if you delegate management of your investments to a professional manager. This framework is useful for seeing where and whether the professional is adding value for you.

Let me describe the framework. Although I said there is no simple, easy-to-follow recipe for investing in the real world, you can think of the framework as being similar to one of the "mother" sauces in French cuisine. There are six such sauces: the milk-and-flour based Béchamel, the light-and-dark-stock-based Velouté and Espagnole, and the emulsified egg-based Hollandaise and Mayonnaise, and, finally, the Vinaigrette, based on oil and some sort of acid like vinegar or citrus juice. Each one of these mother sauces has its own basic recipe.

The mother sauce for my investing framework is a completely passive portfolio. In French cooking, you add ingredients to the mother sauce to get the different variants. For example, if you add tarragon to a hollandaise, you get a béarnaise sauce. Cheese to a béchamel yields a sauce mornay, and red wine to an espagnole produces a bordelaise, and so on. With the investment framework, you don't add different securities. Rather, you add different types of active investment strategies on top of the passive mother portfolio.

So, to summarize, the investing framework consists of two main steps. Step one is to form the mother sauce. Step two is to add layers of activity. Later in the course, we will discuss a critical step three, which is to evaluate the efficacy of the activity in step two. Let's discuss each one of these first two steps in turn.

In principle, the mother portfolio should be a completely passive portfolio that mirrors the market. What do I mean by a passive portfolio? By passive I mean a portfolio that doesn't need tending—one that doesn't need you to actively trade. As we will see there is no perfectly passive portfolio. You'll have to do a certain amount of maintenance that I'll describe in later lectures, but for now, simply think of it as a buy-and-hold strategy.

Next, what do I mean by "the market"? Well, theoretically speaking, I mean every security in the world. Of course, that's not going to be practical, so let me expand on what I mean by "the market," and why such a portfolio might be desirable, at least in theory. After that, we can discuss how you can get close to that ideal in the real world.

Theoretically, the market portfolio consists of all the assets, including stocks and bonds, in the world, in proportion to each asset's contribution to the total value of assets in the world. This last part is really important. In general, a portfolio is defined by two things. One, the set of securities contained in it, and two, the fraction of the portfolio's total value contained in each security. If we consider only portfolios that contains every asset in the world—a long list indeed—then the difference between any two portfolios can be characterized solely by how the total portfolio is allocated across the assets. That is, different portfolios have different portfolio weights, where the weight placed on any one asset is the fraction of the total portfolio value invested in that asset.

You can think of these weights as the weights in a weighted average. The weights all sum to one. Those assets that get more weight will have a bigger impact on the average. For example, let's say you have $500,000 in which to build a portfolio. An equally weighted portfolio of the equities in the S&P 500 firms (the 500 largest companies in the United States) will have no weight placed on fixed income securities, such as government or corporate bonds, but will have 1/500 of the total value—or, in this case, $1000—invested in each of the stocks of the firms on the S&P 500 list.

Contrast this with a value-weighted S&P 500 portfolio. A value-weighted S&P 500 portfolio will again just allocate weights to the equities of S&P 500 firms, but now, in contrast to the equally-weighted portfolio, the weight placed on the 3-M Corporation, for example, will be approximately 21 times larger than the weight placed on Abercrombie and Fitch, because the value of the outstanding shares of stock in Abercrombie and Fitch is only $3.85 billion, whereas the market value of 3-M is about 21 times bigger at $81 billion. The return on the value-weighted S&P 500 portfolio will be more sensitive to the return on 3-M than on Abercrombie and Fitch. And the return on the equally-weighted S&P 500 portfolio is equally sensitive to Abercrombie and Fitch as 3-M.

Back to my original question. What do I mean by "the market"? I mean a value-weighted portfolio of all of the assets in the world. Thus, in addition to including the stocks in the S&P 500, we also need to include the stocks of large non-U.S. firms, the stocks of mid-sized and small companies, both domestic and foreign, the corporate bonds of these firms, the government bonds of every country, the securities included under alternative investments, such as REITs and MLPs, and commodities, like gold, oil, wheat, silver, et cetera.

The idea of passive investing is that you give up trying to pick winners, but you still want the return from those winners. So, instead of the spending effort trying to identify the set of securities that might be winners, you simply hold everything to ensure that you don't miss out on the returns from the winners.

Of course, I'm sure you are saying to yourself, "But don't I also not miss out on the losers?" That's true, but that might be okay on average. If everyone is worried about the losers like you, then the market prices of all those assets will reflect discounts such that, on average, you will be able to make money. Given this discounting, those securities that turn out to be winners will go up by more than without the discounting, and those that turn out to be losers will go down by less. On average, you're good, and you haven't spent much effort.

This actually reminds me of something that happened while I was in graduate school. One of my officemates shared a house with somebody who attended the Culinary Institute of America and worked as a line cook at a high-end restaurant downtown. We all liked to cook and eat, and we'd get together periodically to make elaborate meals of things like salmon and *duxelles en croute*. It was the '80s, after all.

The line cook heard about a customer at the restaurant whose husband, a wine lover and collector, had recently passed. Prior to his passing he had amassed what some thought was a pretty good collection of wine, consisting of thousands of cases—more than anyone could drink in many lifetimes. Many of the cases were unmarked and still in boxes. Since his wife didn't care about or know about wine, she decided to sell it all. And, since she didn't want to go to the trouble of opening all the unmarked cases, she decided just to auction them off blind.

The debate at one of our dinners was whether this made any sense, whether this was good for her, or good for the buyers, and did we want to pool our meager resources and bid on a case. In the end, as a line cook and a couple of Ph.D. students on miniscule stipends, we just couldn't justify the expense of a luxury item like wine. But, we did conclude that it would be likely be a good deal for most buyers and a bad deal for her.

Given the uncertainty about the quality of the wine, buyers would likely pay fairly little, so that the average return compensated them for the risk. We also concluded that the people that would do best would be those who could buy many cases. Anyone who bought a representative random sample of many cases would likely to get some above-average cases that would offset the below-average cases. If we just bought one unmarked case, there was no chance that half would be good and the other half bad. Rather, it would either be all be good or all bad, and that was too risky for us. Since we could afford, at most, one case, we decided to pass.

This is very similar to the situation with a passive portfolio. If you buy a portfolio of everything, there will be winners that offset the losers. And, since most people can't tell which is which a priori, the average price of the whole is likely to generate a decent return.

So, this is why, to start, I want a portfolio of everything. But why a value-weighted portfolio? There are a couple of reasons for that. First, what's the alternative? To buy one share of everything? Realize that the number of shares a company issues is fairly arbitrary. They could have issued twice as many shares at half the price. If they had, your one share would represent only half the exposure to the firm's prospects than if they had issued half those shares. Furthermore, many firms are comprised of divisions or subsidiaries that could be, and in many cases have been, spun off and traded as separate entities. So, one share in a conglomerate represents a different amount of resources than one share in a single division firm. We don't want our passive portfolio to be determined by these somewhat arbitrary things. Rather, we want our passive portfolio, like the wine cases, to be a representative selection. A value-weighted portfolio is just that; it is equivalent to owning a fixed fraction of all of the productive resources in the world. If 3-M controls stuff worth 21 times the value of the stuff controlled by Abercrombie and Fitch, then your fair share of the world portfolio of productive resources should have 21 times more dollars in 3-M than in Abercrombie and Fitch.

While you cannot practically form such a market portfolio, mutual fund companies, like Fidelity or Vanguard, can. That's because they can pool a lot of people's monies together and buy a very large portfolio. In addition, many financial services companies offer index funds that are designed to mirror broad-based indexes, which themselves are like portfolios of securities. For example, many firms offer S&P 500 index funds. There are funds for the Russell 2000, which is an index that represents a portfolio of 2000 small market cap stocks traded in U.S. markets, with approximately half having a market capitalization—now, that's the number of shares outstanding times the price per share—the outstanding market capitalization of these firms is less than $500 million, so not very big firms. The MSCI Index, which was created originally by Morgan Stanley Capital International, is a portfolio of about 1600 equities across the globe. They have a fund that includes the U.S., and also one that is everything but the U.S. By the way, all you need to do is spend some time looking on the web and you can find lots of funds. There's lots of information about what's included in the funds and what they're supposed to cover.

An index fund is simply supposed to track its index. That is, when the value of the index changes, say x%, on a given day, then the value of the fund is supposed to change exactly x% on that day, too. Any difference is referred to as tracking error. While there is some skill in forming a portfolio that has very little tracking error, since the managers of these funds are not actively trying to outperform the index, the fees on index funds should be very low on average. But, there is some variation in both the fees and tracking error. A few minutes on the web and you should be able to find an index fund with the best combination of low fees and tracking error. Information on fees and tracking error is readily available on the web.

There are also Exchange-Traded Funds (or ETFs), which are funds formed to mirror the returns of a specific sector—say, consumer goods, financials, health care, technology, utilities, services. The big difference between an ETF and a passive index mutual fund is that you can trade ETFs during the day like stocks. With a mutual fund, you must redeem shares in the fund at the closing value at the end of the day.

For the student-run fund, I did not want them to hold a passive position simply by holding a single broad index, like the MSCI all-country index. Rather, I wanted them to form a fund of funds, where portions of the money could be held in individual ETFs. The students would determine the portions held in each ETF so that the collection of the ETFs represented the market.

That is, we determined the fraction of the total amount of money invested in the world that is invested in U.S. manufacturing and invested that fraction in a fund of U.S. manufacturing firms. We did this for as many sectors as possible, trying to cover all the sectors, being careful also to invest in global ETFs or indexes in order to gain exposure to the returns of the global capital market. In the end, we had a portfolio of ETFs and index funds that represented a sizable fraction of the world portfolio.

The reason we formed a portfolio of ETFs and index funds was because it allowed the students to be both active and passive. If we wanted to just be passive, we would have put all of our money into the broadest possible ETF, like the MSCI All Country World Index fund, or the ACWI. That would have saved on transactions costs.

So what's step number two in this process? Once we formed the portfolio of funds, I challenged the students to beat it. For this, there are a few things that could be done. We'll discuss in detail throughout the course how to do the analysis to decide what to do exactly. For now, let's just examine the kinds of things that you can do.

I'm going to start with the first activity and this has the highest level of thing that you can do, and then work down to the most detailed thing that you can do. So let's start with this highest-level thing.

The first thing that you can do is to time the market. Timing the market means to get out of the market if you think it's going to do poorly and get back into the market when you think it's going to do well. When you get out of the market, you'll want to put your money somewhere really safe—some low-risk treasury bonds, say. Then, when you think the market is going to rebound, you get out of the bonds and back into the market. This is like standing on the sidelines when the game gets rough and putting yourself back in when the game turns out in your favor.

Of course, this begs a bunch of questions. When you want to stand on the sidelines, which bonds do you buy? Short-term treasuries that mature in a year? A longer-term treasury that matures in, say, 10 to 20 years? What recommends one over the other? We'll discuss these issues and other relevant questions in subsequent lectures. But, for now, the point I want to make is simply that you can try to beat the market by plunging in and out of the market.

A less extreme approach would be to always hold some riskless and risky securities. For example, start out with 40% in safe treasuries and 60% in a global ETF. Then you can try to do better by upping the 60% in the market when you think the market is going to do well and upping the 40% in treasuries when you think that the market will tank. Let's call this asset allocation. That is, you must decide how to allocate your investment across asset types, with stocks and bonds being the two most common types. So this sort of timing behavior, that's the type of activity now called Type I activity.

What's Type II activity? The second type of activity is holding fixed the amount that you have in the market versus treasuries. The second thing that you want to do is to reallocate money across sectors. This is easy to do if you have sector funds or ETFs. You just sell off one of your positions in one ETF and use the proceeds to buy more of another ETF in a different sector. This makes sense if you think that the return in the sector you sell will be lower than the return in the sector you buy into. In a sense, you are timing, not the market, but you are timing across sectors. Okay, so that's the second type of activity.

So what's the third thing you can do in terms of activity? Holding fixed the amount that you have in risky securities and holding fixed the amount that you have within each sector, the third thing you can do is try to find individual securities within a sector that you think will outperform that sector. Let's call this stock picking, or security selection. The idea here is that you can, by studying individual securities, find those that you think are undervalued and will go up a lot. While this stock may be in your ETF already, it will likely represent a very small fraction of the ETF. For some ETFs for fairly broadly defined sectors, the biggest stock held by the ETF will represent only a couple of percent, with many ETFs holding hundreds of securities. For example, for BlackRock's iShares Global Consumer Discretionary ETF, the largest holding is Toyota at 6%, with McDonalds and Home Depot around 3–3.5%. For some sectors defined by a very few very large firms, a single firm may be 10–15% of the ETF. For example, AT&T,

Vodafone, and Verizon represent about 40% of the iShares Global Telecom ETF offered by BlackRock.

So, if you think that McDonald's is undervalued, you can exploit this by selling off some of the Consumer Discretionary ETF and using the proceeds to buy McDonald's stock. In this way, you will still have exposure to the benefits and the risks in the consumer discretionary sector, but you will have a portfolio that overweights McDonalds relative to the market weight of McDonalds in that sector. If McDonalds does better than the sector as a whole, then your overweighting, your adjusted consumer discretionary sector portfolio, will have a bigger return, given the outperformance of McDonalds.

What's the fourth type of activity you can undertake? So far, we have only discussed strategies in which you figure out how much in each security to hold. When you want to change your portfolio weights, you sell something and use the proceeds to buy other things. The three types of activities discussed above were different only regarding the set of things that you would sell and the set of things that you would buy. There is, however, another logical possibility for active management that you can do, but I, and the University Investment Committee, will not let my student managers do. That's any strategy that requires shorting, or taking a short position. So, first, let me explain what a short position is. Then I'll explain the two types of things you can do that require such positions.

A short position is when you sell something that you don't own. How do you do that? Well, you have to borrow the item first, and then you sell it. At some point in the future, the person you borrowed it from will want it back. Perhaps they want to sell it. Since you sold it, you don't have it to give back. So you have to go back into the market to buy it back. We'll discuss the mechanics of this in a later lecture. For now, simply think of it as selling something that you've borrowed and returning it later. Since each stock certificate for a firm is the same as any another, you don't need to return exactly that same stock certificate that you borrowed. Instead, you can buy back any of the stock in the open market to return it. But the gain that you get depends upon the price you sold it for versus the price you had to buy it back for.

A short sale allows you to profit from a price decline. For example, say you think that a particular firm's stock will fall from its current value of $100 to $90. If you owned that stock, you could just sell it before it fell, and use the proceeds to buy something that you think will rise in value. But, if you don't own it, you could borrow it, sell it for $100, and wait for it to drop to $90. Then buy it back, and return it to the person you borrowed it from. You will get $10 per share.

You can use short sales to speculate on price drops. So that's one of the things that you could do. The reason the student managers are not allowed to do this is because you can lose a lot—more than you have. If, after you borrowed the share, the price climbs to $130, then you will have to return the shares by paying $130 per share, for something you just sold for $100, for a $30 loss per share. If you buy and hold shares, the most you can lose is the amount you initially invested. When you short, you're not really investing, you're borrowing. And when the price climbs, the amount that you have to pay, the amount that you owe, climbs as well.

Besides outright speculation, the other active management strategy you can undertake is something called arbitrage. With arbitrage, you find two securities that have the same risk and, as a result, should have the same value, but are priced differently in the market. We will see how to identify such situations in subsequent lectures. An arbitrage opportunity exploits the fact that relative to one another, one security is overpriced and the other security is underpriced. To exploit this, you should short the expensive security and use the proceeds to buy the cheap security. An investor makes a profit when the market recognizes their actual values and the market prices come together. That is, you make money twice—first, when the shorted overvalued security's price falls, and then second, when the price of the undervalued security rises. We will see many examples of this throughout the course.

In this lecture, we have seen how you can layer various types of active management strategies on top of a passive portfolio. I like this way of thinking about an investment portfolio for a couple of reasons. First, I think it makes clear what you need to do to justify moving away from a passive market portfolio. In the student-run fund, this is exactly the point I try to make. In order for the student-run fund to do any of the three things discussed above, the students have to make clear arguments as to either (1) why they think risky securities will underperform risk-free securities, (2) why one sector or industry will do better than some other sector or industry, or (3) why an individual stock that they want to buy will do better than the sector or industry that that stock resides in. I think this is a good standard to set for yourself, too. Since you have the ability to short, you also can try to exploit relative mispricing by using arbitrage. For that, you need to convince yourself that you know that two things are the same, but priced differently.

The remainder of the course is all about methods for quantifying risks and values so that you can convince yourself when an opportunity actually exists. Equally important is to be able to convince yourself when an opportunity does not exist. Finally, there is something that I have always said to my daughters that I think is relevant for investing. They would come from school after an exam and I would ask them how they did. Initially they would say, "I don't know." And I would say, "Then you must not have done very well, because part of knowing is knowing when you know and knowing when you don't know." With respect to investing, if you don't know that you know there is an opportunity, then you better not act on that, because it's essentially just a hunch. My goal with the remaining lectures is to get you to know how to measure and how to recognize real opportunities when they do exist.

Mistakes Investors Make

Lecture 3

In this lecture, you will learn about three cognitive biases that can impair a person's investment performance: framing, biased self-attribution, and seeing patterns when none exist. You will learn about these cognitive mistakes for two main reasons. First, while it may be true that you personally do not make such cognitive mistakes, that is not true for the majority of people. In addition, one of the most common cognitive mistakes people make is in assessing their own susceptibility for making systematic cognitive mistakes. A second reason to examine the types of cognitive errors human make is to potentially profit from any systematic pricing errors that such biases might create.

Framing ✓

- That people can suffer from a framing bias is something that psychologists have documented many times in experiments. Framing involves making different choices based on how a problem is presented—not based on fundamental differences among the choices. What this implies is kind of disturbing.

- First, it implies that our choices can be manipulated by framing. Marketing people make a living doing that, so that is not surprising. Second, the systematic difference in responses also implies that, completely independent of the facts of the statistics, context may drive our decisions.

- An example of this is the phenomenon that investors tend to sell winners and hold on to losers—even when there is no relationship between future returns and past returns. Even if, regardless of whether the stock just went up or just went down, there is a 50-50 chance of winning or losing over the next period, most people would prefer to sell the past winner and hold on to the past loser.

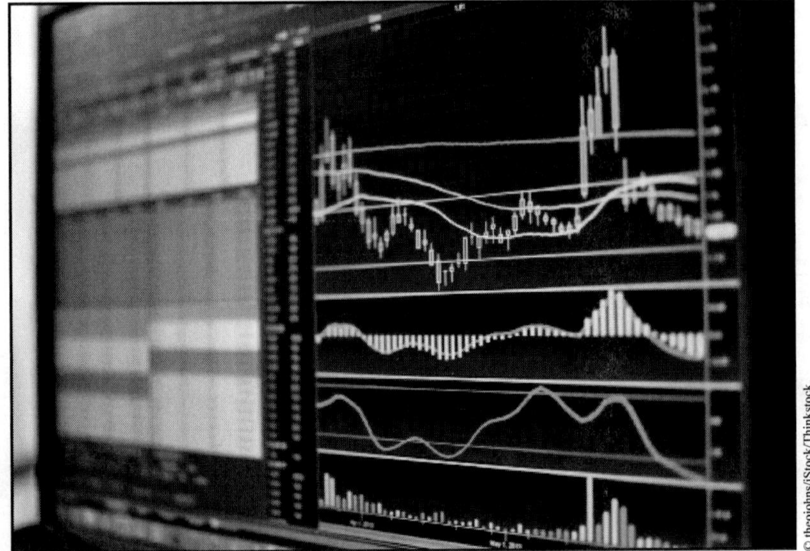

Many stockholders make cognitive mistakes that lead them to make bad decisions regarding buying and selling their stocks.

- Having an asymmetry based on past performance is just like the framing bias; although the past has nothing to do with your future opportunities, people typically make systematically different decisions depending on the past return. Similarly, although the possible outcomes have nothing to do with whether the outcomes are expressed in terms of saving lives or death, people systematically make different decisions depending on the framing.

- One possible explanation for why investors sell winners faster than losers is because, deep down, they do not want to admit failure. By selling a stock that just went down, they are realizing the loss, which prevents them from being able to claim, if only in their own heads, that it really was a good investment because it's going to come back. However, if they sell a winner, they get to claim that they are good investors, before it has a chance to go down and prove them wrong.

- However, to the extent that their actions are driven by something nonmonetary (i.e., their pride), such asymmetries may reduce their investment performance. If there is no relation between past returns and future returns, then such an asymmetry will not be costly. But if there is momentum in returns, the asymmetry locks in a subsequent loss and forecloses on a subsequent gain.

Biased Self-Attribution

- Another thing that people tend to do on average is called biased self-attribution, which is when a person doesn't assign blame or credit fairly. Consider a woman named Jane, who heard a report on CNN on a biotech firm that is creating what the report said was a series of compounds that might increase the effectiveness of certain treatments for diabetes. Jane thought that the CEO not only seemed to be a nice guy who genuinely cared about diabetics having more effective treatments, but was also a smart guy who seemed to have a lot of integrity. On the basis of that report, Jane bought 200 shares of the company at $15 per share.

- The next day, Jane was watching CNN again and saw a report on a cybersecurity firm that had developed a firewall based on an innovative structure designed to protect information passed by mobile devices. She could tell, just by listening to the CEO speak about the varied applications, that this new design could uniquely protect and that he, too, was a smart guy with integrity and a passion for his product. So, she bought 100 shares of that firm, which were selling for $50 per share.

- A month later, she saw that the cybersecurity firm had risen from $50 to $56, a 12% return in just over a month; at that rate, her initial investment of $5000 would grow almost 4 times that after a year. She knew that it was unreasonable to expect that she would get a 12% return every month, but still she felt pretty good.

- The next day, news came out that one of the bio products the biotech firm thought had such promise failed to pass some tests of the Food and Drug Administration, tests that had to be passed before they could turn it into a drug that could be widely distributed. The stock price fell from the level she paid of $15 all the way down to $9, for a $1200 loss (or 40%—in just a month). That night, she complained to her husband that she would have done well on this investment if it weren't for the FDA. Not only did she feel that the firm was wronged, but she also felt that she was wronged, having lost 40% of her investment based on what appeared to be an unreliable test.

- Jane suffers from biased self-attribution, which is when a person gives themselves credit for what turned out to be a good decision but places blame elsewhere when a decision you made turns out poorly. In Jane's case, she took credit for her seeing something in the cybersecurity CEO but blamed the FDA for the loss on the biotech firm.

- Biased self-attribution can be really costly in terms of your ability to accumulate wealth because, if you believe what Jane believes, you will teach yourself to be overconfident. If every time something good happens, it's because of your skill, but every time something bad happens, it's not because of your skill, then you will get a false sense of ability. In Jane's case, she will get the sense that she can judge a good investment just by seeing the CEO speak. If she has this sense, then she may neglect doing the kinds of analyses that will actually identify opportunities and risks.

Seeing Patterns When None Exist

- Consider the plot of a stock price over the course of day. Do you see any patterns, or are the price changes completely random? Experimental psychologists find that most people tend to believe that there is a pattern in the random sequence—that is, they see a pattern when there is none. This is problematic when it comes to investing because patterns typically imply trade opportunities.

- If you knew there was a stock with the property that every time it went up, the next day it had a 60% chance of going up again, and every time it went down, there was a 60% change it would go down the next day, then you could make a lot of money buying after up days and selling after down days.

- People look for patterns, even patterns that aren't sure. But what if you see a pattern when none exists? Reacting to nonexistent patterns can be costly. And even if a slight pattern exists, you can lose a significant amount of money in the short run.

- A good question is why we see patterns when none exist. One explanation is that this is a throwback to when we lived in more primitive times, when sabre-toothed tigers existed. If, back then, we believed that every time the grass rustled, we were more likely than not to get attacked by a sabre-toothed tiger, then whenever we heard the grass rustle, we would run for our lives. Of course, we probably did a lot of unnecessary running, but that was OK.

- There are two types of errors we can make. In statistics, there are labeled as type I and type II errors. Type I error is rejecting a hypothesis that is true. Type II error is accepting (actually, failing to reject) a hypothesis that is false.

- If a person is presumed innocent unless proven guilty, then we say that a court commits a type I error when they convict an innocent person; the court commits a type II error when they let a guilty person go free. In this court example, it may not be clear which type of error is worse.

- But for the sabre-toothed tiger case, the maintained hypothesis is that rustling grass is a tiger. Thus, a type I error is not running when a tiger is there while a type II error is running when there is no tiger there. Clearly, there is a big difference in the costs of these two errors. The cost of the type I error is being eaten by a tiger while the cost of the type II error is getting out of breath and maybe having sore legs. Thus, humans may have a bias to believe something is there even when it is not fairly frequently.

- You may do this to yourself when looking for patterns in returns or prices. In fact, it is fairly easy to do because the types of patterns we think we see are often not easily quantified. Chartists are people who do technical analysis to look for and trade on patterns. If you use a chartist to describe the patterns, they typically explain that it's not a set pattern so much as the sense of a pattern—that no two patterns look exactly the same, but they are very similar in shape.

- In other words, it's like interpreting shapes in clouds. If it were easy to quantify, then you could do that and reject some patterns. But because it's difficult to quantify, it's more difficult to reject—or easier to believe. So, be careful.

Suggested Reading

Ariely, *Predictably Irrational, Revised and Expanded Edition.*

Barber and Odean, "Trading Is Hazardous to Your Wealth."

Bhattacharya, Loos, Meyer, Hackethal, and Kaesler, "The Dark Side of ETFs and Index Funds."

Kahneman, *Thinking, Fast and Slow.*

Questions to Consider

1. Biased self-attribution is when you give yourself credit for good things that happen but blame others when bad things happen. Do you have biased self-attribution with respect to certain types of decisions you make but not others? What is the difference between these types of decisions? What about with investment decisions?

2. Are you overconfident? How would you know if you are overconfident?

Mistakes Investors Make
Lecture 3—Transcript

A big part of what investors do is to react to information they receive. And now more than ever, an investor has access to a bunch of qualitative and quantitative information on markets and individual securities. In some cases, this information is provided by news organizations via the web, such as the information you can get throughout the day on movements in market indexes and individual securities on Yahoo! Finance or Google Finance. Information is also available through brokers, either personally or via news feeds provided by on-line trade platforms. These sources provide you with information on lots of different things, such as what the Fed chairman said or didn't say, if a CEO was fired or not, if a freeze in Florida will affect the orange juice yield.

In addition to this kind of information, there are now many sources on either platforms that allow you to conduct your own analysis or provide you with the results of such analysis. This type of information is usually in the form of some sort of special measure or summary statistic based upon past data. In this course, we'll look at some of these metrics. This course will be especially helpful to you as a consumer of this kind of information, since many of the measures these platforms provide are the result of fairly complex calculations and unless you know the details of how these measures are calculated or what they are supposed to tell you, they can be very hard to interpret. In this course, we will examine the justification and interpretation of these measures.

While it is clearly useful to know what these measures are and what they are supposed to tell you, not only do you need to worry about what they are, you also need to worry about how you react to these measures. The bottom line is that, although you are a thinking machine, you are a human thinking machine, and there is mounting evidence that, on average, humans make a number of systematic cognitive mistakes when processing information. In this lecture, we're going to look at some of these cognitive biases to see how that might impair a person's investment performance.

We will look at these cognitive mistakes for two main reasons. First, while it may be true that you personally do not make such cognitive mistakes, I know that that can't be true for the majority of people. One of the most common cognitive mistakes people make is in assessing their own susceptibility for making systematic cognitive mistakes. So, even if you don't think these mistakes apply to you, since the majority of us think that and make systematic mistakes, many of us are just kidding ourselves.

Rather than rely on our potentially mistaken perception of our own ability, I want to use this discussion of cognitive errors as a way to motivate the need for methodical, non-emotional methods for evaluating your reactions to information. Moreover, since many professionals are subjective to cognitive biases, too, these methods are equally important for you to know if you opt to delegate the management of your investments to a professional. A second reason to examine the types of cognitive errors humans make is to potentially profit from any systematic pricing errors that such biases might create.

Let's look at some of these behavioral biases. I'm going to tell you about three in particular. One is called "framing," two, "biased self-attribution," and three is "seeing patterns when none exist."

Let's look at framing. That people can suffer from a framing bias is something that psychologists have been documenting many times in experiments, and I have actually been able to replicate in my university classroom. For the experiment, I split the class into two parts of about 50 to 60 students each. So that you are convinced that this is a phenomenon I'm about to talk about has nothing to do with differences in intelligence, but rather is a common cognitive mistake that even smart people make, I am careful to split the groups so that there's no selection bias in the groupings. So, I don't split the groups according to their physical location in the class room. Undergraduate students are fairly cliquish, with a high likelihood that one-half will have more cliques of smarter people than the other half. I also don't split by alphabetical order of their last name, since that may disproportionately group one set of people by country of origin, which might be correlated with cultural effects that might systematically effect how they answer the questions. Since student numbers are random, I split them by the last digit in their student number. So that they don't feel subordinated, I say that odds are in group 1 and evens are in group A.

I tell group 1 to find something on the Internet—for example, Albert Einstein's birthstone. And, while group 1 is doing that, I tell group A that they are in charge of public health in the United States and there is going to be an outbreak of a new infectious disease that is expected to kill 600 people if nothing is done. They have a choice. Under program L, 200 people will be saved. Under program M, there is a 1/3 chance that all 600 will be saved, but there is a 2/3 chance that no one will be saved. Then I ask each person in group A to pick the program they prefer.

I then get the attention of group 1 and tell group A to find how many times a Nobel Prize in Economics was awarded to somebody from England. While group A is distracted, I tell group 1 that they are in charge of public health in the United States and that there is going to be an outbreak of a new infectious disease that is expected to kill 600 people if nothing is done. They have a choice. Under program X, 400 people will die, whereas under program Z there is a 1/3 chance that no one will die and a 2/3 chance that all 600 will die.

I have a couple of comments before I reveal the results. First, notice that I really asked the two groups the same question. For group A, I framed the question in terms of saving people, while for group 1 I framed the question in terms of their decision killing people. In both first choices, there are 400 people alive and 200 people dead. With group A, they saved 200 people, which is equivalent to having 600 minus 200, equals 400 dead. With group 1, however, the decision results in 400 people dead, which, of course, is equivalent to having 600 minus 400, equals 200 alive. That is, the first choice for each group is exactly the same. For both groups, the second choices are also equivalent, but one, the one for the group A, is again framed in terms of saving lives, while for group 1 it's framed in terms of killing people. For both second choices, there is a 1/3 chance of having 600 alive and no one dead, and a 2/3 chance at having no one saved or all dead.

Second, while there is a clear choice between the two different options, there is no right or wrong answer. It depends upon how risk-averse you are, and that is something that is completely personal. The first choice presented to both groups can be characterized as a sure thing—200 alive and 400 dead for sure. The second choice offered to each group is risky—a 1/3 chance of 600 alive and zero dead, or a 2/3 chance at zero alive, 600 dead, for an expected number alive of (1/3)600 = 200, or an expected number of dead of (2/3)600 = 400. The expected number alive and dead is the same in both choices, but some people may strictly prefer to have a chance at having every one alive, thus they will like the second options better. Other people may strictly prefer to avoid the chance of having everyone dead, thus they will prefer the first option.

Thus, if there are no systematic differences in the composition of the two groups, say due to cultural differences or differences in intelligence, then the fraction that prefers the first to the second option should be basically the same across the two groups. That is, unless the way the decision was framed affects people's perception of the problem systematically. Only the framing is different. In fact, when this experiment is conducted, the typical responses are very consistent, with the fraction that prefers the sure option over the random option when the question is framed in terms of "saving lives" is 3 to 1: 75% sure to 25% random. But, when the options are framed in terms of "killing people," preferences completely flip, with 3 out of 4 preferring the random option over the sure option; 25% sure to 75% random. Furthermore, these ratios are fairly consistent across all times people have conducted this experiment, including when I have done it in the classroom. Thus, it seems to me that it clearly has something to do with the framing and not the fundamental differences across the groups.

What this implies is kind of disturbing. First, it implies that our choices can be manipulated by framing. I think marketing people know that. But, second, the systematic differences in responses also implies that completely independent of the cold, hard facts of statistics context may drive our decisions.

Another example of this is a phenomenon that investors tend to sell winners and hold on to losers, even when there is no relationship between the future returns and past returns. Even if, regardless of whether the stock just when up or just went down, there is a 50-50 chance of winning or losing over the next period, most people would prefer to sell the past winner and hold on to the past loser.

Having an asymmetry based on past performance is just like a framing bias with the disease. Although the past has nothing to do with the future opportunities, people typically make systematically different decisions depending upon the past return. Similarly, although the possible outcomes have nothing to do with whether the outcomes are expressed in terms of saving lives or death, people systematically make different decisions depending upon the framing.

By the way, one possible explanation for why investors sell winners faster than losers is because, deep down, they do not want to admit failure. By selling a stock that just went down, they are realizing a loss, which prevents them from being able to claim, if only in their own heads, that it was really a good investment. But, if they sell a winner, they get to claim that they're good investors, before it has a chance to go down and prove them wrong. But, to the extent that the actions are driven by something non-monetary (i.e., their pride), such asymmetries may reduce their investment performance. If there is no relationship between past returns and future returns, then such an asymmetry will not be costly. But, what happens if there is what we call momentum in returns? In that case, the asymmetry locks in a substantial loss and forecloses on a substantial gain.

The second thing that we want to talk about is biased self-attribution. This is another thing that people tend to do on average. Biased self-attribution is when a person doesn't assign blame or credit fairly. Consider a person—let's call her Jane—who, while watching CNN, heard a report on a biotech firm that is creating what the report said was a series of compounds that might increase the effectiveness of certain treatments for diabetes. During the report, the CEO was asked if the compounds where sufficiently unique that they could be protected via a patent. Jane thought that the CEO not only seemed to be a nice guy who genuinely cared about diabetics having more effective treatments, but also he was a very smart guy who, even though he may have had the incentive to exaggerate the potential for the firm's products, seemed to have a lot of integrity. On the basis of that report, Jane bought 200 shares of the company at $15 per share.

The next day, Jane was watching CNN again and saw a report on a cyber-security firm that had developed a firewall based on an innovative structure designed to protect information passed by mobile devices. This firm had many clients in financial services and in medical-record processing. She could also tell, just by listening to the CEO speak about the varied applications of this new design that could be uniquely served by this product, that he too was a smart guy with integrity and a passion for his product—all traits of someone destined for success. So, of course, she bought 100 shares of that firm, which were selling for $50 per share.

A month later, she saw that the cyber-security firm had risen from $50 to $56, a 12% return in just over a month. At that rate, her initial investment of $5000 would grow almost four times that after a year. She knew that it was unreasonable to expect that she would get 12% every month, but still she felt pretty good. That night, over a nice bottle of wine, she bragged to her husband that she knew that that CEO had something on the ball. She was not only a good investor, but a good judge of character.

Of course, the next day, news came out that one of the biotech products of the biotech firm thought had such promise failed to pass some of the FDA's drug tests—tests that had to be passed before they could turn the drug into something that could be widely distributed. In response, the CEO issued a press release stating that the compound had passed their own extremely rigorous testing process and that he believed they would ultimately be successful after they appealed the results.

The market was not convinced, and the stock price fell from the level she paid of $15 all the way down to $9, for a $1200 loss, or 40%, in just a month. That night, over a stiff shot of scotch, she complained to her husband that she could have done well on that investment if it weren't for the FDA. Not only did she feel that the firm was wronged, but she also felt that she was wronged, having lost 40% of her investment based on what appeared to an unreliable test.

In addition to a potential drinking problem, Jane suffers from biased self-attribution, which is when a person gives themselves credit for what turned out to be a good decision but places blame elsewhere when a decision they made turns out poorly. In Jane's case, she took credit for her seeing something in the cyber-security CEO, but blamed the FDA for the loss on the biotech firm.

How many times have you done this? Although not within investing, I think I do this fairly often. For example, every Thanksgiving I roast a turkey. To be honest, I think it's hard to roast a turkey well, to consistently keep it moist but make sure it is cooked enough that salmonella is not an issue. I don't know how many times I have said, after presenting an over-cooked, dry bird, "We must have gotten an old bird." But when it turns out nice and juicy, I say "Boy, do I know how to cook or what?"

While biased self-attribution may be just a bit annoying at the Thanksgiving dinner table, it can be really costly in terms of your ability to accumulate wealth. Why? Because, if you believe what Jane believes, you will teach yourself to be overconfident. If every time something good happens it's because of your skill, but every time something bad happens, it's not because of your skill, then you will get a false sense of ability. In Jane's case, she will get the sense that she can judge a good investment just by seeing the CEO speak. If she has this sense, then she may neglect doing the kinds of analyses that will actually identify opportunities and risks.

Let's consider another behavioral bias. Here is something else that people do that is kind of related. Consider a plot of a stock price over the course of a day. If you look at it, do you see any patterns? Any patterns in the price level, or any patterns in the price changes, or are they just completely random? I often ask my students this, and most see patterns. Experimental psychologists have documented this, too. They find that most people tend to believe there is a pattern in a random sequence. That is, they see a pattern where there really is none.

This is problematic when it comes to investing, because patterns typically imply trade opportunities. If you knew there was a stock in which every time it when up, the next day it had a 60% chance of going up again and, if every time it went down, there was a 60% chance it would go down the next day, then you could make a lot of money buying after up days and selling after down days. To see this, consider the following simple example. Let's say yesterday at the close of the market, the price of Sleaze Co. was \$10 per share. By the way, don't ask what Sleaze Co. makes. Today, there is a 50-50 chance that it's going to go up or down. If it goes up to \$11, and if it goes down it will fall to \$9. If it goes up to \$11 today, let the probability that it will go up another dollar to \$12 be p and the probability it will fall \$10 be $(1 - p)$. That is, p is the probability that it will continue, or change in the same direction. $(1 - p)$ is the probability that it will reverse.

Similarly, if the price goes down to \$9 today, then let the probability that it will continue to fall another to \$8 be p, while the probability that it will reverse by a dollar and rise to \$10 be $(1 - p)$.

If p equals 0.5, 50%, and thus $1 - p$ also equals 50%, then knowing whether the price went up or down today doesn't help you predict where it will go at the close of the market tomorrow. But, if p is greater than 0.5, then if it goes up today, it's more likely than not that it'll go up again, and if it goes down today it's more likely than not it'll go down again. That is, there's a pattern. It's not for sure, but it's probabilistically a pattern. So, if it goes up today, you should buy and if it goes down, you should short. Recall that shorting is when you sell something that you don't own. Rather, you borrow it, sell it, buy it back in the future, and return it. If the price you sell it for is larger than the price you have to pay when you buy it back, then you will make money. But, if the price rises, you'll have to buy it back for more than you sold it for. In that case, you're out some money. You've experienced a loss.

So, if you think there's a pattern and you buy after the price rises and sell short after it falls, what is your expected gain? Well, let's see what happens if the price goes up. If the price goes up today, you will buy, say, 1000 shares. That is, you will pay \$11 times 1000. You're going to spend \$11,000 to get 1000 shares. Then, you'll be able to sell those shares the day after today for either \$12 per share p% of the time or at \$10 $(1 - p)$% of the time, for an average price at the close tomorrow of $p \times \$12 + (1 - p) \times \$10$, which, by the way, is equivalent to just $\$10 + p \times \$2$. Thus, on average you will get $(\$10 + p \times \$2)$, all of that multiplied by 1000 for shares, which equals $\$10{,}000 + \$2000 \times p$. If p is greater than 50%, 0.5, then you will sell for more than \$11,000, which is an expected gain.

Similarly, if the price goes down to \$9, then you will sell short 1000 shares and get what? \$9 × 1000—\$9000. After a day, at the close tomorrow, you will buy the shares back to close out your short position. And you will pay what? $P \times \$8 + (1 - p) \times \$10$, which, by the way, equals \$10, minus $\$2 \times p$ per share. If p is greater than 0.5, then you again will make a gain. You short sell at \$9 per share and buy them back for less than \$9 per share.

In fact, a little algebraic manipulation shows that your expected gain is actually going to be, what, $\$2 \times p - \$1$. Thus, if p is 0.6, or 60%, your expected gain is going to be \$0.20 per share. If p is 0.8, your expected gain is \$0.60 per share, for a one-day gain. For a one-day gain, that's going to be \$0.6 × 1000 shares. That's \$600. If p is equal to 1, then the expected gain is \$1 per share for one day. A gain of \$1000. If you could do that every trading day, that's \$252,000 a year. By the way, there's 252 trading days per year. Not bad. So, you can see why people look for patterns, even patterns they're not even sure about.

But, what if you see a pattern and none really exists? If we make this a little bit more realistic, then let's say that regardless of whether you're buying or selling, there's a transaction cost of 20 cents per share. As we'll discuss later, bid/ask spreads—the difference between the price you have to pay and what you have to sell it for at any given moment—create this kind of transaction cost.

Now, if there's no pattern and p equals 0.5, then transaction costs will eat you up, and other traders will make a living trading with you, and it's worse if you're paying an online broker something like \$5 to \$10 per trade.

In fact, a little more algebra shows that if the price change in any given day is $\$\Delta$, and the transaction cost is $\$t$, and the probability of continuation is p, then your one day expected profit per share is $(2p - 1)\Delta - 2t$.

So, for example, if p is less than 0.5, then you will lose money for any positive transaction cost. But, even if p is greater than 0.5, you can also lose money if the transaction costs are big enough. For example, if the transaction cost is 20 cents and the Δ is \$1, then you will lose money for any p less than 0.7.

So, bottom line is if you react to non-existent patterns, that can be really costly to you. And even if a slight pattern exists, you can lose a significant amount of money in the short run if you trade too frequently.

By the way, a really good question is "Why do we see patterns when none exist?" Well, so one explanation is that it's a throwback to when we lived in more primitive times, when saber-toothed tigers roamed the earth. If, back then, we believed that every time the grass rustled, we were more likely than not to get attacked by a saber-toothed tiger, then whenever we heard the grass rustle, we would run for our lives. Of course, we probably did a lot of unnecessary running, especially on windy days.

But that's okay. There are two types of errors that we can make. In statistics, these are labeled type-one and type-two errors. Type-I error is rejecting a hypothesis that's true. Type-II error is accepting—actually, failing to reject—a hypothesis that is false. If a person is presumed innocent until proven guilty, then we would say a court commits a type-I error when they convict an innocent person. But the court commits a type-II error if they let a guilty person go free.

In this example, it may not be clear which type of error is worse from a societal perspective. But for the saber-toothed tiger case, the maintained hypothesis is that rustling grass is a tiger. Thus, type-I error is not running when a tiger is there, while type-II error is running when there is no tiger there. Clearly, there is a big difference in the costs of these two errors. The cost of type-I error is being eaten by a tiger, while the cost of type-II error is maybe getting out of breath and maybe having sore legs. So humans may have a bias to believe something is there, even when it is not there.

Another example comes from the chickens of behavioral psychologist B. F. Skinner. Skinner would put chickens in a cage that had a device that would randomly eject a food pellet. Next to the pellet tube was a little red circle that had nothing to do with the dispensing of the pellet. Many of the chickens would peck the red circle. In some cases, a pellet would fall purely by chance. After a while, whenever the chicken wanted a pellet, however, it would peck at the red circle, thinking that pecking produced a pellet. In fact, since the pellet arrived randomly, they didn't have to wait long. But the point that they interpreted the pecking and the arrival as causal—as a pattern—is what's consistent with what we do as humans. In fact, some chickens might have turned around prior to pecking the red circle and, by pure chance, received a pellet. These chickens then started to believe that it wasn't just the pecking that produced the results, but also the turning around and the pecking. In fact, some chickens developed sort of elaborate dances to produce pellets. But, the arrival of the pellet was purely random. The chickens saw a pattern when none existed. Perhaps this is why athletes don't shave when they are put in the playoffs, or they don't change their socks. They think, just like Skinner's chickens, that they think there's a pattern when none actually exists.

You may do this yourself when you're looking for patterns in returns or prices. In fact, it's fairly easy to do this, since the types of patterns we think we see are often very hard to sort of quantify. Chartists are people that do technical analysis. These are people that look for and trade on patterns. If you ask a chartist to describe the pattern, they typically explain that it's not a set pattern so much as the sense of a pattern—that no two head-and-shoulders patterns look exactly the same, but they're very similar in shape, sometimes occurring within a day, sometimes over a week, sometimes with high shoulders, other times with lower shoulders. In other words, it's like interpreting the shapes in clouds, or interpreting the dances of chickens that produce pellets. If it were easy to quantify, then we could do that and then reject some patterns. But, because it's hard to quantify, it's harder to systematically reject it, and therefore easier to believe in. So, I want you to be very careful about this.

Throughout this lecture, we've seen how investors can make costly cognitive errors in reacting to information. In subsequent lectures, we'll examine some concrete techniques that will allow you to evaluate how you react to things that generate performance. That way, you don't have to rely on your feelings, which we have seen can be unreliable and subject to cognitive errors. We will also discuss how such cognitive errors may generate trade opportunities. Of course, you'll want to use the performance evaluation tools we develop later to evaluate whether or not these potential trade opportunities are there or not, whether there's a saber-toothed tiger there, or whether it's just the rustling in the wind.

The Characteristics of Security Returns

Lecture 4

In this lecture, you will be introduced to a set of concepts and formulas from probability and statistics that you should think about and use whenever you think about investing. These concepts and formulas are the building blocks of slow, deliberative, purposeful thinking about investments. In particular, these concepts and formulas allow you to quantify how the characteristics of individual securities affect the risk of portfolios that you can build. The goal is for you to have an intuitive understanding of what these measures mean.

Returns

- There are many securities in which you could invest; the issue is not which ones you should invest in but how much you should invest in each. In order to be able to optimize over the set of possible portfolios, we first need to be able to quantify certain characteristics of the behavior of asset returns as inputs to that process. We will characterize each individual asset according to its expected return, its return variance (or volatility), and the covariance (or correlation) of its return with the returns on other assets.

- Consider the situation in which you want to hold all securities for a fixed interval of time (or period). We will let t denote time. That is, any arbitrary point in time might be generically labeled t; one period, hence, will be $t + 1$. The length of the period may vary according to the specific investment issues being considered. For now, think of a period as a quarter (3 months) or a year.

- Next, consider the return of an individual security over a period—from t to $t + 1$. There are two components to any return. The first is due to any change in the price of the security. This is called the capital gain (or loss, if the price falls). The second is due to any cash flow generated during the interval; for stocks, the payment of a dividend creates such a cash flow, while coupon payments are a source of cash flows for bonds. The return due to the payment of a dividend is referred to as the dividend yield.

- Regardless of whether we are taking about a stock, bond, or derivative security (such as a call option), we will let P_t denote the price at t, P_{t+1} denote the price one period hence—at $t + 1$—and D_{t+1} be the value at $t + 1$ of any cash flows generated during the interval from t to $t + 1$.

- Given these conventions, the return of a security from t to $t + 1$ (which we will denoted by R_t) is defined as follows.
    - $R_t = \dfrac{P_{t+1} - P_t}{P_t} + \dfrac{D_{t+1}}{P_t}$

- That is, the first part is your percentage capital gain—what you sold it for (i.e., P_{t+1}) minus what you paid (i.e., P_t)—relative to what you paid, P_t. The second part is the dividend yield equals the dividend or cash flow during the period divided by the price you paid.

Returns as Random Variables

- At the time when an asset or security is purchased, the return on any security can be viewed as a random variable. Given the way that we have defined returns, there are two sources of randomness that can creep in. One source of randomness is due to changes in the market value of the security as reflected in the future price, P_{t+1}, relative to the current price, P_t.

- The market value of the security changes when there is new information that comes to light concerning the future cash flows of the security. Because news by its very nature is unpredictable, the future arrival of news is random, and as a result, the future price will differ from the current price in random ways.

- A second source comes from any unpredictable changes in the cash flows D_{t+1}. The dividends paid on common stock are not fixed; rather, it is up to the firm's management to decide how much to pay out as a dividend. Whatever they decide, the value of D_{t+1} is not fully predictable at t. However, firms try to keep dividends fairly constant over time.

- For bonds, in which the D_{t+1} represents a coupon payment, there can be randomness in D_{t+1} due to the possibility of default, in which the bond issuers cannot satisfy their promised payments.

- In addition to the direct effect of a random D_{t+1} on the randomness of the return, the realized value of D_{t+1} may also affect the market's beliefs about the security's value, which will affect P_{t+1} and contribute to the randomness of the return via the first channel.

How to Characterize Randomness Mathematically

- The way mathematicians (and financial economists) typically think about randomness is with the concept of a frequency distribution or a probability density function. A frequency distribution specifies how frequently each of the possible values that could be realized would appear in a very large sample. Alternatively, the frequency distribution specifies how likely it is that a particular value will occur in one sampling.

- Similarly, a probability density function specifies how much probability (or density) is associated with each possible outcome.

- In general, when certain quantities are random, there are a few measures used to characterize the randomness. The first is the expected value, which is often referred to as a measure of central tendency. The second is the variance, which captures the degree of dispersion of the possible values about its central tendency. These first two characterize the behavior of a single random variable—for example, the return on a single security. A third measure, the covariance or the related correlation coefficient, measures how two random variables are related to each other.

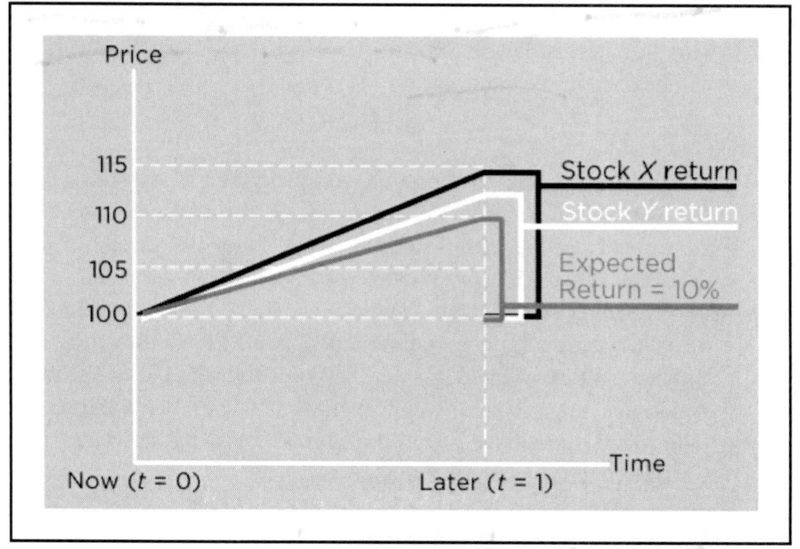

Expected Return

- A security's expected return is defined as the probability weighted average of the possible values the return might end up being. Mathematically, the expected return is $E(R) = (\text{Prob}(R = R_1)(R_1)) + \ldots + (\text{Prob}(R = R_k)(R_k))$. Let the set of possible values of returns be ranked and numbered—that is, let R_1 be the lowest possible return and R_2 be the next, all the way up to R_k, which is the highest possible value.

- The expected return can be thought of as the average value that would occur if you were to "sample" the return many, many times (for example, 1 million times). A simple average is the sum of all the values divided by the number of observations. In the expected value formula, the probability associated with a particular return represents how frequently that return will appear in a large sample. As such, the formula for the expected value as a weighted average, with probabilities for weights, quantifies the simple average return one would get in repeated sampling.

- Statisticians also refer to the expected value as the "mean." Throughout this course, "mean," "average," and "expected value" will be used interchangeably.

Variance

- The expected value does not tell you everything. How close you will get to the expected value depends on the variance, which is the expected value of the squared deviation of the variable from its mean. There are many possible deviations from the mean, with some realized values above the mean and some below the mean. If we take each possible deviation and square it, the squares are all positive. And associated with each value from the set of squared deviations is a probability. The variance is simply the expected value of the possible squared deviations. Thus, the variance is a measure of dispersion about the mean.

- Mathematically, the variance is as follows.
  - $\text{Var}(R) = E((R - E(R))^2) =$
  - $(\text{Prob}(R = R_1))(R_1 - E(R))^2 + \ldots + (\text{Prob}(R = R_k))(R_k - E(R))^2$.

- This is just like the expected value, but instead of $\text{Prob}(R = R_i)$ multiplying R_i, it multiplies the squared deviation of R_i from its mean (i.e., $R_i - E(R))^2$).
  - $\text{Var}(R) = E((R - E(R))^2) = (\text{Prob}(R = R_1))(R_1 - E(R))^2 + \ldots + (\text{Prob}(R = R_k))(R_k - E(R))^2$
  - $E(R) = (\text{Prob}(R = R_1))(R_1) + \ldots + (\text{Prob}(R = R_k)(R_k)$.

- A measure that is related to variance is the standard deviation. The standard deviation is simply defined as $\text{SD}(R) = \sigma = \text{Var}(R)^{(1/2)}$. The standard deviation of return SD(R) is more intuitive because it is in percentages; a variance is in percent squared. Think of the standard deviation as kind of an average for the size of a deviation from the mean return percent.

- Also, the convention is to call the standard deviation of returns "volatility." In standard conversational English, there is no distinction between variance and volatility; both mean variability around some norm. But in investments, there is a big difference—the square root.

Covariance

- Mathematical statistics has a way to quantify the relationship between any two random variables. One concept is that of a joint distribution. The joint distribution between any two random variables (e.g., returns) is a specification of the probabilities associated with each possible pair of values.

- Being able to calculate means and variances from marginal probabilities is not why a joint distribution is useful, however. Importantly, the joint distribution tells you how likely it is that two variables move together, independently, or in opposite directions—on average. Mathematically, using the information contained in the joint distribution between any two random variables, the covariance is defined as follows.
    - $\text{Cov}(R_1, R_2) = E((R_1 - E(R_1))(R_2 - E(R_2)))$

- That is, the covariance is the expected value of the possible paired deviations of each from their mean.

- If, according to the joint distribution, there is a lot of probability associated with cases in which (a) the first is above its mean and the second is below its mean and (b) the first is below its mean and the second is above its mean, then the covariance will be negative. This is true because most of the values of $(R_1 - E(R_1))(R_2 - E(R_2))$ are negative (because either a negative times a positive or a positive times a negative is negative).

- If, instead, most of the probability is associated with cases in which (a) the first is above its mean and the second is, too; and (b) the first is below its mean and so is the second, then the covariance is positive. This is true because most of the values of $(R_1 - E(R_1))$

$(R_2 - E(R_2))$ are positive (because a positive times a positive and a negative times a negative are both positive).

- The correlation coefficient scales the covariance for the size of the variance of each.
    - $\text{Corr} = \rho = \text{rho} = \text{Cov}(R_1, R_2)/(\text{SD}_1 \times \text{SD}_2)$.

- In general, correlation coefficients range from 1 to −1. If the correlation between two variables is 1, then it is the case that one of the variables is a constant positive multiple of the other. That is, if you know the value of one, you can know the value of the other exactly. At the other extreme, two variables can be perfectly negatively correlated (and the correlation coefficient will be −1). Again, you can perfectly predict the other knowing the one.

- If the correlation is 0, that means that knowing something about the one tells you nothing about the other. This makes sense in that the correlation is 0 when the covariance is 0. And the covariance is 0 when it is as equally likely that when one variable (or return) is above its mean, the other may be above or below its mean.

- A correlation between 0 and 1 means that the two variables vary in the same direction, but not perfectly; knowing one gives you a general idea of what the other will be. A correlation between 0 and −1 means that the two variables vary in the opposite direction, but not perfectly. The closer the magnitude of the correlation is to 0, the weaker the relationship. The closer the magnitude of the correlation is to 1, the stronger the relationship.

Suggested Reading

Bodie, Kane, and Marcus, *Essentials of Investments*.

Ross, Westerfield, Jaffe, and Jordan, *Corporate Finance*.

Taleb, *The Black Swan*.

Questions to Consider

1. Can you think of two firms that have returns that are negatively correlated with each other? What are two firms that are positively correlated? What two firms do you think have as little correlation (positive or negative) as possible?

2. You have $1,000,000 invested in the market; over the next year, the market is expected to return 10% with a standard deviation of 15%. Alternatively, you can invest at the risk-free T-bill rate of 1.5%. Thus, if you invest in the market, after a year, you will have $1,100,000 on average, for a $100,000 average gain; if you invest in the risk-free T-bills, you will have $1,015,000, a $15,000 gain. If returns are normally distributed, then the probability that you will have less than 1,015,000 by investing in the market is around 30%. (That is, there is a 70% chance you will do better investing in the market than investing in the risk-free T-bills.) Which do you prefer: investing in the market or the risk-free T-bills?

The Characteristics of Security Returns
Lecture 4—Transcript

In the last lecture, we've seen how human beings can make cognitive errors. Usually, we make these mistakes when we react emotionally—when we don't take the time to carefully analyze the situation, to systematically identify and characterize the set of available alternative decisions, and to reflect on what is best for us. Psychologists have a few phrases for this. Some call it fast thinking versus slow thinking. Fast thinking occurs when time is of the essence. You need react to a stimulus. You're thinking fast when you duck after hearing a car backfire on a street corner.

In contrast, consider the following riddle: You are given a bouquet of flowers. All but two of the flowers are of the daisy variety, and all but two of the flowers are of the rose variety, and finally, all but two of the flowers are of the tulip variety. How many flowers are in the bouquet? At first, I'm sure you were doing some fast thinking. You wanted to categorize the riddle in some way. Do I need mathematical operations like add, subtract, multiple, and divide? Or will I need to list things out? Or is it just like a play on words? But soon, your fast thinking will give way to slow thinking. If you weren't watching this lecture—and, by the way, don't stop the lecture—you would stop and deliberate on the various elements of the riddle. You would approach it methodically, not emotionally. Typically, if you have no systematic way of thinking about something, your fast thinking drives your decision.

As we've discussed before, there are many stimuli for you to respond to in financial markets, and there is often a sense of urgency, as in "better act quick before word gets out of this great investment," or "better act out now before the bottom falls out." In this lecture, I want to go over a set of concepts and formulas from probability and statistics that I want you to think about whenever you think about investing. These concepts and formulas are the building blocks of slow, deliberative, purposeful thinking about investments. In particular, these concepts and formulas will allow us to quantify how the characteristics of individual securities affect the risk of portfolios that you can build. My primary goal for you is to have an intuitive understanding of what these mathematical constructs and formulas mean.

So, just to set the stage, let's say that you have a million dollars to invest. There are many securities in which you could invest. The correct question is not which, but how much you should invest in each. That is, the question of what is the best portfolio of securities to buy with your million dollars?

In order to be able to optimize over the set of possible portfolios, which we'll discuss how to do in subsequent lectures, we first need to be able to quantify certain characteristics of the behavior of asset returns as inputs into that process. Here we will characterize each individual asset according to: (1) its expected return, (2) its return variance, or volatility, and (3) the covariance, or correlation of its return with the return on other assets.

Note that I have said asset returns. That is, let's not limit ourselves to just stock or bonds. In fact, everything we discuss here applies to any asset, including housing and human capital in addition to stocks and bonds. Throughout this series of lectures, I will typically refer to securities and security returns, because we'll mostly be discussing things that are actively traded in financial markets. While you do trade your human capital in a market when you relocate from one job to another, you don't do that very frequently. So, I will typically use the word security to represent a financial instrument that is being bought or sold. But you should realize that everything I say here also applies to things like human capital and housing. You should definitely keep your investment in such assets in mind when forming portfolios.

Before we get to the probability and statistical concepts, we first need to define a few timing conventions. This will allow us to precisely define a security's return. Later, we will discuss why you might want to hold a security for a shorter period of time, while you might want to hold another security for a longer interval. For now, let's just consider a situation in which you want to hold all securities for a fixed interval of time, or period.

We will let t denote time. That is, any arbitrary point in time might be generically labeled t. One period hence will be $t + 1$. The length of the period may vary according to the specific investment issue being considered. For example, an investment in a college education could easily return over 60 to 80 years. If the investment is in a house, then the typical period for a mortgage might be something like 15 to 30 years. But now, with an increase in mobility and greater job turnover, maybe the period is more like 4 to 5 to 6 to 10 years. If you're thinking of a relatively long buy-and-hold strategy for a stock, that period might be one or two years, or three years.

At the other extreme, there are many professional investment firms that seek to exploit very short-run trends created by a temporary drying-up of market liquidity. These firms use computer algorithms to both identify such trends and to submit trades in fractions of seconds. These strategies are referred to as high-frequency trading, or HFT. Such HFT firms compete by being able to execute trades in less than a millisecond. For perspective, realize that the reaction time of a top athlete in the Beijing Olympics was clocked at between 160 and 190 milliseconds. Thus, these firms have to use computers. While you could train Olympic athletes to trade, they are just too slow.

We will discuss reasons why we might want to vary the length of period later. But, for now, think of the period as something like a quarter, say, three months or a year.

Next, consider the return of an individual security over a period, from t to $t + 1$. There are two components to any return. The first is due the change in the price of the security. This is called the capital gain. It might be a capital loss if the price falls. The second is due to any cash flow generated during that interval. For stocks, the payment of a dividend creates such a cash flow, while coupon payments are the source of cash flows for bonds. The return due to the payment of a dividend is referred to as the dividend yield.

Regardless of whether we are talking about a stock, a bond, or a derivative security, such as a call option, we are going to let P_t denote the price at t. Now, notice what I've said here. P_t—that stands for P with a subscript of t. We're going to let $P_t + 1$ denote the price one period hence at $t + 1$. And we're going to let $D_t + 1$ be the value at $t + 1$ of any cash flows generated during the interval from t to $t + 1$.

Given these conventions, the return of a security from t to $t + 1$, which we will denote by R_t is defined as following: $R_t = D_{t+1}/P_t + (P_{t+1} - \mathrm{P}_t)$ all of that divided by the price you paid, *Pt*. That is, the first part is the percentage due to the dividend payment, and the second part is the percentage capital gain.

If you paid, for example, \$100 for a security that paid a \$5 dividend and sold for \$93 at the end of the period, your return is comprised of the dividend yield of \$5/\$100, or 5%. But a capital gain of (\$93 − \$100)/\$100, which is equal to −7%. Thus, the total return is 5% minus 7%, or −2%.

At the time when an asset or a security is purchased, the return on that security over the next period may be viewed as a random variable. It may seem kind of strange to reduce the behavior of a firm and its return to a number, and a random number at that. Finance people are not trying to be demeaning or diminish the importance of all the hard work that managers and employees contribute to the profitability of the firm. Rather, quite the contrary.

They are simply highlighting the fact that, relative to most people's information, there are so many things that affect the performance of a firm that it is almost impossible to predict how those things will evolve over time. Although some of those things may be predictable, many are not. As such, we model the implications of these unpredictable things as random variables. Furthermore, as we will see in lectures 5 and 6, there are good justifications for why returns should be random. We'll discuss that later.

Given the way we have defined returns, there are two sources of randomness that might creep in. One source of randomness is due to changes in the market value of the securities as reflected in the future price $P_t + 1$ relative to the current price P_t.

As we'll discuss in detail in Lecture 5, the market value of the security changes when there is new information that comes to light concerning the future cash flows of the security. Since news by its very nature is unpredictable, else it would not be news, the future arrival of news is random and, as a result, the future price will differ from the current price in random ways.

A second source comes from any unpredictable changes in the cash flows $D_t + 1$. The dividends paid on common stock are not fixed. Rather, it is up to the firm's management to decide how much to pay out as a dividend. If the management thinks that it has a better use for the money than their shareholders, they may cut their dividend and keep the money in the firm. On the other hand, they may not have enough money on hand—say, due to poor sales—to pay what they have paid in the past. In either case, the value of $D_t + 1$ is not fully predictable at t. Having said that though, firms try to keep their dividends fairly constant over time. The management is said to "smooth" dividends as they try to make them less random.

For bonds, in which $D_t + 1$ represents a coupon payment, there can be randomness in $D_t + 1$ due to the possibility of default, in which the bond issuers cannot satisfy their promised payments.

In addition to the direct effect of a random $D_t + 1$ on the randomness of the return, the realized value of $D_t + 1$ may also affect the market's belief about the security's value, which can affect $P_t + 1$ and contribute to the randomness of the return via the first channel we talked about—the capital gain. In the case of stocks, a drop in the current dividend may signal to the market that the firm is not going to pay dividends at the same rate as they paid in the past, thus lowering the market's value of the stock. In the case of bonds, if a bond issuer fails to make a coupon payment, then the market will think it's highly likely that the issuer won't be able to make all of the subsequent payments and the market value of the bond at $P_t + 1$ will also fall.

Now let's see that if returns are random, let's consider how we might want to quantify various aspects of their randomness. So, in other words, we need a structured way to think about something that seems unstructured. The way mathematicians and financial economists typically think about randomness is with the concept of a frequency distribution or a probability density function, sometimes referred to as a "PDF."

A frequency distribution specifies how frequently each of the possible values that could be realized would appear in a very large sample. Alternatively, the frequency distribution specifies how likely it is that a particular value will occur in one sampling. Similarly, a probability density function specifies how much probability, or density, is associated with each possible outcome.

In some cases, the set of possible values are discrete. For example, the number of children a randomly chosen woman will give birth to in her lifetime. The possible values are 0, 1, 2, 3; I don't know what the upper limit is. In other cases, the set of possible values is continuous—that is, the variable can take on any number. For example, the length of time it takes to get from the airport to the Teaching Company headquarters. While our measurements are likely only to be taken to the second, and, as a result, the measured time is discrete, actual time seems continuous and, even if it isn't, we probably might want to model it as such.

Another example is the average number of children that a random sample of women will give birth to in their lifetime. That is different from the discrete case of a single woman, since the average for the sample might be something like 2.14, 2.67, something like that.

In general, when certain quantities are random, there are a couple of measures used to characterize the randomness. The first is the expected value, which is often referred to as a measure of central tendency. The second is the variance, which captures the degree of dispersion of the possible values about its central tendency.

These first two characterize the behavior of a single random variable, say, the return on a single security. A third measure, the covariance, or the related correlation coefficient, measures how two random variables are related to one another.

All right, so let's look at each in turn. Let's consider the expected return. A security's expected return is defined as the probability weighted average of the possible values the return might end up being. Mathematically, the expected return is denoted by $E(R) = \text{Prob}(R = R_1) \times R_1 + \ldots + \text{Prob}(R = R_k) \times R_k$.

What's the first return? Let the set of possible values of returns be ranked and numbered. That is, let R_1 be the lowest possible return. Let R_2 be the next lowest, all the way up to R_k, which is the highest possible value. By the way, the ranking from lowest to highest is arbitrary and inconsequential for this discussion of expected value. If we consider every possible return, then there may be many millions of possibilities.

Okay, so that's not practical. As an alternative, we often simplify things by putting things into buckets, or ranges. In some cases, we simply assume that the values of the return are continuous (i.e., not discrete or distinct separate values) and replace the summation above with a formula that has an integral. We integrate over all of the values.

The expected return can be thought of as an average value that would occur if you were to sample the return many, many times—say, a million times. A simple average is simply the sum of all the values divided by the number of observations. The expected value formula, the probability associated with a particular return, represents how frequently that return will appear in large samples. As such, the formula for the expected value as a weighted average, with probabilities for weights, quantifies the simple average return one would get in repeated samplings.

By the way, statisticians also refer to the expected value as the mean. Throughout the course, I will use mean, average, and expected value interchangeably.

Next, let's consider the variants. The expected value does not tell you everything. For example, just because the average height of a male in the U.S. is, say, 5 foot 9 inches, that does not mean that, if you were to randomly pick a male, off the street, say, that his height would be 5 foot 9. Similarly, even if the expected return on a security is 10%, the likelihood that you will get a return of exactly 10% over the next year is probably pretty small. How close you will get to the expected value depends upon the variance, which we define next.

The variance is defined as the expected value of the squared deviations of that variable from its mean. There are many possible deviations from the mean, with some realized values above the mean and some below the mean. If we take those possible deviations and square them, the squares are all positive. And associated with each of the values from the set of the squared deviations, there is a probability. The variance is simply the expected value of the possible squared deviations. Thus, the variance is a measure of dispersion about the mean.

Alright, so we square the deviations in the variance because it gives us a directionless measure of distance from the mean. But, in the variance, a deviation of 2 units when squared is 4 times bigger than a deviation of 1 when that is squared. Thus, bigger deviations tend to get amplified when calculating the variance. An alternative measure of dispersion might use the absolute value of the deviation rather than the square of the deviation. In that measure, a 2-unit deviation above or below would simply be twice as big as a 1-unit deviation, again, above or below, not four times as big when we get it squared in the variance measure. By the way, there is really no deep justification for using the square rather than using the absolute value, but the variance seems to be fairly standard and commonly used.

Mathematically, formula for the variance is as following: $\text{Var}(R) = E([R - E(R)]^2)$. So that's going to be equal to $\text{Prob}(R = R1) \times [R1 - E(R)]^2 + \text{Prob}(R = R_k) \times [R_k - E(R)]^2$. This is just like the expected value, but instead of $\text{Prob}(R = R_i)$ multiplying R_i, instead it multiplies the squared deviation of R_i from the mean. 1

Thus, if we consider the variance of a stock that returns 10% half the time and −10% the other half the time, the variance will be calculated as follows: The mean return is $0.5 \times 0.10 + 0.5 \times -0.10 = 0$. Thus, the two possible squared deviations are going to be $(0.10)^2$ and also $(-0.10)^2$, both of which equal 0.01. The variance as the expected squared deviation is thus $0.5 \times 0.01 + 0.5 \times 0.01$. So that equals 0.01.

A measure that is related to the variance is called a standard deviation. The standard deviation is simply defined as: $SDr = \sigma = \text{Var}(R)^{(1/2)}$. The standard deviation of return is more intuitive, since it is in percentages. A variance, instead, is in percent squared. Think of the standard deviation as a kind of average for the size of a deviation from the mean return percent. So, for example, for the 10% + minus 10% stock, the variance is 0.01% squared, while the standard deviation is going to be the square root of 0.01% squared, which is equal to 0.1, or 10%.

Another thing I want to mention here is that the convention is to call the standard deviation in returns volatility. In standard conversational English, there is really no distinction between variance and volatility. Both mean variability around some norm. But in investments, there is a big difference, and that difference is the square root. So, the standard deviation is always the square root of the variance.

The standard deviation as a measure of average deviation is really useful. In fact, if returns are normally distributed, like a bell-shaped curve, then a return in a given period will land somewhere between the expected return plus or minus one standard deviation approximately 2/3 of the time. Plus or minus two standard deviations covers almost 95% of the outcomes on average. That is, the return will be less than the mean minus two standard deviations only 2.5% of the time, and the return will be the mean plus two standard deviations above that only 2.5% of the time. Thus, the extreme values account for only approximately 5% when combined. For example, say you've got a million dollars to invest in a portfolio of securities that has a mean return of 10% per year and a standard deviation of 15%. This is not unrealistic. By the end of the year, you will have, on average, $1,000,000 × 1.1, which gives you $1,100,000 on average. But, approximately 2.5% of the time, your $1,000,000 will have fallen below $800,000. This is true, since two standard deviations is 2 × 0.15, or our standard deviation is 15%. That equals 30%. Thus, a return of 1.1, or 10%, − 30% is a loss of 20%. If the standard deviation is smaller, then such a fall is much less likely to happen.

Next, let's consider the covariance and correlation. Before we get to the definition, however, let me motivate why it is important. Recall that the variance or the volatility quantifies how unpredictable a variable is. As such, you might be tempted to think of the variance or the standard deviation as a measure of risk. The most important idea of this course, however, is the notion that one cannot measure the risk of an individual security without considering it in the portfolio in which it will be held. If one holds a portfolio of securities—a collection of various amounts of money invested in a variety of different securities—then the variance of the return on the portfolio will represent risk to that investor. But, how does the variance of an individual security contribute to the variance of the return on the whole portfolio?

The variance of a portfolio return is much more complicated than that of an individual security because we need to know how the return of one security is related to the return of another. This is true because we need to know how the combined return of the securities deviates from the combined mean return for the portfolio.

Mathematical statistics has a way to quantify the relationship between any two random variables. One concept is that of a joint distribution. The joint distribution between any two random variables—say, returns—is a specification of the probabilities associated with each possible pair of values. For example, consider the following description of IBM and Ford. For simplicity, we will assume that Ford can only take on two returns and that IBM can only take on two values. Clearly, this is a simplification since, in reality, Ford and IBM can take on lots of values, but let's assume two values for the time being. Let the two values for Ford be −48% and +21%, and the two values for IBM be −2% and +12%. Thus, there are going to be four possible combinations of Ford and IBM returns. For example, Ford at −0.048, or −4.8%, and IBM at −0.02, or −2%, is one of the possible four combinations. Let's say that the joint distribution is such that the probability of each possible pair is the same across all pairs at 0.25, or 25%.

The joint distribution can be used to calculate both expected values as well as variances for each of the returns. In this case, we would use something called marginal probabilities. A marginal probability is the probability that you get if you just add up all the probabilities for one given value for one of the variables. It's called a marginal probability because it's what you would get if you were to add things up and put them in the margins, with the possible values of Ford running across the top of, say, a table, and all of the values of IBM running down the side. In that example, what you'd have is you'd have the marginal probabilities for IBM along the side and you'd have the marginal probabilities for Ford at the bottom.

So, in this case, if there's 25% for each of the four possible pairs, what that says is for any one of the values for Ford, we add those up as a 50%-chance for Ford being −4.8%. There's a 50%-chance that it'll return the 21%.

Being able to calculate means and variances from marginal probabilities is not why joint distribution are useful. The joint distribution tells you how likely two variables are going to move together, or whether they're going to move independently, or whether they're going to move in opposite directions. Mathematically, using the information contained in the joint distribution between any two random variables, the covariance is defined as follows: The covariance, say, between the return on Ford and the return on IBM, is equal to the expectation of a product of deviations from the mean for each of the two. So it will take the return on Ford minus its mean, but multiple that by the return on IBM minus its mean. That is, the covariance is the expected value of the possible paired deviations of each from their mean.

What does this tell you intuitively? If, according to the joint distribution, there's a lot of probability associated with cases in which, first, Ford is above its mean and, second, IBM is below its mean and the first is below its mean and the second is above its mean. If so, then the covariance will be negative. This is true since most of the values in this expectation are negative, since either a negative is being multiplied by a positive or a positive being multiplied by a negative.

If, instead, most of the possibilities are associated with cases in which the first is above its mean and the second is, too, and when the first is below its mean, so is the second one, then the covariance will be positive. This is true since most of the values in the expected value are both positive at the same time.

Given the joint distribution in which the probabilities are all paired up to be 0.25, the covariance is essentially zero. This makes sense, since if IBM is below its mean, then the value of Ford will be equally likely to be above or below its mean.

Now let's consider what happens if we move some probability around. Let's take 5% away from Ford at −0.048 and at IBM at −2% and give it to Ford at −0.048 and IBM at 12%. Similarly, let's take 5% away from Ford at 21% and IBM at 12% and give it to Ford at 21% but IBM at −2%. Such a reallocation does not affect the expected value, since the marginal probabilities do not change. It does, however, change the variances, and it also changes the covariance. The covariance now becomes −0.00181. This makes sense that the covariance would be negative, because we've reallocated probability so that now, whenever Ford is above its means, it's also less likely that IBM will be above its mean, and whenever Ford is below its mean, it's less likely that IBM will also be below. Now this number is difficult to interpret, as it is a percent deviation times a percent deviation.

A more intuitively informative value is the correlation coefficient, which scales the covariance for the size of the variance of each. Specifically, the correlation coefficient, which is often denoted with a rho, is equal to the covariance between any two of *R*s, divided by the standard deviation of one times the standard deviation of the other. In the case of Ford, by the way, and IBM, we have a covariance of −0.00181. We're going to divide that by the variance. The variance of Ford is 0.01664, and the variance of IBM is 0.0049. If you do that calculation, what you see is the correlation ends up being −0.2. In general, correlation coefficients range from 1 to −1.

If the correlation between two variables is 1, then it is the case that one of the variables is a constant multiple of the other. That is, you know the value of one, you're going to know what the value of the other one is. For example, if the return on Sleaze Co. is always half the return on Ford, then knowing that the return on Ford is 10% allows you to perfectly predict that the return on Sleaze Co. is going to be 5%. Knowing one allows you to perfectly predict the other.

At the other extreme, two variables can be perfectly negatively correlated. When one is up, the other one is exactly down. And then, at a middle ground they can be completely uncorrelated with the correlation being zero. So, to summarize, the sign of the correlation tells you something about what's the direction of the relationship. If it's zero, there really is no relationship. The closer you get to 1, or the closer you get to −1, that tells you something about the strength of the relationship.

So what we've seen throughout this lecture is a sort of standard set of ways to characterize the randomness of random variables. We will use these techniques, we will use these measures in order to get at how to combine securities together to affect the risk of the overall portfolio.

The Theory of Efficient Markets

Lecture 5

In this lecture, you will begin to learn about the efficient market hypothesis in detail. First, the efficient market hypothesis will be defined. Second, you will explore what the hypothesis implies with respect to both security price movements and the ability of various market participants to make excess returns. Third, you will examine the empirical evidence on whether the implications of the efficient market hypothesis hold in data from actual markets. This third step will be done in a later lecture.

The Efficient Market Hypothesis

- The efficient market hypothesis (EMH) is that financial markets are efficient. There are two senses of the word "efficient," one of which is what the EMH refers to directly. The other meaning sometimes is considered an indirect implication of the first meaning.

- The EMH is directly about informational efficiency. The market for a particular security is said to be informationally efficient if all available information that is relevant with respect to the future value of that security is reflected in the current price of that security. The key is that the current price reflects everything available of relevance to future value.

- An efficient market for a security is one in which newly available information is reflected quickly. If it takes time for new information to be reflected in the price of a security, then there is a significant amount of time in which the price of that security does not reflect that available information, which is a violation of the EMH.

The Weak Form

- There are three forms to the EMH, which differ in terms of what is considered "available." One is the so-called weak form of the EMH. It is the weakest form in the sense that it is the easiest form to satisfy—that is, it is the form with the fewest conditions. The weak form states that any information that can be gleaned about future prices from past prices (or returns) will be reflected in the current price. That is, it defines "available" information as including only past prices. This is a weak form because, while it may be difficult for many people to know about, and understand the implications of, the firm's strategic plans say that it should be easy for people to get past price information.

- The principle implication of the weak form is that there are no predictable patterns in returns. A predictable pattern might be something like the following: After the market drops by more than 1%, 90% of the time, the return the next day is bigger than the average return over the previous year. This is a violation of the EMH because, if one can predict with reasonable accuracy (in this case, 90%) that the price is going to be significantly higher tomorrow, then the price today should be higher in anticipation of this.

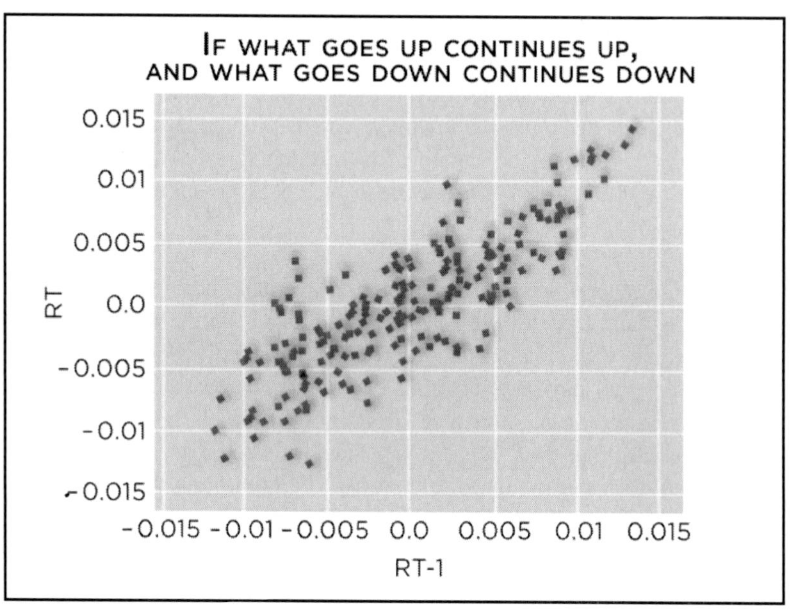

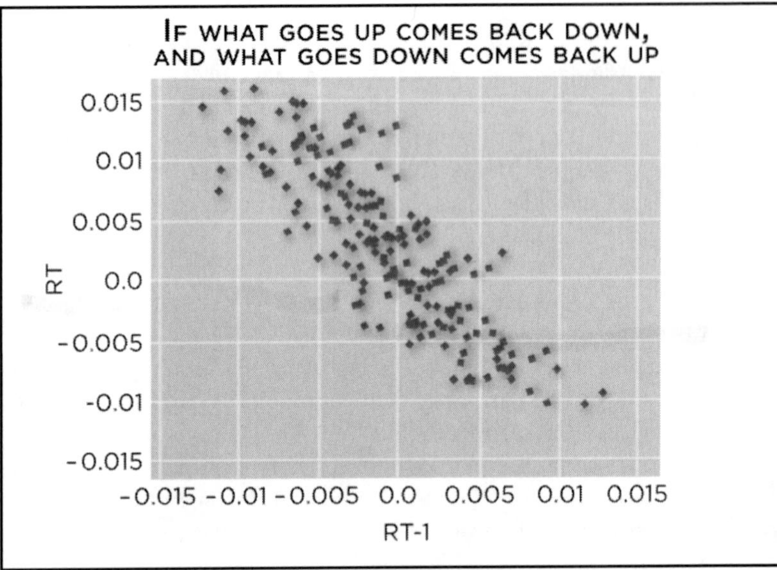

- If the above fact is true for a particular security, then that fact is typically taken as evidence that, on average, the market for that security overreacts to bad news—and following that overreaction, it corrects itself the next day. If the market overreacts to good news, too, then the return following a day with a large positive return will, on average, be negative, overturning some of the prior day's reaction. That is, what goes up comes back down, and what goes down comes back up.

- If the market were to underreact on average, then following good news (and a positive return), there would be another positive return the next day, on average. And following bad news—and a negative return that day—there would be another negative return the next day. These cases are also violations of the EMH because the average price level the next day is not reflected in the current price. If investors know that the price will be higher the day after good news, then why don't they bid up the price today? If they don't, then the current price does not reflect their expectation, which is a violation of the EMH.

- Thus, the weak form of the EMH implies that you can't "time" the market by trading in advance of predictable price changes. It is sometimes said that the weak form implies that price changes are unpredictable. Equivalently, it is said that under the weak form, prices follow what is called a random walk.

- Note that the unpredictable price change and random walk implication is really only an implication of the weak form in markets where no one cares about risk; that is, these features only hold in markets populated solely by risk-neutral people, which are people who only care about the average return, not the possible variability in the return.

- In a risk-neutral world, the average returns will be just the risk-free return, which is the return that induces people to give up current consumption in exchange for future consumption. That is, the risk-free rate is the rate that only reflects the time trade-off—not the risk trade-off. Because no one cares about risk in this risk-neutral world, all interest rates (or returns) are the same.

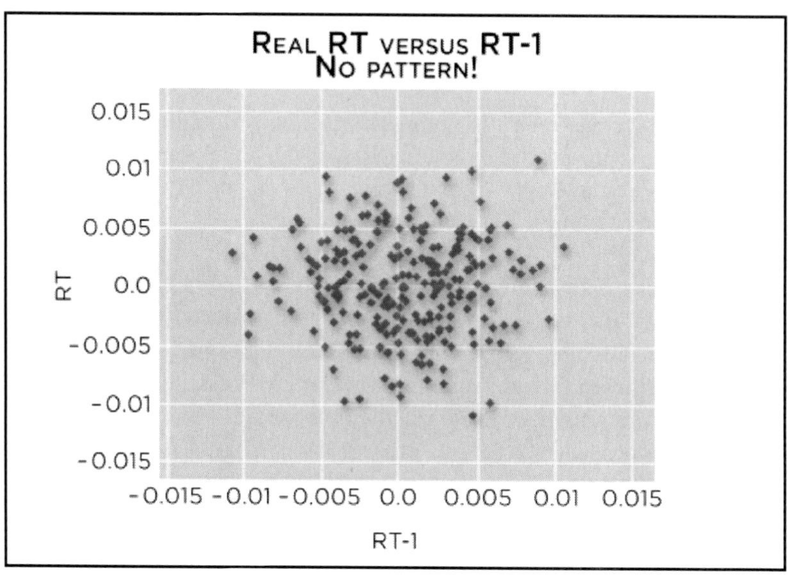

- At very short intervals—for example, over a day—the return you need is typically very small. When risk-free rates are on the order of 1% (as they were following the financial crisis in 2008), then the daily return is 0.03 of a basis point. That's very, very small—in fact, hardly discernible.

- So, if the daily return on all securities is essentially zero on average, then the frequency with which prices rise will be essentially equal to the frequency with which they go down. The changes in price levels are due to the arrival of news. Because news is by definition unpredictable, the price changes must also be unpredictable.

- This is consistent with the image of someone taking a random walk, whereby every step is independent of the previous step. Security prices are similar. If there is good news the next day, the price takes a step up; if there is bad news on that day, the price takes a step down. If you could systematically, perfectly predict the arrival of good news after some observable event, then the price would go up more when that event was observed, but not when the news actually came out. When the news actually came out, people would say that it's not news. Rather, it's old news (which is already reflected in the current price).

- If the average return is significant, then that would imply that the prices would drift up over time. That is, the price changes would be positive on average: When the price rises on one day, it is likely to rise the next day.

- The only extent to which the future return is predictable is by the amount that generates an average return that compensates risk-averse investors for bearing the risk over that period. With risk-averse investors, the weak form of the EMH essentially says that excess returns (i.e., those returns in excess of the average return to compensate savers) are unpredictable. That is, if we were to subtract the average return from each return, the return that is left over is unpredictable.

- The weak form of the EMF implies that you cannot make any excess returns by plunging in and out of the market on the basis of what you can glean from past prices. So, the issue is whether you can spot patterns or not. Consider a chart that shows a time series plot of a year's worth of prices for a stock. If you see a pattern, you are not alone—but is there really a pattern? Plots of price levels can be difficult to interpret; maybe more accurately, they can be easy to overinterpret.

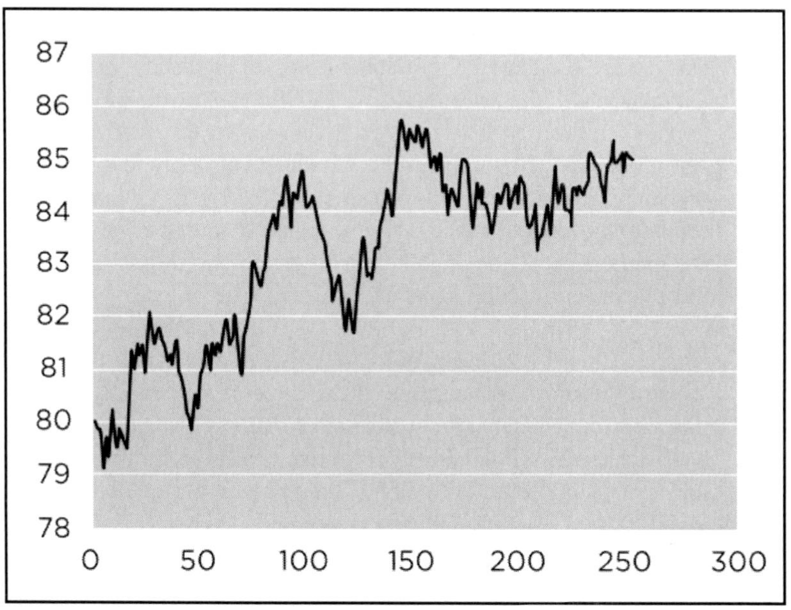

- There is not much argument about the existence of predictability. However, there is significant argument as to whether that predictability represents predictability in excess returns or whether it is predictable variation in fair returns.

The Semi-Strong Form

- The semi-strong form of the EMH is that available information includes past prices/returns and any public information (e.g., Procter & Gamble and Gillette are going to merge). This is less weak because prices have to reflect that which is reflected under the weak form plus the addition of public information. The semi-strong form implies that you cannot make excess returns using a trading strategy that reacts to public announcement of events or policies.

- An example of a violation of semi-strong-form efficiency might entail the announcement of a corporate policy such as a dividend cut. Let's say that the firm announces a dividend cut; at the announcement, the price declines. But on average, the price gains half of the drop back in the next week. Given this rebound, you can make money by buying after dividend cuts: Buy low and sell higher on average the following week. If there is a violation of semi-strong-form efficiency, then the market must not be valuing the implication of the announcement accurately; in this example, there is an overreaction.

- Underreaction to an event will also produce a violation of semi-strong efficiency. For example, if the price of a publically traded firm falls immediately after it announces that it is going to sell more equity, that by itself would not constitute evidence of a violation of the semi-strong form. However, if the price on average continued to fall for a year after the announcement, then the reaction at the announcement is not efficient—there was an underreaction, on average.

The Strong Form

- The strong form of the EMH is that in addition to the stuff that should be reflected under the semi-strong form, it must also reflect private information. If markets are strong-form efficient, then even insiders cannot make trading profits by trading on insider information. This is called the strong form because it seems very unlikely to hold.

- In addition, the strong form implies that right after the decision to adopt a given corporate policy is made—but before it is announced—the impact of the policy will be reflected in prices. There is some evidence that such information does leak out into prices. This is probably because of insider trading (which, although illegal, still happens).

- There is something ironic about strong-form efficiency, however. Although it would be great to have prices be fully efficient and reflect everything, in such a world, there is no incentive to collect costly information in the first place. If a person cannot profitably trade on his or her superior information or analysis of value because prices reflect that information before they can trade, then no one will engage in that kind of activity—and prices will actually be less informative on average. The good news is that no one thinks that markets are strong-form efficient.

Suggested Reading

Bernstein, *Capital Ideas*.

Fox, *The Myth of the Rational Market*.

Malkiel, *A Random Walk Down Wall Street*.

Questions to Consider

1. Go to Yahoo! Finance and create a plot of the prices of a stock you are interested in for over the last five years. Do you see any patterns in the prices? Do you think you know where the prices will be in a year?

2. What kind of publicly available information do you think is relevant for value but might not be accurately reflected in stock prices? Do you think that investors systematically interpret that information wrongly, or do you think that investors just don't pay enough attention to it? Is the market inefficient either way?

The Theory of Efficient Markets

Lecture 5—Transcript

There is a very old story about two financial economists walking down the street. One is a finance professor from the University of Chicago, the birthplace of what is called the efficient market hypothesis. In this lecture, we will discuss this hypothesis in detail. But, in brief, it essentially says that competition among market participants prevents people from getting a "free lunch," or making excessive amounts of money. The other economist is from Wall Street, a place presumably that thrives on making excessive amounts of money. As they talk, they pass what appears to be a $20 bill lying on the sidewalk. In a moment of uncharacteristic generosity, the Wall Streeter points at the bill and says to the professor, "Go ahead." The professor, looking quizzical, says, "What?" And the Wall Streeter says, "Aren't you going to pick up that $20 bill?" The professor says, "Of course not. If it were a real $20 bill, someone would have picked it up already." And with that, the Wall Streeter bends down and picks it up.

Later, they stop at the nearby sandwich shop for lunch and the professor asks, "Aren't you going to buy me a sandwich with the money that you found?" And the Wall Streeter replies, "No. There's no such thing as a free lunch—for you, at least."

In this lecture, we will discuss the extent to which you can make money actively trading in the market. As we discussed in Lecture 2, there are a number of ways in which you can be active. You can be active trying to time the market as a whole, taking money out of the market when you think it will do poorly and putting it in to safe investments like T-bills. You can also be active by reallocating money across sectors or industries, taking money out of the sectors you think will do relatively poorly and putting it in those you think will do relatively well. You can also be active by stock picking, by trying to find individual securities that you think will do better than the market as a whole, or as the sector or the industry that they're in.

In this and the next lecture, I want to talk to you about how often you can expect to find $20 bills lying around. While the Chicago professor may seem silly for not picking up what was obviously a $20 bill, the question you really need to ask is whether it makes sense for you to work through lunch or go for a walk during lunch, and, if it does make sense for you to go for a walk, should you walk down a busy main thoroughfare or a less-well-traveled side street looking for $20 bills?

One way to summarize the intent of this whole course is that it seeks to develop techniques for judging whether a potential investment is a good deal or not. With this intent, the course focuses on essentially a two-part process. First, determine how best to characterize risk. Second, given a good measure of risk, determine whether a security is a good or a bad deal in terms of its ability to, on average, generate returns that will compensate you for its risk.

A good deal is one in which the market price of the security is below its value, and a bad deal is one in which the market price is above its value. That is, anything is potentially a good deal if it's cheap enough and everything is potentially a bad deal if it's too expensive.

In this and the next lecture, we'll examine the evidence on whether or not the premise of this process is folly. The actual process may be folly if the specific techniques people use to measure risk and calculate value are not very good at identifying good and bad deals. But the premise of this process is that there are good and bad deals in the market—that there are $20 bills lying around to be found. Notice that, regardless of what we find in this lecture, it will be good news. If we find that there are no good or bad deals to be found, then the good news is that all deals are just right. That is, prices reflect true value. Thus, you can invest, say, in order to save for retirement without worrying about whether you are being taken advantage of.

And, if we find that there are good and bad deals to be found, then that's good news that you may be able to earn a return on any effort that you want to put into finding those opportunities. If there are good and bad deals, then the only possible bad news is, in order to not be taken advantage of, you have to spend a significant amount of effort protecting yourself from being exploited. And in this lecture, we'll examine this possibility, too.

Just given the fact that there are 19 lectures that follow this lecture, you might guess that there must be $20 bills lying around—else there would be no reason to go through a bunch of lectures on techniques for finding them. This logic is flawed, however, and here's why. Even if you cannot find $20 bills lying around, there is a decent—but not excessive—return to be earned simply by investing. In the story of the financial economists walking to lunch, $20 bills are meant to represent money that you don't have to earn. From now on, I will refer to any money that you get in excess of what you should earn as an excess return.

I keep saying earn. What do I mean by earn? How do you earn returns? And how much should you earn? Well, at any given time in financial markets, there are a bunch of people who have ideas, but not enough money to implement them. At the same time, there's a bunch of people who have some money that they could either consume or save. Since most people are impatient by their very nature, the people with the money now need to be induced to save. If they're going to give up some consumption today, they need to get more consumption in the future than they give up today. That is, they need to get interest on their savings. They earn that interest by forgoing consumption.

You could also say that they're earning interest by providing a service. By giving up something of value, current consumption, they are providing something of value to the people with the ideas, capital to implement their ideas.

In addition to earning a return giving up the consumption-now-versus-consumption-later trade-off, the people who save will also need to be induced to bear risk, the risk associated with some of the ideas turning out to be good, while others of them turn out to be bad. The riskier the idea, the greater the return savers need to be induced to save by investing in that idea. A fair return is a return that balances the amount savers need to be induced to save and the amount the people with ideas are willing to pay to fund their ideas. So, savers earn a fair return by bearing risk and providing capital. An excess return is one that is in excess of the return needed to induce someone to invest. If you like ice cream enough to eat it without whipped cream, an excess return is free whipped cream on your ice cream.

So, what does this have to do with the 19 lectures that follow? Before we investigate whether there are $20 bills, or excess returns, to be had in the market, the point I want to make is that even if there are no excess returns, there are still many things that you need to think about and do with your investments in order to ensure that you get just even a fair return. Many of the 19 lectures that follow will concern these types of issues.

More specifically, even if there are no excess returns to be had in the market for securities, there may be inefficiencies in the market for financial services. Much of the material in the course will put you in a position to make sure that you can get a fair share of your returns if you decide to delegate the management of your investments to a portfolio manager. And if you invest on your own, many of the issues we discuss subsequently will make sure that you don't make mistakes and miss opportunities for even fair returns. Furthermore, the market is not very sympathetic. It won't compensate you for any risk that you might be taking mistakenly. So it's important for us to figure out what risk is so you can avoid it when necessary.

So, let's look at the efficient market hypothesis in detail. We'll do this in three steps. First, I will define the hypothesis exactly. Second, we will explore what the hypothesis implies with respect to both security price movements and the ability of various market participants to make excess returns. Third, we will examine the empirical evidence on whether the implications of the efficient market hypothesis hold in the data from actual markets. This third step will be done in Lecture 7.

The efficient market hypothesis, or EMH for short, is that financial markets are efficient. What does "efficient" mean? There are two senses of the word, one of which is what the efficient market hypothesis refers to directly. The other meaning sometimes is considered an indirect implication of the first meaning.

The EMH is directly related to informational efficiency. The market for a particular security is said to be informationally efficient if all available information that is relevant with respect to the future value of that security is reflected in the current price of that security. The key thing here is that the current price reflects everything available of relevance to future value. This means that if there is information available now that the profitability of a particular company is going to increase significantly in two years, then the current stock price will reflect that future increase in profitability now.

An efficient market for a security is one in which newly available information is also reflected very quickly. If it takes time for the new information to be reflected in the price of a security, then there is a significant amount of time in which the price of that security does not reflect that available information, which would be a violation of the EMH.

There are three forms of the EMH which differ in terms of what is considered available information. The weakest form is the so-called "weak form" of the EMH. It is the weakest form in the sense that it is the easiest form to satisfy. That is, it is the form with the fewest conditions. The weak form states that any information that can be gleaned about future prices from past prices or returns will be reflected in the current price. That is, it defines available information as including only past prices or returns. This is a weak form since, while it may be hard for many people to know about—and understand the implications of—the firm's strategic plans, say, it should be easy for people to get past price information.

The principle implication of the weak form is that there is no predictable pattern in returns. A predictable pattern might be something like "after the market drops more than 1%, 90% of the time the return the next day is bigger than the average return over the previous year." This is a violation of the EMH, because if one could predict with reasonable accuracy, in this case 90%, that the price is going to be significantly higher tomorrow, then the price today should be higher in anticipation of this.

If the above fact is true for a particular security, that fact is typically taken as evidence that, on average, the market for that security overreacts to bad news. And following that overreaction, it corrects itself the next day. If the market overreacts to good news, too, then the return the following day after a large positive return will, on average, be negative, overturning some of the prior day's reaction. That is, what goes up comes back down, and what goes down comes back up.

If the market were to underreact on average, then following good news and a positive return there would be another positive return the next day on average. And following bad news, and a negative return that day, there would be another negative return the next day. These cases are also violations of the weak form of the EMH, since the average price level the next day is not reflected in the current price. If investors know that the price will be higher the day after good news, then why don't they bid up the price today? And if they don't, then the current price does not reflect that expectation, which is a violation of the EMH.

Thus, the weak form of the EMH implies that you can't time the market by trading in advance of predictable price changes. It is sometimes said that the weak form implies that price changes are unpredictable. Equivalently, it is also said that under the weak form prices follow what is called a random walk. I will define what a random walk is shortly, but, I must disclose first that the unpredictable price change and random walk implication is really only an implication of the weak form in markets where no one cares about risk. That is, these features only hold in markets populated solely by risk-neutral people.

Risk-neutral people are those who only care about average return, not the possible variability in the return. Such people view the following two securities as equivalent in terms of returns. Let's say security A has a 50-50 chance at a 10%-return and a 20%-return, for an average return of 15%, while security B always returns 15%. Risk-neutral people are neutral to the risk. All they care about is the average return. So, although there is uncertainty about the return that will occur for security A, since A has an average return that is the same as the average return for B, a risk-neutral investor would view them as equivalent as an investment. A risk-neutral person would also prefer security A to, say, security C, which generates 14% always. Thus, a risk-neutral person always looks solely at what the average return is to rank alternative investments.

So, before we think about the more realistic, but also more complex case in which people care about risk, let's think about how the weak form would manifest itself in the simpler case of a market with only risk-neutral people.

Once we understand that, we can more easily see the added impact of people caring about risk on the implications of the weak form on the EMH.

Let's start with a little thought experiment. In a market with just risk-neutral people, what would be the average return on any security? It would be the same for all securities. Why? Well, let's consider what would happen if there were just two securities in this world; say, security A and security C from before. Although security A's return is uncertain, no one cares. Since it has a higher average return than C, 15% versus 14 for C, everyone would like A and dislike C. As a result, everyone would buy A and sell C. And as they buy A, the price of A will rise, and, as they sell C, the price of C will fall. As the price of A rises, the average return on A will fall, and as the price of C falls, the return on C will rise.

To see this, let's say that we have the price of A as currently at $10. In the event that the return on A is 10% over the next period, then the price of A will be $11 at the end of that period. Similarly, if the return over the next period turns out to be 20%, then the price of A will be $12 at the end of the period. If people want to buy A at the current price, then the price will rise—say, to $10.05. If so, then the price of A turns out to be $11 at the end of the next period, then the return is going to be what? It's going to be ($11 − $10.05)/$10.05, and that's a 9.45%-return. If the price turns out to be $12, then the return is ($12 − $10.05)/$10.05, and that's a 19.4%-return. The average return, then, is $0.5 \times 9.45 + 0.5 \times 19.4$, which is equal to 14.43%, which is lower than the initial 15%. So, similarly, if people were to sell C, the current price of C will fall, which would make the return rise.

By buying and selling A and C, what they're going to do is they are going to make these returns adjust, and people are going to be buying and selling C until the returns actually end up being exactly the same. Thus, in a risk-neutral world, the average returns will be just the risk-free return, which is the return that induces people to give up current consumption in exchange for future consumption. That is, the risk-free rate is the rate that only reflects the time trade-off, not the risk trade-off. Since no one cares about risk in this risk-neutral world, all interest rates and returns are the same.

At very short intervals—say, over a day—the return you need is typically very small. For example, if the annual return is 14%, which is huge, by the way, then the daily return is about 5 basis points, where 100 basis points equals 1%. That is, 5 basis points is 5/100 of a percent—very, very small. When risk-free rates are on the order of 1%, as they were following the financial crisis in 2008, then the daily return is 3/100 of a basis point. That's very, very, very small—in fact, hardly discernible.

So, if the daily return on all securities is essentially zero on average, then the frequency with which prices rise will be essentially equal to the frequency in which they go down. The changes in the price levels are due to the arrival of news. Since news is by the very definition unpredictable—else it's not news, it's olds—the price changes must also be unpredictable.

This is consistent with the image of someone taking a random walk, whereby every step is independent of the previous step. To see what I mean by a random walk, consider my position in the front of the studio here on the carpet. If I start in the middle, and then I flip a coin, if it comes up heads, I'm going to take one step to the left. If it comes up tails, I'll take a step to the right. Where I go from there is going to be completely unpredictable.

Security prices are similar. If there's good news the next day, the price will step up, and if there's bad news on that day, the price will take a step down. If you could systematically predict the arrival of good news after some observable event, then the price would go up more when that event was observed, but not when the news was actually coming out. When the news actually came out, people would say that it's not news. Rather, it's old news, which is already reflected in the current price.

So that's what a random walk is. You go up and you go down randomly. Price changes are not predictable. But what about the average return, what if that is actually a significant number? Then what would that imply the prices would do over time? They would essentially drift up over time. That is, price changes would be positive on average. When the price rises on one day, it's likely to rise the next day. Is that a violation of the weak form? In spirit, no. The only extent to which the future return is predictable is by the amount that generates an average return that compensates risk-averse investors for bearing the risk over that period.

With risk-averse investors, the weak form of the efficient market hypothesis essentially says that excess returns—those returns in excess of the average return to compensate savers—is unpredictable. That is, if we were to subtract the average return from each return, the return that is left over is unpredictable. You can predict that you will get a fair return by holding the security. You just can't predict when you will get a return that exceeds that return or is inferior relative to that return.

If you could, then you would buy more before the return exceeds what you should get and sell before the return is insufficient given the risk. And by doing so, the price will rise before positive excess returns, which lowers that return, and will drop before a negative excess return, which will raise the return. Thus, by exploiting the predictability, your trades either moderate the effect or completely eliminate it. The weak form of the efficient market hypothesis states that active investors are active enough to eliminate the predictability in excess returns. And that means that, on average, investors who just hold securities will earn a fair return, but not an excessive return.

To put this into the context of the framework for investing we developed in Lecture 2, the weak form of the efficient market hypothesis implies that you cannot make any excess returns by plunging in and out of the market on the basis of what you can glean from past prices. If you hold a single index fund or an ETF that represents most of the market, you might be tempted to use that fund to time the market. If you think the market will fall, sell it and put all the money into cash. And if you think the market will rise, take all your money out of cash and put it into the market. The weak form of the EMH implies that you will not make any money doing that. In fact, given that there are transaction costs associated with such trading, the weak form says that you will actually lose money relative to what you could earn simply by buying and holding.

So, the issue is whether you can spot a pattern or not. Consider a chart that shows a time-series plot of a year's worth of prices for a stock. Say, go to any web site and download the data. Do you see any patterns? If you do, you're not alone. But, is there really a pattern?

Alright, so let's consider how we might detect predictability. Specifically, let's consider a plot of return at, say, t, against the return at $t - 1$. So what we're going to do is, on one of the axes we're going to plot the current return, and then on the other axis we're going to plot the return that occurred before that, or last period's return. On the plot, you can draw a vertical line emanating up from the horizontal axis to indicate the average of last period's returns—the lag returns. Any return from that period that was bigger than this average will be on the right of the line. Anything to the left corresponds to returns that are lower than average. Similarly, you could draw a line perpendicular to the vertical axis that indicates the average for the subsequent period's returns, RT.

What would predictability look like in such a plot of data? If there is predictability, then you should have a scatter of data points that either trend up or trend down. For example, if you have overreaction to information, then you would have "that which goes up comes back down," and "that which goes down comes back up." A plot of RT against RT-1 that has a general downward trend in the scatter of data is consistent with the overreaction violation of the weak form. With this kind of scatter, you would see that when the previous return was above average, more often than not, the returns on the next day are lower than average. Similarly, when the prior return is below average, the next day's return will be above average more often than not. Furthermore, if we calculate the average of the returns for the next day for different ranges of last period's returns, we see that the lower the last period return is, the higher is the average the next day.

In contrast, a scatter plot with a general upward trend is consistent with an under-reaction violation of the weak form efficiency. That is, what goes up continues up and that which goes down, continues down.

Let's return to the plot of the prices of your randomly selected stock. Do you see a pattern? I've done this with students at the university, by the way. I'll show them a scatter plot, but this is actually a scatter plot from data that I have created using a process that has no predictability in it. Most of my students will say that they actually do see a pattern. And then I will show them a plot of RT against RT-1 that proves that there is no pattern. The data are evenly distributed throughout the plot. There's no upward trend or downward trend. If the last period's return is high or low, then the next day's return is equally likely to be above or below its average. There's no predictability. By the way, most people end up arguing with me when they look at the level of the prices. They see patterns in the level of the prices. This illustrates that plots of price level can be really hard to interpret. Maybe more accurately, they can be easy to over-interpret.

What is the empirical evidence about the weak form? One of the reasons that the University of Chicago is associated with the EMH is because of Professor Eugene Fama, one of the fathers of modern finance. Professor Fama was particularly adept at computers back in a time when a computer less powerful than the one that typically sits in your lap took up whole basements of large academic buildings. Because he was so adept, he was the first to do the monumental task of systematically looking to see if there was any predictability. And, at that time, he found none.

More recently, as computing power because cheaper and more convenient to wield, closer looks at data have shown some predictability. In fact, there is not much argument about the existence of predictability. However, there is significant argument as to whether this predictability represents predictability in excess returns or whether it is predictability in the variation in fair returns.

Let's move on to the next form. There's the semi-strong form of the EMH. It's that available information includes past prices and returns and any public information. For example, whether Procter and Gamble or Gillette are going to merge. This is less weak, since prices have to reflect that which is reflected under the weak form plus any additional public information. The semi-strong form implies that you cannot make excess returns using a trade strategy that reacts to public announcements of events or policies.

An example of a violation of the semi-strong form of efficiency might entail the announcement of a corporate policy such as a dividend cut. Let's say the firm announces a dividend cut. At the announcement, the price declines. But on average, the price gains half of the drop back in the next week. Given this rebound, you can make money by buying after dividend cuts. Buy low and sell higher on average the following week. If there is a violation of the semi-strong form efficiency, then the market must not be valuing the implication of the announcement accurately. In this example, there is an overreaction.

An under-reaction to an event will also produce a violation of the semi-strong form of efficiency. For example, if the price of a publically-traded firm falls immediately after it announces that it is going to sell more equity, that by itself would not constitute evidence of a violation of the semi-strong form. But, if the price on average continued to fall for a year after the announcement, then the reaction at the announcement must not be efficient; there was an under-reaction on average.

Now let's consider the strong form. The strong form of the EMH is that in addition to the stuff that should be reflected under the semi-strong form and the weak form, it must also reflect private information. If markets are strong form efficient, even insiders cannot make trading profits by trading on inside information. This is called the strong form because it seems very unlikely to hold. In addition, the strong form also implies that right after the decision to adopt a given corporate policy is made, but before it's actually announced, the impact of that policy will be reflected in prices. There is some evidence that some of this information does leak out into prices. This is probably because of insider trading, while, although illegal, still does happen.

There is actually something very ironic about the strong-form efficiency. Although it would be great to have prices fully efficient and reflect everything, in such a world there is really no incentive to collect costly information in the first place. If a person cannot profitably trade on his or her superior information or analysis of value because the price reflects that information before they can trade, then no one will engage in that kind of activity, and prices will actually be less informative on average. This is called the Grossman paradox, named after Sanford Grossman, the professor who pioneered the way we think about information and security prices. The good news is that no one really thinks that markets are strong-form efficient.

The point of this lecture has been to discuss the implications of market prices reflecting information about value. It is often said that an economist knows the price of everything, but the value of nothing. The question examined here is whether there is at least a theoretical case to be made that prices might equal value. In the next lecture, we'll examine the empirical implications regarding this theoretical case.

Evidence on Efficient Markets

Lecture 6

The last lecture examined the efficient market hypothesis and its implications. In this lecture, you will examine the body of empirical evidence on whether these implications are borne out in the data from actual markets. By examining this evidence, you will get a sense of where you might want to look for trading opportunities and where you need not bother. While most of the academic evidence is that markets are fairly efficient, even the academics have found a number of phenomena that seem to put chinks in the armor of the efficient market hypothesis. This lecture will look at some of the most notable phenomena.

Momentum

- The first set of anomalies concerns predictable patterns in returns. These might be violations of the weak form of the EMH in that, presumably, you can make excess profits simply by executing trade strategies conditional on past returns or price levels.

- There are a few of these anomalies; the first is the momentum phenomenon. To understand what this phenomenon is, consider the following strategy. Step 1 is to take a list of many securities—for example, those traded on the NYSE and NASDAQ—and calculate their returns over some past period. For example, calculate their return over the last 6 months.

- Step 2 is to rank these securities from highest return to lowest return. Step 3 is to buy all of the securities in the top 10% (let's call them the winners) and sell short all those securities in the bottom 10% (let's call them the losers).

- The final step is to hold this portfolio for 6 months. Then, after those 6 months, do it again—that is, rerank all the securities on the NYSE and NASDAQ on the basis of the just-past 6-month return, and go long those securities in the winner 10% and sell short those in the loser 10%. Hold for another 6 months, and then repeat.

- It has been shown that, on average, the returns from this strategy dominate the returns from a passive strategy of just holding a "market" portfolio consisting of all the securities on your original list. It has also been shown that such phenomena exist if you use different horizons. Furthermore, the magnitude of the extra return is fairly large; if you rebalance once a month, you can get about 1% extra return, which is approximately 12% per year when compounded over 12 months.

- According to the weak form of the EMH, you should not be able to beat the market by trading on the basis of past returns. However, this momentum strategy, as the name suggests, indicates that stocks that go up continue to go up, and stocks that go down continue to go down. This is a predictable pattern that is not supposed to happen if markets are weak-form efficient.

Possible Efficient Explanations

- There are many retorts to this conclusion that appear in the academic literature. One retort is that it fails to consider transactions costs. Such a strategy is costly to implement, especially for a small investor. If you consider all the stocks on the NYSE and NASDAQ, you're talking about thousands and thousands of stocks—around 7000 in total.

- If you do the rebalancing each month, it turns out that many of the stocks that were in the winner portfolio over one period are not in the winner portfolio the next period. The same is true for the loser stocks. So, to implement this strategy, you have to trade a lot of stocks each period. And if you have to pay a brokerage fee, such fees will eat up any gain.

- A second retort to momentum being evidence of inefficiency is that the excess return from the momentum strategy is really not excessive. Rather, the return is fair compensation for risk. While the momentum strategy is seemingly innocuous in terms of risk, the retort claims that it actually has you load up on risk. The argument is that the mechanics of the strategy result in the selection of a risky portfolio.

- The idea starts from the position that over 6 months, the mean returns on securities are not negligible. Unlike at the daily level (where we ignored mean returns), a 6-month return may be big enough that variation in mean returns across stocks may matter.

- If markets are efficient, then those securities that have more risk should have higher average returns than those that have less risk. What will you get when you sort stocks on the basis of their past returns? Although the label of "winners" for the top 10% of securities indicates a set of securities that have "won," perhaps these are just securities that have a bunch of risk. The reason they are in the winner portfolio is because, due to their higher average return, they would have fairly higher return anyway.

- The bottom 10% returning may simply be securities that are not very risky on average; thus, their average return is relatively small. A portfolio that is long really risky securities and short low-risk securities has more than the average amount of risk. Because the risk of this strategy is riskier than holding the market, then this strategy will generate higher returns than the market on average.

- It is kind of difficult to confirm or dispute the possibility that momentum returns are just compensation for risk. That's because it is difficult to measure risk. If we had a sure way to measure risk, then we could see if the winner portfolio is actually riskier than the loser portfolio. Researchers have examined this using a set of standard asset pricing models to define risk, and they have found that risk explains very little of the extra return.

Volatility Anomalies

- A different type of evidence regarding market efficiency concerns the volatility of stock returns. The EMH states that the arrival of new (i.e., unanticipated) information will create changes in the value of securities. The changes in prices reflect change in the state of knowledge about the future. Thus, the variation in price changes must be related to the arrival of information. In addition, if the markets are going to send signals regarding where to allocate resources, then the information price reflected should only be relevant to fundamental value.

- There are two types of phenomena that would be very disturbing with respect to the EMH. First, it would be disturbing if the amount of variation in prices or returns were not plausibly related to the arrival of relevant information regarding fundamental value. If markets were too volatile or not volatile enough, both would be bad.

- A second thing to look at is whether price changes are permanent or temporary. If markets are efficient, then any price changes caused by the arrival of new information should be permanent in the sense that they will not be reversed on average. If, on average, some reaction is reversed, then the markets must be overreacting.

- One way to examine the appropriateness of volatility is to compare short-run versus long-run volatility. If price changes are permanent (i.e., they are not reversed on average), then the amount of variation in price changes over two days should be pretty close to twice that over one day. If, however, there is overreaction to some information that arrives that is eventually corrected, then we would expect to see the variance of prices over 10 days, for example, to be less than 10 times the variance over a single day.

- Researchers have compared short-term versus long-term variance and have found that, in fact, the variance of price changes over longer intervals of time (for example, over five years) seems too small relative to the variance of price changes over shorter intervals (for example, over a year) to be consistent with market efficiency. That is, it seems that the amount of variance in the market in the short run is too high.

- The idea is that, in the short run, prices fluctuate too much either due to investors' reactions to things that are not ultimately relevant or due to overreactions to things that are relevant. Either way, this implies that prices deviate from the fundamental values of the securities in significant ways in the short run. Thus, someone who has a strong sense of the fundamental value of a security should be able to make an excess return by buying low and selling high (relative to fundamental value).

- Some very interesting evidence on this "excess volatility" notion at shorter intervals was also discovered while considering the difference between trading-time versus elapsed-time volatility. Studies in the 1980s compared the variance of returns over two types of intervals: from market open to market close (i.e., during the day) and from market close to market open (i.e., overnight).

- While the number of hours in each interval has changed periodically, the open-to-close interval is always much shorter than the overnight close-to-open interval. When researchers compared the open-to-close variance with the close-to-open variance, they found that the variance from open to close was many times larger than the variance from close to open. Thus, we would expect the bulk of the variance to happen when markets are open. This is completely consistent with market efficiency.

- However, there is some really interesting evidence that is counter to the EMH that comes from a paper by Ken French and Richard Roll. Their result is that the variance of returns or price changes are more related to trading than the flow of information during normal business hours.

Efficient Explanation

- An alternative hypothesis is that the information that gets reflected in prices is relevant to fundamental value, but the market itself facilitates aggregating people's potentially disparate views on the implications of that information. That is, the market process itself may serve to come up with a consensus view on the implications of new information. Without the market process that produces prices, it is difficult to know what the information means.

- If the market does serve the useful purpose of aggregating the value implications of new (relevant) information, then that might explain the French-Roll results. If the market is closed on Wednesday, perhaps it takes longer than the time during Thursday's market for the market to form that consensus. If so, then the drop in volatility is simply because there is less information conveyed by the market—because the market is not open enough time to fully convey that information.

- This is both good and bad news. It suggests that the market is actually doing something useful; it not only reflects relevant information, but it also conveys relevant information. That's good. The bad part is that it takes longer than a day for it to do that. That is not too bad, but it does indicate that if you have a superior idea on fundamental value, then you may have a window of opportunity (at least a day) in which to exploit your superior view.

Track Record of Professionals

- Given these results, it appears that prices may be wrong for a while. The question, then, is whether you or others can effectively exploit this fact. For this, there is a significant body of literature that examines the ability of professional fund managers to "beat the market."

- Professionals spend all day looking for and exploiting market inefficiencies. Because they spend a significant amount of time and resources on such activities, they might be able to beat the market. The evidence on this is fairly clear: On average, professional fund managers *do not* beat the market.

Suggested Reading

Bernstein, *Capital Ideas*.

Conrad and Kaul, "An Anatomy of Trading Strategies."

Daniel, Grinblatt, Titman, and Wermers, "Measuring Mutual Fund Performance with Characteristic-Based Benchmarks."

Fox, *The Myth of the Rational Market*.

Jegadeesh and Titman, "Profitability of Momentum Strategies."

———, "Returns to Buying Winners and Selling Losers."

Lesmond, Schill, and Zhou, "The Illusory Nature of Momentum Profits."

Malkiel, *A Random Walk Down Wall Street*.

Questions to Consider

1. Do you think that markets are too volatile? Do you think the market is volatile because it overreacts to information on average or because it simply reacts to things that are really relevant?

2. Various markets throughout the world have circuit breakers that prevent prices from moving too much in one day; when prices move sufficiently far to trigger the circuit breaker, the markets close for a period of time. Many people believe that on those days in which a circuit breaker is triggered, the circuit breaker impedes investors' ability to trade at efficient prices that would exist if the markets were to remain open. Would you feel more or less comfortable trading in a market with such circuit breakers? Why or why not?

Evidence on Efficient Markets

Lecture 6—Transcript

Remember the two finance professionals who went to lunch in the last lecture? Well, they live fairly close to each other and, at the end of the day, they typically walk home together, at least for part of the journey. One night, while walking home late—it was dark at that time—they saw a well-dressed guy crawling on his hands and knees next to a car. As they passed, they asked him if they could help, and the guy replied that he was looking for some money that he had dropped earlier. He wasn't sure if he had or hadn't and, if he did, whether he dropped it there or elsewhere. The academic professor suggested that they look under the light across the street. If there was any money to be found, it would be easiest to find it under the light, and if no money was found, that would be strong evidence that the guy did not actually drop any money and that he could stop searching. The Wall Streeter resisted and said to the academic, in hushed tones, that he knew where the money was, but wasn't going to tell so that he could have it all to himself.

In the last lecture, we examined the efficient market hypothesis and its implications. In this lecture, we'll examine the body of empirical evidence on whether these implications are actually borne out by the data in actual markets. By examining this evidence, we'll get a sense of where you might want to look for trading opportunities and where you need not bother.

But, the point of the above story is that the finance academic and the practitioner is that you are in a bit of a quandary. The academics have studied the issue of market efficiency for a long time. Some critics claim that it's hard to trust their conclusions because the academics always look for inefficiency—and find little or none—by looking at publicly-available data, like under the light. Furthermore, most academics are not motivated or compensated by profits and, as a result, they have a muted incentive to find market efficiency. Lastly, if they were motivated by money—which, I can attest many are, just like any other person—then if they did find some market inefficiency, they would probably not publish their findings. Finance practitioners, however, are motivated by profits, and many of them sell their services for managing your money—the service of finding money for you—and they sell this for a fee. Thus, they have every incentive to claim that they, of course, know where there's market inefficiency and that they are the only ones who can find it.

The bottom line is that while most of the academic evidence is that markets are that the markets are fairly efficient, even the academics have found a number of phenomenon that seem to put chinks in the armor of the efficient market hypothesis. This lecture will look at some of the most notable phenomena.

I should warn you, however, that some academics are not convinced that these phenomena constitute excessive profit opportunities. Rather, they view them as anomalies with respect to our simple models and continue to entertain the possibility that the models are flawed and sometimes indicate false opportunities. We'll discuss this view in this lecture, too. It'll be up to you to decide, and potentially act on, which view you find most compelling.

As we discuss each phenomenon, I hope you will get a sense that each phenomenon is fairly involved. The fact that these are the phenomena that keep cropping up in discussions is evidence that markets are fairly efficient. If they were wildly inefficient, then there would not be much debate about these potential few phenomena.

The first set of anomalies we'll discuss concerns predictable patterns in returns. These might be violations of the weak form of the efficient market hypothesis in that, presumably, you can make excess profits simply by executing trade strategies conditional on past returns or price levels.

There are a few of these phenomena, but let me start with the momentum phenomenon. To understand what this phenomenon is, consider the following strategy. Step one is to take a list of many securities, say those traded on the NYSE and the NASDAQ, and calculate the returns over some past period. For example, calculate their returns over the past six months. Step two is to rank these securities from highest return to lowest return. Step three is to buy all of the securities in the top 10%, let's call them winners, and sell short all the securities in the bottom 10%, let's call them losers.

The final step is to hold this portfolio for six months. Then, after six months, do it again. That is, re-rank all the securities on the NYSE and the NASDAQ on the basis of the past return in the last six months, and then go long those securities in the winner 10% and short those in the loser 10%. Hold for another six months, and then repeat.

It's been shown that, on average, the returns from this strategy dominate the returns from a passive strategy of just holding a market portfolio consisting of all the securities on the original list. It has also been shown that such phenomena exist if you use different horizons, say, only go back a few months and only hold the portfolio for a month before rebalancing. Furthermore, the magnitude of the extra return is fairly large. If you rebalance once a month, you can get about 1% extra return, which, when compounded over 12 months, is approximately 12% per year, and that's significant.

According to the weak form of the efficient market hypothesis, you should not be able to beat the market by trading on the basis of past returns. But, this momentum strategy, as the name suggests, indicates that stocks go up, and they continue to go up, and the stocks that go down continue to go down. There is some sort of momentum. This is a predictable pattern that is not supposed to happen if markets are weak-form efficient.

Let's think of some explanations here. There are many retorts to the conclusion that this appears to be inefficiency. Let's examine each of these retorts in turn.

One retort is that it fails to consider transaction costs. Such a strategy is costly to implement, especially for a small investor. If you consider all the stocks on the NYSE and the NASDAQ, we're talking thousands and thousands of stock, around 7000 in total. If you do the rebalancing each month, say, it turns out that many of the stocks that were in the winner portfolio over one period are not in the winner portfolio the next period. So, too, it's true with the loser stocks as well. So, to implement this strategy, you have to trade a lot of stocks in each period, and if you have to pay a brokerage fee, such fees are going to eat up any gain that you had.

In addition, if financial institutions seek to exploit this phenomenon, even though they have much lower transactions costs—they don't have to pay a broker—it turns out most of the stocks in the winner and loser portfolios are stocks that are what are called thinly traded. Thinly traded stocks are those with little volume and, when people trade even small quantities, they move the price significantly. What this implies is that when you go to sell your winners after holding them, you will push the price down, reducing their return. When the academics study these phenomena, they don't do so by actually trading, rather, they just look at the prices that occurred in the market. For the thinly traded stocks, the data does not reflect the cost of an actual trade that would be made. Thus, the returns on paper look much larger than they would be if you actually tried to implement the strategy for real.

A second retort to momentum being evidence of inefficiency is that the excess return from the momentum strategy is really not excessive. Rather, it is a fair return, a fair compensation for risk. While the momentum strategy is seemingly innocuous in terms of risk, the retort claims that it actually has you load up on risk. The argument is that the mechanics of the strategy result in a selection of a risky portfolio. Let's see why.

The idea starts from the position that over six months the mean returns on securities are not negligible. Unlike at the daily level, where we ignored mean returns, like in the last lecture, a six-month return may be big enough that variation in mean returns across stocks may matter.

If markets are efficient, then those securities that have more risk should have higher returns than those that have less risk. What will you get when you sort stocks on the basis of their past return? Although the label of winners for the top 10% of securities indicates a set of securities that have won, perhaps there's just a bunch of securities that have a bunch of risk. The reason they are in the winner portfolio is because, due to their higher average return, due to their higher risk, they have gone up more on average. They would have gone higher anyway.

This is similar to the following situation. Consider a set of 100 people. All are men from age 20 to 29. This set of people was randomly selected. Fifty men were chosen at random from Bolivia, while 50 men were chosen at random from the United States. We then measure each person's height and rank them from highest to lowest. We then look at the top 10 and the bottom 10. What fraction of the top 10 do you expect will be from the U.S.? What fraction from Bolivia? And for the bottom 10%, what fraction will be from the U.S.? What fraction from Bolivia?

What if the average height of men aged 20 to 29 in the U.S. is 5 foot 9 inches, but the average height of men aged 20 to 29 in Bolivia is only 5 foot 3 inches? Given that, it probably would not be surprising that there will be more men in the top 10 group that are from the United States and more men from Bolivia from the bottom 10 group.

Similarly, it might not be surprising that the top 10% returning securities overrepresented or oversampled from riskier securities, which have higher returns on average.

What about the bottom 10% returning securities? They may simply be securities that are not very risky on average. Thus, their average return is relatively small.

So, what happens when you hold a portfolio that is long, risky assets—you buy them—and short, low-risk securities? That portfolio has more risk than the average amount of risk. This is true because the strategy has you take a long position in risky ones and a short position in low-risk ones. If you take a long position in each, say splitting your money equally between the winners and losers, then that group will have an average amount of risk. But, the momentum strategy has you buy very risky securities by essentially borrowing the money by shorting low-risk securities; this is a very, very risky strategy.

The argument is that since the risk of this strategy is riskier than holding the market, then this strategy will generate higher returns than the market on average. As we will discuss later, after we examine some asset pricing models, it is kind of hard to confirm or dispute the possibility that momentum returns are just compensation for risk. And that's because it is hard to measure risk.

If we had a sure way to measure risk, then we could test this possibility. Specifically, we could see if the winner portfolio is actually riskier than the loser portfolio. Researchers have examined this using a set of standard asset pricing models to define risk. And they have found that risk explains very little of this extra return.

Okay then. It must be inefficiency. Not so fast. Note that I was careful to say, "if we had a sure way to measure risk." What if researchers can identify a bunch of risks, but not all of them? Then, it is still possible that the winner portfolio consists of more securities with unknown, hard-to-measure risks than the loser portfolio does. If so, then the extra return is simply compensation for investors bearing these hard-to-identify risks. Of course, this extra risk has to be risk that the investors know is there, this is why they discounted those securities more, that academics and professionals can't measure or quantify. If it's not a hidden risk, then the market might be inefficiently pricing things.

One last fact that I want to share with you that might sway you one way or the other as to whether it is inefficiency (i.e., a profit opportunity), or it's efficiently pricing of hard-to-identify risks.

Initially, it seemed that momentum profits were fairly persistent across time and location. Researchers showed that the momentum phenomena occurred over multiple time periods and in both domestic and foreign stock exchanges. However, momentum appears to be less pronounced over the last decade. As we discussed last lecture, if there is a pattern in a return, then we would expect that as investors traded to exploit these patterns the patterns would moderate or disappear. That seems to be what happened with momentum.

A similar phenomenon has occurred with something called the "turn of the year" effect. It used to be the case that small stocks that did poorly during the prior year would have very sizable returns during the first five trading days after the turn of the year. This was a very strong effect, occurring year after year. Now it does not happen, on average.

Let's examine another type of evidence of inefficiency. The evidence concerns the volatility of stock returns. Recall what the efficient market hypothesis says about what generates volatility. The efficient market hypothesis states that the arrival of new (i.e., unanticipated) information will create changes in the value of securities. The changes in prices reflect a change in the state of knowledge about the future. Thus, the variation in price changes must be related to the arrival of information. In addition, if the markets are going to send the signals regarding where to allocate resources, then the information prices should reflect should be only relevant with respect to fundamental value.

There are two types of phenomena that would be very disturbing with respect to the efficient market hypothesis. First, it would be disturbing if the amount of variation in prices or returns was not plausibly related to the arrival of relevant information regarding fundamental value. If markets are too volatile or not volatile enough, both would be bad.

If the markets are not volatile enough, then prices clearly do not update frequently or by enough. Then, resources will be allocated on the basis of old information. If markets are too volatile, then clearly the prices are reflecting something irrelevant, letting capital be allocated on the basis of who knows what.

A second thing to look at is whether price changes are permanent or temporary. If markets are efficient, then any price change caused by the arrival of new information should be permanent in the sense that it will not be reversed on average. If, on average, some reaction is reversed, then the markets must be overreacting.

One way to examine the appropriateness of volatility is to compare short-run versus long-run volatility. If price changes are permanent (i.e., they are not reversed on average), then the amount of variation in price changes over two days should be pretty close to twice that over one day. If, however, there is overreaction to some information that arrives that is eventually corrected, then we would expect to see the variance of prices over, say, 10 days say to be less than 10 times the variance over a single day.

Researchers have compared short-term versus long-term variance and have found, in fact, that the variance of price changes over longer intervals of time, say, over five years, seem too small relative to the variance of price changes over shorter intervals of time, say, over a year, to be consistent with market efficiency. That is, it seems that the amount of variance in the market in the short-run is too high. The idea is that, in the short run, prices fluctuate too much either due to investors' reacting to things that are not ultimately relevant or due to overreaction to things that are relevant. Either way, this implies that price deviations from the fundamental values of the security are significant in the short run. Thus, someone who has a strong sense of fundamental value for a security should be able to make an excess return by buying low and selling high relative to the fundamental value.

Some very interesting evidence on this excess volatility notion at shorter intervals was discovered while considering differences between trading-time versus elapsed-time volatility. Studies back in the 1980s compared the variance of returns over two types of intervals—from a market open to a market close (i.e., during the day), and from the market close to the market open (i.e., overnight). While the hours in each interval has changed periodically, the open-to-close interval is always much shorter than the overnight close-to-open interval.

When researchers compared the open-to-close variance with the close-to-open variance, they found what you would expect—namely, that the variance from the open-to-close was many times larger than the variance from close-to-open. Even though the close-to-open period is longer than the open-to-close period, this comparison makes sense. The amount of information that is produced during the day, especially during the '70s and '80s, the period from which this data came, is much greater than the amount of information that's produced overnight. Thus, we'd expect the bulk of the variance to happen when the markets are open, when the information is being produced. This is completely consistent with market efficiency.

But, there is some really interesting evidence that is counter to the efficient market hypothesis that comes from a paper by Ken French and Richard Roll. Their result, which I affectionately call the "French Roll" or the "baguette" effect, is that the variance of returns of price changes are more related to trading than to the flow of information during normal business hours.

Let me explain further. French and Roll studied a period in 1968 when the market was closed on Wednesdays. Apparently, there was too much trade volume to keep track of and clear, so they closed the markets on Wednesdays for half the year in 1968 in order to catch up.

French and Roll computed the variance of returns from Tuesday-close to Thursday-close and compared the variance that occurred during the period with Wednesday closures to that which occurred during the period in which the market was open on Wednesdays.

They found that the variance of returns between Tuesday-close to Thursday-close when the market was open on Wednesdays was almost exactly twice that of the variance of the returns between Tuesday-close and Thursday-close when the market was closed on Wednesdays. Thus, the variance of the returns seems to be more related to trading time than to business-hour time.

This is a bit disturbing, in that one would expect that any information that people discovered or was announced on a Wednesday when the market was closed would have been reflected during the trading day on Thursday. Except for the fact that the stock market was closed these Wednesdays, these Wednesdays were normal business days. As such, the average amount of news regarding non-market-related items of relevance to the fundamental value of firms and their securities should have been the same during the period in '68 when the market was open as when it was closed.

Thus, the closure/non-closure Tuesday-close to Thursday-close returns should have been the same amount, given the same flow of news. But, when the market was closed on Wednesdays, it's as if that day—and its news—just dropped off the face of the earth. It's as if the bulk of what generates volatility must be information about market-related phenomena, not related to fundamental value.

The French-and-Roll result has been taken by many as very strong evidence of what Keynes referred to as "animal spirits"—that the markets mostly reflect information about how peoples' animal spirits will be reflected in the market.

Now that markets are open around the globe, and many securities from one country can be traded in multiple venues, it's hard to make the kinds of comparisons that French and Roll did. But, what if the effects they document are due to the markets reflecting speculative phenomena unrelated to fundamental value? Then, especially given that globally markets are open for even more hours in the day, there might even be a greater amount of excess market volatility.

Let's consider an explanation of this phenomenon. An alternative hypothesis is that the information that gets reflected in prices is actually relevant for fundamental value, but the market itself facilitates aggregating people's potentially disparate views on the implications of that information. That is, the market process itself may serve to come up with a consensus view of the implications of new information. Without the market process that produces prices, it's hard to know what that information means.

There is a well-known exercise that gets at this notion. By the way, this exercise is based upon a gentleman that used to travel to English county fairs and ask people to guess the weight of a prize cow. I actually conduct a variant of this experiment in some of my university courses.

Prior to class, I fill an empty jar—and this jar used to hold about 32 ounces of rice—with coins, including pennies, nickels, dimes, and quarters. I then pass the jar around the class of about 100 people and ask them to guess the number—not the value, but the number of the coins in the jar. I have them write down their guesses on a piece of paper and hand it in to me.

To give them the incentive to think about it, I tell them that I will give them extra credit points if their guess is closer to the truth than the average of the guesses. That is, in order to get points, they have to be more accurate than the average. For example, if the actual number of coins is 1200 and the average is 1175, to get extra credit they will have to guess between 1175 and 1225.

The idea is that the average of the guesses is close to what the market would determine the price to be. The price would be the average of peoples' beliefs simply to let supply equal demand. There has to be as many people who want to sell as who want to buy. So the average price sort of makes this balance.

As it turns out, I very rarely give any extra credit. The average of the wide range of guesses is better than most people's individual guess. Thus, the averaging process of the market may actually produce useful information.

If the market does serve the useful purpose of aggregating the value implications of new and relevant information, then that might explain the French-Roll results. If the market is closed on Wednesday, perhaps it takes longer than the time during Thursday's market for the market to form that consensus. If so, then the drop in volatility is simply because there's less information conveyed by the market, because the market is not open enough time to fully convey that information.

This is both good and bad news. It suggests that the market is actually doing something useful. It's not only reflecting relevant information, it's also conveying relevant information. That's good.

The bad part is that it takes longer than a day for it to do this. In my mind, that's not too bad, but it does indicate that if you have a superior idea of fundamental value, then you may have a window of opportunity—at least a day—in which to exploit your superior view.

By the way, during the 1968 closure period, the variance of returns per week were only slightly more than 4/5 of the weekly variance when market was open. So, it's not that it took longer than Thursday for the Wednesday information to get reflected in prices. Rather, it appears that the Wednesday information was lost for good.

Given these results, it seems that the prices may be wrong for a while. The question then is whether others can effectively exploit this fact. For this, there is a significant body of literature that examines the ability of professional fund managers to beat the market. Professionals spend all day looking for and exploiting market inefficiency. Since they spend a significant amount of time and resources on such activities, they might be able to beat the market. The evidence on this is actually fairly clear. On average, professional fund managers do not beat the market.

On average, fund managers underperform their benchmarks. That is, they have a particular set of securities they are trying to outperform, but they are unsuccessful on average.

Of course, this is just an average result. There are clearly fund managers who do beat the market in any given year. The question is whether this is skill or luck. If it were skill, then we would expect good managers to be able to outperform many other managers in other periods as well. The empirical evidence on persistence is that most managers that outperform the market do not have much, if any, persistence in their superior performance over time. In fact, the only category that has persistent performance is the category of very poorly performing managers. It's actually surprising that they survive, given their extreme poor performance. That they do survive should tell you to be careful when picking a professional manager. Bad managers are out there.

Among the set of managers that do outperform, there's a small set that have outperformed over many periods. On these managers I have three comments.

First, in many cases, their persistent out-performance is due to their carrying over returns from previous years. What you want to do is look at whether most of the manager's long-term return is from one or two years only. I have seen studies that show that many managers that have very good performance typically shift into very low-risk strategies thereafter in order to be able to protect their past performance. They do this so that they can claim persistent performance, when in fact it's just luck in one period.

My second point is even if managers do have superior performance over multiple periods, that fact is only weak evidence of superior skill and ability. To see this, consider another experiment I always conduct in one of my university courses. In the course, I ask students to see if they have any telepathic ability. To see if they do, I have them flip a coin six times in a row and keep track of whether it's heads or tails on each flip. I ask them to concentrate and try to get the coin to come up heads.

After they flip, I ask everyone if there was anyone that got six heads in a row. In a typical class size of 70, it almost always happens that at least one person gets six heads in a row. If they were managing a portfolio and they beat the market six years in a row, they would be worshiped as an investing god. But, clearly, the person who gets six heads in a row is just lucky. Yet, the likelihood that we would get one lucky person out of 70 is actually fairly high. In contrast, if I were to single out someone beforehand, then the probability that that person would get six heads in a row is extremely low. In fact it is 0.56 = 0.0156—1.56%. However, the probability that out of 70 people there will be at least one person who gets six heads in a row is surprisingly close to 1. In fact, in all the years I've done this experiment in class, I've never failed to get at least five or six heads in a row. This is very similar to the answer to the question, "What's the probability that out of *N* people, two have the same birthday?" The answer is a surprising 99% for *N* around 60. Similarly, out of thousands and thousands of professional fund managers, it's not surprising that we can find a few managers who beat the market over many periods.

The third thing I want to say is in most cases, the people that have superior performance charge higher fees. In these cases, the after-fee returns that you will get will likely not beat the market. So, even if there are some market inefficiencies that some people with superior skill can exploit, the market for their services does not seem to be inefficient.

In this lecture, we have seen some conflicting evidence regarding market efficiency. In my mind, this evidence is whether individuals can make excess returns on average. It is clear that on average they cannot, but that doesn't mean that there aren't some people who can't. Perhaps you're one of those people. But, since most people are overconfident, again I want to suggest that you make sure you evaluate your performance systematically. And for that, you need to know how to account for risk, and that we're going to do shortly.

Valuation Formulas

Lecture 7

In this lecture, you will examine one of the most basic building blocks of any financial valuation method—namely, the concept of the time value of money. From this, you will obtain various formulas for present value, future value, and net present value. With these concepts, and their formulas, you will be able to calculate a number of values of interest, including how much money you need to save for retirement given an expected return on your investments, the value of a bond, and the value of a stock.

The Time Value of Money

- The time value of money is a concept that is fundamental to finance in that it allows us to compare cash flows that arrive at different points in time. The time value of money is at the center of any investment decision because you are always deciding whether it makes sense to pay the market price for a security now in order to get something (usually uncertain) in the future.

The time value of money allows for the comparison of cash flows that arrive at different points in time.

- The concept of the time value of money is the notion that, for most people, a dollar today is worth more than a dollar tomorrow. Consider how you would react if someone were to offer to sell you a promise to pay you a dollar a year from now. You would probably be willing to pay less than a dollar for this promise.

- This difference manifests itself in financial markets as a positive interest rate. The interest rate is the fraction of the initial amount paid you get extra for giving up that amount today. If you paid 95 cents to get a dollar in a year, then the annual interest rate is 5/95 = 0.0526 (or 5.26%). You get 5 cents more than the 95 cents you paid. Because 5 cents is 5.26% of 95 cents, the interest rate is 5.26%.

- There are many other names for the interest rate, including the discount rate, the opportunity cost of capital, the required rate of return, and the capitalization rate. They all mean the same thing.

- The notion of the time value of money gives rise to two formulas. The first is the future value formula; the second is the present value formula. In terms of the timing convention we will use throughout the course, we will say that payments occur at specific times relative to the current period, which we will denote by $t = 0$. We will count time relative to the current period in years. Thus, one year later is $t = 1$, while four-and-a-half years from now is $t = 4.5$. Exactly one year ago is denoted by $t = -1$.

- Consider a specific cash flow in the current period (CF_0). The future value formula translates CF_0 into its equivalent future value after t years given an annual interest rate. Let the future value after t years be denoted FV_t, and let the annual interest rate be denoted by r.

- To do this translation, we take the current cash flow CF_0 and multiply it by the quantity (1 plus the interest rate) for each year until we get to the target future date. That is, after one year, the future value is $CF_0(1 + r)$. After another year, that value grows to $CF_0(1 + r)(1 + r)$. After t years, the CF_0 has grown to its future value: $FV_t = CF_0(1 + r)^t$.

Table 7.1

Year = t	Interest rate = r	Future value = FV_t	Value
0	10%	CF_0	\$100.00
1	10%	$CF_0(1 + r)$	\$110.00
2	10%	$CF_0(1 + r)^2$	\$121.00
3	10%	$CF_0(1 + r)^3$	\$133.10
4	10%	$CF_0(1 + r)^4$	\$146.41
5	10%	$CF_0(1 + r)^5$	\$161.05
6	10%	$CF_0(1 + r)^6$	\$177.16
7	10%	$CF_0(1 + r)^7$	\$194.87
8	10%	$CF_0(1 + r)^8$	\$214.36
9	10%	$CF_0(1 + r)^9$	\$235.79
10	10%	$CF_0(1 + r)^{10}$	\$259.37

- The notion of the present value simply puts the future value notion on its head. If someone were to promise you a cash flow CF_t in t years from now, you would view that promise as equivalent to $CF_t/(1 + r)^t$ now. This is true because, according to the future value formula, you can take this current amount and generate $(CF_t/(1 + r)^t)(1 + r)^t$ in the future. Notice that $(CF_t/(1 + r)^t)(1 + r)^t$ is simply CF_t, which is the amount you were promised at t. Thus, a cash flow of CF_t t years in the future is worth $CF_t/(1 + r)^t$ now.

Table 7.2

Year = t	Interest rate = r	Calculation	Value
0	5%	$CF_0(1+r)^5$	\$78.35
1	5%	$CF_0(1+r)^4$	\$82.27
2	5%	$CF_0(1+r)^3$	\$86.38
3	5%	$CF_0(1+r)^2$	\$90.70
4	5%	$CF_0(1+r)$	\$95.24
5	5%	CF_0	\$100.00

- The future value CF_t promised is discounted to get a present value in the sense that it is multiplied by a number $(1/(1 + r))^t$, which is less than 1. The more years into the future, the greater the discount. That is, over t years, the future value is multiplied by $(1/(1 + r))^t$. As the time into the future gets bigger, the present value is a smaller fraction of the future value. Thus, the discount is larger. Also, the greater the interest rate r, the greater the discounting (i.e., the smaller the fraction $(1/(1 + r))^t$).

Table 7.3

Year = t	Interest rate = r	Calculation	Value
0	10%	$FV/(1+r)$	$0.909
1	10%	FV	$1.00
0	10%	$FV/(1+r)^2$	$0.826
1	10%	$FV/(1+r)$	$0.909
2	10%	FV	$1.000

Value Additivity

- These methods described can be applied to a set of multiple payments because of something called value additivity, which implies that the present value of a collection of future payments, with each individual payment at a different future date, is simply the sum of the individual present values associated with each of the different future payments.

- Put more simply, value additivity is the notion that the whole is worth the sum of its parts. While this may not be true for nonfinancial things (such as a marriage, a corporation comprised of synergistic divisions, or a work of art), it is true for financial securities and cash flows.

- Given value additivity, we can calculate the present value of a stream of cash flows. Let the stream be denoted by $(CF_{t1}, CF_{t2}, CF_{t3}, \ldots, CF_{tT})$, where CF_{t1} denotes the first cash flow, which occurs at time $t1$ (in years); CF_{t2} is the second cash flow, which occurs at time $t2$ (in years); and on up to CF_{tT}, which is the terminal (or last) cash flow, occurring at time tT. According to value additivity, the present value of this stream is simply the following.

- $$PV = \frac{CF_{t1}}{(1+r)^{t1}} + \frac{CF_{t2}}{(1+r)^{t2}} + \frac{CF_{t3}}{(1+r)^{t3}} + \ldots + \frac{CF_{tT}}{(1+r)^{tT}}$$

Net Present Value

- The net present value (NPV) is calculated to evaluate the quality of an investment. Whether it is an investment in a financial security or an investment in real assets, such as a project in a corporation or privately owned business, the key feature of most investments is that you have to spend something to get future cash flows. The net present value is the difference between the present value of what you get and the present value of what you have to spend to get it. That is, it is the net of the present values.

- Because what you spend is typically known with certainty and is spent now, that value is not discounted. That is the cost of the investment. If you are investing in a financial security, it is the price of the security now. If you are investing in a project for a corporation, it is the cost of starting that project now.

- The NPV of an investment is simply the present value of the future cash flows from the investment minus its cost. If the NPV is positive, then your investment gives you a stream of future payments that is worth more than what you paid; that's a good investment. If the NPV is negative, then what you get is worth less than what you have to pay; that's clearly a bad investment.

Special Cases

- In some cases, the payments from a security or a real investment have a fixed structure. In some of these cases, there are special formulas that simplify the calculation of the present value of the stream. For example, some investments generate a stream of equal cash flows at regular and identical time intervals.

- For example, any fixed rate, fixed term loan is like this; the borrower pays a fixed amount every month for 60 months (or 5 years). A rental agreement or lease is also like this. The renter pays a fixed rent every month for the length of the lease.

- Anything that has a stream of equal payments is called an annuity. We can still calculate the present value as the sum of present values of single sums, but there is a shortcut formula that can be applied. We will be able to understand the formula for an annuity if we first consider something called a perpetuity.

Perpetuity

- A perpetuity is the generic name for a security that promises a fixed payment at evenly spaced intervals forever. In the case of a perpetuity, we cannot simply add up the present values of each of the future payments because there is an infinite number of these payments into the future. However, a result from the mathematics of infinite sequences and series actually allows us to come up with an analytical formula for this infinite sum.

- The present value of each subsequent payment is smaller than the one before. If each present value were the same, then the infinite sum would be infinity (the same as the sum of an infinite series of 1s). However, because the subsequent present values are smaller and smaller, the infinite sum is finite.

- The formula for the present value of a perpetuity that pays \$$C$ every period with the first payment exactly one period from now and a periodic rate r is \$$C/r$.

Annuity

- An annuity is something that pays a fixed payment every period for a finite number of periods. If the number of payments is fairly small, then you can just calculate the present value of each payment and add them up. But if we are talking about a 30-year mortgage, then you have to calculate $12 \times 30 = 360$ individual present values, and then add them all up.

- We can use a trick to determine the present value of any annuity that comes from value additivity and the fact that an annuity is simply perpetuity with the tail cut off. Thus, the value of an annuity is the value of perpetuity minus the value of the tail.

- In general, the formula for an annuity is as follows.
    - $PV_{\text{annuity}} = \left(\frac{CF}{r}\right)\left(1 - \left(\frac{1}{1+r}\right)^t\right)$ or $\left(\frac{CF}{r}\right) - \left(\left(\frac{CF}{r}\right)\left(\left(\frac{1}{(1+r)}\right)^t\right)\right)$

What is the value of a 5-year annuity that pays \$300 a year with the first payment in a year?

Let the interest rate be 15% (or 0.15).

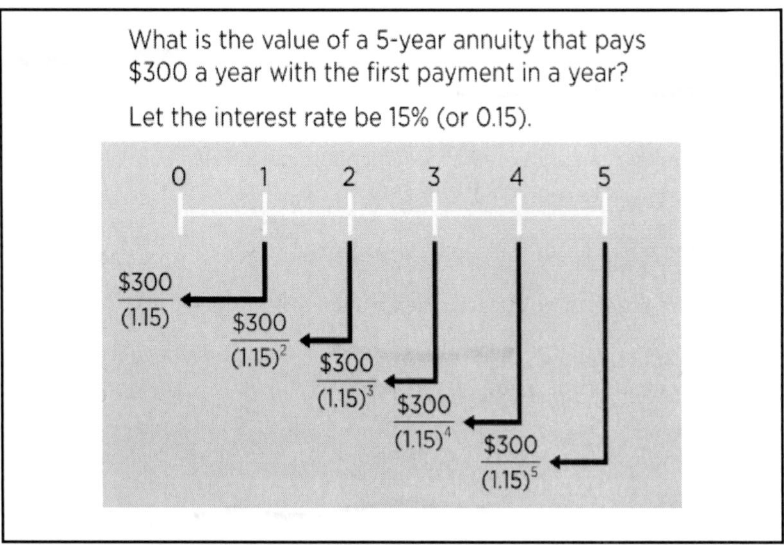

Growing Annuities and Perpetuities

- The last set of formulas is for both annuities and perpetuities in which the payments are not fixed, but are growing at a constant rate each period. These are called growing annuities and growing perpetuities.

- A growing perpetuity is one in which the periodic payments grow at a fixed rate g (where, for example, $g = 0.05$ is 5% growth rate). If the first payment, paid 1 period from now, is C_1, then the next payment is $C_2 = (1 + g)C_1$, and the payment after that is $C_3 = (1 + g)C_2 = (1 + g)^2C_1$. Given this structure, the present value of this stream is $PV_{GP} = \left(\frac{C_1}{r - g}\right)$.

- One way to think about this is that, without growth in the payment, the future values are discounted; the farther in the future, the greater the discount. However, if the cash flows are growing, that offsets the discounting. So, think of $r - g$ as the net amount of discounting given the growth in the cash flows.

- Note, however, that if the growth is equal to or is outstripping the discounting—if g is equal to or greater than r—then the growth outpaces the discounting. In that case, the infinite sum is actually infinity. When g is greater than or equal to r, then the formula generates a bogus answer; it generates a negative number, when the answer is in fact positive infinity.

- When the stream of payments lasts for t years, it is known as a growing annuity. The formula for that is $PV_{GA} = \left(\frac{C}{r}\right)\left(1 - \left(\frac{(1+g)^t}{(1+r)^t}\right)\right)$. Like the annuity, a growing annuity is just the difference between the values of two growing perpetuities.

Suggested Reading

Brealey, Myers, and Allen, *Principles of Corporate Finance.*

Ross, Westerfield, Jaffe, and Jordan, *Corporate Finance.*

Sharpe, "The Arithmetic of Active Management."

Questions to Consider

1. When the discount rate increases, what happens to the present value of a given stream of payments?

2. If you do not know anything about the interest on 1-year deposits at your bank, how much would you be willing to pay now to get \$100 in 1 year? What discount rate did you apply? Was your discount rate based on impatience, an expectation of inflation, both, or something else entirely?

3. The value of a 30-year fixed-rate mortgage is simply the present value of the fixed monthly payments discounted using the monthly interest rate. Similarly, you can determine the monthly payments associated by borrowing \$500,000 by finding the value of X such that the present value of X every month for the next $30 \times 12 = 360$ months is equal to \$500,000. At any point in time, the remaining principle the borrower owes is simply the present value of the remaining payments at the interest rate quoted when the loan was made. If the interest rate is 0.3 % per month (for an annual effective rate of $(1.003)^{12} - 1 = 0.0366$ or 3.66%), what is the monthly payment on a \$500,000 30-year monthly payment loan?

Valuation Formulas

Lecture 7—Transcript

So far, over the first six lectures in this course, we've discussed some very fundamental and general issues concerning an effective investment strategy. All of this discussion was done at a mostly conceptual level.

As you no doubt were thinking, many of these general and conceptual discussions begged questions such as, "But, how do I actually decide exactly what to do?" "How do I decide whether to buy 100 shares or 1000 shares?" "What exactly should I be willing to pay for a particular security?" "What critical values of what variables indicate whether or how much I should invest in international securities?" "How much interest rate risk does my portfolio contain and what sized position in what kinds of securities will help me reduce my exposure?" All of these questions are quantitative questions. In the next few lectures we'll develop a set of tools that are used in subsequent lectures to answer these very specific quantitative questions.

In this lecture, we'll start by examining one of the most basic building blocks in any financial valuation method, namely the concept of the time value of money. From this, we will obtain various formulae for the present value, future value, and the net present value.

With these concepts, and formulae, we'll be able to calculate a number of variables in values of interest, including: How much money do you need to save for retirement, given an expected return on your investments? What's the value of a bond? And what's the value of a stock?

So, let's start by defining the concept of the time value of money. This concept is fundamental to finance in that it allows us to compare cash flows that arrive at different points in time. The time value of money is at the center of any investment decision, since you are always deciding whether it makes sense to pay the market price for a security now in order to get something, usually uncertain, in the future. The time value of money part takes care of the difference between now and the future. That's actually the easy part. Most of the rest of the course is focused on the hard part—the uncertain part. What is the value of some uncertain payment?

The concept of the time value of money is the notion that, for most people, a dollar today is worth more than a dollar tomorrow. To see whether this is true or not, consider how you would react if someone were to offer to sell you a promise to pay you one dollar a year from now. How much would you be willing to pay for this promise? Probably less than a dollar. But why?

There are a couple of obvious possible answers. One has to do with the expectation of inflation. If the price of goods will be higher in a year, the dollar you give up today will buy less consumption in a year. So, you will want to give up less than a dollar today so that you get at least as much consumption in the future as you gave up today.

Another answer has to do with the postponement of consumption. If you give up the price of the security today, you can't buy anything with that money today. In order to want to postpone consumption, you will need to be rewarded with the expectation of more future consumption than you give up today.

The third answer concerns default risk. There's a chance that the person promising you a dollar a year from now may not actually pay you a dollar a year from now (i.e., that person might default). Given the possibility that you might not get all of your dollar back in a year, you don't want to give up a whole dollar today.

These three reasons all make it such that a dollar in the future is worth less than a dollar today. This difference manifests itself in financial markets as a positive interest rate. The interest rate is simply the fraction of the initial amount paid that you get extra for giving up that amount today. If you paid 95 cents to get a dollar in a year, then the annual interest rate is 5/95, or 0.0526, or 5.26%. You get 5 cents more than the 95 cents you paid. Since 5 cents is 5.26% of 95 cents, the interest rate is 5.26%.

By the way, there are many other names for the interest rate, including the discount rate, the opportunity cost of capital, the required rate of return, and the capitalization, or simply cap rate. They all mean the same thing.

A final reason for the time value of money is the fact that the market pays an interest rate. The market requires that you give up less than a dollar to get a dollar in a year. That is, one reason a dollar in a year is worth less than a dollar today is because of opportunity costs.

The opportunity cost of some action, say, for example, an investment, is that you give up something by not doing that action. So, one reason you would pay less than a dollar for a promise to get a dollar in a year is because, if you did give up a whole dollar, you would be missing the opportunity to give up less than a dollar to the market to get a dollar in a year. That is, a dollar in the future is worth less to you today because the market gives you the opportunity to give up less than a dollar to get a dollar in the future.

This time-value of money notion gives rise to two formulas. The first is the future value formula, while the second is the present value formula. In terms of the timing convention we'll use throughout the course, we will say that payments occur at specific times relative to the current period, which we will denote by $t = 0$. We will count time relative to the current period in years. Thus, one year later is $t = 1$, while four-and-a-half years from now is $t = 4.5$. Exactly one year ago will be denoted $t = -1$.

Consider a specific cash flow in the current period. Let's call this CF_0. The future value formula translates CF_0 into its equivalent future value after t years given an annual interest rate. Let the future value after t be denoted FV_t. And let the annual interest rate be denoted by r. To do this translation, we take the current cash flow, CF_0, and merely multiply it by the quantity (1 + the interest rate) for each year until we get to the targeted future date. That is, after one year, the future value is $CF_0 \times (1 + r)$. After another year, the value grows for one more year to $CF_0 \times (1 + r)(1 + r)$. After t years, CF_0 has grown to its future value of $FV_t = CF_0 \times (1 + r)^t$. So, for example, if you have a current cash flow of \$100 and the interest rate is 10%, then the future value of this \$100 after 10 years is $\$100 \times (1.1)^{10}$, and that's equal to \$259.37.

The notion of the present value simply puts the future value notion on its head. Rather than answer the question "What future value is equivalent to a given cash flow now?" it asks, "What value now, in the present period, is equivalent to a given payment in the future?" Thus, if someone were to give you a promise to pay a cash flow of CF_t in t years from now, you would view that as a promise that is equivalent to what? $CF_t/(1 + r)^t$ now. This is true because according to the future value formula you can take the current amount and generate what? CF_t in the future. Notice that $CF_t/(1 + r)^t \times (1 + r)^t$ that set simply equals CF_t, which is the amount that you were promised at t. Thus, a cash flow of CF_t at t years into the future is exactly worth $CF_t/(1 + r)^t$ now. For example, a cash flow of $259.37 in 10 years is equivalent to $100 now, or if we take $259.37/(1.1)^{10}$, that's equal to 100. Similarly, $100 in five years at 5% annual interest is going to be worth what? $\$100/(1.05)^5$, and that's $78.35. Note that in all of these calculations, you should use the decimal version of percent. That is, use 0.05 for 5%. Do not use 5 for 5%.

The future value CF_t promised in the future is discounted to get the present value in the sense that it is multiplied by a number which is less than 1, and that number is $[1/(1 + r)]^t$. For example, if r is equal to 10% (0.10), then $1/(1 + r)$ is equal to what? 0.909. Thus, a dollar one year from now is worth the discounted value of 90.9% of that dollar.

A dollar two years from now would be the discounted value of its discounted value next year. Next year, you will get a dollar in a year. Thus, next year, that promise will be worth what? 1(0.909), or 90.9 cents. If that's what it's worth next year, then its present value today must be worth 90.9% of that, or 90.9×90.9, which is equal to 82.6 % of that one dollar two years from now. Thus, the present value of a dollar in two years is equal to $[(1/(1 + 0.1)^2]$, which is the same as $1 \times (0.909)^2$. That is, the future value two years in the future is discounted twice—once for each year.

Note that the more years into the future, the greater the discount. That is, over t years into the future, you get multiplied by $(1/(1 + r))^t$. As time into the future gets bigger, the present value is a smaller fraction of that future value. Thus, the discount is larger. Also, the greater the interest rate r, the greater the discounting—the smaller is the fraction $(1/(1 + r))^t$.

Let's do an example. Say you have your eye on a BMW, but you don't have enough money right now. And that BMW is going to cost $48,000, say, in two years. How much do you have to save today if you're going to have \$48,000 in two years, let's say, if you can invest at 6%? The answer is, what's the present value of \$48,000 discounted back two years? So take $\$48{,}000/(1 + 0.06)^2$. That equals \$42,719.83.

The methods described above can be applied to a set of multiple payments because of something called value additivity. Basically, what we did above was we figured out what is the present value of a single payment. Now what we're going to do is we're going to consider a stream of multiple payments. Value additivity implies that the present value of a collection of future payments, with each individual payment at some different future date, is simply the sum of the individual present values associated with each of the different future payments.

Put more simply, value additivity is simply that the whole is worth the sum of the parts. While this may not be true for some non-financial things, like marriage, or a corporation comprised of synergistic divisions, or a work of art, it is true for financial securities and cash flows.

Value additivity is true in finance because of financial engineering, which allows us to combine individual cash flows or dismantle combination cash flows into separate parts.

If value additivity did not hold, then financial engineers would be able to make excessive profits from something called arbitrage. We will see how to do such financial engineering in subsequent lectures. The basic idea of financial engineering is to mimic, or replicate, the cash flows from one security by building a replicating portfolio out of other securities.

If you can form such a replicating portfolio, then it must be the case that the price of the thing that you can replicate must be related to the price of the parts used to build the replicating portfolio. Arbitrage is defined as the situation in which the cost of the replicating portfolio is different than the price of the security you're replicating. If such an arbitrage opportunity exists, then you can make money by buying the cheap one and selling the expensive one.

Since many professional investors spend all day looking for such opportunities, we typically assume that value additivity holds. If it doesn't, it will hold fairly quickly. This is true, because to exploit arbitrage the traders buy the cheap one, which bids the price up, and then you sell the expensive one, which lowers the price. They will continue to do this until the two prices converge and the arbitrage opportunity disappears. Thus, by exploiting arbitrage opportunities, professional traders make them go away. And, to the extent that traders can only make profits for a short while, they must trade quickly. Thus, value additivity is going to mostly hold most of the time.

Given value additivity, we can calculate the present value of a stream of future cash flows. Let the stream be denoted by CF_{t1}, CF_{t2}, CF_{t3}, all the way up to CF_{tT}, where CF_{t1} denotes the first cash flow that occurs at time $t1$, where $t1$ is measured in years. Let CF_{t2} denote the cash flow that occurs at time 2, where $t2$ is the time that that cash flow occurs, et cetera, et cetera. According to value additivity, the present value of this stream is simply going to be equal to $CF_{t1}/(1 + r)^{t1} + CF_{t2}/(1 + r)^{t2} + CF_{t3}/(1 + r)^{t3}$ all the way up to the cash flow of the last payment that occurs after $CF_{tT}/(1 + r)^{tT}$. For example, with $r = 0.05$ (or 5%), what's the present value of receiving the following stream of payments: \$100 at $t = 1$, \$200 at $t = 2$, and \$300 at $t = 3$? The answer is: $PV = \$100/(1 + 0.05)^1 + \$200/(1 + 0.05)^2 + \$300/(1 + 0.05)^3 = \$535.80$.

Now, we can also consider situations in which we get and make payments. For example, consider the following situation. Let $r = 0.2$ (20%). What's the present value of receiving a payment of \$200 at $t = 2$ and \$100 at $t = 6$, but making a payment of \$300 at $t = 3$? In that case, the present value is going to be $PV = \$200/(1 + 0.20)^2 + -\$300/(1 + 0.20)^3 + \$100/(1 + 0.20)^6$. When we add all that up, that turns out to be −\$1.23.

The concept of the net present value is related to the last example. The net present value, or NPV for short, is calculated to evaluate the quality of an investment. Whether it is an investment in a financial security or an investment in real assets, such as a project in a corporation or a privately owned business, the key feature of most investments is that you spend something now to get future cash flows. The net present value is the difference between the present value of what you get and the present value of what you have to spend to get it. That is, it is the net of the present values.

Since what you spend is typically known and certain and is spent now, the value is not discounted. That is, the cost of the investment. If you're investing in a financial security, it's the price of the security in the market now. If you're investing in a project for a corporation, it's the cost of starting that project now.

The NPV of an investment is simply the present value of the future cash flows from the investments minus its cost. If the NPV is positive, your investment gives you a stream of future payments that is worth more than what you paid. That's a good investment. If the NPV is negative, then what you get is worth less than what you have to pay. That's certainly a bad investment.

In some cases, the payments from a security or a real investment have a fixed structure. In some of these cases, there are special formulae that simplify the calculation of the present value of that stream. For example, some investments generate a stream of equal cash flows at regular intervals that are identical in time space. For example, any fixed rate, or fixed term loan is like this. The borrower pays a fixed amount every month for 60 months—say, for five years. A rental agreement or a lease is also like this. The renter pays a fixed rent every month for the length of the lease.

Anything that has a stream of equal payments is called an annuity. We can still calculate the present value of the sum of the *PV*s of the single parts, but there's a shortcut formula that can be applied. We will be able to understand the formula for the annuity if we first consider something called a perpetuity.

A perpetuity is a generic name for a security that promises a fixed payment at evenly spaced intervals forever. The closest thing to a real-world perpetuity that I know of is the British consol, which was a security issued in 1751 that was to replace existing British government debt. It consolidated debt, thus it was called a consol. This debt promised to pay an annual fixed payment of 3.5% forever. It turns out that it is not actually a perpetuity, because they have reduced the coupon payment a few times since 1751. Thus, the payments for the consol are really not fixed forever, as they are with an actual perpetuity.

In the case of a perpetuity, we cannot simply add up the present values of each of the future payments, since there are an infinity of number of payments. However, as a result of some mathematics on infinite sequences and series, this actually allows us to come up with an analytic formula for this infinite sum. I'll show you the formula for this in a minute. But first, to give you an intuitive feel for how this infinite sum of values works, consider the following infinite sum.

Let's say I'm standing in the studio six feet from the edge of the rug in the studio. Every time I take a step, I step half way toward the edge. So, my first step is three feet, putting me three feet from the edge. The next step is half of three feet, putting me within 1.5 feet from the edge. The next step is 1.5 divided by 2, or 0.75 feet. And so on, and so on. I keep on taking half-steps. Notice that since I'm always halving the distance to the edge of the rug, I never actually get to the edge of the rug.

While I have an increasingly hard time making increasingly exactly-half steps, if I could, I would never reach the end of the rug. I would continue to take half-steps into the infinite future—a boring life for sure.

But notice that through time I will get closer and closer to the edge of the rug. So, if we add up the total distance I've traveled, equivalent to the infinite sum of each step size I took, the sum must be six feet—the original distance to the edge of the rug. That is, the limit of the sum of a number of steps doesn't go to infinity. It goes to six feet. So, an infinite sum is actually a finite number.

This is similar to the infinite sum of discounted future values. With the half-step problem, each subsequent step is smaller and smaller than the one before. With the present value problem, the present value of each subsequent payment is smaller than the one before. If each step size was the same, then the infinite sum would be infinity—that's the same as an infinite series of a series of ones. But, because the subsequent present values, or step sizes, are smaller and smaller and smaller, the infinite sum is actually finite.

In fact, the formula for the present value of a perpetuity that pays $\$C$ every period with the first payment exactly one period from now and a periodic rate of r is $\$C/r$. For example, what is the present value of a perpetuity that pays \$1000 per year, with the first payment occurring after one year from today, if the annual discount rate is 12%? The answer is \$1000/0.12, or \$8333.33.

Let's look at the value of an annuity. Recall that an annuity is something that pays a fixed payment every period for a finite number of periods. If the number of payments is fairly small, then you can just calculate the present value of each payment and add them up. But if we're talking about a 30-year mortgage, then you have to calculate 12×30 for 360 individual payments, and then calculate the present value of each one of those individual payments, and then add them all up. What a pain in the neck.

By the way, this reminds me of a story I once heard about Carl Friedrich Gauss, the famous German mathematician. When Gauss was just a kid, the teacher made him add up all of the integers from 1 to 100. And Gauss turned the answer in after 10 seconds. Rather than brute force the answer by calculating $1 + 2 = 3$, $3 + 3 = 6$, $6 + 4 = 10$, $10 + 5 = 15$, et cetera, ad nauseum, Gauss noted that $1 + 100 = 101$, $2 + 99 = 101$, $3 + 98 = 101$, etc., on up to the 50th pair of $50 + 51 = 101$. Thus, the answer was $50 \times 101 = 5050$. Done.

We can use a similar trick to determine the present value of any annuity. The trick comes from value additivity and the fact that an annuity is simply a perpetuity with the tail cut off. Thus, the value of an annuity is the value of perpetuity minus the value of the tail.

To see this, let's look at an example. What is the value of a five-year annuity that pays \$300 a year with the first payment in a year? Let the interest rate be 15%, or 0.15. Note that the value of a perpetuity that pays \$300 every year, with the first payment exactly one year from now, when the interest rate is $r = 0.15$ is, what? \$300/0.15, which is equal to \$2000. Note that after five years pass and the perpetuity has paid five \$300 payments, that perpetuity will also be worth \$2000. In present value terms, that \$2000 value in year five is worth what? $\$2000/(1 + 0.15)^5$. It's equal to \$994.35 now. Thus, an annuity that pays \$300 every year for five years, with the first payment being made exactly a year from now, is worth \$2000 – \$994.35, which is \$1005.65. In general, the formula for an annuity is equal to the *PV* of an annuity is equal to $(CF/r) \times (1 - 1/(1 + r)^T)$. For the example, if we have \$300/0.15 – (\$300/0.15) × $(1/(1.15)^5)$, then we have what? The \$2000 – \$994.35. That gives us the value of the annuity, at \$1005.65.

The last set of formulae we will consider for both annuities and perpetuities are payments in which they're not fixed, but they're growing at a constant rate each period. These are called growing annuities and growing perpetuities.

A growing perpetuity is one in which the periodic payments grow at a fixed rate g (where g, for example, would be something like 0.05 for 5%). If the first payment, paid one period from now, is C_1, then the next payment is C_2, which is equal to $(1 + g)C_1$. And the payment after that will be $C_3 = (1 + g)C_2 = (1 + g)^2C_1$. Given this structure, the present value of this stream is $PV_{GP} = C_1/(r - g)$.

One way to think about this, without any growth in the payment, the future values are discounted. The farther in the future, the greater the discount. But, if the cash flows are growing, that offsets this discounting. So, think of the $r - g$ as the net amount of the discounting, given the growth in the level of the cash flows.

Note that if the growth is equal to or is outstripping the discounting—that is, if g is equal to r or greater than r—then the growth outpaces this discounting. In that case, the infinite sum is actually infinity.

But when g is greater than or equal to r, then the formula gives you a bogus answer. It generates a negative number, when, in fact the answer is really positive infinity. So be careful. If you ever use g that's greater than r, you're going to get a crazy answer. Don't use that formula.

When the stream of payments lasts for t years, it is known as a growing annuity. The formula for that is $(C/r) \times [1 - (1 + g)^t/(1 + r)^t]$. Like the annuity, a growing annuity is just the difference between the values of two growing perpetuities.

Now that we have a set of tools, let's see how we might use them to answer some very basic but important questions. For example, if you're 40 years old now, making a salary of $120,000 per year, how much do you need to save each year until you retire in order to have a nice retirement?

There are lots of unknowns in this question, so we'll have to make a few assumptions about a few things, like what kind of return on savings can you expect to get on average, how long might you live, when you're likely retire, how much of the current purchasing power you have in your annual salary do you think you will want in retirement?

So, let's make some assumptions and then, on the basis of these assumptions, we'll be able to use the formulae we've developed to answer that question. We can change some of the assumptions to see how sensitive our answer is to these assumptions. I'll let you do that.

I should mention there are numerous websites that have calculators that do these kinds of calculations for you. One thing I have noticed is that you can get wildly different answers depending upon which site you go to. Since they do not show you exactly how they came up with the answers, all I conclude is that they make wildly different assumptions in the details of the calculations. So, if you really want to know what's being assumed to see if that really applies to you, then you really need to make your own calculations based upon your own assumptions. So, let's go through this example, and you'll see how to do that.

Let's say you expect to retire at age 65. If you are 40 now, you have 25 years to set aside a portion of your salary. According to the Social Security Administration, if you are currently 40 years old, you are expected to live for another 38 years if you are a male and 42 years if you're a female.

But, let's say both your mother and father lived well into their late 80s. So, since you want to make sure that you have enough, let's figure it out if you live to be, say 85. Thus, you're going to need to save for 25 years and then live off the savings for 20 years. Let's ignore inflation and just look in real terms. Once you retire, you're not going to need to be paying off your house. So, let's say that you want to consume in real terms the equivalent to $120,000 per year. Some years you may consume more—say, go to Greece for a month—while other years you may consume less, spending more time with your grandkids as they grow up. But, on average, you're going to need \$120,000 per year.

The next thing you need to assume is what kind of return you can expect to earn on your money while in retirement. If you will want to not risk your savings, then we need to assume a fairly low number that is consistent with having your nest egg invested in low-risk securities. So, in real terms, let's assume you're able only to get 2%.

So, at age 65 you will need to have an amount of money that is equivalent to \$120,000 per year for the next 20 years, at a discount rate of 2%. That's just an annuity. For simplicity, let's assume that you get the money at the end of the year. So, at 65 you retire and one year later you have to pay yourself an equivalent of \$120,000 at the end of that year. An annuity of \$120,000 per year for 20 years at 2% is worth \$1,962,172, or \$1.96 million. So, you need to save an amount, let's call it $\$X$, every year for the next 25 years so that you have \$1.962 million at the end of that 25 years.

Notice that 1.962 million dollars 25 years in the future is equivalent to what? Its equivalent to its present value, which is $\$1{,}962{,}172/(1 + 0.1)^{25}$, and that's equal to \$181,100 now, if the interest rate is 10%.

So, to figure out what is equivalent to \$1.962 million in 25 years—which is equivalent to \$181,100 now—you need to figure out what annuity with payments at the end of the year for the next 25 years is equivalent to \$181,100 now. That is, you need to solve the following formula: $\$181{,}100 = (\$X/0.1)(1 - 1/(1.1)^{25})) \rightarrow \$X = \$181.100/(1/0.1)(1 - 1/(1.1)^{25})) = \$19{,}951$ per year, and we simply divide that by 12 to come up with a monthly value that is approximately \$1662 per month. Better start saving now.

So what we can see from these formulas is that we can answer some very interesting quantitative questions. And in subsequent lectures, we'll use these over and over again to do just that.

Bond Pricing

Lecture 8

When most people think of investing, they think of stocks. But what about the bond market—the market for fixed income? In terms of sheer size, the money in fixed income dominates the amount of money tied up in equity or stock by about 5 to 1 in the United States. In this lecture, you will learn how to price bonds given an interest rate. You will also learn how the interest rates on bonds are quoted.

Bonds

- A "plain vanilla" bond is defined by the following features: maturity (the final date of the last promised payment), face value (the principal due at maturity), coupon rate (the percent of the face value that is the annual payment), and payment frequency (the number of times over which the annual payment is made).

- "Plain vanilla" refers to the structure of payments that will be discussed in this lecture—that is, the structure defined by the maturity, face value, coupon rate, and payments per year. There are many bonds that have the basic bond structure but also have some bells and whistles added on.

- A zero coupon bond is a special case in which the coupon rate is zero; it promises only one future payment equal to the face value at maturity. An example of a zero coupon bond is a U.S. treasury bill, which is a bond issued by the U.S. Treasury with a maturity less than a year.

- The price (or market value) of a zero coupon bond is simply the present value (PV) of that single payment at maturity. That is, price $= PV = \frac{FV}{(1+r)^T}$, where FV is the face value, r is the appropriate annualized discount rate, and T is the number of years into the future when the bond matures and pays FV.

- For a zero coupon bond, the price is always less than its face value when interest rates are positive. Thus, sometimes these instruments are referred to as pure discount instruments, because they always sell at a discount to the face value.

- Most bonds pay a positive coupon. In addition, most bonds (either corporate debt or government debt) pay the annual coupon in 2 installments, one every 6 months. For these bonds, the coupons paid every 6 months are the coupon rate multiplied by the face value of the bond divided by 2. The last coupon paid is when the bond matures; at that maturity date, the bond also pays its face value.

- For example, consider a 4% coupon bond that makes coupon payments twice a year and matures in 10 years. A timeline might show payments of \$20 every 6 months with a final payment of \$1020, which is the face value plus the final \$20 coupon.

- If the appropriate interest rate is an annualized effective 3%, then we can determine the price by taking the present value (using that rate) of this stream. This raises the first messy issue with bonds. The 3% is an annualized *effective* rate. What does that mean? What is the alternative to an annualized effective rate?

- This issue has to do with how we discount payments received at 6-month intervals. There are two things we could do. First, we could just use 0.03/2 to be the 6-month rate and, using that 6-month rate, discount each cash flow back by the number of 6-month periods that payment is in the future. That is, the present value of the first \$20 payment is simply \$20/1.015 = \$19.70443; similarly, the present value of the second \$20 coupon is $\$20/(1.015)^2 = \$19.41323$.

- The second thing we could do instead is to use the annual 3% rate and count time in years. With this approach, the present value of the first \$20 coupon is $\$20/(1.03)^{0.5} = \$19.70659$; the second payment (at a year from now) is \$20/(1.03) = \$19.41748.

$10,000 at 1.5% every 6 months for 1 year

Payback at 6 months
(principal + interest)
$10,000 + $150 = $10,150.00

Payback at 12 months
(6-month interest + interest on the $150 interest)
$150 + $2.25 = $152.25 + principal = $10,302.25

Stated rate = 3% Annual effective rate = 3.0225%

- Although the differences are minor, they will add up, especially when we have 20 coupon payments for a 10-year bond. These differences are due to compounding. The first method is consistent with the 6-month rate being 1.5% (or half of 3%). The greater the stated rate or the number of years, the present value is a smaller fraction of the future payment.

- You should think of the differences as just resulting from a difference in the convention used for quoting rates. Although the effective rate tells you something about what you pay if you are borrowing or what you get if you are lending, there may be some good reasons to use a noneffective rate when quoting rates.

- Let's go back to pricing the 10-year 4% semiannual paying coupon bond. In general, if the effective periodic rate is r%, the face value is FV, the coupon rate is c, the number of compounding periods is K per year, and T is the time to maturity, then the price of such a bond is given by the following formula.
    - $$P = \left(\frac{c/K (FV)}{r_K} \right) \left(1 - \left(\frac{1}{1 + r_K} \right)^{TK} \right) + \frac{FV}{(1 + r_K)^{TK}}$$

$10,000 at 10% for 1 year:

Compounding	P	I	
once a year:	$10,000	$1000	$11,000.00
twice a year:	$10,000	$1025	$11,025.00
monthly:	$10,000	$1047.13	$11,047.13
daily:	$10,000	$1051.56	$11,051.56
continuously:	Pe^{rt} = $10,000$e^{(0.10 \times 1)}$ =		$11,051.71

- If you have an annualized stated rate with compounding frequency equal to the frequency of the payments, then all you have to do to get r_k is simply divide the stated rate by the number of compounding periods. If the payment frequency is different than the compounding frequency used to define the annualized stated rate, then convert the stated rate to an annualized effective rate (r_e) first.

- For example, if the stated rate is 4% compounded continuously, then the effective rate is Exp(0.04) − 1 = 0.040811 (or 4.0811%). Then, use this effective annual rate to convert to an effective period rate according to the payment frequency on the bond. So, if the payment frequency is twice a year, then the right rate to use in the formula is $r_K = (1+r)^{\frac{1}{K}} - 1 = (1+0.040811)^{\frac{1}{2}} - 1 = 0.020201 = 2.0201\%$ for the effective 6-month rate.

- Note that the first part of the formula is just the formula for the present value of an annuity. The coupons are an annuity that pays the annual coupon rate divided by the number of compounding periods times the *FV* every *K* periods per year over all of the years—for a total of *TK* periods. That is, we have $10 \times 2 = 20$ $20 payments.

- In order to use the standard annuity formula, we need the effective 6-month rate. Let's price the bond as if the effective annual rate is 3%, for example. Then, the 6-month rate is simply $r_K = (1+r)^{\frac{1}{K}} - 1 = (1+0.03)^{\frac{1}{2}} - 1 = 0.014889 = 1.4889\%$.

Using the formula, the present value of the coupons is \$343.75. And the present value of the face value is simply \$744.096. Thus, the whole bond is worth \$343.749 + \$744.096 = \$1087.845.

- One of the reasons bond rates may not be quoted in effective terms can be seen in the following example. Consider the price of a standard plain vanilla 4% coupon semiannual paying bond that matures in 10 years. What is the price of this bond if the *stated* rate is the same as the coupon rate and is compounded as frequently as the coupon is paid (in this case, twice a year)? Then, the periodic effective 6-month rate is 0.04/2 = 0.02. Plugging that into the formula, we get a price for this bond at \$1000.

- Such a bond is said to sell at par. That is, when the bond sells for its face value, it is a par bond. In this case, if you buy the bond, it is as if you are lending the firm \$1000 now (i.e., the price you paid for the bond), and in exchange, you get 6 months of interest every 6 months (i.e., \$20) until, after 10 years has passed, you get your original loaned amount back. That is, the coupons pay you enough interest to compensate you for lending the \$1000 in the first place. Thus, when they pay you back, they don't owe you any more than you lent originally. The coupons cover your time value.

- Notice that if we used an effective annual rate of 4%, then the periodic rate would be $(1.04)^{0.5} - 1 = 0.019804$, which is less than 2%. If that was the competitive rate, then you would have to pay more than \$1000 to get the \$20 interest and the \$1000 back after 10 years. In fact, the price is \$1111.30. This makes sense because with an *effective* annual rate of 4%, the return is less than with a stated 4% annual rate compounded *semiannually*. Thus, with the lower effective rate, for the same fixed payments in the future, you just pay more.

- The convention is to quote the rates on bonds that pay coupons semiannually as the stated rate based on compounding twice a year. That is, the stated rate is twice the effective 6-month rate. If rates are quoted in that way, then if the stated rate is equal to the coupon rate, the price of the bond sells at par. If the stated rate exceeds the coupon rate, then the bond will sell at a discount (i.e., it is a discount bond); by paying less to get the same stream of future payments, you get a bigger return. And if the stated rate is less than the coupon rate, the bond sells at a premium (it is a premium bond).

Yield to Maturity

- So far, we have looked at what the price would be given an interest rate. Actually, what happens in the markets is that investors decide how much they are willing to pay for something, and then the financial press reports a rate that is consistent with that price. The rate they report is something called a yield to maturity (YTM).

- A yield to maturity is a special case of something referred to as an internal rate of return (IRR), which is a general concept that doesn't just apply to bonds. It also applies to any investment. The IRR is the rate such that when that rate is applied to the cash flows for any project, the net present value of that project is zero.

- In most cases, you can think of an IRR as a breakeven value of interest. In most cases, if the interest rate in the market for a project is less than the IRR for that project, then when you use the market rate to discount the cash flows, the project will be positive NPV. If the market rate of interest is greater, then the NPV will be negative.

- Thus, the IRR is the dividing line (in terms of interest rate) between the project being good (i.e., positive NPV) or bad (negative NPV). If the cash flow stream has both positive and negative values, then there are some odd cases in which an increase in the discount rate might actually raise the NPV—and a decrease in the discount rate might lower the NPV. This doesn't happen with bonds because the cash flows on a bond are always positive.

- The yield to maturity is the IRR on the project buying the bond at its current market price and holding it to maturity. Thus, it is the return you get when you pay the current price and hold it until it matures. The YTM is kind of an average of returns over all the years until maturity.

Suggested Reading

Fabozzi, *Fixed Income Mathematics, 4E.*

Jha, *Interest Rate Markets*.

Sharpe, "The Arithmetic of Active Management."

Smith, *Bond Math.*

Tuckman and Serrat, *Fixed Income Securities*.

Questions to Consider

1. Which would you be willing to pay more for: a 5% annual coupon bond that pays the annual coupon 1 time per year or a 5% annual coupon bond that pays the annual coupon in 2 installments, one every 6 months?

2. For a given effective annual rate, which of these two bonds has a higher present value?

Bond Pricing

Lecture 8—Transcript

When most people think about investing, they think about stocks. If you watch a variety of financial news programs, except for a few notable exceptions, most of them focus on the stock market. We also have lots of market indices to watch and prognosticate about that track stocks. But what about the bond market, the market for fixed income? It turns out that in terms of sheer size, the money in fixed income dominates the amount of the money tied up in equity or stocks by about 5 to 1 in the United States.

In addition to the sheer size, and thus its importance, of fixed income as an asset class, I personally find fixed income very satisfying and attractive. The pricing relationships are quite elegant and beautiful. In comparison, as we'll see in detail in later lectures, the pricing of equity is a bit of a mess. To put it in perspective, bonds are referred to as fixed income because the income they provide, via coupon payments are specified contractually. When you buy a bond, you know what the seller is promising to pay you. Of course, as we will discuss further later, sometimes the seller doesn't follow through on the promise, but this is fairly rare. But in the vast majority of the cases, you know exactly what you're going to get.

In contrast, with equity, the cash streams you'll get—say, in terms of the dividend payments—are completely up to the discretion of the firm's management, which they exercise sometime in the future. Thus, the payments on fixed income are easy to predict because they are fixed, while the payment stream on equity is essentially what many people refer to as a WAG (or a wild ass guess). A second nice feature of bonds is that they are fairly easy to see what the appropriate discount rate is for discounting the bond's fixed payments by looking at the prices of other bonds. As we will see, while it is hard to find comparable equities, it's relatively easy to find good comparisons with bonds. In contrast, for equity, it's essentially a life-long struggle to determine the appropriate measures of risk and the appropriate discount rate that goes with that risk. Basically, there are only two things that go into the price of a security—the future cash flow stream and the appropriate discount rate. For equity, both are WAGs. For fixed income, both are relatively easy to pin down.

Having proclaimed my love for fixed income let me complain about a few things. Fixed income can be a bit confusing because of the usually many ways in which they quote interest rates. There are many interest rates floating around at any point in time. In fact, if you simply spend a few minutes on the web looking for the interest rate you'll see that there are many. It is sometimes hard to figure out what the difference is.

Sometimes the differences in rates have something to do with reporting conventions. Not all bonds are quoted with the same conventions concerning how to count time, for example. Other times, the differences in rates are substantive. In this lecture, I will discuss the reporting conventions, which generate numerical differences that are not substantive.

In this lecture, I will punt on the substantive differences in the rates, leaving those issues for another lecture. Once we have a better feel for bond pricing, understanding why interest rates vary across different bonds will be easier to understand. So, for the purposes of this lecture, there will be one interest rate, which is in effect for all periods. This is clearly a simplification. Realize that we will remove this simplification starting with the very next lecture.

So, let's take a closer look at fixed income so that we can appreciate its beauty and see through all its messy parts. Let's start by defining the basic features of any bond. With this, we'll have a common language.

A plain vanilla bond is defined by the following features: (1) its maturity, (2) its face value, (3) the coupon rate, and (4) the payment frequency. Before I define each of these features, I do want to explain what I mean by plain vanilla. By plain vanilla, I mean the structure of payments that we'll discuss in this lecture. That is, the structure defined by the maturity, the face value, the coupon rate, and the payments per year.

There are many bonds that have this basic bond structure, but they also have other bells and whistles that are added on. For example, there are convertible bonds that give the owner the option to convert the bond of the firm into so many shares of stock in that firm at some interval of time in the future. A convertible bond can be thought of as a plain vanilla bond plus an option to swap one security for another. Value additivity says that we should be able to price the convertible bond as the value of the plain vanilla bond component plus the value of the option to swap. In this lecture, we will see how to price plain vanilla bonds. In subsequent lectures, we will examine how to price options in general. These lectures will allow us to price the value of the option to the swap part.

The features of a plain vanilla bond are, one, maturity. Maturity is the final date of the last promised payment. The second feature is the face value. That's the principal that's due at maturity. Then there's the coupon rate. That's the percent of the face value that is the annual payment. Then there's payments per year—the number of times over which you get the annual payment, over which those payments are made.

A zero coupon bond is a special case in which the coupon rate is zero, thus the name. It promises only one future payment equal to the face value at maturity. An example of a zero coupon bond is a U.S. treasury bill, which is a bond issued by the U.S. Treasury with a maturity less than one year. The price, or market value, of a zero coupon bond is simply the present value of that single payment at maturity. That is, the price $= PV = FV/(1 + r)^t$, where the future value, the face value, is the principle; r is the appropriate discount rate, and t is the number of years in which the payment is made. If, for example, the 1-year annualized discount rate is 2% ($r = 0.02$), then the present value of a 1-year zero coupon bond with a face value of \$1000 is going to be $1000/(1 + r)^1$, that's equal to \$980.39.

For a zero coupon bond, or a zero for short, the price is always less than its face value when the interest rates are positive. Thus, sometimes these instruments are referred to as pure discount instruments because they always sell at a discount to their face value. The only time that the price might be above the face value is when the nominal interest rate is negative. This only happens when the market expects significant deflation (i.e., a drop in the prices of goods at maturity). In that case, the purchasing power of a dollar in the future will be greater than the current purchasing power of the dollar. Thus, if one gives up \$1 now to get \$1 in the future, they're giving up a dollar's worth of consumption at current prices to get more consumption in the future. If deflation is not expected to be large enough that the increase in consumption in the future is not sufficient to compensate the investor for his or her having to postpone consumption, then the interest rate will still have to be positive. But, if the expected deflation is high enough, the interest rate might become negative. Following the financial crisis in 2008, there was much talk about the global economy collapsing and, given high amounts of unemployment, the prices of goods would fall due to a lack of demand. At that time, there was much discussion about the possibility of negative interest rates.

We will return to zeroes in a bit. Next, let's consider a coupon-paying bond. Most bonds pay a positive coupon. In addition, most bonds, either corporate debt or government debt, pay an annual coupon in two installments, every six months. For these bonds, the coupons paid every six months are the coupon rate multiplied by the face value of the bond divided by 2.

The last coupon paid is when the bond matures, at the maturity date. The bond also pays its face value. For example, consider a 4%-coupon bond that makes coupon payments twice a year and matures in 10 years. A timeline of the payments might show payments of $20 every six months with a final payment of $1000 plus $20, or $1020, which is the face value plus the final $20 coupon.

If the appropriate interest rate is an annualized effective 3%, then we can determine the price by taking the present value, using that rate, of this stream of payments. This raises the first messiness issue that has to do with bonds. I was very careful to say that the 3% was an annualized effective rate. What does that mean? What is the alternative to an effective annualized rate?

The issue has to do with how we discount payments received at six-month intervals. There are two obvious things we could do. We could just use the interest rate—3% in this case—divided by 2 to be the six-month rate, and then using that six-month rate, discount the cash flows back by the number of six-month periods that that payment is in the future. That is, the present value of the first $20 would simply be $20/1 + 0.015 = $19.70443. By the way, I've added a lot of decimal places here so you can check my numbers. Make sure that you're following along. Similarly, the present value of the second coupon payment is going to be $\$20/(1.015)^2$, and that's equal to $19.41323.

The second thing we could do instead is just to use the annual rate and count time in years. With this approach, the present value of the first \$20 coupon is what? It's $\$20/(1.03)^{0.5}$, where 0.5 is counting half a year. That's equal to \$19.70659. The second payment at a year from now is $\$20/(1.03)^{1}$. That's \$19.41748. Now you can see the difference from what we did when we took the annual rate and divided it by 2.

Although the differences are minor, they do add up, especially if we have 20 coupon payments for a 10-year bond. These differences are due to something called compounding. The first method is consistent with the six-month rate being 1.5%, or half of 3%.

Let's say you took out a loan in which you had to pay an interest rate that was compounded every six months. That is, the six-month rate is 1.5% every six months. What would you owe at the end of a year if you borrowed \$10,000? After six months you would owe what? \$10,000 × (1.015), or \$10,150. Then after another six months, you would owe 1.5% on the original \$10,000 but also 1.5 on the \$150 in interest you owed after six months but didn't pay yet. That is, you owe \$10,150 + 150 + (0.015 × 150). You owe \$10,302.25, since the interest on the interest is 0.015 × 150, that's \$2.25.

Thus, if you take the annual rate and divide by 2 to get the six-month rate, you're actually paying an effective rate more than 3%. Right? Thus, you would say that the 3% is not an effective annual rate. Rather, if the stated rate is 3% compounded every six months, I would say that the equivalent annualized effective rate is really 3.0225%. In terms of nomenclature, I may quote a stated rate and a number of compounding periods per year. With such a stated rate, you should divide by the number of compounding periods per year to get what is referred to as the periodic rate.

This is the effective rate for a period, which is something like half a year, or 1/12 of a year. Then, add that periodic rate to 1 and raise the whole thing to the number of compounding periods per year. The answer to this is how much you owe for every dollar that you borrowed at the stated rate. If you then subtract 1 from that number, you get the effective annual rate. For example, if I said that the stated rate was 3%, compounded semi-annually, every six months, then the periodic rate (i.e., the six-month rate) is 0.03/2, or 1.5%. Then, what would you owe after a year, or after two six-month periods, would be $1.015^2 = 1.030225$. Thus, the effective annual rate is $1.030225 - 1$, which is equal to 0.030225 or 3.0225%.

Conversely, if we say that the effective annual rate is 3%, I am saying that the six-month rate is the rate when applied twice, for two six-month periods, that generates a payment of 3%. That is, the effective six-month rate is the six-month rate raised to second power such that that = 1.03, or we're going to take $(1.03)^{0.5} - 1$, that gives us a six-month rate of 1.4889%. That is, if the effective annual rate is 3%, then the effective six-month rate is going to be less than half of 3%. Thus, if you're borrowing money, the effective rate that you pay will be larger than the stated rate when the interest is compounded frequently. The more frequently interest is compounded, then the greater is the effective annual rate above the stated rate.

A stated rate of 10% is a larger and larger effective annual rate as the frequency compounding period increases. However, there is a limit to how large the effective rate can get. In fact, if interest is compounded continuously, say, every nano-fraction of a nanosecond, then there's a mathematical result that the effective rate is simply $\exp^{(r \times t)} - 1$, where r is the stated rate, and t is going to be 1 to make it an annual rate. Similarly, if the stated rate is r and it is continuously compounded, then the present value of \$1 t years from now is simply $\$1 \times \exp^{(-r \times t)}$. Note that $\exp^{(-r \times t)}$ is a number less than 1. Thus, the present value is a fraction of the future value.

The greater the stated rate or the number of years, the present value is a smaller fraction of that future payment. You should think of the differences as just resulting from the differences in the convention used for quoting rates. As we will see, although the effective rate tells you something about what you pay if you're borrowing and what you get if you're lending, there may be some good reasons why you use a non-effective stated rate. We'll return to this later when we see how to price a bond given an effective rate.

That was a long but necessary aside. Let's go back to our pricing of our 10-year 4% semi-annual paying coupon bond. In general, if the effective periodic rate is r, the face value is FV, the coupon rate is c, the number of compounding periods is K per year, and T is the time to maturity, then the price of the bond will be given by the following formula. $P = ((c/K) \times FV)/r_K \times [1 - 1/(1 + r_K)^{(T \times K)}] + FV/(1 + r_K)^{(T \times K)}$, where $r_K = (1 + r)(1/K) - 1$.

If you have an annualized stated rate with compounding frequency equal to the frequency of the payments, then all you have to do is get the periodic rate is simply by dividing the stated rate by the number of compounding periods. If the payment frequency is different than the compounding frequency used to define the annualized stated rate, then convert the stated rate to an annualized effective rate. For example, if the stated rate is 4% compounded continuously, then the effective rate is going to be $\exp^{(0.04)} - 1$, and that's equal to 0.040811, or 4.0811%. Then use this effective annual rate to convert to an effective period rate according to the payment frequency of the bond. So, if the payment frequency is twice a year, the right rate to use in the formula would be $r_K = (1 + r)^{(1/K)} - 1 = (1 + 0.040811)^{1/2} - 1 = 0.020201$ for the effective six-month rate. You see what I mean by messiness.

Note that the first part of the formula is just the formula for the present value of an annuity, which we saw in previous lectures. The coupons are an annuity that pays the annual coupon rate divided by the number of compounding periods times the face value every K periods per year over all those years, for a total of $T \times K$ periods. That is, we're going to have $10 \times 2 = 20$, \$20 payments.

In order to use the standard annuity formula, we need the effective six-month rate. Let's price the bond as if the effective annual rate was 3%, say. Then, the six-month rate is simply $rK = (1 + r)^K - 1 = (1 + 0.03)^{1/2} - 1 =$ 0.014889. Using the formula, the present value of the coupons is then going to be \$343.75. And the present value of the face value is simply going to be the face value divided by that annual effective rate raised to the 20th, which is \$744.096. Thus, the whole bond is worth \$343.749 + 744.096, which is equal to \$1087.84.

One of the reasons bond rates may not be quoted in effective terms can be seen in the following example. Let's consider the price of a standard plain vanilla 4% coupon semi-annual paying bond that matures in 10 years. What is the price of the bond if the stated rate is the same as the coupon rate and its compound frequency is same as the rate at which the coupons are paid—that is, in this case, say, twice a year. Then, the periodic effective six-month rate is going to be what? 0.04/2, or 2%. And, plugging that into the formula, we get the price of a 4%-coupon paying bond equal exactly to its face value of $1000.

Such a bond is said to sell at par. That is, when the bond sells at its face value, it is a par bond. In this case, if you buy the bond, it is as if you were lending the firm $1000 now (i.e., you lend it to them when you pay for the price of the bond). In exchange, you get six months of interest every six months, or $20, until, after 10 years has passed, you get your original loaned amount back. That is, the coupons pay enough interest to compensate you for lending them $1000 in the first place. Thus, when they pay you back, they don't owe you any more than you originally lent to them. The coupons cover the time value.

Notice that if we have used an effective annual rate of 4%, then the periodic rate would be what? $(1.04)^{0.5} - 1 = 0.019804$, which is less than 2%. If that was the competitive rate, then you would have to pay more than $1000 to get $20 in interest and then the $1000 back after 10 years. In fact, at that effective rate, the price is $1111.30. This makes sense, since with an effective annual rate of 4%, the return is less than the stated rate of 4% compounded semi-annually. Thus, the lower the effective rate, for the same fixed payments in the future, you just pay more.

The convention is to quote rates for bonds that pay coupons semi-annually as the stated rate based upon compounding twice a year. That is, the stated rate is twice the effective six-month rate. If rates are quoted in this way, then if the stated rate is equal to the coupon rate, the price of the bond sells at par. If the stated rate exceeds the coupon rate, then the bond will sell at a discount (i.e., it's a discount bond). By paying less to get the same stream of future payments, you get a bigger return. And if the stated rate is less than the coupon rate, then the bond sells at a premium. It is called a premium bond.

So far, we have looked at what the price would be given an interest rate. Actually, what happens in the markets is that investors decide how much they are willing to pay for something and then the financial press reports a rate that is consistent with that price. The rate that they report is something called the yield to maturity, or YTM for short.

We will look at how to calculate an YTM in a second. But first, I should note that the yield to maturity is a special case of something referred to as an internal rate of return, or IRR for short. An IRR is a general concept that doesn't just apply to bonds. It also applies to any investment.

So what is an IRR? The IRR is the rate—let's call it r_{IRR}—such that when that rate is applied to the cash flows from any project, the net present value of that project is zero. In most cases, you can think of an IRR as a break-even value of interest. In most cases, if the interest rate in the market for the project is less than the IRR for that project, then that means that the market discounts the cash flows such that this is a positive NPV project. If the market rate of interest is greater than that, then the NPV will actually be negative.

Thus, the IRR is sort of a dividing line in terms of the interest rate between a project being a good idea, a positive NPV, and being a bad idea, being negative NPV project. I keep qualifying the statement "in most cases" because there are some cash flow streams in which there are both positive and negative values, for which the IRR actually does not do a good job of ranking NPVs. This doesn't happen with bonds with the cash flows that bonds typically have because all of those cash flows are always positive.

The yield to maturity is the IRR on the project buying the bond at its current market price and holding it to maturity. Thus, it is the return you get when you pay the current price and hold it until it matures. As we will see, the YTM is kind of an average of returns over all the years until maturity. We'll return to this in a subsequent lecture when we consider yield curves, in which there's not a single interest rate.

Let's consider some examples of yield to maturity. Consider the yield to maturity of a perpetuity that pays $1 every year with the next payment exactly one year from now. Let's say that this bond is currently selling for $20. What is its yield to maturity?

The perpetuity formula says that, for an effective annual rate of r, the value of a perpetuity that pays a dollar in yearly intervals is $\$1/r$. Thus, to get the yield to maturity we need to solve for the r that satisfies the following equation: $\$1/r = \$20$. That is, $r = \$1/\$20 = 0.05$, or 5%. So, the annualized effective yield to maturity is 5% in this case. Clearly, if the market price is lower than $20, then the yield to maturity is higher than 5%. To get the present value to be lower, we have to discount at a higher rate. Similarly, if the price is above $20, then the yield to maturity has to be less than 5%.

Let's consider the yield to maturity on the bond discussed earlier that pays a 4% coupon every six months and has a face value of $1000. If the current market price is $1000, then we know that the effective six-month rate that generates such a present value is what? It's 0.02. Thus, on an effective annualized basis, the yield to maturity is what? $(1.02)^2 - 1 = 0.0404$, or 4.04%. Equivalently, we could simply say that it is 4%, compounded semi-annually. In fact, the convention for reporting the yield to maturity for standard bonds is simply to quote two times the effective six-month yield.

Thus, if the price of the bond was $1000, the financial press would say that the yield to maturity is simply 4%. Realize that such a bond is really paying slightly more than that because you can invest the coupons sooner if it pays them every six months rather than every year. A $1000 face value bond that pays 4% coupons once a year that sells for $1000 has an annualized effective yield to maturity of 4%. If you were to discount such a payment stream at 4.04%, the price would actually be less than $1000. Thus, you would prefer to buy a bond that pays a 4%-coupon, paying it in two six-month installments for $1000 rather than pay $1000 for a bond that pays a 4%-coupon only once a year. The yield to maturity associated with the semi-annual payments is larger than the yield to maturity on the equally priced annual coupon paying bond.

What if the yield to maturity if the price of the semi-annual 4% coupon $1000 face value bond is $975? We know it must be greater than 4% semi-annually compounded yield to maturity. But how much more? The financial press will calculate it for you. And, you can also use canned functions on financial calculators or in spreadsheet programs. But, it is kind of instructive to see how these programs would calculate it.

Consider the bond we've been talking about. Consider a spreadsheet of how you might calculate the value of this bond for any given quoted yield to maturity. In such a spreadsheet, you would list all the cash flows and the times in which they occur. And then, for a given discount rate, you would calculate the present value of that stream of payments. For starters, let's say that you use the yield to maturity at 0.04. This yield to maturity abides by the reporting conventions and, as such, it is twice the effective six-month rate, which is 2%.

Thus, the present value of the first payment of \$20 at $t = 0.5$ is going to be $\$20/(1 + (0.04/2))^{(1)}$. That is, the six-month rate is 0.04/2, and exponent is the number of six-month periods. That's going to be one six-month period. 0.5 years from now, after one six-month period, that's when we need to discount that value back. The value is then the sum of each of the present values for each of these payments. As we've shown before, the present value of this bond is going to be \$1000 if the yield to maturity is 4% compounded semi-annually.

But remember, the price is what? \$975. Thus, we need to change the yield to maturity until the value drops to \$975. Do you want to increase the yield or decrease the yield? You want the price to fall from \$1000 to \$975, so you want to increase the yield to pull down the present value. But how much do you need to lower the yield? How can you get an exact number? Well, you can either keep guessing by plugging in a new number each time, or you can use your spreadsheet solve it. Most spreadsheets have some sort of optimization routine that you can use. By the way, if you do that in this case, the answer to the yield to maturity is 4.3104%. At the yield to maturity, the present value of that stream at this yield to maturity is 4.3%, the value is \$975.

In this lecture, we've seen how to price bonds given an interest rate. We've also seen how interest rates on bonds are quoted. In this lecture, we either (1) took the interest rate as given and determined the price, or (2) took the price as given and determined the yield to maturity. Interest rates and prices convey the same information. In the next lecture, we'll explore in detail the information content in interest rates and bond prices. In that lecture, we will explore the nature of bond risk as well.

The Term Structure of Interest Rates
Lecture 9

In this lecture, you will learn how to glean information about the future from yield curves. You will examine the yield curve and the term structure of interest rates. First, you will learn what a yield curve is. Second, you will examine how to use the yield curve to determine the present values of a series of future expected cash flows. Third, you will examine the information content of the yield curve.

Yield Curves

- So far, we have considered present and future value calculations given a single interest rate. However, there are many interest rates; rates often differ because they correspond to very different borrowing/lending activities.

- A yield curve is simply a plot of the relationship between yields to maturity and time to maturity. With any yield curve, time to maturity is across the horizontal axis; yield to maturity is on the vertical axis.

- The term structure of interest rates refers to the structure or the shape of the relationship between yields and time to maturity.

- You are going to see how current rates relate to future rates. There are two types of markets. One market is one in which people trade bonds that mature in the future for delivery now. This is referred to as the spot market. There are other markets where people trade contracts for trades in the future. These are the markets for forwards or futures contracts.

- Most yield curves are based on the prices of zero coupon bonds. For example, the yield to maturity for the 10-year time to maturity is the yield for a bond that makes a single payment in 10 years.

- You can have a yield curve based on the yield of nonzero coupon bonds. The zero coupon yield curve is cleaner because it reflects for any given time to maturity just the rate for lending or borrowing for just that length of time.

- The yields on a zero yield curve plot are obtained from the market prices of zero coupon bonds. Specifically, for a given price per $100 in face value, the yield (y) for a given time to maturity (t years) is simply the rate that solves the following equation.
    - $\text{Price} = \dfrac{\$100}{(1+y)^t}$

- For example, if the price of a 10-year bond is $75 per $100 in face value, the 10-year yield is y such that $\dfrac{\$100}{(1+y)^{10}} = \$75$. The solution is $y = \left(\dfrac{\$100}{\$75}\right)^{\frac{1}{10}} - 1 = 0.029186 = 2.9186\%$. Note that this is an annualized effective rate.

- Typically, yields increase with time to maturity. That is, a typical term structure is one in which the yield curve is upward sloping.

- To keep things simple, let's consider a hypothetical yield curve for zero coupon bonds that mature in 1, 2, and 3 years. Let's say that the yield on the 1-year zero is 0.04 (or 4%); with such a yield, a $1000 face value 1-year zero would sell for $961.54.

- Let's say that the yield on the 2-year zero is 0.06 (or 6%); with that yield, the price of a $1000 face value 2-year zero would be $\$1000/(1.06)^2 = \$890.00$.

- Finally, let's say that the yield on the 3-year zero is 0.07 (7%), implying the price per $1000 in face value is $816.30.

- Because the 3-year yield is bigger than the 2-year rate, which is bigger than the 1-year yield, the yield curve has the more typical upward slope.

- Next, let's consider how you might use the yields for zero coupon bonds to price nonzero coupon bonds. By value additivity, the present value of a stream of payments—for example, the coupons and face value on a coupon-paying bond—is simply the sum of the present values of each of the separate parts of the stream.

- So, let's consider a simple bond that has a face value of $1000 and pays an annual 5% coupon only once a year that matures in 3 years. The cash flows on this bond are 0.05 × $1000 = $50 at $t = 1$, another $50 at $t = 2$, and then the face value (of $1000) plus the final $50 coupon payment for a total payment of $1050 at $t = 3$.

- To figure out the value of this coupon bond, we need to figure out the present value of each of its payments. What is the present value of the first $50 coupon payment at $t = 1$ year? For this, we can use the yield curve for zeros. For that yield curve, we know that the value of $1000 in one year is $961.54.

- Given that, what must be the value of $50 in one year? Because $50 is 5% of $1000, then $50 in a year must be worth exactly 5% on the value of $1000 in a year. That is, $50 in a year is worth 0.05 × 961.54 = $48.077.

- Equivalently, $50 in a year is just $50 discounted back using the 1-year yield off the zero yield curve. That is, the present value of $50 in a year is $\$50/(1 + 0.04)^1 = \$48.077$. You get the same answer.

- To get the present value for the whole stream of payments on the coupon-paying bond, simply discount each of the payments from that bond at the zero yield that corresponds to when each payment is made. Then, add up all of the individual present values. The result is $949.69.

Why a Given Shape?

- A typical term structure is an upward-sloping yield curve. Why is that typical? To understand why, consider how you would feel investing in zeros with different times to maturity. If you invest in a bond with a long time to maturity, you are *implicitly* "tying your money up" for long time. If you invest in a shorter-term bond, you are *implicitly* tying your money up for less time. As a result, you may need a greater return to induce you to *implicitly* tie your money up for longer periods of time. Thus, the yield will increase with time to maturity.

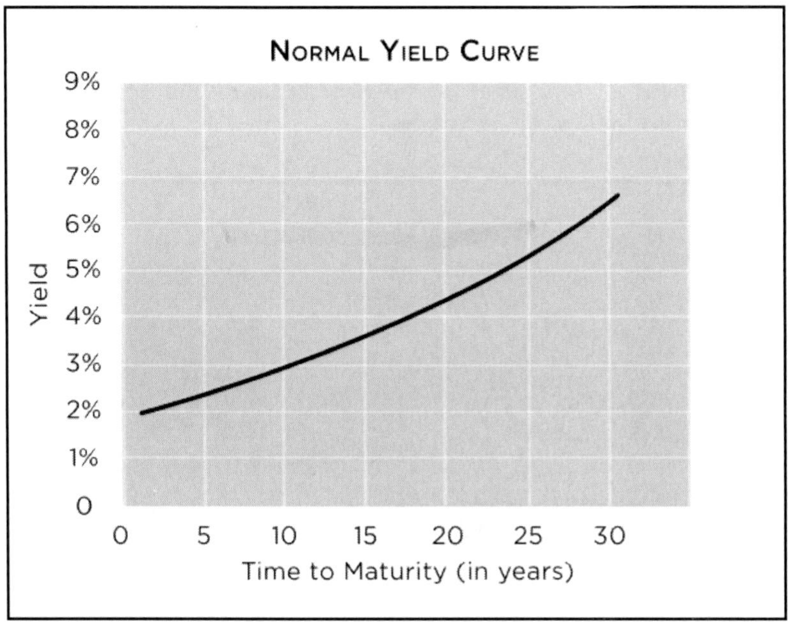

- The term "implicitly" is stressed because you personally are not forced to tie your money up until maturity. You do not have to hold a 10-year bond for 10 years; rather, you can sell it to someone else prior to maturity if you need liquidity.

- However, the person you sell it to will either have to hold it to maturity or will have to sell early to someone who will either have to hold it to maturity or find someone else to sell it, too—until there is some last person who will hold it to maturity. So, even though you do not have to hold it to maturity, somebody will have to.

- Thus, the rate at the time you buy it is based on what people are willing to pay given that someone must hold it to maturity. Because someone is tying their money up for a longer period of time, the return per year demanded is typically higher, making the yield curve slope upward. The extra return is called a term premium.

- In some cases, however, the yield curve can be downward sloping. That is, the yields on longer-term treasuries are lower than those for shorter-term treasuries. To highlight that this is not typical, this is called an inverted yield curve.

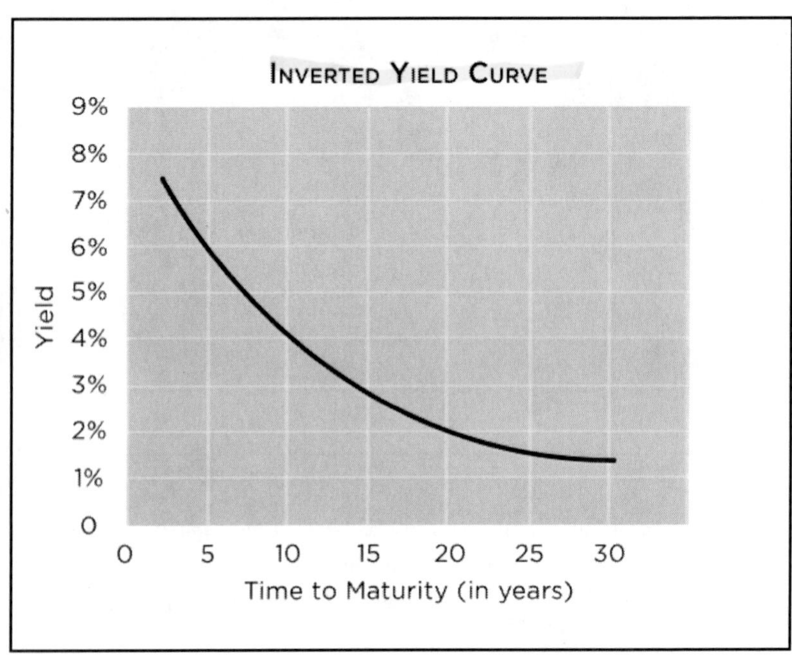

- Let's see why the shape of the yield curve might tell us something about the future. Suppose that your investment horizon is 2 years. Let $t = 0$, and let your end point be $t = 2$.

- Consider two ways to get a return over 2 years. The first way is to invest in the 1-year zero at the 1-year yield of 4%; then, when the zero matures at $t = 1$, roll over the amount you get at maturity into another 1-year investment (one that matures at $t = 2$). Let's call this the rollover strategy. The second way is to directly invest in the 2-year zero at the annual 6% yield. Let's call this the direct strategy.

- Note that for the rollover strategy, you have some uncertainty about what the 1-year rate will be next year. If you could know next year's 1-year rate for sure, what would it have to be to make you indifferent between these two strategies? The answer to that question is called the forward rate.

- Note that for the direct strategy, per dollar invested, you will get $\$1(1.06)^2 = \$1.1236$ after 2 years. If you do the rollover strategy, each dollar you invest will grow to $\$1(1.04) = \$1.04$ after 1 year (to $t = 1$). Then, take that amount and invest at the 1-year rate available at $t = 1$ for 1 more year.

- At $t = 1$, there will be many 1-year zeros that you can invest in. For example, there may be a zero that was initially issued with a time to maturity of 10 years that at $t = 1$ is 9 years old; thus, it matures at $t = 2$. There may be a new zero issued that matures in 1 year (at $t = 2$). Because all of these zeros just make a single payment at $t = 2$, the rates on all of these will be the same. The rate will be reflected on the yield curve at $t = 1$.

- Specifically, on the $t = 1$ yield curve, the rate will be that which is associated with a time to maturity of 1 year. Let's call this rate r_{11}, for the rate on a 1-year zero at $t = 1$. Let the first number be the date of the spot market and the second number be the time to maturity.

- What does that rate have to be for the rollover strategy to generate the same 2-year return as the direct strategy? That is, what is the forward rate? The answer is the solution to the following equation: $(1 + 0.04)(1 + r_{11}) = (1 + 0.06)^2$.
- Thus, the answer is $r_{11} = \frac{(1+0.06)^2}{(1+0.04)} - 1 = 0.080385 = 8.0385\%$.
- Thus, if the 1-year rate is 8.0385% next year, then the rollover strategy will generate the same 2-year return as the direct 2-year strategy. Thus, 8.0385% is the forward rate.

The Expectations Hypothesis

- For a given expectation in the future, the current yields adjust until the forward rates are equal to the market's expectation of the future spot rate. This is the expectations hypothesis—that, in a risk-neutral world, forward rates are expectations of future short-term rates.
- If you don't have a view on what interest rates will be in the future, then you can use the yield curve to calculate a series of forward rates, and under the interpretation of forward rates as expected future rates, these rates will give you a forecast of the market consensus view.

Downward-Sloping Yield Curves

- Periodically, there are downward-sloping yield curves. That is, the yield curve is inverted. That means the market expects the short-term rates to decline. This is typically associated with the expectation of a future recession and very slow economic growth.
- When the economy is in a recession, the Federal Reserve typically increases the money supply in order to lower interest rates in the hopes that low rates will spur investment and greater economic activity. The Fed typically does this by keeping short-term rates low. Thus, when the yield curve becomes inverted, the market is expecting the Fed to act in this way.

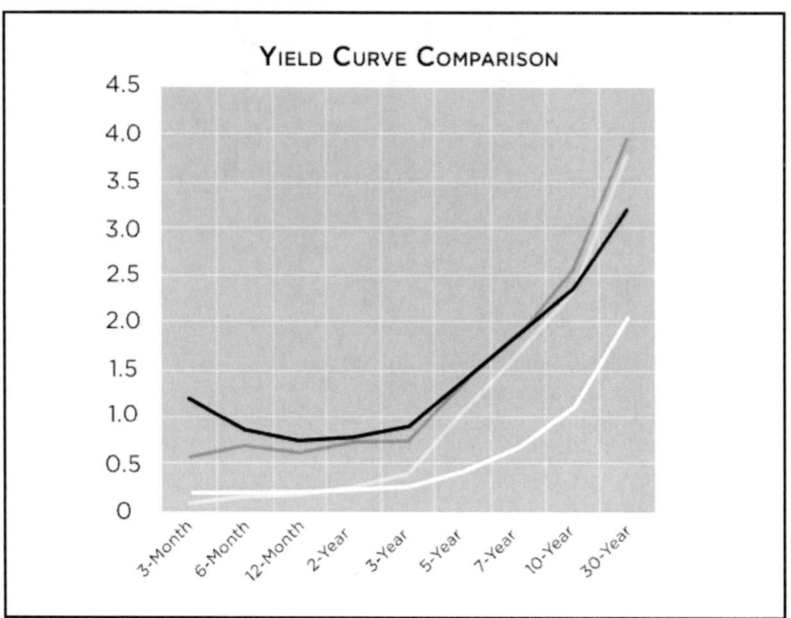

Term Premia

- In a risk-neutral world, forward rates are expectations of future spot rates. So, why do yield curves typically slope up? Does the market always expect short-term rates to rise? And, because they don't always rise and keep on rising, does this mean that the market is systematically wrong?

- The answer is that forward rates would have an additional component when the market is risk averse that generates a persistent upward slope. These additional components are called term premia.

- Term premia come from the fact that longer-term bonds are riskier than shorter-term bonds. Thus, term premia reflect the extra risk in longer-term bonds. As the term of the bond gets longer, the term premia get bigger and bigger. As a result, even if the market expects yield curves to say pretty much the same, yield curves will have an upward slope, reflecting increasing term premia.

Suggested Reading

Fabozzi, *Fixed Income Mathematics, 4E.*

Jha, *Interest Rate Markets*.

Sharpe, "The Arithmetic of Active Management."

Smith, *Bond Math.*

Tuckman and Serrat, *Fixed Income Securities*.

Questions to Consider

1. If the market expects short-term interest rates to fall in the future, can the yield curve still be upward sloping? How does the existence of term premia affect your answer?

2. When the market predicts a future recession, the yield curve becomes inverted. Does that imply that you should not invest in long-term bonds?

The Term Structure of Interest Rates
Lecture 9—Transcript

When people find out that I'm a finance professor at a party, I usually get asked lots of questions. Many people want to know if interest rates are going to rise or fall. Should they refinance now or should they wait? Should they lock in the rate or let it float until closing? Is the bond market going to tank, or will it be a safe harbor?

To be honest, these conversations usually aren't very satisfying for either of us, and that's because the very nature of these questions implies that they expect me to have a crystal ball that allows me to see into the future. I don't. However, there is a bunch of information about the future contained in bond prices.

But explaining how to get at that information is fairly involved and requires quite a bit of background. But for you, my students, in this lecture we're going to take a close look at how you can get the information in those fixed income markets. Specifically, we'll examine how, at any given moment in time, interest rates vary with time to maturity. We will then examine what that tells us about how interest rates might change over time.

In this lecture, we'll spend most of our time discussing expected returns. The two lectures after this one will explore the nature of bond risk and how to measure it. In this lecture, we'll examine the yield curve and the term structure of interest rates.

First, we will define the yield curve. Second, we will then examine how you can use the yield curve to determine the present values of a series of future expected cash flows. Then, third, we'll examine the information content of the yield curve.

Let's start by defining what a yield curve is. So far, we've considered present and future value calculations given a single interest rate. But, if you were to spend a couple of minutes searching the web for the interest rate, you would see that there are many interest rates. The rates often differ because they correspond to very different borrowing and lending activities.

One example is that interest rates differ by the maturity of the bond. For example, if you invest in a one-year T-bill, you will get a different interest rate than if you invest in a 10-year treasury bond.

A yield curve is simply a plot of the relationship between the yields to maturity and time to maturity. With any yield curve, time to maturity is across the horizontal axis, and yield to maturity is on the vertical axis. The term structure of interest rates refers to the structure or the shape of the relationships between yields and time to maturity.

To see the current yield curve on U.S. Treasury securities, you can go to Bloomberg.com and click on the "U.S. Treasuries" link under the "Rates and Bonds" under the "Market Data" pull-down tab on the homepage.

A word about some nomenclature. As I've hinted, we're going to be talking about how current rates relate to future rates. There are two types of markets. One market is one in which people trade bonds that mature in the future for delivery now. This is referred to as the spot market. There are other markets where people trade contracts for trades in the future. These are markets for forwards or futures contracts.

We will not be discussing forward and futures markets in this lecture. We will just be looking at the information about future spot market rates that can be gleaned from the rates in the current spot market.

Most yields are based on the prices of zero coupon bonds. For example, the yield to maturity for the 10-year time to maturity is the yield for a bond that makes a single payment in exactly 10 years.

As it turns out, there are many zero coupon bonds traded in the market for all maturities up to 30 years, and that's because there are bonds called STRIPS, which stands for Separate Trading in Registered Interest and Principle Securities. These zero coupon bonds are the separate coupon payments and the face value of the principal from coupon-paying Treasury bonds. That is, the coupons and the principle payments from coupon-paying bonds have been stripped apart and are sold separately. Each payment is a zero coupon bond.

You can have a yield curve that's based upon yields from non-zero coupon bonds. The zero-coupon yield curve is cleaner, since it reflects at any given time to maturity just the rate for lending or borrowing for just that length of time.

The yields on a zero yield curve plot are obtained from the market prices of zero coupon bonds. Specifically, for a given price per \$100 in face value, the yield, (let's call it y) for a given time to maturity (say, t years) is simply the rate that solves the following equation: Price = $\$100/(1 + y)^t$.

For example, if the price of a 10-year bond is \$75 per \$100 in face value, then the 10-year yield is y such that $\$100/(1 + y)^{10} = \$75$. The solution is simply $y = (\$100/\$75)^{(1/10)} - 1 = 0.029186$ (or 2.9186%). Note that this is an annualized effective rate.

Typically, yields increase with time to maturity. That is, the typical term structure is one in which the yield curve is upward sloping. We will see why later this lecture.

Let's do two things first. First, let's consider a hypothetical yield curve to solidify our understanding. Then, given that yield curve, let's see how you would use it to discount a stream of future expected cash flows.

To keep things simple, let's consider a hypothetical yield curve for zero coupon bonds that mature in one, two, and three years. Let's say that the yield on the one-year zero is 4%, or 0.04. With such a yield, for a \$1000 face value, a one-year zero would sell for \$961.54.

Let's say the yield on the two-year zero is 6%, or 0.06. With that yield, the price of \$1000 in face value for the two-year zero would be $\$1000/(1.06)^2 =$ \$890.00.

Finally, let's say that the yield on the three-year zero is 7%, implying that the price per \$1000 in face value would be \$816.30. Since the three-year yield is bigger than the two-year yield, which is also bigger than the one-year yield, this yield curve has the typical upward slope.

Next let's consider how you might use the yields for zero coupon bonds to price non-zero coupon bonds. Recall, by value additivity, the present value of a stream of payments—say, the coupons and the face value of a coupon-paying bond—is simply the sum of the present values of each of the separate parts of that stream.

So, let's consider a simple bond that has a face value of $1000 and pays an annual 5% coupon only once a year that matures in three years. The cash flows on this bond are going to be $0.05 \times \$1000 = \$50$ at $t = 1$, after one year, another $50 at $t = 2$, and then the face value (of $1000) plus the final $50 coupon payment for a total value of $1050 at $t = 3$.

To figure out the value of this coupon bond, we need to figure out the present value of each of its payments. What is the present value of the first $50 coupon payment at $t = 1$ year?

For this, we can use the yield curve for zeroes. For that yield curve, we know that the value of $1000 in one year is what? $961.54. Given that, what must be the value of $50 in one year? Well, since $50 is just 5% of $1000, then $50 in one year must be exactly worth 5% of the value of $1000 in a year. That is, $50 in one year is worth $0.05 \times 961.54 = \$48.077$.

Equivalently, $50 in a year is just $50 discounted back using the one-year yield off the zero yield curve. That is, the present value of $50 in a year is going to be $\$50/(1 + 0.04)^1 = \$48.077$. You get the same answer.

To get the present value of the whole stream of payments on the coupon-paying bond, simply discount each of the payments from that bond at the zero yields that correspond to when each payment is made. Then add up all of the individual present values. The result in this case is $949.69.

Now that we've seen some of the ins and outs of the yield curve, let's see why a yield curve might have a particular shape. As I said earlier, a typical term structure is an upward sloping yield curve. Why is that typical?

To understand why, consider how you would feel investing in zeroes with different times to maturity. If you invest in a bond with a long time to maturity, you are implicitly tying up your money for a long time. If you invest in a shorter-term bond, you are implicitly tying up your money for less time. As a result, you may need to get a greater return to induce you to implicitly tie up your money for a longer period of time. Thus, the yield will increase with time to maturity.

I keep qualifying my statements with the word implicitly. I say implicitly because you personally are not forced to tie up your money until maturity. You do not have to hold a 10-year bond for 10 years. Rather, you can sell it to someone else prior to maturity if you need the liquidity.

But, the person you sell it to will either (1) have to hold it to maturity, or (2) will have to sell it to somebody else early who will either have to (a) hold it to maturity, or (b) find someone else to sell it to who will … until some last person who has to hold it to maturity. So, even though you do not have to hold it to maturity, someone will have to. It's just like you're passing a hot potato. Just because you don't have to hold it doesn't mean it's not hot.

Thus, the rate at the time that you buy is based on what people are willing to pay, given that someone must hold it to maturity. Since someone is tying their money up for a longer period of time, the return per year demanded is typically higher, making the yield curve slope upward. The extra return is called a term premium. We will return to term premium at the end of the lecture.

In some cases, however, the yield curves have been downward sloping. That is, the yields on longer term treasuries are lower than those on shorter term treasuries. To highlight that this is not typical, this is called an inverted yield curve.

There was an inverted yield curve starting in August of 2006 that lasted about 10 months. At the time of the inversion, the financial press was rife with articles quoting experts claiming that such a shape was forecasting a coming recession. Seven months after the inversion period ended, in January 2008, the U.S. economy was in the first stages of the so-called Great Recession that happened in the 2008 financial crisis.

To see why the shape of the yield curve might tell us something about the future, let's go back to our hypothetical upward-sloping yield curve and see what that might tell us.

The way we're going to investigate the determinants of the shape of the yield curve is by considering a couple of alternative multi-year investment strategies. The efficacy of such strategies will depend upon what the future rates turn out to be. Thus, your willingness to adopt one of these strategies will depend upon your expectations regarding future yields.

Let's say your investment horizon is two years. Let now be $t = 0$ and let the endpoint of your strategy be $t = 2$. Let's consider two ways in which you can get a return over two years. One, the first way is to invest in the one-year zero at the one-year yield of 4%. Then, when that zero matures at $t = 1$, roll over the amount that you get at maturity into another one-year investment that matures, say at $t = 2$. Let's call this the roll-over strategy.

The second way is just to directly invest in the two-year zero at its annual 6% yield. Let's call this the direct strategy.

Note that for the roll-over strategy, you have some uncertainty about what the one-year rate will be next year. If you could know next-year's one-year rate for sure, what would it have to be to make you indifferent between these two strategies? The answer to that question is called the forward rate. Note that for the direct strategy, per dollar invested, you are going to get $\$1 \times (1.06)^2 = \$1.1236$ after two years.

If you do the roll-over strategy, each dollar you invest will grow to $\$1(1.04) = \$1.04$ after one year at $t = 1$. Then, if you take that amount and invest it at the one-year rate available at $t = 1$ for one more year, what are you going to get? At $t = 1$, there may be many one-year zeros that you can invest in. For example, there may be a zero that was initially issued with a time to maturity of 10 years that at $t = 1$ is now nine years old. Thus, it matures at $t = 2$. There may be a new zero issued that matures in one year (at $t = 2$). Since all of these zeroes just make a single payment at $t = 2$, the rates on all of these will be the same. The rate will be reflected on the yield curve at $t = 1$. Specifically, on the $t = 1$ yield curve, the rate will be that which is associated with the time to maturity of one year. Let's call this rate r_{11}, for the rate on a one-year zero at $t = 1$. Let's let the first number be the date of the spot market and the second number be the time to maturity.

What does this rate have to be for the roll-over strategy to generate the same two-year return as the direct strategy? That is, what is the forward rate? The answer is the solution to the following equation: $(1 + 0.04) \times (1 + r_{11}) = (1 + 0.06)^2$. Thus, the answer to this question is $r_{11} = (1 + 0.06)^2/(1 + 0.04) - 1 = 0.080385$. Thus, if the one-year rate is 8.0385% next year, then the roll-over strategy will generate the same two-year return as the direct two-year strategy.

Thus, 8.0385% is the forward rate. Now, you may have the intuition that the forward rate is the value when averaged with the one-year yield generates the two-year rate. If so, that's good. Unfortunately, you can't really get a forward rate simply by saying that 4 and 8 averages to 6. While 8 is close, that process does not take into consideration compounding. Due to compounding, it cannot be a simple average, where you just add the values and divide by 2. Rather, due to compounding, the forward is based upon a geometric average. Although the numbers are slightly different, you can still use your intuition based upon simple averages to understand what's going on.

Now, to see what you might do with the forward rate, let's consider some examples. And, for now, just to keep things easy, let's say that all you care about this the expected return—that you are risk neutral. We'll examine risk and risk aversion later once we see what's going on with this simpler case.

Let's say you think that the yield to maturity on one-year zeroes will be 7% next year. If you want to get a good return over the next year (between now and one year hence), do you want to invest in the one-year zero or do you want to invest in the two-year zero and sell it next year and realize the capital gain at that time?

If you invest in the one-year zero, you get the yield to maturity on that one-year bond. That is, you get $r = 0.04$ (4%) for sure. Always.

What if you invest in the two-year zero and sell it early? What do you expect to get on your investment over one year? Well, it depends upon what you expect the one-year zero yield will be next year. Recall that the price per \$1000 in face value for a two-year zero was \$890.00.

If you think that the one-year yield to maturity will be equal to the forward rate of 8.038% next year, then what do you expect you will be able to sell the current two-year zero for next year when it's a one-year zero? You must think that you should be able to sell it for what? \$1000/(1.08038) = \$925.60. The return over that year is r such that \$890.00 = \$925.60/(1 + r) → r = \$925.60/\$890.00 − 1. That's equal to 4%. That is, you get exactly the same return from investing in the two-year and selling it early as you would get by directly investing in the one-year.

Now, what if you were to expect the rate to be lower than the forward rate? For example, let's say that the one-year yield to maturity will be 7% next year—not the 8%. If so, then you must expect that you will be able to sell the current two-year zero for what? \$1000/(1.07) = \$934.58. In one year, you'll be able to get that price. In that case, the one-year return is the r such that \$890.00 = \$934.58/(1 + r) → r = \$934.58/\$890.00 − 1. That gives you a return of 0.05, or 5%. That is, you will get a larger return than if you were to just go out and get the one-year zero if it's the case that you expect short-term rates, the one-year rate next year, to be what? Less than the forward rate in the current yield curve.

And if you think the one-year yield to maturity next year is going to be 9%, then (1) you expected to sell the two-year zero next year for \$917.43, and (2) your one-year return from investing in the two-year zero will be only 3.083%. That is, it would be less than if you were to directly invest in the one-year zero.

So, if you think the one-year rate next year will be higher than the forward rate—for example, 9% versus 8.038%, then you should invest directly in the one-year. But, if you think the one-year rate next year will be lower than the forward rate—for example, 7% being lower than the 8.038%, then you should invest in the two-year and sell it early, next year. Only if you think the one-year rate will equal the forward rate will you be indifferent between the one-year and the two-year zeroes.

What if everyone in the market is just like you (i.e., they only care about expected returns)? Then what would be the forward rate? What would the forward rate have to equal?

Well, let's consider some supply-and-demand forces. Let's say that the yields are as in this example: the one-year yield is 4%, the two-year yield is 6%, for a forward rate of 8.038%. And let's say that everyone thinks that the one-year rate next year is going to be 7%. Then what would everyone do?

Since in this case the return from investing in the one-year and holding it to maturity is 4% but the return from buying the two-year and selling it next year is 5%, as we calculated earlier, everyone would rather buy the two-year and sell it early.

But, if everyone did that, what would happen to the prices of these bonds? We have many people buying the two-year bond, which bids up its price. And as the price rises, the yield will fall. So, the two-year rate will drop from 6% to some lower value.

And then, if we have everyone avoiding the one-year zero, the price of the one-year will fall. And as it falls, the yield on the one-year zero will rise. It will rise from 4% to some higher value.

All this buying of the two-year and selling of the one-year will stop when the investors are indifferent between investing the one-year versus the other. For example, if the one-year rate turns out to be 4.23% and the two-year rate turns out to be 5.606%, then the market is indifferent, and they will want to hold both types of bonds. With these rates, the forward rate is calculated as $(1 + 0.05606)^2/(1 + 0.0423) - 1 = 0.07\%$, which is the market's expectation of the one-year rate for next year.

That is, for a given expectation in the future, the current yields adjust until the forward rates are equal to the market's expectation of the future spot rate. This is called the expectations hypothesis—that forward rates are expectations of the future short-term rates. So, to summarize, if you don't have a view on what interest rates will be in the future, then you can use the yield curve to calculate a series of forward rates and, under the interpretation of forward rates as expected future rates that will occur in the future, you can use these to get a sense of what the consensus view is from the market as to what those future rates will be.

We have seen that in a risk-neutral world, the forward rate is the market's expectation of the future short-term rate. Under this, what does an upward-sloping yield curve imply about the market's expectations of future short term rates—not just next year, but years beyond that?

What if everyone thought that the one-year rate was going to stay at 4% every year for the next few years? In that case, the forward rate would just equal 4%. The two-year yield would be $(1 + r02)^2$ would have to be equal to $(1 + 0.04) \times (1 + 0.04)$. So it's got to be the case that the two-year zero would also have a yield of 4%. Similarly, if the market expects that the one-year yield will be 4% in two years, then the annualized yield on the three-year zero will also be 4%. That is, the yield curve will be completely flat.

In the simple example we had before, the yield curve was upward sloping. And the forward rate for the one-year yield next year was greater than the current one-year rate. That is, the reason the two-year yield is bigger than the one-year yield is because it's the average of 4% and the higher one-year yield that we expect next year. The expectation is rising, and that expectation pulls up the two-year rate.

What is the forward rate for the one-year two years from now? It's going to be the rate that solves $(1 + 0.06)^2 \times (1 + ?) = (1 + 0.07)^3$. In the case we had with the original yield curve, the solution is 9.0284%. So, it continues to slope up because the market expects short-term rates to continue to rise.

Note that the increase in yields from the one-year to the two-year was bigger than the increase in the yields from the two-year to the three-year. This happens because there was a big expected jump from $t = 0$ to $t = 1$ in the one-year rate, from 4% to approximately 8%. But the jump in the one-year between $t = 1$ and $t = 2$ is expected to be smaller—from approximately 8%

to approximately 9%. This results in the slope of that part of the yield curve increasing, but increasing at a slower rate.

Recall that periodically we've had downward-sloping yield curves. That is, the yield curve is inverted. What does this mean? That means that the market expects short-term rates to decline. This is typically associated with the expectation of a future recession and very slow economic growth. When the economy is in a recession, the Federal Reserve typically increases the money supply in order to lower interest rates in the hopes that low rates will spur investment and greater economic activity. The Fed typically does this by keeping short-term rates low. Thus, when the yield curve becomes inverted, the market is expecting the Fed to act in this way. The inverted yield curve in 2006 did a very good job of predicting the recession and the low rates that followed.

We have seen that in a risk-neutral world, forward rates are expectations of future spot rates. So, why do yield curves typically slope up? Does the market always expect short-term rates to rise? And, since they don't always rise and keep on rising, does this mean the market is systematically wrong?

The answer is that forward rates have an additional component when the market is risk-averse, and that additional component generates the upward slope. These additional components are called term premium. Term premium come from the fact that longer-term bonds are riskier than shorter-term bonds—that they are hotter potatoes than shorter-term bonds.

Why does this imply the upward slope? Well, let's consider the case in which everyone thinks the one-year yield will be 4% on average for the next two years. Under risk neutrality, then the one-year and the two-year yields will both be 4%, as we argued before. And the forward rate will, again, be 4%.

For reference, the price of the two-year is $\$100/(1 + 0.04)^2 = 92.4556$. But, if the two-year bond is riskier than the one-year, then risk-averse investors will be willing to pay less than that \$92.4556. If the price is lower, then the two-year yield is higher. Say it rises to 4% plus a quarter of a percent.

At this two-year yield, what is the forward rate? It has to be bigger than 4%, the expected one-year rate next year. In fact, the forward rate in this case is equal to $(1 + 0.0425)^2/(1 + 0.04) - 1 = 0.05$ (or 5%). Five percent is the forward rate in this case. The difference in the forward rate and the expected future spot rate next year is the term premium. In this case, it's 1%.

This term premium reflects the extra risk in longer-term bonds. As the term of the bond gets longer, the term premium get bigger and bigger. As a result, even if the market expects yield curves to stay pretty much the same, yield curves will have an upward slope, reflecting increasing term premium.

In this lecture, we've seen how you can glean information about the future from yield curves. We have also seen that, aside from the market's expectations about future interest rates, term premia make forward rates harder to interpret.

For many securities in the fixed-income markets, there are many people all looking at the same data. And the kind of data they're all looking at is pretty much public information. It depends upon how you read the subtle messages in what the Federal Reserve chairman says or what he doesn't say. It depends upon GNP growth and inflation. It's not like stocks and corporate debt, where knowing a lot about an individual firm may give you an advantage. Rather, with things like the U.S. treasuries, knowing a lot puts you merely on par with a lot of other people whose job it is to spend time running the numbers. So trust what the market rates are telling you.

The Risks in Bonds

Lecture 10

This lecture will investigate why and how long-term bonds are riskier than short-term bonds. Specifically, this lecture will examine two things that might happen that increase in likelihood over longer intervals of time: defaults and actual (rather than expected) changes in interest rates. The first creates default risk while the second creates interest rate risk. In this lecture, you will learn about the nature of both types of risk.

Interest Rate Risk

- Consider the following situation: You have a 2-year investment horizon and have just purchased a zero coupon bond that matures in 2 years. The yield to maturity (YTM) on that bond is 4%, that is, the yield curve is flat at 4% for all maturities. Thus, per \$1000 in face value, you paid $\frac{\$1000}{(1.04)^2} = \$924.5562$.

- With this zero coupon bond, you don't get any intervening coupons. If you hold it to maturity, then you get the YTM or 4% for each year. That is, you paid \$924.5562, and you get $\$924.5562(1.04)^2 = \$1000$ after two years. Note that in this case, even if interest rates fell to zero or skyrocketed, you would still get 4% annual growth on your initial investment of \$924.5562.

Reinvestment Risk

- Now, consider if you had purchased a 2-year bond that pays a 5% annual coupon. If the YTM is the same on all maturities at 4%, then, per \$1000 in face value, you pay $\frac{\$50}{(1.04)^1} + \frac{\$1050}{(1.04)^2} = \$1018.861$.

- Importantly, if the yield curve stays flat at 4% from now until maturity and you hold it to maturity, then you will also get 4% on your money—as with the 2-year zero. After 1 year, you will get \$50. At that time, if the yields have not changed, then you will be able to invest that \$50 at 4% for another year. That is, \$50 at $t = 1$ will grow to \$50(1.04) = \$52 at $t = 2$. Thus, at $t = 2$, you will have that \$52 plus \$1050 from the face value and the last coupon, for a total of \$1102.

- So, you gave up \$1018.861 at $t = 0$ and received \$1102 at $t = 2$. That would be equivalent to investing at a rate r such that $\$1018.861(1+r)^2 = \left(\dfrac{\$1102}{\$1018.861}\right)^{\frac{1}{2}} - 1 = 0.04 = 4\%$.

- What would your return be if the yield curve had shifted down to 2%, for example, after 1 year? Then, you would have paid \$1018.861, but you would have received after 2 years only \$1050 + \$50(1.02) = \$1101; then, this is equivalent to receiving a return of $\left(\dfrac{\$1101}{\$1018.861}\right)^{\frac{1}{2}} - 1 = 0.0395 = 3.95\%$ (as opposed to 4%).

- So, even though the YTM when you purchased the bond was 4% and you held it to maturity, you didn't receive that 4%. That's because the yield when you reinvested the coupon had changed from the original YTM. Of course, no such problem exists with a zero coupon bond, because you have no coupons to reinvest.

- With coupon bonds, you face what is referred to as reinvestment risk, which occurs when your investments have some cash flows that occur at a shorter horizon than your investment horizon (for example, the $t = 1$ coupon in this example).

Price Risk

- Reinvestment risk is one of two kinds of interest rate risk. The other kind is price risk, which refers to the change in the value of a bond as a result of a change in yields. This occurs when you invest in securities that are longer term than your investment horizon.

- Depending on a bond's time to maturity relative to your investment horizon, bonds that pay coupons will have both reinvestment risk and price risk. To understand price risk as clearly as possible, let's consider an example in which there is no reinvestment risk; these examples consider zero coupon bonds.

- Let's say that the current yield curve is flat at 2% for all maturities. Let's say that you want to invest for 5 years and are considering the following three strategies: buy a 5-year zero, buy a 10-year zero and sell it at the end of the 5 years, or buy a 15-year zero and sell it at the end of 5 years.

- The returns on the last two investments are uncertain because the prices of the current 10- and 15-year zeros 5 years from now (when they will be 5- and 10-year zeros, respectively) are unknown now.

- If you invest $1,000,000 in the 5-year zero, you will get 2% because that is the YTM and you will hold it until maturity. What will you get if you invest $1,000,000 in the 10-year zero now but sell it after 5 years?

- The holding period yield (HPY) is defined as the yield that, when applied to the realized cash flows, makes your investment a zero net present value (NPV) investment. That is, the HPY is the internal rate of return you realized on your investment in that bond. Notice that the HPY can only be calculated ex post, once you know what you sold the bond for at the end of your holding period. Given the cash flows you actually received, when you discount at the holding period yield, the result is the price you paid for the security.

- If the yields don't change, then the holding period yield for the longer-term zero will be the same as your original yield to maturity. Similarly, if the yield curve stays flat at 2% and you invest in the 15-year zero, your holding period yield over 5 years will be 2%, too. Thus, the maturity of the bond has no influence on your HPY, provided that the yields don't change—but they do change.

- In that case, is there a difference in the HPY between the three bonds? The HPY for the 5-year bond over 5 years is simply its original YTM of 2%. Thus, if your horizon is 5 years, then a 5-year zero locks in your yield.

- Given shifting yield curves, will there be a difference between the 10- and 15-year bonds? In both cases, you get less than if you had invested in the 5-year zero.

- Although the 15-year has a higher HPY when rates fall, you typically can't get the possibility of that upside unless you also face the possibility of rates rising. If the current yield curve incorporates the market's view on the expected future level of interest rates, then the yield curve is as likely to shift up as down. As a result, the holding period yields for longer-term bonds are more variable than those of short-term bonds. Thus, long-term zeros are riskier than shorter-term zeros.

Let the current yield curve be flat at 2% for zero coupon bonds:

Table 10.1

Maturity (in years)	Annual yield (in percent)	Zero price (per $1000 in face value)
5	2	$\$1000 / (1.02)^5 = \$905.73$
10	2	$\$1000 / (1.02)^{10} = \$820.35$
15	2	$\$1000 / (1.02)^{15} = \$743.01$

Let's say you want to invest for 5 years and are considering the following 3 strategies:

1. Buy a 5-year zero
2. Buy a 10-year zero and sell it at the end of 5 years
3. Buy a 15-year zero and sell it at the end of 5 years

What is your HPY if the yield curve shifts up to 4% in 5 years?

Table 10.2

Maturity (in years)	Annual yield (in percent)	Zero price (per $1000 in face value)
5	2	$1000 / (1.04)^5 = $821.93
10	2	$1000 / (1.04)^{10} = $675.56
15	2	$1000 / (1.04)^{15} = $555.26

When you sell a $1000 face value 10-year zero 5 years later, it is worth $1000 / (1.04)5 = $821.93.

Because you paid $820.35 per $1000 initially, your HPY is:

$$\$820.35 = \$821.93 / (1 + HPY)^5 \rightarrow HPY$$
$$= (\$821.93 / \$820.35)^{1/5} - 1$$
$$= 0.000385 = .0385\% < 2\%$$

You get less than if you had invested in the 5-year zero!

What happens if the yield curve shifts down to 1% at all maturities instead?

Table 10.3

	t = 5 yield curve flat at				
	1%		2%		4%
HPY for 5-year zero	2%		2%		2%
HPY for 10-year zero	3.01%	>	2%	>	0.008%
HPY for 15-year zero	4.03%	>	2%	>	−0.018%

Credit Risk

- Credit risk is the risk that you won't get all your promised payments. Credit rating agencies, such as Moody's, Standard & Poor's, and Fitch, provide ratings in the form of letter grades that specify something about the likelihood of a default.

- Aggregate data on the default experience of a collection of bonds by original credit rating is available from Standard & Poor's and academic papers. The typical information that a credit rating agency has to summarize credit risk is contained in a matrix of cumulative average default rates based on historical data. Such a matrix shows the probability of a company defaulting on a security they issued within a number of years as a function of that issue's credit rating.

- A typical matrix is structured as follows (see **Table 10.4**): Across the top are different horizons, measured in number of years. The first column is for within 1 year; the second column is for within 2 years. This extends all the way up to within 10 years. Down the side is the credit rating, with the best rating at the top, falling to the worst rating at the bottom.

- The numbers in the matrix answer the following question: For a bond originally issued at rating *X*, what is the probability that it will default within *Y* years? By subtracting the entry in the column to the immediate left of a given entry within a given row, you can determine the probability of an issue of that rating defaulting the year corresponding to that column. This is called the incremental or marginal probability of default for that year for that original rating.

- The marginal probabilities obtained from a matrix are the answers to the following question: For a bond originally issued at rating *X*, what is the probability that it will default in year *Y* of its life? For any given row, corresponding to a given rating at issue, the entries in the table increase from left to right. This simply reflects that it is more likely that more defaults will occur the longer we wait.

Table 10.4

Years after Issuance		1	2	3	4	5	6	7	8	9	10
Aaa	Marginal	0.00%	0.00%	0.00%	0.00%	0.05%	0.03%	0.01%	0.00%	0.00%	0.00%
	Cumulative	0.00%	0.00%	0.00%	0.00%	0.05%	0.08%	0.09%	0.09%	0.09%	0.09%
Aa	Marginal	0.00%	0.00%	0.30%	0.14%	0.02%	0.02%	0.00%	0.00%	0.05%	0.01%
	Cumulative	0.00%	0.00%	0.30%	0.44%	0.46%	0.48%	0.48%	0.48%	0.53%	0.54%
A	Marginal	0.01%	0.08%	0.02%	0.06%	0.06%	0.09%	0.05%	0.20%	0.09%	0.05%
	Cumulative	0.01%	0.09%	0.11%	0.17%	0.23%	0.32%	0.37%	0.57%	0.66%	0.71%
Baa	Marginal	0.20%	0.40%	1.34%	1.24%	0.74%	0.31%	0.19%	0.25%	0.14%	0.40%
	Cumulative	0.20%	0.60%	1.94%	3.18%	3.92%	4.23%	4.42%	4.67%	4.81%	5.21%
Ba	Marginal	1.15%	2.42%	4.32%	2.26%	2.53%	1.27%	1.11%	1.61%	1.71%	3.47%
	Cumulative	1.15%	3.57%	7.89%	10.15%	12.68%	13.95%	15.06%	16.67%	18.38%	21.85%
B	Marginal	2.84%	6.78%	7.35%	8.49%	6.01%	4.32%	2.40%	3.95%	1.96%	0.83%
	Cumulative	2.84%	9.62%	16.97%	25.46%	31.47%	35.79%	38.19%	42.14%	44.10%	44.30%
C	Marginal	24.97	15.12%	8.04%	6.76%	4.14%	4.33%	2.70%	1.79%	0.85%	0.90%
	Cumulative	24.97	40.09%	48.13%	54.89%	61.03%	65.36%	68.06%	69.85%	70.7%	71.60%

- What may not be obvious is how the marginal probabilities of default change with time to default across ratings levels. Continuing down the rows, the incremental probabilities typically continue to fall.

- The difference between each adjacent entry gets bigger as you move to the right. Thus, the pattern of incremental probabilities for higher-rated issues is the opposite of that for lower-rated issues.

- These probabilities are all from the perspective of when the bond was issued. That is, they are unconditional probabilities in the sense that the probabilities are based solely on the kind of information someone would have at the time of the issue. That is, these probabilities are based on *not* knowing any part of an issue's realized experience (e.g., whether they made it through the first year or not.)

- However, you might be interested in investing in a bond that has been around awhile. Thus, you might want to answer the following question: What is the probability that it will default given that it has survived so far? This is a conditional probability.

- Although the probabilities in a cumulative default probability matrix are unconditional probabilities, they can be used to calculate conditional probabilities. Specifically, you can calculate something called a default intensity or a hazard rate. Both are defined as the probability of a default over a particular year after issue, conditional on it not having defaulted yet.

Recovery Rates and Pricing Default-Prone Bonds

- Once you have these probabilities, you still need some additional information to help you figure out what is the value of a risky bond. The additional piece of information you need is something called a recovery rate.

- A default triggers a potentially long and drawn out legal process by which many people argue about who gets what. Because the firm's assets are unlikely to be worth nothing, the outcome of this process is that debt holders will get some fraction of what was promised to them.

- The recovery rate is defined as the fraction of the bond's face value that the bond sells at when the default occurs. Recovery rate varies across bonds according to their seniority (for example, senior secured bonds have priority over junior subordinated bonds).

- For a given recovery rate, you can get an estimate of the market's belief about the likelihood that there will be a default on that bond. If there is a positive risk of default for a bond, then that bond will have a yield that is bigger than the yield on a similar risk-free bond. The difference on the yield on the default-prone bond and the risk-free bond is called the credit or default spread. The extra yield from the spread compensates the holder for the greater chance of a default.

EXAMPLE BOND

Default Free				
Time (t) (in years)	Zero YTM	Bond CF	Bond PV	YTM = 4.2795% PV
0.5	3.0%	$2	$1.97	$1.96
1	3.5%	$2	$1.93	$1.92
1.5	3.8%	$2	$1.89	$1.88
2	4.0%	$2	$1.85	$1.84
2.5	4.2%	$2	$1.81	$1.80
3	4.3%	$102	$89.90	$89.95
	Default-free bond price = $99.35			$99.35

- Assuming that the world is risk neutral, for a given probability of default (P) and a given recovery rate (R), it must be the case that the spread (s) is such that $s = P(1 - R)$. That is, per dollar invested, you will lose \$1 − \$$R$ if the default occurs. The extra return per dollar invested, which is the spread s, must equal your expected loss. Your expected loss is simply P(\$1 − \$$R$). Thus, the "risk neutral" probability of the default is $P = \frac{s}{(1-R)}$.

Suggested Reading

Fabozzi, *Fixed Income Mathematics, 4E.*

Jha, *Interest Rate Markets.*

Smith, *Bond Math.*

Tuckman and Serrat, *Fixed Income Securities.*

Questions to Consider

1. Is there more or less reinvestment risk in a 5% coupon-paying bond than in a 10% coupon-paying bond? If both mature at the same time, does your answer depend on how far in the future they mature?

2. When there is news that indicates that a firm may default on a bond that it has issued, the price of those bonds falls. What happens to the credit spread and, for a given recovery rate, the implied probability of default?

3. What will happen to the yield to maturity on a risky bond if the yields on risk-free bonds increase but both the likelihood of default and the recovery rate for a risky corporate bond stays the same?

The Risks in Bonds

Lecture 10—Transcript

In the last lecture, we examined how, for any given point in time, there is variation in interest rates that apply to different times to maturity. We saw that some of variation has to do with expectations that interest rates would change over time. In addition, I argued that some of the variation was due to something called term premium. These premium were based on the notion that long-term bonds are riskier than short-term bonds.

You may have noticed, however, that we didn't really investigate why or how longer-term bonds are riskier. We'll do that in this lecture. Specifically, we'll examine two specific things that might happen that increase in likelihood over longer intervals of time. One is defaults, and two is actual—rather than expected—changes in interest rates. The first creates default risk while the second creates interest rate risk.

In this lecture, we'll examine the nature of both types of risks via a series of examples. In the next lecture, we'll develop a set of metrics that will allow us to quantify interest rate risk in particular.

There are very many quantitative methods for measuring default risk, too. Unfortunately, most of those are beyond the scope of this course. My hope is that the material on defaults in this lecture will give you a good intuitive idea of how to think about the effects of possible defaults. We will start by considering interest rate risk and then, in the second half, consider credit risk.

Let's start examining interest rate risk by thinking about a specific problem you might face. We will start simply and then add more complexity. By the way, many of the magnitudes of the changes in these examples that are to follow are not meant to be realistic. They are extreme so that you can clearly see the effect of the changes.

So, to start, let's consider the following situation. You have a two-year investment horizon and have just purchased a zero coupon bond that matures in two years. Let's say that the yield on that bond is 4%. That is, the yield curve is flat at 4% at all maturities. Thus, per \$1000 in face value, you will have paid what? $\$1000/(1.04)^2 = \$924.55$.

With this zero coupon bond, you don't get any intervening coupons. If you hold it to maturity, then you get the yield to maturity, or 4%, for each year. That is, you paid \$924.55 and you get $\$924.55 \times (1.04)^2 = \$1000$ after two years. Note that in this case, even if interest rates fell to zero or they skyrocketed, you would still get a 4% annual growth on your initial investment of \$924.55.

Now, consider if you had purchased a two-year bond that pays 5% annual coupons. If the yield to maturity is the same on all maturities at 4%—that is, the yield curve is flat at 4%, then per \$1000 in face value, you would pay: $\$50/(1.04)^1 + \$1050/(1.04)^2 = \$1018.86$.

Importantly, if the yield curve stays flat at 4% from now until maturity and you hold it to maturity, then you will also get 4% on your money, as with the two-year zero.

To see this, realize that after one year you will get \$50. At that time, if the yields have not changed, then you'll be able to invest that \$50 at 4% for another year. That is, the \$50 at $t = 1$ will grow to $\$50 \times (1.04) = \$52$ at $t = 2$. Thus, at $t = 2$, you'll have \$52 plus \$1050 from the face value plus the last coupon, for a total of \$1102.

So, you gave up \$1018.86 at $t = 0$ and you received \$1102 at $t = 2$. That would be equivalent to investing at a rate r such that $\$1018.86 \times (1 + r)^2 = \$1102 = r = (1102/1018.861)^{1/2} - 1 = 0.04$, or 4%. In other words, your return would have been 4% over those two years, too.

Now, what would your return be if the yield curve had shifted, say, down to 2% after a year? That is, it was flat at 4 and it shifted down to 2. Then you still will have paid \$1018.86, but you would have received after two years only $\$1050 + (1.02) \times \$50 = \$1101$. This is then equivalent to receiving a return of $\$(1101/1018.86)^{1/2} - 1 = 0.0395$ (or 3.95%). Not 4%. It's less.

So, even though the yield to maturity when you purchased the bond was 4% and you held it to maturity, you didn't receive 4%. You received less. That's because the yield when you reinvested the coupon had changed from the original yield to maturity. Of course, no such problem exists with a zero coupon bond, because there's no coupons to reinvest.

With coupon bonds, you face what is called reinvestment risk. Reinvestment risk occurs when your investments have some cash flows that occur at a shorter horizon than your investment horizon. For example, at $t = 1$ for the coupon in the last example, whereas our horizon was $t = 2$.

Reinvestment risk is one of two kinds of interest rate risk. The other kind is price risk. Price risk refers to the change in the value of a bond as the result of a change in yields. This occurs when you invest in securities that are longer-term than your investment horizon.

Depending upon a bond's time to maturity relative to your investment horizon, bonds that pay coupons will have both reinvestment risk as well as price risk. To see price risk as clearly as possible, let's consider an example in which there is no reinvestment risk. These examples we'll have to consider zero coupon bonds only.

Let's say that the current yield curve is flat at 2% for all maturities. Let's say that you want to invest for five years and are considering the following three strategies: (1) buy a 5-year zero, (2) buy a 10-year zero and then sell it at the end of five years, and then (3) buy a 15-year zero and sell it at the end of 5 years.

The returns on the last two investments are uncertain, because the prices of the current 10- and 15-year zeroes five years from now, when they are then 5- and 10-year zeroes, they are unknown now.

If you invest $1,000,000 in the five-year zero, you will get 2%, since that is the yield to maturity and you will hold it until maturity. What will you get if you invest $1,000,000 in the 10-year zero but sell it after five years?

The holding period yield, or HPY for short, is defined as the yield that when applied to the realized cash flows, makes your investment a zero NPV investment. That is, the holding period yield is the internal rate of return you realized on your investment in that bond. Notice that the holding period yield can only be calculated ex-post, once you know what you sold the bond for at the end of your holding period. Given the cash flows you actually received, when you discount at that holding period yield, the result is the price that you paid for that security. That's what defines the holding period yield.

For example, let's figure out what your holding period yield would be if you invested \$1,000,000 in a 10-year zero and sold it after five years, when it's a five-year zero. The answer depends upon what happens to the yield curve over time. For reference, let's see what the holding period yield will be if the yield curve stays flat at 2%, so at $t = 5$, let the yield curve be flat at 2%.

If so, then, per \$1000 in face value, you will be able to sell it for $\$1000/(1.02)^5 = \$905.73$, since the original 10-year zero is now a five- year zero. You discount it back at 2% for five years.

Since you paid \$820.35 per \$1000 in face value originally, your holding period yield is such that $\$820.35 = \$905.73/(1 + \text{HPY})^5 \rightarrow \text{HPY} = (\$905.73/\$820.35)^5 - 1 = 0.02$, or 2%. So, if the yields don't change, then the holding period yield for the longer-term bond will be the same as your original yield to maturity. Similarly, if the yield curve stays flat at 2% and you invest in the 15-year zero, your holding period yield over the five years will also be 2%.

Thus, the maturity of the bond has no influence on your holding period yield, provided that yields don't change. But yields do change. In that case, there's going to be a difference in the holding period yield between these three different strategies.

Clearly, the holding period yield for the five-year bond over five years is simply the original yield to maturity of 2%. Thus, if your horizon is five years, then the five-year zero locks in that yield. Given shifting yield curves, there will be a difference between the 10- and the 15-year bonds.

So let's see. What is your holding period yield if the yield curve shifts up to 4% in the next five years? When you sell a $1000 in face value for the 10-year zero five years later, it's going to be worth $\$1000/(1.04)^5 = \$821.93$.

Since you paid $820.35 per $1000 initially, your holding period yield is going to be $\$820.35 = \$821.93/(1 + \text{HPY})^5 \rightarrow \text{HPY} = (\$821.93/\$820.35)^{(1/5)} - 1 = 0.000385 < 0.02$. So you're going to get less than if you had invested in the five-year zero. And when you sell the $1000 face value original 15-year zero five years later, when it is then a 10-year zero, it's going to be worth $\$1000/(1.04)^{10} = \$675.56$. In that case, your holding period yield is actually going to be −0.01885. That's a loss of about 1.885%.

You can work out for yourself the holding period yields if the yield curve shifts down to, say, 1%. In that case, the holding period yield on the original five-year, again, is 2%, the original 10-year yield is going to be 3.01%, and the original 15-year is going to be 4.03%.

Although the 15-year has the higher holding period yield when rates fall, you typically can't get the possibility of that upside unless you also face the possibility of rates rising, and the downside that comes with that. If the current yield curve incorporates the market's view of the expected future level of interest rates, as we argued in the previous lecture, then the yield curve shifts are going to be as likely to shift up as shift down. As a result, the holding period yields for longer-term bonds are more variable than those for short-term bonds. Thus, long-term zeroes are riskier than shorter-term zeroes.

So far, we've gone through some examples which illustrate two sources of interest rate risk—reinvestment risk and price risk. Most bonds have both. In the next lecture, we'll develop a summary metric that will allow us to quantify the sum of both types of risk present in a single bond or a portfolio of bonds. This metric is fairly involved, so we're going to have to dedicate a whole lecture to it.

Next, let's consider credit risk. Credit risk is the risk that you won't get all your promised payments. Credit rating agencies such as Moody's, Standard & Poor's, Fitch, and A.M. Best, which specializes in insurance companies, provide ratings in the form of letter grades that specify something about the likelihood of default. You can easily find information online about what these letter grades are supposed to mean.

Realize, however, that these ratings can be hard to compare across rating agencies. One reason is that the ratings are difficult to compare is because these companies have different methods for evaluating the creditworthiness of a company. Another reason comparisons are difficult is because they use different letter schemes. For example, Moody's uses BAA, but S&P uses BBB for a similar category. You just need to spend some time on the Internet to see the differences.

In this part of the lecture, I want to spend time focused on the numbers, not the letters. In this section of the lecture, we will examine the kind of information that is used to measure or summarize the risks associated with default events. We will examine two important parts—information on (1) default probabilities, and (2) recovery rates. Both will be necessary to be able to price a bond with default risk.

We will also examine a technique for inferring the likelihood of default from market prices. This method is fairly crude, but it does allow you to use the prices of other default-prone bonds to see if the price of an alternative bond is fair or not. That is, it allows you to get a sense if the bonds are priced fairly relative to one another. If they are not, then this suggests a potential trading strategy.

Aggregate data on default experience of a collection of bonds by original credit rating is available from Standard & Poor's and also in academic papers. For example, Edward Altman, a professor from NYU, is one of the foremost authorities on default, and he has a lot of information on his own personal website.

The typical information that a credit rating agency has to summarize credit risk is contained in a matrix of "cumulative average default rates" based upon historical data. Such a matrix shows the probability of a company defaulting on a security they issued within a number of years as a function of that issue's credit rating.

A typical matrix is structured as follows: across the top, there are different horizons, measured in number of years. The first column is for within one year. The second column is for within two years. This extends all the way up to within 10 years. Down the side is the credit rating, the best rating at the top, falling to the worst rating at the bottom.

The numbers in the matrix answer the following question: "For a bond originally issued at rating *x*, what is the probability that it will default within *y* years?" For concreteness, let's think about the row associated with the BAA-rated bonds.

The entry under one-year column specifies the probability that a bond rated BAA when issued will default within a year after it was issued. Let's say that that probability is 0.2%. That is, only 2 out of 1000 such issues really defaulted within a year.

The next entry over to the right specifies the probability that an original BAA issue will default within two years after its issue. For example, let's let this probability be 0.6%, or 6 out of 1000. Note that the entry is for within two years. Thus, this category includes issues that defaulted within one year and those that default within the second year.

Since we know that the likelihood is going to be 2 out of 1000 that there is a default within the first year, then the entry in the second-year column indicates that there's only going to be four additional issues that default in the second year, for a cumulative number of defaults of 6 out of 1000. By subtracting the entry in the column to the immediate left of a given entry within that given row, then you determine the probability in an issue of that rating will default in the year corresponding to that column. This is called the incremental or marginal probability of default for that year for that original rating.

The marginal probabilities obtained from a matrix are the answer to the following question: "For a bond originally issued at rating *x*, what is the probability that it will default in year *y* of its life?" Not before, but in that year. For a given row, corresponding to a given rating at issue, the entries in the table increase from left to right. This simply reflects that it's more likely to have more defaults the longer we wait.

What may not be obvious is how the marginal probabilities of default change over time given the differences in default ratings. Let's compare BAA firms with CAA firms. What is typical is that a CAA issue is very likely to default within a year—say, almost a quarter of the CAA firms default within a year. The incremental probability of defaulting in the second year will be something like 13%. For CAA, the typical likelihood of default in the third year will be less than the incremental default for the second year, say at 10%, not 13%. Continuing down the row, the incremental probabilities typically continue to fall.

Next consider the row for the BAA firms. For BAA firms, the incremental probabilities typically grow as you move from 1 year to 10 years. That is, the difference between each adjacent entry gets bigger as you move to the right. Thus, the pattern of incremental probabilities for the higher-rated issues is the opposite of that for the lower-rated issues.

So why? It's actually intuitive. An issue that is originally rated at CAA is very likely to default very early on and, given that it doesn't default early on, it's less likely to default later on. The higher-rated BAA issues are less likely to default early on—they're highly rated for a reason, right? And then, given these bonds don't default early on, it will take more time for the defaults to actually occur.

Note that these probabilities are all from the perspective of when the bond was issued. That is, they are unconditional probabilities in the sense that the probabilities are based solely on the kind of information someone would have at the time of the issue. That is, these probabilities are not based on knowing anything about the realized experience (i.e., whether they survived the first year or not).

But, you might be interested in investing in a bond that's been around for a while. Thus, you might want the answer to the following question: "What is the probability that it will default given that it has survived so far?" This is a conditional probability.

Although the probabilities in a cumulative default probability matrix are unconditional probabilities, they can be used to calculate conditional probabilities. Specifically, you can calculate something called a default intensity or a hazard rate. Both are defined as the probability of a default over a particular year of issue conditional on it not having defaulted yet.

Again, let's think about the CAA issue. Let's say that you are considering buying a bond that was originally issued as a CAA bond two years ago that has not defaulted. For this bond, what is the likelihood that it will default in the next year? The answer to this question is the hazard rate, or the default intensity, for the third year.

To answer this question, realize that the probability that it survives until the beginning of the third year is simply 1 minus the cumulative probability for two years. In the CAA case, if the cumulative entry for the two years is 40%, then the probability it survives until $t = 3$ is $1 - 0.4 = 0.6$ or 60%.

And what is the probability that it defaults during the third year? If the entry for two years is 40% and the entry for 3 years is 48%, then the probability it defaults in the third year is simply the marginal probability. It's 48% – 40% = 8%. Then, out of the 60% of the times that it gets to year three, only 8% of those times does it default in the third year. That is, the hazard rate for the third year is $8/60 = 0.133$ or 13.3%.

So, once you have these probabilities, you still need some additional information to help you figure out what is the value of a risky bond. The additional piece of information you need is something called a recovery rate. A default triggers a potentially long and drawn-out legal process by which many people argue about who gets what. Since the firm's assets are unlikely to be worth nothing, the outcome of this process is that the debt holders will get some fraction of what was promised to them. Because it's very uncertain what this fraction will be, and when the bondholders will get it, it's very hard to come up with an estimate at default of the present value of its final payment.

The good news is that there's a good estimate of the value. It's simply the value of the bond once the default occurs. The "recovery rate" is defined as the fraction of the bond's face value that the bond sells at when the default occurs.

Recovery rates vary across bonds according to their seniority. For example, senior secured bonds have priority over junior subordinated bonds. Thus, holders of junior subordinated bonds will only get something if there's anything left over after the senior secured bondholders and other higher priority bondholders get their share. Thus, the recovery rates are higher for senior secured bonds than for junior subordinated debt. Senior secured might recover 60%, whereas junior subordinated debt might only recover about 30%.

Now that we see the typical kinds of information we have concerning default, let's examine what you can do with this information. For a given recovery rate, you can get an estimate of the market's belief about the likelihood that there will be a default on that bond. If there's a positive risk associated with default for the bond, then that bond will have a yield that is bigger than the yield on a similar risk-free bond. The difference on the yield in the default-prone bond and the risk-free bond is called the "credit or default spread." The extra yield from the spread compensates the holder for the greater chance of a default.

Let's see how to infer the likelihood of a default from the spread. Let's just start by assuming that we are in a risk-neutral world. For a given probability of default, let's say, denoted P, and a given recovery rate R, it must be the case that the spread, denoted s, is such that: $s = P \times (1 - R)$. That is, per dollar invested, you lose \$1 − \$$R$ if the default occurs. For example, if the recovery rate is 60%, you're going to lose 40% in value. The extra return per dollar invested, which is the spread s, must equal your expected loss. Your expected loss is simply the probability of default times the loss when you're in default, plus the probability of no default times no default. So, it's just $P \times (1 - R)$.

So, how do you get the spread? You essentially reverse-engineer using a zero-yield curve in order to get the spread under the risk-neutral pricing. Let's do an example of this. Let's say you have a 4% coupon bond that pays coupons semi-annually, with the next coupon in exactly six months. This bond was a five-year bond that was issued initially two years ago, so now it's a three-year bond. Thus, the cash flows on the bond going forward are, per $100 in face value, $2 after six months, $2 after another six months, on up to $102 after three years.

Let's say that the bond is currently selling at $96 per $100 in face value. The first question is: "Does the market think that there's any default risk?" To see if it does, let's see what the value of the bond would be if we had risk-free rates that we applied to this bond. To do that, we should just discount the cash flows using the risk-free rates off the zero yield curve. Let's say that when we use those rates off the zero yield curve, the present value of the cash flow is $99.34. Thus, if our 4% coupon bond was really default-free, the price would be $99.34 per $100 in face value, not $96. Thus, the market must think that there is default risk. The yields off the yield curve account for the interest rate risk through the term structure. The difference tells us something about credit risk.

To figure out how risky, we need to determine the spread between the yield on the risk-free bond and this risky bond. To get the yield on the risk-free bond, what we need to do is assume a single rate that, when applied to the cash flow, generates the price we get as the risk-free bond. So, we're looking for that single rate—that single yield—that's consistent with a price of $99.34. So, what we're going to do is we're going to keep changing the rate we have assumed until we get a price that's equal to $99.43. In this case, the final rate that we're going to get is going to be the yield to maturity on a risk-free version of the bond that we're interested in. In this example, the answer is 4.2795%. This is the default-free yield.

Next, we need to find the single yield when applied to the 4% coupon bond generates a price of $96 per $100 in face value. This is going to be the yield to maturity on a default-prone bond. Again, we apply the same technique we used to get the yield for the equivalent risk-free bond. This time, we need a single yield, such that when we apply it to the cash flows we get a price of not $99.34, but $96. The result, then, is the risky yield, and in this case, it's 5.54%.

Thus, the spread is going to be 5.54% – 4.27%, which gives us a spread of 1.25%. If we assume a recovery rate of 0.6, then the probability of default is going to be = 0.012/(1 – 0.6) = 0.0315 (or 3.15%).

So what does this mean? Should we sell? Should we buy? This number allows you to price other bonds with similar risks. And that will help you to decide. For example, let's say you find a junior subordinated bond that has similar characteristics, but it has a 3% coupon that matures in three years. It's currently priced at $95 per $100 in face value. Is this a good deal? Well, let's see. If it's similar to the bond that we just determined the spread for, then we can discount back the cash flows on this default risk-prone bond and get its value using the spread. If the result is $93.27 per $100 in face value, then the 3% coupon bond is overpriced at $95. So, in fact, that's the price you get when you discount it back at the risky default rate. So, do not buy it. And, if you own it, sell it.

In this section of the lecture, we have examined how default or credit risk affects the yields on bonds. While most investors only want to consider highly rated bonds, there is a significant amount of return to be earned by bearing default risk. Once you get an estimate of the default-risk premium, or the spread, you have to decide if it's big enough to induce you to invest.

Of course, you will want to look at the returns on equally risky bonds to see if the return is even in the ball park. If the premium doesn't meet what you can get elsewhere, then walk away. But if the premium is comparable, you will need to decide if it's big enough. Given the market price, there is going to be some sense in which the premium must be big enough for the average investor present in the market. If not, the price would be lower.

So, you just need to figure out if you are more or less willing or more or less able to bear default risk or more or less risk-averse than the average investor in the market. If you are less risk-averse or more able, then you can make a lot of return on these default-prone bonds.

Quantifying Interest Rate Risk

Lecture 11

This lecture will examine a measure of interest rate risk that accounts for both reinvestment risk and price risk. In this lecture, you will learn how to calculate this measure for an individual bond. You will also learn that you can apply the metric to portfolios of bonds as well. While you may never actually calculate this metric yourself, you will examine the formula so that you know exactly what the metric is—and what it is not. The goal of this lecture is to give you an intuitive feel for the features of bonds that raise or lower interest rate risk.

Balance Sheet Risk

- A balance sheet (see **Table 11.1**) is a snapshot at a moment in time of the various parts that comprise the assets and liabilities of a firm. There are two sides to the balance sheet that, as the name makes explicit, must balance. The right-hand side lists all of the liabilities that a firm has issued in order to fund its activities.

Table 11.1 Balance Sheet

Assets (*A*)		Liabilities (*L*)	
Plant	\$190	Debt	\$150
Cash	\$10		
		Equity (*E*)	\$50
Firm value	\$200		\$200

- Firms sell two basic types of liabilities. The first type is fixed claims, in which the firm promises to pay back what it borrowed plus interest at a set schedule. These claims are debt or bonds. The second is residual claims, in which the owners of these claims get whatever is left over after all the other claimants are paid. These claims are equity. This liability side shows the value of the debt and the equity of the firm.

- The left-hand side of the balance sheet measures the value of all the assets the firm has or has created with the money it raised by issuing the liabilities and selling equity listed on the other side of the balance sheet.

- Think of the asset side of the balance sheet as the value of everything the firm has purchased, including raw materials, plants and equipment, human capital, the infrastructure it has to make and sell its products and services, etc. The hope is that the unique and creative manner in which the management deploys all these assets makes the assets worth more when controlled by the firm than just the sum of their individual values alone.

- The value of the equity is simply the difference between what the enterprise is worth minus the market value of what is owed on the fixed liabilities. That is, the market value of equity (E) is equal to the market value of the assets (A) minus the market value of the debt liabilities (L).

- Because the balance sheet must balance, we have equity always equal to the value of assets minus the value of the debt liabilities: $E = A - L$. Thus, if either the value of A or the value of L changes, so does E. That is, the balancing of the balance sheet then implies that $\Delta E = \Delta A - \Delta L$, where Δ stands for "the change in."

Asset/Liability Management

- A bank issues a bunch of different types of debt liabilities. For example, they issue liabilities in the form of demand deposits. These are checking and savings accounts. They are called demand deposits because the holder of the liability (i.e., the depositor) can get their money back on demand. Thus, these can be very short-term liabilities. A bank might also issue slightly longer-term debt-like liabilities, such as 1- to 5-year certificates of deposit.

- All of these liabilities have a market value. They are promises the bank has made to pay something in the future. As a consequence, the market value of these liabilities depends on the position of the yield curve.

- The bank takes the deposits and then makes investments—in loans to business and loans to people buying homes. These are the assets the bank has on its balance sheet. These loans are assets that are like investments in the sense that they will be making a series of cash flow payments to the bank over time. And these assets have a market value.

- An important feature of these investments is that they are typically very long term in nature. For example, a 30-year mortgage is around a long time.

- Bank and other financial institutions engage in something called asset/liability management, which is all about controlling changes in equity. Financial institutions have to work at this because, by the very nature of their business, they have a mismatch between the long-term versus short-term nature of their assets and liabilities.

- For a depository institution, they issue short-term liabilities and invest in long-term assets. This means that the asset side and the liability side of the balance sheet have differing sensitivities to change in interest rates.

Duration

- Bonds with identical maturities will respond differently to interest rate changes when the coupon rates differ. We need a metric that considers all of the dimensions of the bond in determining its sensitivity. Such a metric is duration.

- Although duration means something in common parlance, it has a very specific meaning in fixed income analysis. Duration is the elasticity of the bond's value with respect to a change in the yield to maturity of the bond.

- The concept of elasticity is from microeconomics. There, economists use elasticity as a unit-less measure of how sensitive the demand for a product is to various variables of interest, such as the price of the good, the price of a substitute, or the wealth of a consumer. In general, elasticity is the percentage change in something given a percentage change in something else. Often, what matters is whether the elasticity is bigger than, equal to, or smaller than 1.

- The duration in fixed income is the elasticity of the price of a bond to the change in the yield to maturity. That is, it is defined by the following formula.
    - $\frac{\Delta P}{P} \div \frac{\Delta y}{(1+y)} = -D$, where P is the price, Δ is the change in, y is the yield, and D is the duration.

- Think of the duration as telling you the magnitude—not the direction—of the change. Because the direction of the change in the bond price is obvious, we ignore the sign when discussing the duration. Thus, durations are always positive.

- Sometimes you will hear someone refer to a Macaulay duration, which is the duration that was just defined—i.e., it is the magnitude of the percentage change in the price given a percentage change in the yield.

- You might also hear someone refer to the modified duration of a bond, which is simply the Macaulay duration divided by 1 plus the current yield. That is, $MD = \frac{D}{(1+y)}$. If the duration is not qualified with a first name, the default is that we are referring to the Macaulay duration.

- The Macaulay duration implies that $\left|\frac{\Delta P}{P}\right| = \text{D}\left|\frac{\Delta y}{1+y}\right|$. In words, the absolute value of the percent change in the price is the duration times the absolute percentage change in the yield, where the percent is measured as the change in the yield divided by 1 plus the yield (i.e., not the net yield, but the gross yield).

- One of the reasons people use modified duration is because, after hitting the expression above with a stick, you get the following expression: $\left|\frac{\Delta P}{P}\right| = MD\left|\Delta R\right|$. In words, the percentage change in the bond price is equal to the modified duration times the absolute change in the yield. That is, the price change is linear in the yield change, where the modified duration is the magnitude of the linear multiple.

Formula for Duration

- The duration of a bond is calculated as the weighted average of the times in which the bond makes its payments. The weight for a specific time a payment is made is the fraction of the total value of the bond that that payment contributes to the total value.

- We have a set of periods in which the bond makes its payments. If it pays coupons semiannually, then the first payment will be at t = 0.5, the second at t = 1, and on up to the maturity—for example, at t = 10 (for a 10-year bond). The duration is a weighted average of each of these times.

- The value of the bond is simply the sum of the present values of each of the individual payments. The weight of the first payment will be the present value of that payment divided by the value of the bond. That is, the weight is the fraction of the total value that that first payment contributes to the value of the whole bond.

Computing Duration

Duration of 2-year, 8% bond:
Face value = $1000, YTM = 12%

t	Years	CF_t	$PV(CF_t)$	Weight (W)	W × years
1	0.5	40	37.736	0.041	0.020
2	1.0	40	35.600	0.038	0.038
3	1.5	40	33.585	0.036	0.054
4	2.0	1040	823.777	0.885	1.770
		P =	930.698	1.000	D = 1.883

Thus, the weight on t = 2 is $\frac{\$823.78}{\$930.70}$ = 0.885 = 88.5%

- For example, if we consider a bond that makes annual payments, let CF_1 be the first cash flow that occurs at $t = 1$. Similarly, let CF_2 be for the cash flow at $t = 2$. Continue this way until we get to the final year (for example, T); the CF_T is the final cash flow at $t = T$. The duration is then the following formula.
    - $D = \frac{PV(CF_1)}{PV(all)}1 + \frac{PV(CF_2)}{PV(all)}2 + ... + \frac{PV(CF_T)}{PV(all)}T$, where PV(CFT) is the present value of the cash flow at t, t is the period when a payment is made, and $PV(all) = PV(CF_1) + PV(CF_2) + ... + PV(CF_T)$ is the present value of the whole stream of payments.

- Because the duration is based on all of the payments, it combines the effects of differences in coupon rates and differences in maturity. In addition, note that because the duration is a weighted average based on values, the duration of a portfolio of bonds is simply the weighted average of the durations of each of the individual bonds in the portfolio. The weight to be applied to the duration of an individual bond is simply the fraction of the portfolio's value that bond represents.

Intuition

- Based on the idea of duration as a weighted average, we can get an intuitive feel for what affects the duration of a bond or portfolio of bonds.

- Note that for a zero coupon bond, duration equals maturity because 100% of its present value is generated by the payment of the face value, at maturity. For coupon bonds, the duration is less than its time to maturity (TTM). There is positive weight on the earlier payments. As a result, the average is pulled down relative to what it would be with no coupons.

- Holding everything else fixed, as the TTM increases, the duration increases. In addition, as the coupon rate increases, the duration falls. Less intuitive is what happens to the duration when the yields are high versus low.

Bond Sensitivity to Interest Rates

Years	5.00%	6.00%	7.00%	Range/2
5	$1043.29	$1000	$959.00	$42.15
10	$1077.22	$1000	$929.76	$73.73
20	$1124.62	$1000	$894.06	$115.28

FV: $1000
Coupon rate: 6%
Coupon value: $60 a year
Interest rate: 5%-7%

Years	6.00%	7.00%	8.00%	Range/2
5	$1042.12	$1000	$960.07	$41.03
10	$1073.60	$1000	$932.90	$70.35
20	$1114.70	$1000	$901.82	$106.44

FV: $1000
Coupon rate: 7%
Coupon value: $70 a year
Interest rate: 6%-8%

Years	5.00%	6.00%	7.00%	Range/2
5	$1086.59	$1042.12	$1000	$43.29
10	$1154.43	$1073.60	$1000	$77.22
20	$1249.24	$1114.70	$1000	$124.62

FV: $1000
Coupon rate: 7%
Coupon value: $70 a year
Interest rate: 5%-7%

- Under which situation would you be more worried about losing your value? Would you lose more value given a percentage increase in yields in the high- or the low-yield cases? Use your intuition that duration is the weighted average. As the yields increase, how are the weights reallocated over the times of the payments?

- As the yields increase, the payments that are farther out are worth relatively less because they are discounted at a higher rate. As a result, the weights on later periods are smaller when yields are higher versus when yields are lower. This means that, holding everything else fixed, the duration is smaller when yields are higher. Thus, when yields are low, the duration is higher. As a result, a given percentage increase in yields will result in a much larger drop in the value of the bond in a low-interest-rate environment.

Suggested Reading

Bodie, Kane, and Marcus, *Essentials of Investments*.

Fabozzi, *Fixed Income Mathematics, 4E*.

Jha, *Interest Rate Markets*.

Smith, *Bond Math*.

Tuckman and Serrat, *Fixed Income Securities*.

Questions to Consider

1. Based on duration, which bond is subject to more interest rate risk: a 30-year fixed-rate mortgage or a 20-year zero coupon bond?

2. Consider a 30-year fixed-rate mortgage that requires monthly payments and has an annual interest rate of 5%. In the duration calculation for this mortgage, how much more weight is on the first cash flow at 1 month versus the last cash flow after 30 years? How does your answer change if the interest rate is 1% or 10%?

Quantifying Interest Rate Risk
Lecture 11—Transcript

In the last two lectures, we have seen that there are two types of categories of risk for bonds. One is interest rate risk and the other is credit risk. Within the category of interest rate risk, there are two distinct types—reinvestment risk and price risk. The last lecture illustrated the nature of these risks.

In that lecture, we saw the following relationships. When your investment horizon is longer than the time in which a bond makes a payment, you're exposed to reinvestment risk. This can happen when you invest in a bond that matures before your horizon. It can also happen if your bond matures on or after your horizon, but it pays a coupon during the intervening years. Price risk occurs when you invest in a bond with a time to maturity beyond your investment horizon. Most bonds have both reinvestment risk and price risk bundled together.

In this lecture, we will examine a measure of interest rate risk that accounts for both reinvestment risk and price risk. With this lecture, you will see how to calculate this measure for an individual bond. We will also see that you can apply this metric to portfolios of bonds. While you may never actually calculate this metric yourself, we will examine the formula so that you know exactly what this metric is, and what it is not. My goal in this section is to give you an intuitive feel for the features of bonds that raise or lower interest rate risk.

In addition, this metric is commonly used and provided in information concerning the activities of managed bond funds. Since these funds are actively managed, the composition of the portfolio changes sufficiently often that knowing the average of the metric is more informative than knowing the individual metric for each security at a particular point in time.

Finally, these metrics are extremely important for understanding the balance sheet risks of a financial institution. As we've seen with the financial crisis of 2008, such balance sheet risks can have a devastating impact on the institution's ability to make good on promises they might make you regarding wealth management services or specific investments they might offer.

The lecture is going to unfold as follows. First, we'll examine a few reasons why you might care about interest rate risk. Second, we'll examine the balance sheet risk of any firm, but we will highlight financial institutions, since many of these are especially prone to interest rate risk. And then, third, we're going to define the duration metric and examine exactly what it's supposed to measure. Fourth, we will see how to calculate the duration and develop intuition on what makes it large or small.

You may care about interest rate risk for a couple of reasons. First, it may affect you directly. Following the financial crisis of 2008, the Federal Reserve embarked upon a protracted period of time in which its monetary policy was aimed at keeping interest rates low in an effort to stimulate business activity. Anyone who was retired and living off the coupons of risk-free investments can attest to the fact that such policies made it hard to get enough interest income to cover expenses. These people then had to sell off some of the principal just to make ends meet. But, selling off principal would reduce the amount of earnings potential in the future. Perhaps if these people had a better measure of interest rate risk, they would have been able to form a more defensive portfolio prior to the crisis.

A second reason to measure interest rate risk is to recognize and quantify the interest rate risks embedded in the stocks you might hold in your portfolio. To illustrate this, I will provide a simple example of balance sheet risk next.

Consider a typical firm's balance sheet. A balance sheet is a snapshot at a moment in time of the various parts that comprise the assets and liabilities of a firm. There are two sides to the balance sheet that, as the name explains, must balance.

The right-hand side lists all of the liabilities that the firm has issued in order to fund its activities. Firms sell two basic types of liabilities. One, fixed claims, in which the firm promises to pay back what it borrowed plus interest at a set schedule. These claims are debt or bonds.

Then there are residual claims, in which the owners of these claims get whatever is left over after all the other claimants are paid. These claims are equity. This liability side shows the value of the debt and the equity of the firm.

The left side of the balance sheet measures the value of all the assets the firm has or has created with the money it raised by issuing the liabilities and selling equity listed on the other side of the balance sheet.

Think of the asset side of the balance sheet as the value of everything the firm has purchased, including raw materials, plant and equipment, human capital, the infrastructure it has to make and sell its products and services, all those things. As we will see in a subsequent lecture, the hope is that the unique and creative manner in which the management deploys all of these assets makes the assets worth more when controlled by the firm than just the sum of their individual values alone.

The value of the equity is simply the difference between what the enterprise is worth minus the market value of what is owed to the fixed liabilities. That is, the market value of equity, denoted E, is equal to the market value of the assets, denoted A, minus the market value of debt liabilities, denoted L, for liabilities.

Since the balance sheet must balance, we have equity always equal to the value of assets (A) minus the value of the debt liabilities (L), or: $E = A - L$. Thus, if either the value of A or the value of L changes, so does E. That is, the balancing of the balance sheet implies that: $\Delta E = \Delta A - \Delta L$.

If you own equity in a firm, you need to be concerned about anything that changes the value of the assets and the liabilities, because that ends up affecting the value of your equity. For example, let's consider a financial institution that you might own stock in. To make it even more concrete, let's consider a depository institution like a savings and loan or a commercial bank. A bank issues a bunch of different types of debt liabilities. For example, they issue liabilities in the form of demand deposits. These are things like checking accounts and savings accounts. They're called demand deposits because the holder of the liability, i.e., the depositor, can get their money back on demand. Thus, these are very short-term liabilities. Now, by the way, this is the first thing that I've said so far that might hint at where we're going with this in terms of balance sheet risk.

A bank might also issue slightly longer-term debt-like liabilities, like a one or a five-year certificate of deposit. All of these liabilities have a market value. They are promises that the bank has made to pay somebody in the future. As a consequence, the market value of these liabilities depends upon the position of the yield curve.

The bank takes the deposits and then does what? It makes investments. In what? Loans to business. Loans to people buying houses. These are the assets of the bank that they have on their balance sheet. These loans are assets that are like investments in the sense that they will be making a series of cash flow payments to the bank over time. And these assets have a market value. An important feature of these investments is that they're typically very long-term in nature. For example, a 30-year mortgage is around for a long time.

Banks and other financial institutions engage in something called asset–liability management. Asset–liability management is all about controlling changes in equity, or E. Financial institutions have to work at this because, by the very nature of their business, they have a mismatch between the long-term versus short-term nature of their assets and liabilities. For a depository institution, they issue short-term liabilities and invest in very long-term assets.

As we are about to see, this means that the asset side and the liability side of the balance sheet have differing sensitivities to changes in interest rates. We will return to this after we develop a measure of interest rate sensitivity in a minute.

In this section of the lecture, we will examine a bunch of examples to get a general model of interest rate sensitivity. Again, the examples have been built to illustrate a specific feature or effect. While some of the specific numbers may not seem realistic, I assure you that the effects these examples illustrate are very realistic and relevant.

From previous lectures, we have a sense that the longer the term to maturity, the greater the sensitivity to interest rate changes. But what about coupons? The following series of examples are designed to explore how interest rate sensitivity varies with both, separately and combined. Following the series of examples, we will then develop a unifying quantitative metric called duration.

Consider the following example. This example seeks to isolate the effect of differences in maturity. As a result, the bonds considered pay no coupons. Let bond A pay $1762.34 in five years. Let bond B pay $3105.85 in 10 years. Suppose the zero coupon yield is flat at 12%. At an annual yield of 12%, both are currently priced at $1000. For A, discount $1762.34 back five years at 12%. For B, discount $3105.84 back 10 years at 12%.

Now suppose the interest rate increases by 1 percentage point. What happens to the value of A and B? Well, the value of A drops to $956.53, while the value of B drops to $914.94. Since both were $1000 when the yields were 12%, the price of B falls by a greater percent than A.

The longer maturity bond has the greater drop in price because the payments are discounted a greater number of times. Next, let's consider what happens to interest rate sensitivity as a function of maturity if the bond pays coupons. Specifically, let's consider a variety of different $1000 face value bonds that pay coupons annually. First, let's consider the difference in sensitivities between three different 6% annual paying coupon bonds that vary by time to maturity. Let's consider three different times to maturity: five years, 10 years, and 15 years.

As a crude measure of sensitivity, let's consider the average change in the value of each of these bonds, given a change in the yields by 1 percentage point. That is, calculate the changes in the bond's value given a 1 percentage point increase in yields and then a 1 percentage point decrease in yields. Then take the two price changes, add them up, and divide by two to get the average price change. By comparing across the different times to maturity, we can see if the maturity effect we documented in the last example still holds when coupons are paid.

Let the starting yield be 6%. Since the bonds all pay 6% annual coupon, all of the three bonds will trade at par regardless of whether they mature in five years, 10 years, or 20 years.

Next, let's consider a change in price if the yields drop to 5%. Clearly, the prices all rise. Furthermore, as with the first example that isolated just maturity, the 20-year bond price rises more than the 10-year bond's price, which is more than that of the five-year bond price rise.

Next, consider the change in price if the yields rise to 7%. The prices all fall. Similarly, the 20-year falls more than the 10-year, which is more than the five-year. The average changes in the prices are $42.15 for the five-year bond, $73.73 for the 10-year bond, and $115.28 for the 20-year bond. So, this confirms the intuition from the first example. The longer the time to maturity, the greater the sensitivity to interest rates.

Now, so that we can see how the level of the coupon matters, let's up the coupon rate from 6% to 7% and redo the whole exercise. The goal will be to compare the average change in price between the 6% coupon-paying bond and the 7% coupon-paying bond, holding fixed the time to maturity.

Now, there are two ways we could do this. One is to consider the sensitivity of the 7% coupon bond to changes in interest rates given a starting point of 7% for yields. Then, to simulate changes in interest rates, let them go up 1% to 8%, or down 1% to 6%.

If you do that, you will see that the average changes in prices are smaller for the 7% coupon bond. Specifically, for the 6% bond, the average change is $42.15, but for the 7% coupon-paying bond, the average change was $41.03. That's for the five-year bond.

For the 10-year 6% coupon bond, the average change was $73.73, but the average change for the 10-year 7% coupon bond turns out to be only $70.35. The comparison between the two 20-year bonds is even bigger. It's $115.28 for the 6% coupon bond versus only $106.44 for the 7% coupon bond. Thus, when we consider variation in the yields around 7% for the 7% coupon bond, the 7% coupon bond is less sensitive than the 6% coupon bond.

The second way we could examine the sensitivity is to just by keeping the yields as they were in the first part of the example, starting at 6% and having them either go up to 7% or down to 5%. Then, examine the difference in the average price changes as the coupon rate goes from 6% to 7%.

If you do that analysis, you will see that, holding fixed the time to maturity, the average price changes are actually larger for the 7% coupon bond than they are for the 6% coupon bond. For example, for the five-year bond, the 7% coupon bond will change an average amount of $43.29 when the rates go from 6 to 7 and from 6 to 5. Recall that the average change for the 6% coupon bond was $42.15.

The result is that the bonds with identical maturities will respond differently to interest rate changes when the coupon rates differ. Unfortunately, we got an ambiguous result with the last example. The ranking of sensitivity based on time to maturity was unambiguous. The longer the time to maturity, the greater the sensitivity. But, the ranking of sensitivity to coupons depends upon the level of the interest rate. That is, whether we started at 6 and moved up or down, or we started the yields at 7 and moved up and down.

What we need is some sort of metric that will account for all these issues simultaneously. We need a metric that considers all of the dimensions of the bond in determining its sensitivity. Such a metric is called duration.

What is duration? Although duration means something in common parlance, it has a very specific meaning in fixed income analysis. First, I will discuss its economic meaning, and then I'll show you how to calculate it.

Duration is an elasticity of the bond's value with respect to the change in the yield to maturity of that bond. The concept of elasticity is from microeconomics. There, economists use elasticity as a unit-less measure of how sensitive the demand for a product is to various variables of interest, such as the price of the good, the price of a substitute, or the wealth of the consumer.

In general, elasticity is the percentage change in something given a percentage change in something else. Often, what matters is whether the elasticity is bigger than, equal to, or smaller than one. For example, when gasoline prices skyrocketed during the Carter administration, the question was how much would the demand drop for such a large increase in prices? How much would the demand for gasoline drop? The notion was that the demand for gasoline, at least in the short run, was inelastic in the sense that given a 20% change in the price of gasoline, the percentage drop in the demand would be less than 20%, say only 5%. Thus, the elasticity would be 5/20 = 0.25, meaning that for every percentage point increase in price, the demand would drop by only a quarter of a percentage point.

It is inelastic in the sense that demand is rigid. It doesn't change much. Even when we hit a really big price increase, it's still not going to change much. The demand for gasoline is inelastic in the short run because, at least in the short run, people still live where they live and they still have to drive their car to work. The demand is going to be less inelastic in the long run because if the price of gasoline stays high, people might choose to live closer or ride a bike to work.

The duration in fixed income is the elasticity of the price of the bond to the change in the yield. That is, it's defined by the following formula: $[\Delta P/P]/[\Delta y/(1+y)] = -D$.

In the gasoline example, I referred to the elasticity in terms of its magnitude, ignoring the direction of the change. Although an increase in price lowers demand, the elasticity was 0.25, not −0.25. Thus, since we have a yield curve that rises, or interest rates that rise, the price of the bond will fall. In the formula, the duration is the elasticity. While the bond's price drops, say, 2% for every 1 percentage increase in the yield curve, we will say that the bond's duration is 2, not −2. That is, think of the duration as telling you the magnitude, not the direction of the change. Since the direction of the change in the bond is obvious, we'll just ignore that sign when discussing the duration. Thus, durations are always positive. And when interest rates go up, prices always fall.

Sometimes you will hear someone refer to the Macaulay duration. This is the duration we have just defined. It's the magnitude of the percentage change in the price given a percentage change in the yield. You might also hear someone refer to the modified duration of a bond. The modified duration is simply the Macaulay duration divided by 1 plus the current yield. That is, modified duration, or MD, is = $D/(1 + y)$. If I do not qualify the duration with its first name, I will, by default, be referring to the Macaulay duration.

The Macaulay duration implies that the absolute value of the percentage change in the price is the duration times the absolute percentage change in the yield, where the percentage is measured as the change in the yield divided by 1 plus the yield.

One of the reasons people use modified duration is because, after hitting the expression above with a stick for a little bit, you end up getting the following expression. In words, the percentage change in the bond price is equal to the modified duration times the absolute change in the yield. That is, the price change is linear in the yield change, where the modified duration is the magnitude of this linear multiple.

Now that we have this duration, let's figure out how we would calculate it. The duration of a bond is calculated as the weighted average of the times in which the bond makes its payments. The weight for a specific time a payment is made is the fraction of the total value of the bond that that payment contributes to the total value.

Alright, that was a big mouthful. Let's break this into parts. We have a set of periods in which the bond makes its payments. If it pays coupons semi-annually, then the first payment will be at $t = 0.5$, the second at $t = 1$, on up to maturity, say, at $t = 10$ for the 10-year bond. The duration is the weighted average of each of these times.

By the way, I am counting time in years. In that case, the duration will be so many years. If you want to count time in six-month units, then the first payment would be at $t = 1$, the second at $t = 2$, on up to maturity at $t = 20$ for 10 years, 20 six-month periods from now. If you calculate the duration using six-month periods, you will just get a number that is two times the duration calculated counting time in years. I'm going to always count time in years.

Now let's consider the weights more closely. The value of the bond is simply the sum of the present values of each of the individual payments. The weight on the first payment will be the present value of that payment divided by the total value of the bond. That is, that weight is the fraction of the total value of the bond that that first payment contributes to the value of that whole bond.

For example, if we consider a bond that makes annual payments, let CF_1 be the first cash flow that occurs at $t = 1$. Similarly, let CF_2 be the cash flow associated with $t = 2$, and continue in this way until we get up to the final year (say T), and let CF_T be the final cash flow at $t = T$. The duration, then, is the following formula. $D = (PV(CF_1)/PV(\text{all})) \times 1 + (PV(CF_2)/PV(\text{all})) \times 1 + \ldots + (PV(CF_T)/PV(\text{all})) \times T$, where: $PV(CFt)$ is the present value of the cash flow at t, t is the period when a payment is made, and $PV(\text{all}) = PV(CF_1) + PV(CF_2) + \ldots + PV(CF_T)$ is the present value of the whole stream of payments.

Let's consider an example. Specifically, let's consider a 2-year, 8% coupon bond, with a face value of $1000 and a stated annual yield-to-maturity of 12%. Coupons are paid semi-annually here. Therefore, each coupon payment is going to be $40 and the per-period yield to maturity is going to be half of 12, or 6%. The present value of the whole stream is $930.70.

The present value of the first payment at $t = 0.5$ is $40/(1.06) = $37.74. So, the weight at $t = 0.5$ in the duration measure will be $37.74/$930.70 = 0.041. That is, 4.1% of the total value is due to the payment at $t = 0.5$.

Calculating in a similar fashion, the weight on the payment at $t = 1$ after two six-month periods is going to be 0.038. Note that the weight at $t = 1$ is less than the weight at $t = 0.5$, because it's farther in the future. As such, its present value is less than the present value of the first payment. It contributes a smaller fraction to the whole.

The weight on the final payment, however, is large because it also includes the face value. The cash flow at $t = 2$ is $1040. It has a present value of $823.78. Thus, the weight on $t = 2$ is going to be $823.78/$930.70 = 0.885. Fully 88.5% of the value of the bond comes from the payment at time $t = 2$.

Thus, most of the weight is on $t = 2$. And the duration will just be a little bit below two years. In fact, the duration in this case is 1.883 years.

Since the duration is based upon all the payments, it combines the effects of differences in coupon rates as well as differences in maturity. Also note that because the duration is the weighted average based upon values, the duration of a portfolio of bonds is simply the weighted average of the duration of each of the individual bonds in the portfolio. The weight to be applied to the duration of an individual bond is simply the fraction of the bond's value in that total bond portfolio value.

Based on the idea that duration as a weighted average, we can get kind of an intuitive feel for what affects the duration of a bond or portfolio of bonds. So let's consider some special cases. Note that for a zero coupon bond, the duration equals maturity since 100% of its present value is generated by the payment of the face value at maturity. One hundred percent of the weight is on the time that it matures.

For coupon bonds, the duration is less than the time to maturity. There is positive weight on the earlier payments. As a result, the average is pulled down relative to what it would be with no coupons.

So let's see how good your intuition is. Let's consider two examples. What's the duration of a 30-year fixed-rate mortgage? A fixed-rate mortgage has fixed monthly payments. So, just to get some intuition, let's ignore discounting for the time being. Then, the duration would be just the weighted average of 1/12 for the first month, 2/12 for the second month, 3/12 for the next month, all the way up to $(12 \times 30)/12$ (that's 360/12). So I'm counting time in years here, so 1/12 stands for one month; 360/12 is the last payment after 30 years. If there is no discounting going on, then the weight on each of these time periods is the same. It's 1/360. Thus, the duration would just be the simple average of all those times. The simple average is going to be what? 15 years.

Now, consider the effect of discounting. Recall from the previous example, the weight on the first coupon was bigger than the weight on the second, and so on. The same is true for the mortgage. So, there is actually more weight on the 1/12 time period then there is on 360th 12th period. For interest rates around 4%, the weight on the first payment is three times bigger than the weight on the last payment. As a result, the duration of a 30-year mortgage is much less than 15. It's actually only 12 years.

So far, we have seen that holding everything else fixed, as the time to maturity increases, the duration increases. And, as the coupon rate increases, duration falls. Less intuitive is what happens to the duration when yields are high versus low.

Under which situation would you be more worried about losing the value of a bond that you might hold? Would you lose more value given a percentage increase in yields if the yields were high or if the yields were low? Use your intuition on duration as a weighted average to see what the answer is. As the yields increase, how are the weights re-allocated across the times of the payments? As the yield increases, the farther out payments are worth relatively less because they're discounted at a higher rate. As a result, the weights on the later periods have smaller weights than when the yields are high than when the yields are low. This means that, holding everything else fixed, the duration is smaller when the yields are higher. Thus, when the yields are low, the duration is higher. As a result, a given percentage increase in yields will result in a much larger drop in value of the bond in a low interest rate environment.

In this lecture, we have seen that the sensitivity of bonds to changes in the yield is determined by its duration. We have also seen how to calculate duration. The important lesson to learn from these calculations is that the time to maturity may not be particularly close to the duration of a bond. Thus, you should pay particularly close attention to the actual duration of your bond investments rather than just think about their time to maturity.

Value Creation and Stock Prices

Lecture 12

In this lecture, you will start the process of understanding risk. The lecture will examine the basic notion of value in a corporate setting. Then, given this notion, you will examine where risk might reside. In particular, you will examine how the risk gets allocated among the claimants of the firm on the balance sheet. You will examine the weighted average cost of capital. You will also learn how the structure of the financing of the firm—that is, the firm's capital structure—affects who bears the risk in the firm.

NPV and Value

- The value of a firm as an entity derives solely from its ability to transform a bunch of stuff worth X into some other stuff that is worth more than X. The firm's management adds value only if the present value of the expected cash flows exceeds the certain value paid for the input. This difference is known as the net present value (NPV).

- The only way to get a positive NPV is by buying stuff for X that generates future and uncertain cash flows that are, in present value terms, worth more than X. If it doesn't, then what the firm does is not worth doing.

- What does NPV have to do with the stock price of these companies? Stock is just one source of money for management; it represents only one kind of claim to the cash flows of the firm. The structure of the claims issued to raise money to fund the projects that produce future cash flows is extremely important for understanding the risks of each of the securities you might buy.

- In general, there are two basic types of financial instruments or contracts that are issued to raise money to fund a firm's activities: stocks or equity (ownership) and bonds or debt (borrowing and lending).

- A bond is a fixed-income instrument in which the seller promises the buyer a set of fixed payments. Bond owners have no control rights, but they have priority over equity. Bond owners face default risk and interest rate risk.

- In contrast to bonds, a stock (or equity) is partial ownership in a company. As such, equity holders get what is left over after the firm pays all of its bills, including payments to firms and people who supply the inputs to the firm's processes. Once it pays the bills for the suppliers and sells what it produces, it makes profits. From these profits, the firm must make payments to the debt holders that lent them money in the first place to create this venture.

- If there is anything left over after the debt holders are paid, only then do the equity holders get anything. Thus, sometimes you will hear equity referred to as a "residual claim."

- In return for getting leftovers, equity holders have control rights; that is, they have a say in how the firm is run. Because they get what is left over, they want to make sure the management does not waste their resources.

- The management of the firm gets the money from selling debt and equity and then tries to transform it by creating a unique combination of people and capital that will produce profits into the indefinite future.

- The cash flows from the transformation created by the firm are distributed back to the debt and equity holders. The government also gets some in taxes. For this lecture, imagine that there is no government.

- Because equity is a residual claim, the return on equity depends on the return on the firm's assets (the whole) and the level of debt and other liabilities (the amount of the whole that is promised to someone else).

Balance Sheet and Value Creation

- A firm's balance sheet (see **figures 12.1–12.4)** is a summary of the value of the assets and liabilities of the firm. Think of a small entrepreneurial start-up; the numbers are in millions (not billions). The firm has raised $200 million in capital by selling claims to the cash flows from the venture. It has sold debt worth $150 million, and the owners of the firm (the entrepreneur and partners) have put up $50 million.

Figure 12.1 Balance Sheet

Assets (*A*)		**Liabilities (*L*)**	
Plant	$100	Debt	$150
Inventory	$100		
		Equity (*E*)	$50
Firm value	$200		$200

Figure 12.2 Balance Sheet: Debt Increase

Assets (*A*)		**Liabilities (*L*)**	
Plant	$100	Debt	$160
Inventory	$100		
		Equity (*E*)	$40
Firm value	$200		$200

Figure 12.3 Balance Sheet: Assets Increase

Assets (*A*)		**Liabilities (*L*)**	
Plant	$100	Debt	$160
Inventory	$120		
		Equity (*E*)	$60
Firm value	$220		$220

Figure 12.4 Balance Sheet: Assets Decrease

Assets (A)		Liabilities (L)	
Plant	$100	Debt	$160
Inventory	$80		
		Equity (E)	$20
Firm value	$180		$180

- Initially, they buy some raw materials (worth $100 million) and some equipment (worth $100 million). Given the riskiness of this venture, the debt holders require 5% interest. The equity holders demand 25% interest. Their returns are going to be risky. So, in order to induce them to want to invest, they need to get a higher expected return—or else they would invest their money elsewhere.

- Let's say that the debt holders only require 5% because they view their claim as risk-free. For now, let's assume that there is enough value in the firm—and there will be enough value in the firm—that the firm will always be able to make good on its promises to pay back the debt. Thus, it is risk-free debt.

- The weighted average of the two required rates of return is $(0.75 \times 0.05) + (0.25 \times 0.25) = 0.10$ (or 10%). The weights are the relative amount of money raised in each type of security: 75% in debt and 25% in equity.

- Often, financial professionals refer to this mix by discussing the "debt-to-equity ratio." In this case, the debt-to-equity ratio is 3 because the debt is worth 3 times more than the equity. The 10% in this example is the firm's cost of capital. It is the return that must be promised to the claimants in order to get them to fund the firm's activities.

- Now that the firm has material and equipment, it can transform these items into new stuff that will generate future and risky cash flows. Let's say that, on average, the $200 million worth of stuff generates an average return of 10%. Then, when we discount back the future cash flows the firm generates, what is the value we get?

- What is the risk of the cash flows generated by the firm? In an *efficient market*, it must be such that the discount rate is 10%—because the debt and equity holders are the ones that collectively bear the risk. The bondholders and equity holders get all of the cash flows from the company. Thus, if there is any variation in the future cash flows, they are the ones that must live with the variation in what they get.

- So, if the risk is such that the discount rate is 10% when they bought the firm's liabilities, then we should also discount back the expected cash flows from the capital and the ideas of the firm at 10%. And if the capital and ideas and management generate a 10% expected increase over the initial value of the assets, then the present value of the cash flows from the transformation is simply $200 million. In that case, the debt holders can get their 5%, and the equity holders can get their 25%.

- The market value of the debt is still $150 million, and the market value of the equity is still $50 million. No value was added. And that's because the market was efficient; no one made an excessive return.

- But what if the market is *not* efficient? If there was no valuable transformation, then the equity holders would have received a fair return on 25% even if their $50 million stayed worth $50 million. In the case of a valuable transformation, the equity holders get more than 25%, because they get $3.63 million more in present value.

Capital Structure

- Because equity is a residual claim, the value of equity is the value of the assets minus the value of the liabilities: $E = A - L$. If the value of A or L changes, then E changes in response. Consider what happens if a firm becomes more "levered"—that is, if it increases its debt.

- A pure capital structure change is when we simply change the capital structure without affecting the assets of the firm. Most capital structures changes are also accompanied by investments in the firm. If a firm sells some corporate bonds, they increase the amount of debt relative to equity, and they take the money raised and, for example, develop a new product or expand into a new market. If the firm sells equity, it uses the proceeds to build a state-of-the-art manufacturing and distribution center.

- When a firm does this kind of investment, two things are changing: the capital structure and the portfolio of real projects the firm has.

- Consider a situation in which a firm raises money by issuing securities and then immediately pays out the proceeds to retire or reduce the amount of another security. The returns on equity are levered in the sense that they are more sensitive to the value of assets. Thus, the more debt is used to fund the assets, the more sensitive the value of equity is to changes in the value of the firm. More leverage can make equity have higher returns when asset values increase—but also more negative returns when asset values fall.

Cost of Capital

- Let's consider how the capital structure affects the cost of capital of the firm, which is the return that must be promised to the claimants in order to get them to fund the firm's activities. What happens to the cost of capital as we change the capital structure?

- If the firm is financially sound enough that they will never default on a debt claim, then the required rate of return to the debt will be the risk-free rate. However, because the shareholders of the firm have residual claims, they will require a return that is commensurate with the risk of the equity.

- The greater the leverage (i.e., debt), the more sensitive the equity is to changes in asset values. And the more sensitive the equity is to changes in assets, the more risk. Thus, the required rate of return for equity must be increasing in the leverage (i.e., the debt-to-equity ratio) of the firm.

- In general, the required rate of return on equity r_e is the following function of the required return on debt, the required rate of return on the assets, and the debt-to-equity ratio: $r_e = r_a + \frac{D}{E}(r_a - r_d)$.

- The required rate of return on the assets r_a is the amount investors have to get if they owned all of the assets of the firm. This expression says that as the firm levers up (and $\frac{D}{E}$ gets bigger as D grows and E shrinks), the required rate of return on a firm's equity must rise.

Suggested Reading

Bodie, Kane, and Marcus, *Essentials of Investments*.

Brealey, Myers, and Allen, *Principles of Corporate Finance*.

Ross, Westerfield, Jaffe, and Jordan, *Corporate Finance*.

Questions to Consider

1. The concept of NPV is at the heart of any business enterprise. Can you think of a time in your career when your organization implemented a project that was a negative NPV? Do you think your organization routinely took on negative NPV projects or only positive NPV projects?

2. When you think of business managers and leaders you have known (including yourself), did any of these people instill a value system that encouraged seeking out and implementing positive NPV projects? What did these people do to encourage such activities? Did this process entail formal evaluation of the NPV, or was it implicit in the decision-making process?

Value Creation and Stock Prices

Lecture 12—Transcript

In previous lectures, we've seen how to translate the expectation of uncertain future cash flows from a specific investment into an equivalent sure value today. The key to this method is using an appropriate discount rate. To adjust for the fact that the cash flows are risky or uncertain, the discount rates must reflect risk. That is, the discount rate should be used to be the same as what a person could earn by putting their money in alternative investments that are equally risky. If you could get more elsewhere, you wouldn't want to invest in the specific investment you're considering. That is, if you put your money into that specific investment, you'll be incurring the opportunity cost of forgoing alternative, perhaps superior, rates of return on other investments.

Thus, your required rate of return on any investment should equal your opportunity cost, holding constant the risk of alternatives. Thus, throughout the rest of the course, I'll be using interest rate, discount rate, opportunity cost of capital, required rate of return, all to mean the same thing—namely, the rate that you should use to discount uncertain future cash flows.

One of the most important issues with this approach is the determination of the risk in an investment. And, as we will see, the issues that bear on this question, "What is risk and how can I measure it?" will take many lectures to lay out. In this lecture, we'll start by the process of understanding what risk is. For this, the lecture will examine the basic notion of value in a corporate setting. That is, given this notion, we'll examine where risk might reside. In particular, we will examine how risk gets allocated amongst the claimants of the firm on the balance sheet. Here we will examine the weighted average cost of capital. We will also see how the structure of the financing of the firm—that is, the firm's capital structure—how that affects who bears the risk in the firm.

To start, we need to consider the general relationship between the cash flows of the firm and the value of the firm. The value of the firm as an entity derives solely from its ability to transform a bunch of stuff that's worth x into some other stuff that's worth more than x.

The firm's management adds value only if the present value of the expected cash flows exceeds the certain value it paid for the inputs. This difference is known as the net present value, or NPV for short. The only way to get a positive NPV is by buying stuff for x that generates future and uncertain cash flows that are, in present value terms, worth more than x. If it doesn't do that, then what the firm is doing is not worth doing.

So what does this have to do with the price or the value of the stock? Let's turn to that next. But first, note that I asked a very particular question. What does NPV have to do with the stock price of a company? To understand that, we need to consider how firms raise the x dollars in the first place.

Stock is just one source of money for management. It represents only one kind of claim to the cash flows of the firm. The structure of the claims issued to raise the money to fund the projects that produce the future cash flows is extremely important for understanding the risks to each of the types of the securities that you might buy.

In general, there are two types of financial instruments or contracts that are issued to raise money to fund a firm's activities. They are stock or equity, which is ownership, or bonds or debt, which is borrowing and lending. Recall that a bond is a fixed-income instrument, where the seller promises the buyer a fixed set of payments. Bond owners have no control rights, but they do have priority over equity. As discussed previously, bond owners face default risk and interest rate risk.

In contrast to bonds, a stock or equity is partial ownership in that company. As such, equity holders get what is left over after the firm pays its bills, and these bills include payments to the firms, to other firms, and to people that supply the inputs to the firm's process. Once it pays the bills to the suppliers and it sells what it produces, it makes profits. And from these profits, the firm must make payments to the debt holders that lent them money in the first place to create that venture. And if there's anything left over after the debt holders are paid, then only then do the equity holders get anything. Thus, sometimes you will hear equity as referred to as a residual claim.

In return for getting leftovers, equity holders have control rights. That is, they have a say in how the firm is run. Since they get whatever is left over, they want to make sure that the management does not waste their resources. Unless three-martini lunches produce leftovers, equity holders want to be able to rein in such practices.

The management of the firm gets the money from selling debt and equity, and then tries to transform it by creating a unique combination of people and capital that will produce profits into the indefinite future. The cash flows from this transformation created by the firm are distributed back to the debt and the equity holders. By the way, the government also gets some in taxes. We will have to discuss this a bit later. For this lecture, let's consider there being no government.

Since equity is a residual claim, the return on equity is going to depend upon the return on the firm's assets—the whole—and the level of debt or other liabilities—the amount of the whole that is promised to somebody else.

A firm's balance sheet is a summary of the value of the assets and the liabilities of the firm. Let's look at a few simplified stylized balance sheets to get an idea of some of the most important relationships that exist. Here I want to affect focus on the value creation process, not on the accounting. The accounting issues are clearly important, as they help you figure out how to interpret financial statements of the firm. Most of the accounting issues concern how to account for the economic benefit and cost of something when it actually occurs.

For example, to reflect the deterioration of a piece of capital equipment over time, even if the firm does not incur an expense to fix it, accountants will recognize this depreciation. The amount of depreciation they recognize is based upon some conventions, for example, something like straight-line depreciation, that may or may not reflect the actual depreciation of the value of that equipment. Thus, the accounting numbers reflect accounting conventions rather than the truth, although the conventions are typically designed to reflect when a benefit or cost is economically incurred rather than when it is actually incurred.

For now, we will focus on some relations that must hold for the market values if investors, debt and equity holders, could see through the accounting conventions to see the actual value of the various elements.

So, let's consider a firm that was just started. Think of a small entrepreneurial start-up where the numbers are in millions, not in billions. The firm has raised $200 million in capital by selling claims to the cash flows from the venture. It has sold debt worth $150 million, and the owners of the firm, the entrepreneurs and partners, have put up $50 million.

Initially, they go out and they buy some raw materials worth, let's say, $100 million and some equipment worth another $100 million. Given the riskiness of the venture, the debt holders require 5% interest on their debt claims.

The equity holders demand 25% interest. As we will see, their returns are going to be risky. So, in order to induce them to want to invest, they need to get a higher expected return. Else, they would invest their money there.

Let's say the debt holders only require 5% because they view their claim as risk-free. As we will see, we'll have to figure that out in a second, whether it is actually risk-free or not. For now, let's assume that there's enough value in the firm that if the firm needs to be liquidated in any way, they have plenty to be able to pay back the debt. Thus, the debt will be risk-free.

The weighted average of the two required rates of return is thus $0.75 \times 0.05 + 0.25 \times 0.25 = 0.10$ or 10%. The weights, the 75% and the 25%, are the relative amounts of money raised by each type of the security. Seventy-five percent was in the debt. That's the weight that was applied to the 5% required rate of return on the debt, and the 25% was on the equity. That was the percentage that was applied to the 25% return on equity.

Often, financial professionals refer to this mix by discussing the debt-to-equity ratio. In this case, the debt-to-equity ratio is three because the debt is worth three times more than the equity. The 10% in this example is called the firm's cost of capital. It's the return that must be promised to all of the claimants in order to get them to fund the firm's activities.

Now that the firm has material and equipment, it can do its magic and transform these items into new stuff that will generate future but risky cash flows. Let's say that on average the $200 million worth of stuff generates an average return of, say, 10%. Then, when we discount back the future cash flows from the firm that it generates, what is the value we're going to get?

Here's a really important point. What is the risk of the cash flows generated by the firm? My claim is that in an efficient market, it must be such that the discount rate is 10%.

Why? Because the debt and the equity holders are the ones that collectively bear the risk. In a bit, we'll discuss how the risk is distributed amongst the various claimants, but for now think of the bond holders and the equity holders being the same people. That set of people gets all of the cash flows from the company. Thus, if there's any variation in the future cash flows, they're the ones that have to live with that variation in what they get.

So, if the risk is such that the discount rate is 10% when they bought the firm's liabilities, then we should also discount back the expected cash flows from the capital and the ideas of the management at a rate of 10%. If the capital and the ideas of the management generate a 10% expected increase over the initial value of the assets, then the present value of the cash flows from the transformation is simply the original $200 million. In that case, the debt holders get their 5% and the equity holders are going to get their 25%.

The market value of the debt is still $150 million, and the market value of the equity is still $50 million. No value was added, and that's because the market was efficient. No one made an excessive return.

But what if the market is not efficient? What happens if someone with a good idea buys $200 million worth of stuff that can produce future cash flows that generate a 12% coupon but has exactly the same risk that something that generates a 10% return would have? In that case, the firm sells $150 million in debt, the entrepreneurs add their $50 million on their own. What happens to the value of the debt and the equity after the firm makes this transformation?

If the firm takes the $200 million and invests it in the capital equipment and raw materials and people that generate a 12% return, then what will you get in the future on average? Just to keep things simple, let's consider a one-period model. The $200 million in assets, once the firm does its magic, will generate a value of equal to [$200 × (1 + 0.12)] = $224 million, or 12% bigger than what it initially was. And, what would be the value now? Given the riskiness, we need to discount that $224 million back at 10%. So, the present value is simply $224 million/1.10 = $203,636,363.

In that case, what is the debt worth? Well, the debt is still worth $150 million. The debt holders are going to get their promised payments, whether the assets generate 10% or 12% return in the future. Thus, their claims are risk-free and they should only get the risk–free rate of return of 5%.

What's the equity worth? It's worth the difference between the value of the firm's assets, which is $203.63 million, and the value of the debt, which is $150 million. Thus, the initial investment of $50 million by the entrepreneurs of the firm is worth $203.63 – $150 = $53.63 million.

Note that if there was no valuable transformation, the equity holders would have received a fair rate of return of 25%, even if their $50 million stayed worth $50 million. In the case of the valuable transformation, the equity holders get more than 25%, since they're getting $3.63 million more in present value terms.

What happened here is that the management of the firm (the entrepreneurs) exploited a positive NPV investment within the context of the corporate form. In the next lecture, we will discuss something called the present value of growth opportunities, which is this effect in spades.

Next, we need to take a closer look at how risk is allocated amongst the various claimants. There are two main reasons to understand these relationships. First, you need to be able to keep track of who bears the risk in any business. If you're investing in that business, you need to know what risk you bear when buying one of the firm's securities.

Second, the market data from other comparable firms can be very useful for assessing the return you should get on a firm in which you are thinking about investing. When looking at the data of other firms, you will see significant differences in the capital structure of these firms. And, as we will see next, the capital structure of the firm can obscure the information you can glean from market data on whether the return on the firm you're considering is appropriate or not. Specifically, if you want to price the stock of one company by looking at the returns of stocks of other companies that have similar risk, you will need to adjust for the capital structure differences between these two comparable firms.

To see the effect of capital structure, let's go back to the original balance sheet when there was no excess return to be made. But, let's use the balance sheet to see who gets the risk.

Since equity is a residual claim, the value of equity is the value of assets minus the value of liabilities: E = A − L. If the value of A or L changes, E changes in response.

Most people are used to thinking of risk in terms of not getting what they expect in the future. But, keeping track of that kind of information is really kind of messy. So, instead, what we're going to do is we are going to use the present value notion to boil down all of these potential outcomes in the future to a value now.

So, when I say something changes, I mean that there is new information that allows us to update our predictions of future outcomes. And when that new information arrives, the present value of our predictions also changes. Thus, the risk contained in any security can be captured, through the present value notion, by how changes in present values affect the current value of that security.

Looking at the original balance sheet, what happens if the value of the assets increases to $220 million because of good news? For example, it's now very likely that there will be a change in regulations that will make your firm more profitable. Recall that, originally, the equity was worth $50 million and the debt was worth $150 million. When the assets increase in value to $220 million, the equity value rises to \$220 – \$150 = \$70 million. This happens because the value of the debt remains at \$150 because it is risk-free and it is still risk-free.

When the good news arrived, the equity value increased by (\$70 – \$50)/\$50 = 0.4 or 40%. So what happens if there is bad news? For example, there's some medical study that indicates the product that your firm produces clogs arteries eventually. With this news, the value of the inventory falls to, say, \$80 million from \$100 million. They're not going to be able to sell artery-clogging products for as high a price anymore. What happens to the value of equity? E is going to fall to \$30 million. The assets are worth \$180 now. The debt is still worth \$150, so E = \$180 – \$150 = \$30.

With the drop in equity value, the equity gains (\$30 – \$50)/\$50 = –0.4, or it loses 40% in value. Notice that the possibility of such good news and bad news has no effect on the value of the debt. Unless the value of A falls by more than \$50, the value of the debt will be unaffected. Thus, equity acts as a buffer, taking the first \$50 million in potential losses first.

If the value of the assets falls below \$150, then the equity is completely wiped out and the value of debt is then reduced. For the purposes of this example, let's say that such a drop in value is impossible. If this is true, then the debt is risk-free. And the return the firm has to pay its debt holders in order to induce them to give up \$150 million is going to be what? The risk-free return—in this example, 5%. Also, in this case, all of the risk is in the equity. And that's why they require a 25% return.

Next let's consider the effect of leverage. Let's consider what happens if the firm becomes more levered, that is, it increases its level of debt. Just to isolate the effect of such a capital structure change, we will consider something called a pure capital structure change. A pure capital structure change is when we simply change the capital structure without affecting the assets of the firm.

Most capital structure changes are also accompanied by investments in the firm. If the firm sells some corporate bonds, they increase the amount of debt relative to the equity and they take the money raised, for example, and develop a new product or expand into a new market. If the firm sells equity, it uses the proceeds to build a new state-of-the-art manufacturing facility somewhere. So, it changes the value of E, or changes the nature of the assets that the firm has. For a pure capital structure change, we're only going to change the capital structure without changing the assets in the firm. When a firm does these kinds of investments, we can isolate the effect of just the capital structure.

Here, I just want to focus solely on the effect of a capital structure change without the nature of the firm's business changing, too. To do that, we will consider a situation in which the firm raises money by issuing securities and then immediately pays out the proceeds to retire or reduce the amount of another security.

For example, let's increase the amount of debt and use the proceeds to pay out a one-time cash dividend to the equity holders. Specifically, let's raise \$10 million in debt and use it to pay out a one-time dividend to equity holders of \$10 million. Then, on the balance sheet, the debt will increase from \$150 million to \$160 million. Since the \$10 million in cash is not in the firm, we paid it out, the assets of the firm have not changed. And, since the firm owes something worth \$160 million, and the value of the assets is still \$200 million, the equity holder's claim has now been reduced from \$50 million to \$40 million. It's been reduced by the amount of the extra debt that we raised.

Are the equity holders mad? No. While they have equity that's worth \$10 million less, they also have \$10 million more in cash in their pocket. So, they are not mad. All that's happening is we're just swapping something worth \$10 million—their equity—for something else worth \$10 million— cash.

The most important thing to notice is that the risk of the firm has not changed. The risk of the firm has not changed. And that's because the actual real assets have not changed. The firm does what it did before the capital structure change. But, under this new capital structure, what happens to the return on equity if there is good or bad news?

First, consider if there is good news. Remember the regulations—they got more favorable—and the value of the inventory rises from $100 million to $120 million. Let's say the plant and equipment is generic, so it doesn't change. In that case, with the good news, the value of assets rises to $220 million, just like it did previously when the firm had less debt. In response, the equity value will be $220 million (the value of the assets) – $160 million (the value of the debt) = $60 million. Given this good news, the equity rose 50% in value, from 40 to 60 [i.e., ($60 – $40)/$40 = 0.5]. Recall, prior to the firm changing its "debt-to-equity ratio," the return from such good news was only $20/$50 = 40%.

Next, consider if there's bad news. The product clogs arteries, and the value of the inventory drops to $80 million. Then, the assets are worth only $180 million, the debt remains risk-free at a value of $160, and the equity falls to $180 million – $160 = $20 million. That is, the equity falls by 50%, from $40 million to $20 million.

Recall that prior to the firm changing the debt to equity ratio, the return on such bad news was only –$20/$50 = –40%, not –50%. Thus, the returns on equities are levered in the sense that they are more sensitive to the value of the assets. Thus, if more debt is used to fund the asset, the more sensitive the value of equity is to changes in the value of the firm. More leverage can make equity have higher returns when the asset values increase, but more negative when the asset values fall.

Next, let's consider how the capital structure affects the cost of capital. Recall that the cost of capital of the firm is the return that must be promised to the claimants in order to get them to want to fund the firm's activities.

What happens to the cost of capital as we change the capital structure? If the firm is financially sound enough that it will never default on the debt claim, then the required rate of return on the debt is still the risk-free rate of 5%. But, because the shareholders of the firm have residual claims, they will require a return that is commensurate with the risk of the equity.

As shown with the balance sheet examples previously, the greater the leverage, the more sensitive the equity is to changes in asset values. And, the more sensitive the equity is to changes in asset values, the more risk the equity has. Thus, the required rate of return for equity must be increasing in the leverage—increasing in the debt-to-equity ratio—of the firm.

So, let's look more closely at what happened to the cost of capital. Let's say that the value of the firm will never drop below \$160. The inventory, if sold as door stops, is worth at least \$60 million. Even after the firm increases the level of debt, the debt remains risk-free, just as it was before the firm levered up. Thus, the required rate of return demanded by the bond holders is still the risk-free rate of 5%. But now, the firm is paying 5% on \$160 million out of \$200 million rather than just \$150 million out of \$200 million.

Has the cost of capital gone down? If yes, why? If no, why? The firm is now paying only 5% on more money than it raised. It must be cheaper, right? Wrong. And here's why. Because the equity is more highly levered, it is riskier. Thus, the equity holders need to have a higher return than when the firm had less leverage. Even if the firm raises more money via cheap, low-debt risk, the risk of the firm is now concentrated into a smaller equity stake.

Since we're considering a pure capital structure change, in which we didn't alter the total risk of the firm, the cost of capital, which is comprised of the average return on both the debt and the equities, must be the same as it was before the capital structure change.

The risk borne by the \$200 million initially, \$150 in debt and \$50 million in equity, is still borne by the \$200 million, but now it's \$160 in debt and \$40 in equity. If the required rate of return on the debt is still 5%, then the required rate of return on the equity must go up by exactly the amount that keeps the weighted average costs of capital the same.

Prior to the capital structure change, the cost of the capital was, let's call it $r(\text{init}) = (\$150/\$200) \times 0.05 + (\$50/\$200) \times 0.25 = 0.10$. After the capital structure change, the new cost of capital, let's call it $r(\text{new})$, must be the same as the original. That is, $r(\text{new}) = r(\text{init})$. The new cost of capital is going to be equal to what? $r(\text{new}) = (\$160/\$200) \times 0.05 + (\$40/\$200) \times r_e(\text{new})$, where $r_e(\text{new})$ is the new required rate of return on the equity. The new required rate of return on equity must be such that

$r(\text{new}) = (\$160/\$200) \times 0.05 + (\$40/\$200) \times r_e(\text{new}) = r(\text{init}) = 0.10$. If we solve for that, what we see here is: $r_e(\text{new}) = 0.30$ (or 30%). That is, $0.8 \times 0.05 + 0.2 \times 0.30 = 0.10$.

In general, the required rate of return on the equity is the following function of the required return on debt, the required return on the assets, and the debt-to-equity ratio: $r_e = r_a + (D/E)(r_a - r_d)$.

The required return on the assets, r_a, is the amount that the investors have to get if they owned all of the assets of the firm. In the example, this is the 10%. Given the riskiness of the cash flows generated by the assets from the firm's management, then the return must be 10%—else it's not worth doing. This expression says that as the firm levers up and D/E gets bigger as D grows and E shrinks, the required rate of return on a firm's equity must rise.

So, let's say that you're looking at two firms in the same business, say, two fast food hamburger chains. You notice that the stock of one of the chains has generated a much larger return on average than the other one. Is that stock that you want to invest in? It might just be that the chain has a significantly higher debt-to-equity ratio and, as a result, has to discount the price of its equity sufficiently to generate a high enough return on the equity to induce the equity investors to invest. While it may have a higher return, it may also have more of its risk concentrated in each of the dollars that equity investors invest. Without looking at its capital structure, you might wrongly conclude that you want to invest in the chain with the higher average rate of return.

This lecture has shown that the required rate of return on securities depends upon the capital structures of the firm. We last considered how the equity returns on two firms that are essentially in the same business can be very different solely on the basis of differences in their capital structure. Both can be efficiently priced, but one will have a much higher return on equity than the other because it has higher leverage. What you need to be able to do is compare the return per unit of risk to see which is the better deal. In subsequent lectures, we will develop an explicit way to calculate what the return per unit of risk is.

Present Value of Growth Opportunities

Lecture 13

In this lecture, you will examine how a firm's growth prospects translate into firm value and stock price and how good (and bad) decisions by the company's leadership can have an amplified effect in the firm's stock price. You need to know how good the leadership team of a firm is at creating a stream of good ideas and good decisions into the future. The goal of this lecture is to give you an idea of what affects the value of firms and how the decisions of management affect the values of the stocks (and bonds) the firm issues.

Dividend Model

- In order to see how good managerial decisions can be amplified in the current stock price, we're going to build a simple (but not simplistic) model that connects three items: the future opportunities and cash flows of the firm, the quality of managerial decision making, and the value of the firm's securities.

- This model is simply that the value of the firm is the present value of the cash flows that the firm generates using its human and physical capital. In general, these cash flows will be random. The way to value these cash flows is to determine their expected or average value and then discount them at a rate that is appropriate for their risk.

- The model is a model of *average* or *expected* cash flows with a given amount of risk into the future. The standard approach is to value the firm as the present value of the stream of profits it generates into the future. The value of the firm is then the present value of the stream of cash flows that can be distributed to the claimants, where the discount rate used to calculate the present value is the firm's cost of capital (or the required rate of return on the firm's assets).

- The approach is as follows: Determine the possible cash flows that can be distributed to claimants. These are called free cash flows. Then, determine the value of the firm by taking the present value of these free cash flows. Then, determine the value of debt. Subtract that from the firm value to get equity value. This is called the free cash flow approach.

Stock Returns

- Let's examine stock returns more closely. Rather than value the whole firm and then subtract the value of the debt, you can also directly value the stock, based solely on the cash flows stockholders are expected to receive.

- The basic approach is to recognize that holding the stock forever provides an infinite stream of dividends. Discounting the infinite stream of dividends at the rate of return investors require for the stock gives us the current value of the stock.

- Let's assume that the stock today trades ex-dividend—that is, the next dividend is one period hence. In other words, if you buy the stock today, you have to wait a period to get the next dividend. Let's say that the stock pays DIV_1 1 year from now, DIV_2 2 years from now, etc. Also let the required rate of return be r. Then, the price of the stock is simply $P_0 = \frac{DIV_1}{(1+r)} + \frac{DIV_2}{(1+r)^2} + \frac{DIV_3}{(1+r)^3} + \ldots$.

- If the discount rate is just 1 percentage point higher or lower, the value of the stock will vary by a wide amount. Therefore, it is extremely important to get the right discount rate given the firm's risk.

Managerial Decisions

- Let's turn to seeing how good decisions taken by the firm's management translate into the current stock price. The price of stock depends crucially on the ability of the firm's management to continually find positive net present value projects to invest in.

- To keep things simple, let's consider an all-equity firm. Thus, all the cash flows of the firm are owned by the shareholders. Let's say that this firm has $50 in capital per share. You can think of the $50 per share as being the value of the transformed "stuff" the management has created. Think of it as stuff that generates a cash flow every year. Because it is an all-equity firm, the equity holders get all of these cash flows (in one way or another).

- Let's say that this capital generates 12% in earnings on average every year. So that we can use perpetuity formulas, let's assume that it generates this 12% in profits at the end of the year. Once the firm gets the profits, it can pay it out to the shareholders. Thus, the $50 per share of capital throws off $6 per share every year.

- Also, just to keep things simple, let's assume that the $50 worth of capital the firm has per share does not depreciate—that is, it doesn't wear out over time. This assumption is not essential, but it makes things easier to keep track of.

- Given the riskiness of this firm's business, let's say that the investors require 10% return on the equity. Because it is an all-equity firm, the cost of capital for this firm is also 10%.

Payout Policy

- Next, consider the decisions that management can make with the cash flow. If the management pays all of this $6 out as a dividend, then it will not retain any earnings to "plow back" into the firm. In that case, the firm will not grow. The $50 in capital per share will just stay at $50.

- If the firm pays out all of its earnings as a dividend, then what is the value of the stock? If the firm will always be able to generate 12% return on capital on average, then it can pay a $6 dividend every year (at the end of the year) on average. In that case, the stock is a perpetuity. Using the PV of a perpetuity formula and the required rate of return of 10%, the per-share value of the firm is simply $P_0 =$ $6/0.10 = $60.

- If this is the current policy of the management, then this is what you should be willing to pay for the stock. If you pay this amount, then you will get a 10% return on average, year after year.

Plowback

- Can the firm increase its stock price by retaining some earnings to reinvest in itself? For example, what will happen if it plows back 40% (and pays out 60%)? Let's say that after 1 year (at $t = 1$), the firm will have \$6. It pays out 0.6 × \$6 = \$3.60 and plows back 0.4 × \$6 = \$2.40. Thus, the dividend per share at $t = 1$ is \$3.60. Under this policy, what will the firm pay as a dividend at $t = 2$?

- At $t = 2$, the firm's capital grew to \$52.40 per share (the original \$50 plus the \$2.40 in retained earnings). If the firm invests the \$2.40 in retained earnings in the same capital as its original \$50 in capital (capital that generates 10% earnings), then between $t = 1$ and $t = 2$, the firm will generate 0.12 × \$52.40 = \$6.288 in earnings.

- And out of that, it pays out 0.6 × \$6.288 = \$3.77 as a dividend at $t = 2$ and plows back 0.4 × \$6.288 = \$2.515. Thus, at $t = 2$, the capital is now \$50 + \$2.40 + \$2.515 = \$54.915.

- Between $t = 2$ and t = 3, the firm generates 0.12 × 54.915 = \$6.59, of which it pays out 0.6 × \$6.59 = \$3.954 as the dividend at $t = 3$ and retains 0.4 × \$6.59 = \$2.636—and so on.

- Thus, the growth between $t = 1$ and $t = 2$ is (3.77 − 3.60)/3.60 = 0.048 (4.8%). And the growth between $t = 2$ and $t = 3$ is (3.954 − 3.77)/3.77 = 0.048 (i.e., also 4.8%).

- If you continue on this way, and the capital continues to generate 12% per year, then the growth in the dividend with the 40% payout ratio will be 4.8% in perpetuity. In fact, the growth rate in the dividend is simply plowback rate times the return on capital. That is, 4.8% is 40% of the required rate of return 12%.

- If you took over the management of the company, would you want to plow back 40%? Right now, the firm pays a dividend of $6 per year, and the stock is worth $60. If you take over and plow back 40%, will the shareholders view you as a hero or a goat?

- There are two effects. First, the dividend is lower if the firm retains more. It was $6. Under your new 40% plowback policy, the next dividend will only be $3.60. That doesn't sound good given that the value of the firm is the discounted stream of dividends. The second effect, however, is that under your potential plowback policy, the dividends will grow.

PERPETUITY FORMULAS

$$PV = \frac{C}{r}$$

$$\$20 = \frac{\$1}{r} \Rightarrow r = \frac{\$1}{\$20} = 0.05 \text{ or } 5\%$$

$$\$18 = \frac{\$1}{r} \Rightarrow r = \frac{1}{18} = 0.0555\ldots \text{ or } 5.55\%$$

$$\$22 = \frac{\$1}{r} \Rightarrow r = \frac{1}{22} = 0.04545 \text{ or} 4.55\%$$

- The efficacy of your policy depends on what happens to the stock price. Now, the share price is the PV of a growing perpetuity, with a 4.8% growth rate from the next dividend at t = 1 of $3.60. Thus, the price is now P_0 = $3.6/(0.10 – 0.048) = $69.23. The price goes up; you are a hero.

- Merely by changing the policy (not by spending any new money, just money that you already had), you make all of the shareholders obtain an instant 15% return (i.e., ($69.23 – $60)/$60 = 0.15).

The Price-to-Earnings Ratio

- The price-to-earnings ratio is typically used by value investors to determine whether a firm's value is too high or too low. Seemingly, a stock with a price 15 to 20 times higher than its earnings is thought to be expensive relative to a stock with a price-to-earnings ratio of 8 to 10. There is a way in which this makes sense: For simplicity, let the earnings be a measure of the amount of money that can be distributed—the potential cash flow of dividends of the firm.

- If the earnings don't grow, then the price is simply $P = E/r$, where E is the earnings and r is the appropriate discount rate. If the price of the stock is the present value of the perpetual stream of average earnings, then the price-to-earnings ratio is simply $P/E = 1/r$.

- This ratio might be too high based on mispricing. It might be that the real value should be E/r, but its market price is higher than that. This might have happened because the market's expected earnings are too high or the discount rate is too low. Either way, the security is overvalued.

- But it also might be that the price is high due to the present value of growth opportunities (PVGO), which is the difference between the value of stock if it doesn't grow and the value of stock if it does grow.

- If the firm has a lot of growth opportunities and a management team that can identify and implement new positive NPV projects, then the value of the firm equity will be $P = E/r + \text{PVGO}$, where (E/r) is the no-growth value of the firm. So, maybe the price of the firm's equity is higher not because it is overvalued; maybe it has significant growth opportunities.

Suggested Reading

Bodie, Kane, and Marcus, *Essentials of Investments*.

Brealey, Myers, and Allen, *Principles of Corporate Finance*.

Ross, Westerfield, Jaffe, and Jordan, *Corporate Finance*.

Questions to Consider

1. Which firms do you think have the ability to consistently create value year after year?

2. If a firm simply expands by continuing to do what it currently is doing, what will likely happen to its return on assets? And how will this affect its PVGO?

Present Value of Growth Opportunities
Lecture 13—Transcript

Everyone wants to be the person who discovers Microsoft in 1986. During its first five to 10 years, the value of Microsoft stock grew at a phenomenal rate of 60% per year. Compare that to more recent IPOs. After Facebook shares started to trade publicly on May 18, 2012, its price fell from its IPO price of $38, bottoming out at around $18. It then hit a snag around $25 about a year after the IPO, and it only got back to its IPO level during the third quarter of 2013. The long-term future of Facebook is yet to be determined. As of the time of the taping in this course, it had only been publicly traded for about a year and a half, as compared to the 27 years that Microsoft had been trading.

What about Tesla Motors? Tesla also did an initial public offering during the post-2008 financial crisis period in the middle of 2010. In contrast to Facebook, it consistently climbed from its IPO level of around $20 a share to over $160 per share by mid-year 2013. Is Tesla the new Microsoft?

There are some obvious differences between Tesla and Facebook. One is a car company, the other a social media company. One received some support from the U.S. government in the form of loans, and the other did not. And Facebook is one-fifth of the size of Tesla. Is there anything fundamentally the same or different about these companies, though?

During this lecture, we're going to examine how a firm's growth prospects translate into a firm's value and their stock price, and how good or bad decisions by the company's leadership can be amplified in effect through the stock price.

The point of this lecture is that, in addition to being able to run the numbers, you need to know how good the leadership team of the firm is at creating a stream of good ideas and good decisions into the future. More specifically, my goal with this lecture is to give you an idea of what affects the value of firms and how the decisions of management affect the values of the stocks and the bonds that the firm issues. We discussed this in the last lecture. This lecture takes a deeper dive into the numbers.

Throughout this session, I want you to keep in mind the cases of Facebook, Tesla, and Microsoft. I also want you to keep in mind Eastman Kodak. I want you to think about Kodak because it is a company that has been everything a firm can possibly be. Kodak has been an iconic U.S. company, entering the Dow Jones Industrial Average Index in 1930, where it stayed for 74 years. In the 1970s, it dominated the market for photographic film and cameras, representing 90 and 85% of the U.S. market, respectively. And it has completely collapsed, declaring bankruptcy in January of 2013.

Since the turn of the 21st century, Kodak's price has fallen off a cliff. In this session, we'll see how future prospects keep prices up. We will see how to quantify these future prospects and how to translate these prospects into current price, or current value. We will see why a company like Kodak has its price fall to zero, while other companies trade at prices many times the cash flows that they generate in a year.

In the lecture, we'll examine the valuation of stock as the present value of its stream of dividends. We will then consider how these dividends can be sustained by the management. These two topics together link the management's decision to the value of the firm's stock.

To start, let's consider a firm that pays dividends. You might often hear that such a firm is a good firm, since it can generate a source of cash flow to you that will allow you to buy groceries, pay down your mortgage, go on vacation, and so on. One of my goals with this lecture is for us to examine how dividend payments affect the return on your investment in that firm.

In this lecture, I want to identify where the magic happens in a well-run firm. I want to point right at the spot in the equations where the value of what goes on inside of corporations generates value for the investor.

As we discussed in the last lecture, this value comes from the management's ability to find positive NPV projects. In this lecture, I want to point right at the spot where the good management manifests itself. In order to do that, I'm going to build a simple model, but not a simplistic model, that connects three different items: (1) the future opportunities and cash flows of the firm, (2) the quality of managerial decisions, and (3) the value of the firm's securities.

With this model, we'll be able to see how good managerial decisions can be amplified in the current stock price. This model also allows us to see the nature of the differences between a company like Tesla and Kodak.

And finally, this model will allow us to see how these differences will manifest themselves in the market variables we can see from various financial information sources. This last step is extremely important because there is lot of misconception regarding how to interpret these numbers. This model will provide some clarity for you on how these numbers are calculated and what they mean.

So let's build the model. The model will utilize the formulas that we developed in Lecture 7 on present value calculations. In particular, we'll use the special-case formulas for infinite streams of payments. In order to use these formulas, we'll have to make some special simplifying assumptions. But, I want you to realize that these assumptions are just for convenience to get you to see the magic more clearly. I hope to convince you that the intuition and the conclusions of the model do not rely on the assumptions in any substantive way.

The model is simply that the value of the firm is the present value of the cash flows that the firm generates using the human and physical capital that it has. In general, these cash flows will be random. The way to value these cash flows is to determine their expected average value and then discount them at the rate that is appropriate for their risk. Subsequent lectures will examine how to get these appropriate rates. Here, I'm just going to provide us with rates that vary with riskiness.

The model I will develop here is a model of average or expected cash flows with a given amount of risk in the future. The standard approach is to value the firm as the present value of the stream of profits it generates into the future. The value of the firm is then the present value of the stream of cash flows that can be distributed to the claimants, where the discount rate used to calculate the present value is the firm's cost of capital, or the required rate of return on the firm's assets.

The approach is as follows. Determine the possible cash flows that can be distributed to claimants. These are called free cash flows. Then, determine the value of the firm by taking the present value of these free cash flows. Then, determine the value of the debt, subtract that from the value of the firm to get the value of the equity. This is called the free cash flow approach.

Now let's examine the stock returns more closely. Rather than value the whole firm and then subtract the value of the debt, you can also directly value the stock, based solely on the cash flows stock holders are expected to receive. We will see how to do this in this section of the lecture.

The basic approach is to recognize that holding the stock forever provides an infinite stream of dividends. Discounting the infinite stream of dividends at the rate of return investors require for the stock gives us the current value of the stock.

Let's assume that the stock today trades ex-dividend. That is, the next dividend is one period hence. If you buy the stock today, you have to wait a period to get the next dividend. Let's say that the stock pays Div_1 one year from now, Div_2 two years from now, et cetera, et cetera. Also, let's let the required rate of return be r. The price of the stock is simply going to be: $P_0 = \text{Div}_1/(1 + r)^1 + \text{Div}_2/(1 + r)^2 + \text{Div}_3/(1 + r)^3 + \ldots$ on and on forever.

Let's do a little example based upon a real company, the American Financial Group. Let's say that they just paid a dividend of $0.78. Let's see what would happen if that annual dividend was expected to stay at $0.78. Let's say that the risk of AFG stock is such that the discount rate is $r = 0.105$ (10.5%). In that case, the present value of AFG should be: $P_0 = \$0.78/0.105 = \$7.43$. By the way, what we're using here is we're using the present value of an infinite stream, the present value of a perpetuity.

By the way, when I did this calculation, the price of AFG was actually $51.58. When I did this calculation, should I have shorted? Well, not so fast. According to Fidelity at that time, the dividend had grown at 9% in the past. If the dividend is expected to grow at 9% every year, then the next dividend will be $\$0.78 \times 1.09 = \$0.85$. Given this growth, we should not use just the present value of a perpetuity. Instead, we should use the present value of a growing perpetuity that we saw back in Lecture 7. Using that formula, we have: $P_0 = \$0.85/(0.105 - 0.09) = \$56.68$.

Recall that the present value of a growing perpetuity formula uses the next payment in the numerator. Thus, we use the dividend expected next year of \$0.85, not the current dividend of \$0.78. The value at the time that AFG was very close to the value that we just got, so this model is working, not bad.

To show you how important the discount rate is, though, notice that if the discount rate just changes by 1 percentage point higher or lower, the value of the stock varies by a wide amount. For example, if instead of the discount rate being 10.5%, it's 11.5%, then the price of the stock is \$34. And instead of it being 10.5%, it's 9.5%, it's \$170. This illustrates how important it is to get the discount rate right for a given firm's risk.

Next, let's turn to seeing how good decisions taken by the firm's management translates into the current stock price. The point I want to make here is that the price of the stock depends crucially on the ability of the firm's management to continually find positive NPV projects to invest in. This will be the difference between Kodak and Tesla, maybe.

To keep things simple, let's consider an all-equity firm. Thus, all of the cash flows of the firm are owned by the shareholders. Let's say that this firm has \$50 in capital per share. We can talk in per-share terms rather than in terms of total values, but if you want to do the analysis in total values, too, you can do that as well. The economics are essentially the same. But we're going to talk about \$50 per share.

Think about the \$50 per share as being the value of the transformed stuff that the management has created with the money that it raised. Think of this as the stuff that generates cash flows every year. Because it's an all-equity firm, the equity holders get all of those cash flows in one way or another. We will see what I mean by in one way or another in a minute.

Let's say that this capital generates 12% in earnings on average every year. So that you can use the perpetuity formulas, let's assume that it generates this 12% in profits at the end of the year—and, again, it does it every year at the end of the year. Once the firm gets the profits from this, it can then pay them out to shareholders. Thus, the $50 per share in capital is going to throw off $6 per share every year.

Also, just to keep things simple, let's assume that the $50 worth of capital the firm has per share does not depreciate. That is, it doesn't wear out over time. This assumption is not essential, but it does make things a lot easier to keep track of.

Given the riskiness of the firm's business, let's say that the investors require a 10% return on their equity. Since it's an all-equity firm, the cost of capital for this firm is also 10%. Next, consider the decisions that management can make with respect to cash flow. If the management pays out all of this $6 as a dividend, it will not retain any earnings to plow back into the firm.

In that case, the firm will not grow. The $50 in capital per share will just stay at $50. If the firm pays all of its earnings out as a dividend, then what's the value of the stock? If the firm will always be able to generate 12% return on capital on average, then it can pay a $6 dividend every year, at the end of the year, on average for every year. In that case, the stock is a perpetuity. Using the present value of a perpetuity formula and the required rate of return of 10%, the per-share value of the firm is simply $P_0 = \$6/0.10 = \$60.00$. If this is the current policy of the management, this is what you should be willing to pay for the stock.

Notice that if you pay this, you're going to get a 10% return on average, year after year after year. To see why, let's decompose your return into two components—the dividend yield and the capital gain. The dividend yield in this case is just going to be $6/60 = 0.10 or 10%.

What will be the capital gain in terms of the return that you get year after year after year? To figure that out, we need to predict what the price will be next year. Well, given the payout policy of the management, the price next year is easy to figure out. Next year, the dividend will also be $6. If the firm is no more or no less risky than it was this year, then the required rate of return will remain at 10%. Thus, the price next year will be $6/0.10 = $60.00

again. Thus, the expected capital gain is zero. All of the return on this stock comes from the dividend yield. Your total return is 10%.

Now, can the firm increase its stock price by retaining some earnings to reinvest in itself? For example, what would happen if it plows back 40% of this money and it pays out 60%? Let's say that after one year at $t = 1$, the firm will have \$6. It pays out $0.6 \times \$6 = \$3.60$ and it plows back the remaining $0.4 \times \$6 = \$2.40$. Thus, the dividend per share at $t = 1$ is \$3.60. Under this policy, what will the firm pay as a dividend at $t = 2$?

At $t = 2$, the firm's capital grew to \$52.40 per share. That's the original \$50 plus the \$2.40 in retained earnings that they plowed back into the firm. If the firm invests that \$2.40 in retained earnings into the same capital as the original \$50 in capital, capital that generates 12% in earnings, then between $t = 1$ and $t = 2$, the firm will generate $0.12 \times \$52.40 = \$6.28$ in earnings. And out of that, if it pays out 60%, it's going to pay a dividend of \$3.77. It's going to plow back 40% of its earnings; that's going to be \$2.51. Thus, at $t = 2$, the capital then becomes $\$50 + \$2.40 + \$2.51 = \$54.91$. Between $t = 2$ and $t = 3$, the firm generates $0.12 \times 54.91 = \$6.59$, of which it's going to pay out $0.6 \times \$6.59 = \$3.95$ as a dividend, at $t = 3$ and retains $0.4 \times \$6.59 = \$2.63$, et cetera, et cetera, et cetera. So every period, we pay out a little bit more, we invest a little bit more.

So, the question is: What is going to be the growth rate of the dividend? The dividend growth between $t = 1$ and $t = 2$ was $(3.77 - 3.60)/3.60 = 0.048$, 4.8%. And the growth between $t = 2$ and $t = 3$ is $(3.95 - 3.77)/3.77 = 0.048$, i.e., also 4.8%. If you continue on this way, and the capital continues to generate 12% per year, then the growth of the dividend with the 40% payout ratio will be 4.8% in perpetuity. In fact, the growth rate in the dividend is simply the plowback rate times the return on capital. That is, 4.8% is 40% of the required rate of the return on the capital of 12%.

If you took over as management of this company, would you want to plow back 40%? Right now, the firm pays out a dividend of \$6 per year and the stock is worth \$60. If you take over and plow back 40%, will the shareholders view you as a hero or as a goat?

So there are two effects. First, the dividend is lower if the firm retains more—if it pays out less and retains more. It was \$6. Under your new 40% plowback policy, the next dividend is only going to be \$3.60. That doesn't sound good, given that the value of the firm, or the value of the stock in this case, is the discounted stream of dividends.

The second effect, however, is that under your potential plowback policy the dividends will grow. The efficacy of your policy depends upon what happens to the stock price.

Now, the share of a price is the present value of a growing perpetuity, with a 4.8% growth rate with the next dividend at $t = 1$ of \$3.60. Thus, the price now is going to be $P_0 = \$3.6/(0.10 - 0.048) = \$69.23$. The price goes up, so you're a hero. Of course you are.

Merely by changing the policy—not by spending any new money, just money that you already had—you made all of the shareholders obtain an instant 15% return (i.e., the price went from \$60 up to \$69.23). That's heroic.

If someone buys the stock now, after the new policy has been implemented, what is their return going forward? The price next year is going to be $P_1 = \$3.77/(0.10 - 0.048) = \$72.55$. This is true because next year, the expected dividend to be paid is going to be \$3.77. Since it will continue to grow at 4.8% thereafter, the value is just the value of a growing perpetuity. As a result, over the next year, a new investor will get a total return based on the following: (1) A purchase price of \$69.23, (2) a dividend payment of \$3.60, and (3) a future price after one year of \$72.55. The total return, then, is $(\$72.55 + \$3.60 - \$69.23)/\$69.23 = 0.10$, 10%.

So, regardless of whether the dividend is \$6 with no growth or \$3.60 growing at 4.8% thereafter, the total return is 10%. This 10% is the amount that is needed to compensate the equity investors for the risk that they bear by owning the stock. The price of the shares adjusts to make the return reflect the required rate of return.

So, if somebody tells you that you should buy a stock because it generates a high dividend, that may not be a very good reason. The firm may be paying a high dividend but not generating any capital gains. The only reason you might care whether the returns are in the form of dividend yield versus capital gains is due to some asymmetries that might exist in the tax code. They typically exist in the tax code because capital gains you typically pay less than if you were to pay on dividends. This is one of the reasons that, more often than not, it's the case that firms have stopped paying dividends in order to lower your tax bill.

Let's return to the issue of plowing back earnings. Why did the price go up? The answer is that, by plowing earnings back into the firm, the firm is exploiting a whole series of positive NPV projects. Intuitively, the firm is essentially borrowing money at 10% and investing it at 12%. The 10% is the rate of discount applied to its equity. Thus, for every dollar the firm receives by selling equity, the firm is essentially promising $1.10 back on average. When the firm then takes that $1 it raised and puts it into the firm's transformational process, it's going to get 12%. That $1 will turn into $1.12. Thus, after it pays back the $1.10 it owes, it has $0.02 left over, which the equity holders are going to get. This $0.02 can be reinvested to generate even more gains in the future.

What if the return on capital is only 8%? Then, without any plowback, the price of the firm would then be ($50 × 0.08)/0.10 = $40.00. With a 40% plowback, the next dividend would be 0.08 × $50 × 0.60 = $2.40. The dividend growth rate is 0.4 × 0.08 = 0.032. Thus, the price at t = 0 is going to be P_0 = $2.40/(0.10 − 0.032) = $35.29—that's less than if there was going to be no growth.

In this case, plowing back destroys value because the firm is investing in a negative NPV project. It borrows at 10% but invests at 8%.

To see the general relationship very clearly, let's take a closer look at exactly what is happening. For this, let's go back to the 12% return on capital and the 10% cost of capital case. In that case, if the firm did not plow back, then the value of the firm is simply $6/0.10 = $60.00. If the firm plows back 40% this year, they are investing 0.40 × $6 = $2.40 in the firm. What do they get? That $2.40 in extra real capital is going to generate 0.12 × $2.40 = $0.288 every year.

What is that perpetual cash flow of this worth? If it is reinvested in the same capital simply to grow in the firm, then the riskiness of that capital is still the same. That is, the cost of the capital is still 10%. As a result, the \$0.288 per year forever is worth \$0.288/0.1 = \$2.88 in present value terms. But what did it cost? It only cost the investment of the \$2.40. Thus, the NPV of this reinvestment in the firm was \$2.88 − \$2.40 = \$0.48.

Most importantly, the shareholders get more than just the \$0.48. The \$0.48 is just the value of the \$2.40 investment this period. What about the extra investments the firm gets to make with the NPV of the \$0.48? To see this, consider what you get next year. Recall that in the second year you have \$52.40 of capital per share. This is going to throw off 12%. That throws off an earnings of \$6.28. Of that \$6.28, the firm is going to invest 0.40 × \$6.28 = \$2.51.

What is the perpetual cash flow generated by this \$2.51 each year? It's 0.12 × \$2.51 = \$0.30. Because you get this each year, this is a perpetual cash flow, and that perpetual cash flow is worth: \$0.30/0.10 = \$3.00. Thus, the NPV is \$3.00 − \$2.51 = \$0.50.

How much bigger is this NPV than the NPV of the investment in the first year? So it's going to be the NPV in this year, which is about (\$0.50 − \$0.48)/\$0.48 = 4.8%. This growth equals something familiar. It equals the plowback rate times the rate of return on the capital, i.e., 0.40 × 0.12 = 0.048, or 4.8%.

Now, what we have here is the NPV is growing. The growth in the NPV is 4.8%. So, in terms of the current stock price, this growing series of NPVs is worth what? We can apply the growing perpetuity formula again and see that the value of the growing perpetuity of NPVs is \$0.48/(0.10 − 0.048) = \$9.23.

Note that the value is simply the difference between the value of the stock if it doesn't grow, which is \$60, and the value of the stock if it does grow. This difference is called the present value of growth opportunities, or PVGO for short.

Note that when the return on capital is less than 10%, the present value of growth opportunities is going to be negative if the firm does not pay out its earnings as a dividend. This is true because anything that the firm plows back in the firm is a negative NPV project, which destroys value.

Let's tie this all together. The price-to-earnings ratio is typically used by value investors to determine whether a firm's value is too high or too low. Seemingly, a stock with a price of 15 to 20 times higher than its earnings is thought to be expensive relative to a stock with a price-to-earnings ratio of about 8 to 10. There is a way in which this makes sense. For simplicity, let the earnings be the measure of the amount of money that can be distributed—the potential cash flows as the dividends of the firm.

If the earnings don't grow, then the price is simply equal to what? P = Earnings/r, where r is the appropriate discount rate. So, if the price of the stock is the present value of the perpetual stream of average earnings, then the price-to-earnings ratio is simply P/Earnings = (1/r).

This ratio might be too high based upon mispricing. It might be that the real value should be Earnings/r, but the market price is higher than that that's being indicated. That might have happened either because the market expects the earnings to be too high or the discount rate to be too low. Either way, the security is overvalued.

But it also might be that the price is high due to the present value of growth opportunities. If the firm has a lot of opportunities to grow and the management team is able to identify and implement new positive NPV projects, then the value of the firm's equity will be P = (Earnings/r) + PVGO, where (Earnings/r) is the no-growth value of the firm. So, maybe the price of the firm's equity is higher not because it is overvalued. Maybe it has significant growth opportunities.

What we have seen in this lecture is that we have created an example in which there's positive NPV in the first period, and with that positive NPV, that allows managers to grow the firm by investing that positive NPV. The point was that current NPV allowed the firm to invest, that would generate future NPV. That would allow them to invest some more, which would generate some more future NPV, and on and on and on. This essentially shows that NPV begets more NPV.

Now, we did make some simplifying assumptions in order to use standard perpetuity formulas. One assumption was that every time the firm invested in capital, it automatically received a 12% return on capital. This is probably unrealistic. In actually, the firm cannot keep doing what it is currently doing and keep achieving the 12% returns. Consider Kodak, for example. Also, consider Starbucks. They went on an expansion binge until they started to put storefronts across the street from each other. The return on each of those new storefronts was not as high as the original storefront that they put up.

In order to get this present value of growth opportunities, the management team needs to create an environment in which the management is constantly looking for new NPV projects. It creates this environment by looking for NPV projects constantly and always implementing them. If they have NPV, they can use that NPV to create new NPV projects.

The risk to an investor who pays for the present value of the growth opportunities is that the management may falter. Thus, as an investor, you might need to have a very clear sense of the ability of management to sustain an environment that continually seeks to generate positive NPV projects. If the management can, then the management's decisions will get amplified, as we've shown. Kodak lost that ability. Perhaps firms like Facebook and Tesla are just getting started.

Modeling Investor Behavior

Lecture 14

In this lecture, you will learn how economists model investor behavior. As is true with any model, the implications of the model may miss something important. For example, a model may tell you that something is not a risk when it is. In that case, investors will discount the prices of securities that have that "something." Then, according to the model, it will look like a good deal when it really isn't. In order for you to have intuition for when that occurs, you need to know how the model was built—not just its implications. All models start from the material presented in this lecture.

Modeling Individual Behavior

- The tradition in economics and finance is to index individuals as i and j (as in the ith person does A and the jth person responds by doing Z). To make this a bit less impersonal, we will use Ichabod (for i) and Jane (for j).

- The atoms of economic analysis—i.e., the most primitive building block—are consumption bundles, preferences, opportunity sets, and choice. A consumption bundle is any combination of goods and services. For example, the following are three different consumption bundles.
    - Consumption bundle A = (12 cans of beer, 4 bags of potato chips, and 1 umbrella)

    - Consumption bundle B = (1 bottle of chardonnay, 12 oysters, and 1 umbrella)

    - Consumption bundle C = (1 bottle of chardonnay, 4 bags of potato chips, and 1 plastic poncho)

- Let any specific consumption bundle consist of a list of the amounts for every single good and service in the universe. The items on the list may also be state dependent, such as "an umbrella on a rainy day in 2015."

- If there are K different goods and services, then a generic consumption bundle (for example, the mth out of many) is a vector $X_m = (x_1, x_2, x_3, \ldots, x_K)$, where x_1 is the number of units of good/service 1, x_2 is the number of units of good/service 2, etc., all the way up to the last—the Kth—good. Note that x denotes a particular number of an individual good whereas X denotes a particular combination of all the goods.

- Next, we can characterize an individual's opportunity set as the subset within the set of all possible consumption bundles that that individual can afford. Sometimes the opportunity set is defined by a budget constraint. That is, out of all the possible combinations of things, a person can only get the combinations that satisfy that person's budget constraint.

Preferences

- Once we have the opportunity set, we need an individual's preferences over those opportunities. Preferences are modeled as follows: A set of preferences is a set of orderings for any two pairs of consumption bundles. For example, if the three consumption bundles previously described are the only possible bundles, then Ichabod's preferences are fully characterized by $A > B$, $A > C$, $B > C$. Jane may have different preferences; she may have the following ranking: $A < B$, $A < C$, $B > C$.

- Rather than have preference rankings for every pair, economists use a utility function that takes as its arguments the number of units of each good and spits out a number that is an index of the happiness the person achieves with that bundle.

- For the purposes of this lecture, the numbers don't have to have any intrinsic meaning. All the utility numbers have to do is rank alternatives. That is, for any given pair of consumption bundles, the utility numbers must be such that the bundle that is preferred results in a higher number than the less-preferred bundle.

- A utility function $u^j(X)$ that represents Jane's preferences must be such that $u^j(X_1) > u^j(X_2)$ if and only if Jane prefers X_1 to X_2, for all possible pairs of consumption bundles.

- At this point, there are a bunch of questions economists like to ask, including the following: For any given set of preferences, does there exist at least one utility function that will represent those preferences? If there exists such a function, does that function have any nice properties? Is it continuous? Does it always have a derivative?

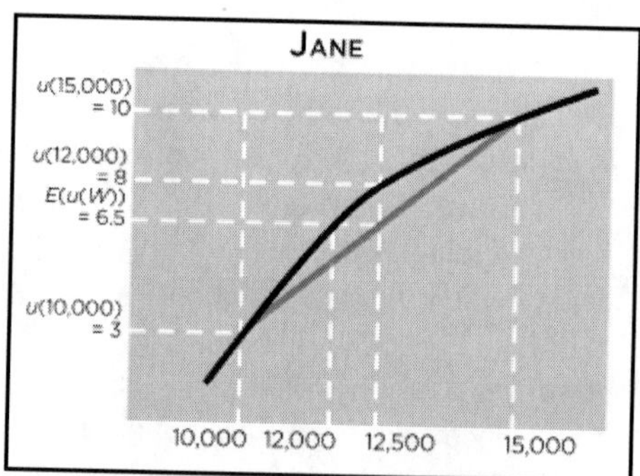

- The answer is that not all preferences have representations that are well-behaved functions. Rather, there are some conditions that, if imposed on preferences, will result in well-behaved utility functions.

- One of the reasons economists want to impose these conditions is not because they think they reflect people's preferences. In fact, in some cases, the conditions needed to generate well-behaved functions are violated by perfectly sensible preferences. The reason we impose these conditions is because we want to use the mathematical tools of constrained optimization—and we can only do that if we have well-behaved functions.

- With well-behaved utility functions, we can use the mathematics of constrained optimization to maximize that person's utility function subject to the budget constraint. The answer to this constrained optimization hopefully is predictive of how people pick among alternative opportunities. However, if the function does not really reflect a person's preference, then the solution might be kind of dicey.

Indirect Utility

- A person's utility must go up if he or she has more income or wealth. As income or wealth increases, the budget constraint lets in more consumption bundles. With more consumption bundles to pick from, the person must be able to do at least as well as before—probably better.

- An indirect utility function is the answer to the following question: For a given person's utility function of consumption bundles, what is the maximal utility that person can achieve with a given level of wealth?

- For example, let's say that you have a monthly budget of \$10,000. There are a bunch of things you could buy in a month with this money, including stocks, bonds, vacations, health care, chardonnay, and potato chips. The stocks and bonds allow you to buy maybe better vacations in the future.

- Let's say that when you pick the consumption bundle you like best, you achieve a level of happiness of 12,000 happiness units. If so, then your indirect utility function is $u(\$10{,}000) = 12{,}000$ happiness units.

- If you were to have a monthly budget of \$15,000 instead, how much happier would you be? Given all the things you can afford with \$15,000 per month, pick the consumption bundle you like best. Let's say that that bundle generates 13,476 units of happiness. Your indirect utility function is then $u(\$10{,}000) = 12{,}000$ and $u(\$15{,}000) = 13{,}476$.

- Once we have an indirect utility of wealth function (i.e., we know $u(\$10{,}000) = 12{,}000$ and $u(\$15{,}000) = 13{,}476$), we can then start to ask how you would feel in happiness units if the amount of wealth you might have is random. Economists refer to this as preferences over lotteries. A lottery is defined as anything that makes our future wealth random.

Expected Utility

- The most popular way for economists to model your preferences over lotteries is according to Von Neumann and Morgenstern's expected utility hypothesis, which states that a person's preferences over lotteries can be captured by the expected value of a carefully chosen indirect utility function.

- Consider three consumption bundles: X_1, X_2, and X_3. Let's say that if you had \$10,000, you would buy X_1 out of all the choices you have available to you with \$10,000. And if you had \$15,000, you would buy X_2. And if you had \$17,000, you would buy X_3.

- In terms of indirect utility functions, it must be the case that $u(\$17{,}000) > u(\$15{,}000) > u(\$10{,}000)$. Note that there may be many such functions that capture your preferences for money. The following will work: $u(\$10{,}000) = 3$, $u(\$15{,}000) = 12$, $u(\$17{,}000) = 13$. This works because the functions maintain order; you like more income to less income. But this different function works just as well: $g(\$10{,}000) = 10$, $g(\$15{,}000) = 15$, $g(\$17{,}000) = 17$.

- Now, let's say that you are facing the following two lotteries.
  - Lottery 1: 50-50 chance at either \$10,000 or \$15,000
  - Lottery 2: 60% chance at \$10,000 and 40% chance at \$17,000.

- Let's say that you prefer lottery 2 to lottery 1. According to the expected utility hypothesis, there exists an indirect utility function (maybe u, or maybe g, or maybe something else entirely) that will capture your preferences if we take the expected value of the utilities that are possible.

- If the u function captures your preferences over lotteries, then the expected utility under lottery 1 should be smaller than the expected utility under lottery 2. The expected utility under lottery 1 is $0.5 \times 3 + 0.5 \times 12 = 7.5$. The expected utility under lottery 2 is $0.6 \times 3 + 0.4 \times 13 = 7$. That is, the u function says that lottery 1 is better than lottery 2. So that function *does not* represent your preferences over lotteries.

- What about the g function? The expected utility of lottery 1 is $0.5 \times 10 + 0.5 \times 15 = 12.5$, and the expected utility of lottery 2 is $0.6 \times 10 + 0.4 \times 17 = 12.8 > 12.5$. This indirect utility function *does* capture your preferences over, at least, these two lotteries.

- It may not work for other lotteries. And there are clearly other functions that will also work for the choice over these two lotteries.

- So, what we need—for each person—is to find a function for that person that captures his or her preferences over all possible lotteries. Once we have that, we can start to predict people's answers to the following questions: How much would I be willing to pay to get rid of a risk I face now? How much would I have to get paid to bear a risk I don't have now?

- The shape of the indirect utility function tells us something about people's aversion to variation in outcomes. How do we get indirect utility functions for people in the market? The answer is that we don't. Rather, we typically just assume some function that has some features we like, such as that it's easy to work with.

- And this is where financial economists may be on thin ice. Many of the functions used in finance are such that *only* the expected value and the variance matter. But there is much evidence to suggest that people care about much more than just the expected value and variance.

- If we use utility functions that imply that only mean and variance matter, then we will have missed some important features of investors' preference. If we use such functions to build an asset pricing model, then the model may imply that something is not important when in fact it is. That means that when we use a model to tell us what risk is and what return we should get for that risk, it may be misleading.

Suggested Reading

Kreps, *A Course in Microeconomic Theory*.

von Neumann and Morgenstern, *Theory of Games and Economic Behavior*.

Questions to Consider

1. Using the choices offered in question 1 for Lecture 1, can you use the expected utility hypothesis to infer the shape of your indirect utility function of wealth?

2. Some people cannot judge how they might feel in the event that they have extreme amounts of wealth or income. Do you think more people overestimate or underestimate how happy they might be if they won the lottery? Given your view, do you think that the expected utility hypothesis would be useful at capturing people's attitudes toward risk and uncertainty?

Modeling Investor Behavior

Lecture 14—Transcript

John Maynard Keynes was a very famous English economist from Cambridge who is well known for, among many other things, his heuristic characterizations of financial markets. In particular, in his famous book *The General Theory of Employment, Money and Interest*, published during the Great Depression in 1936, he characterized the stock market as a beauty contest. He further characterized it as being unstable and volatile due to the speculation of human participants who could not rein in their animal spirits and only take fully deliberative actions.

Keynes was also famous as an investor and is said to have made—and lost—many fortunes. He was also a keen observer of market and human behavior.

In *The General Theory*, Keynes described a beauty contest run by a newspaper. Of course this contest was just a useful invention from Keynes' mind. In the contest, the newspaper would publish photographs of six women. Then, the readers would submit their votes for the woman that they thought was the most beautiful.

I should be more precise here. I should say that the readers supposedly would vote for the woman that each thought was the most beautiful. Although each reader was asked to vote for the woman they thought most beautiful, what were the actual incentives embedded in Keynes' invention? A reader could only win the ultimate prize if that reader had picked the woman that most of the readers had picked as most beautiful. Then, among those that picked the most beautiful woman, there would be a random drawing.

So, if you wanted to get a chance at the prize, you didn't really want to vote for the woman you actually thought was most beautiful. Rather, you wanted to vote for the woman you thought that the most people would vote for as being the woman the most people voted for.

Notice that I did not say that you would vote for the woman you thought the most people thought was the most beautiful. If I did, that would imply that only you understood the game—that all other people were voting for the woman they actually thought was the most beautiful.

But, if you are not the only one who sees the distinction, then some—maybe not all—people would be voting for who they thought the others would be voting for, where the reason they were voting for a particular woman was sometimes because they actually thought she was most beautiful, but other times because they merely thought that others would be voting for her. Wow.

So, this is the crux of why the stock market is a beauty contest. You don't really want to buy the best firm before everyone else does. Rather, before anyone else does, you want to buy the firm that other people will want to buy. And if everyone is doing that, you might get the market chasing its tail, rather than chasing good companies.

Thus, good investors are not necessarily those that can actually find good investments, but those who can predict what stocks others will want to pick. Of course, if everyone is just picking the most beautiful stocks, then there is no problem with picking the stocks that everyone picks. Those are the best. But, if others are not picking the best stocks, then, by trying to pick what they pick, you might not pick the best, or you might pick not the best. And if they are trying to predict what you are picking, they may also not pick the best stocks.

In that sense, the market creates its own alternative reality that has nothing to do with whether it is actually a good investment or not. And, if everyone is trying to predict what everyone else is trying to predict, you can see how this might become very unstable. And, if you also add animal spirits, then it is clearly unstable.

To see this, consider the following simple game some have called the marriage game. There are two people who like opera and sports. Dave likes opera intensely, and he also likes sports, but less intensely. To put some numbers on it, let's say that Dave gets 10 units of happiness out of opera and 8 units of happiness out of sporting events. Sometimes I'll call these units of happiness utils.

Dianne also likes opera and sports. She's a little bit intense about it and she mildly prefers sports to opera. I've done extensive analysis and determined that, relative to Dave, she gets 8 units of happiness out of sports and only 7 out of opera.

Dave and Dianne also like each other and like to spend time together. In fact, if they are together, that generates another two units of happiness for each, independent of what they're doing. Thus, if Dave is with Dianne at the opera, he gets 10 + 2 = 12 units of happiness, and Dianne gets 7 + 2 = 9 units. Similarly, if Dave and Dianne are together at a sporting event, then Dave gets 8 + 2 = 10 and Dianne gets 8 + 2 = 10.

But if they are apart, they like what they like and they're getting just what they get, right? They don't get any extra by being together. They decide that they deserve one night out a week together. On Wednesdays, they either go to a sporting event, or they go to the opera.

One Wednesday, they both went off to work and forgot to discuss where they were going that evening. Just to keep the game interesting, it turns out that Dave works alone and his phone was on the fritz. Also, the music hall is on the other side of town from the sports arena.

The question is where should each go? And which is actually the best? What's going to be the outcome? If you were married to Dave or Dianne, what would you do?

From Dave's perspective, he would try to put himself in Dianne's shoes. What would she do? So, this is just like the beauty contest in that Dave is not thinking about what he wants alone. If alone, he wants what he wants. He wants to go to the opera. But, if he goes to the opera and Dianne picks what she wants to do alone, then she will go to sports, and they will be apart.

So, if Dianne picks sports, the best thing for Dave to do is to also pick sports. But what if Dianne thinks that Dave will pick what he likes to do alone, and she picks opera. If she picks opera, the best thing for Dave to do is to pick opera.

Dave is now confused. He muses, "Is Dianne going to be selfish tonight or is she going to be thinking about what I want?" And then it comes to him, perhaps he should do the same type of analysis he just did, but from Dianne's perspective to see if she has a dominant move.

From her perspective, she thinks if Dave goes to the opera, then the best thing for her to do is also to go to the opera. But if Dave goes to sports, the best thing for her to do is to go to sports. So, what she wants to do depends upon what Dave wants to do, but what Dave wants to do depends upon what Dianne wants to do. There is an indeterminacy here. Not sure what's going to happen. In economics, we would say that there are multiple equilibria.

By the way, what we just went through is consistent with the notion of play in game theory of John Nash, the person the movie "A Beautiful Mind" is based upon.

The idea is that Dave examines what is best for him if Dianne picks one action, say, opera. In this case, Dave should pick opera, too. Then, Dave puts himself in Dianne's shoes and asks if he picks opera, is the conjectured action of Dianne, pick opera, the best thing for her to do? If the answer is yes, which it is in this case, then we have a potential solution.

It is only an actual solution if, when we do the same thing for Dianne, it is the case that if she picks opera, opera is Dave's best response. It is, in this case. This is called a Nash equilibrium.

The important thing to note is that this game has another perfectly reasonable Nash equilibrium. And that's when they both pick sports. This is the beauty contest. And in some sense it is unstable, as Keynes said, because we have to guess which equilibrium strategy people will play.

In fact, Dave and Dianne may just flip coins. And that's too bad, since half the time they are apart and, of those times, half the time someone is going to be at a different venue than they would prefer to be at.

This example also points out the incentive to communicate and coordinate. On the first time they go to a different venue, when they get home they will probably agree that if it ever happens that they forget to discuss where to go on that Wednesday night and either Dave's or Dianne's phone is on the fritz, that they will go to the opera.

Such coordination might work in a game of marriage—maybe not—but when was the last time you coordinated with the market on the stocks they thought were the most beautiful?

This is a very long introduction on our next topic. The point I want to stress out of the preceding discussion is that an investor may need to predict what other people feel. The next topic is to discuss how economists model investor behavior.

Before we get started, I have a few caveats. First, I am not saying after we look at how financial economists model human behavior that you will be able to predict what everyone will like before they like it. Or, to paraphrase Wayne Gretzky, that you will be able to skate to where the puck is going, not where it is now.

The reason we will discuss how financial economists model human investment behavior is because all asset pricing models are based on the notions laid out here. An asset pricing model is a collection of assumptions that generate a set of implications regarding what is risk, and how it is best measured, and how much extra return a person should get in excess of the risk-free rate for bearing it.

That is, an asset pricing model determines the appropriate discount rate to use when determining the present value of an expected future cash flow. Thus, an asset pricing model allows you to price securities. And then, using the price implied by the asset pricing model, you can compare that to the price in the market to determine whether the market price is a good deal or a bad deal.

As is true with any model, the implications of the model may miss something important. For example, a model may tell you something that is not risk when, in fact, it is. In that case, investors will discount the prices of securities that have that something. Then, according to the model, it will look like it's a good deal when it really isn't.

In order for you to have intuition on when that occurs, you need to know how the model was built, not just its implications. All models start from the material discussed in this section. It is important for you to have a sense of the foundation of these models.

As we discuss these models in subsequent lectures, I will highlight the implications that stem from the way humans are modeled in this lecture. In this lecture, I will point out what I think are very strong assumptions that produce overly narrow implications in some of the most often used asset pricing models. By the way, since most of the models in physics can't explain half the matter in the universe, I don't feel so bad about what happens in finance.

So let's consider how financial economists model individual behavior. Let's start with an individual. The tradition in economics is to index individuals as I and J, as in the Ith person does A and the Jth person responds by doing Z. To make this a bit less impersonal, I will refer to Ichabod for I, and Jane for J.

The atoms of economic analysis (i.e., the most primitive building block) are consumption bundles, preferences, opportunity sets, and choice. A consumption bundle is any combination of goods and services. For example, here are three different consumption bundles: Consumption bundle A is 12 cans of beer, four bags of potato chips, and one umbrella. Consumption bundle B is one bottle of chardonnay, 12 oysters, and one umbrella. Consumption bundle C is one bottle of chardonnay, four bags of potato chips, and a plastic poncho.

Let's build a bit more structure so that we can see how this set-up is very general. Let any specific consumption bundle consist of a list of the amounts of every single good and service in the universe. The items on the list may also be state-dependent like an umbrella on a rainy day three years from now. If there are K different goods and services, then a generic consumption bundle—say the mth out of many—is a vector $Xm = (x_1, x_2, x_3,$ all the way up to $x_K)$ where x_1 is the number of units of the good/service 1, x_2 is the number of units of good/service 2, et cetera, all the way up to the last—the Kth—good. Note that lower case x denotes a particular number of an individual good, whereas the cap X denotes a particular combination of all the goods.

Next, we can characterize an individual's opportunity set as the subset within the set of all possible consumption bundles that that individual can afford. Sometimes the opportunity set is defined by a budget constraint. That is, out of all of the possible combinations of things, a person can get only those things that the person can consume with the budget that they have.

Once we have the opportunity set, we need an individual's preferences over those opportunities. Preferences are modeled as follows. A set of preferences is a set of orderings for any two pairs of consumption bundles. For example, if the three consumption bundles previously described are the only possible consumption bundles, then Ichabod's preferences might be fully characterized by A > B, A > C, B > C. Jane may have different preferences. She may have the following ranking: A < B, A < C, B > C.

Here's where things get a little dicey. Rather than have preference rankings for every pair, economists use a utility function that takes as its argument the number of units of each good and spits out a number that is an index of happiness that person achieves with that bundle.

This notion may seem a little strange to some people because it entails assigning a number to a feeling of happiness or satisfaction. How can we do that? Can a single number capture the nuances of your feelings? For our purposes, the numbers don't have to have any intrinsic meaning. All the utility these numbers have to do is rank alternatives. That is, for any pair of consumption bundles, the utility numbers must be such that the bundle that is preferred results in a higher number than the less-preferred bundle.

A utility function, say, $u_J(X)$ that represents Jane's preferences must be such that $u_J(X_1) > u_J(X_2)$ if and only if Jane prefers consumption bundle X_1 to consumption bundle X_2, for all possible pairs of consumption bundles.

Note that I didn't say that Jane has a utility function. Rather, Jane has preferences. An economist might be able to represent her preferences with a utility function provided that function ranks bundles according to her preferences. At this point, there are a bunch of questions that economists like to ask. Such as, for any given set of preferences, does there exist at least one utility function that will represent those preferences? And, if there does exist such a function, does that function have any nice properties? Such as "is it continuous?" "Does it always have a derivative?" Things like that.

The answer is that not all preferences have representations that are well-behaved functions. Rather, there are some conditions that, if imposed on preferences, will result in well-behaved utility functions.

One of the reasons economists want to impose these conditions is not because they think that they reflect people's preferences. In fact, in some cases, the conditions needed to generate well-behaved utility functions are violated by perfectly sensible preferences.

The reason we impose these conditions is because we want to use the mathematical tools of constrained optimization, and we can only do that if we have well-defined or well-behaved functions.

With well-behaved utility functions, we can use the mathematics of constrained optimization to maximize the person's utility function subject to the budget constraint. The answer to this constrained optimization hopefully is predictive of how people pick among alternative opportunities. But, if the function does not really reflect a person's preferences, then that solution is going to be kind of dicey.

Finance is based upon money and wealth. As such, we need to translate utility functions on consumption bundles into preferences over wealth and income levels. This is actually pretty straightforward. A person's utility must go up if they have more income or wealth. As income or wealth increases, the budget constraints let in more consumption bundles. With more consumption bundles to pick from, the person must be able to do at least as well as they did before, probably better.

An indirect utility function is the answer to the following question: "For a given person's utility function over consumption bundles, what is the maximal utility that person can achieve with a given level of wealth?" So, for example, let's say you have a monthly budget of $10,000. There are bunch of things that you could buy with that in a month's time. You could buy stocks, bonds, vacations, health care, chardonnay, potato chips. The stocks and bonds, by the way, allow you to maybe buy better vacations in the future. Let's say that when you pick the consumption bundle you like best, you achieve a level of happiness of 12,000 happiness units. If so, then the indirect utility function you have would be *u*($10,000) = 12,000 units of happiness.

If you were to have a monthly budget of $15,000 instead, how much happier would you be? Given all the things you can afford with $15,000 per month, you pick the consumption bundle you like best. Let's say that the bundle generates 13,476 units of happiness. Your indirect utility function is then *u*($10,000) = 12,000 units, and *u*($15,000) = 13,476.

Once you have an indirect utility of wealth function, i.e., we know that the *u*($10,000) = 12,000 and *u*($15,000) = 13,476, you can then start to ask how you would feel in happiness units if the amount of wealth you had was random. Now we're talking finance and investments. Economists refer to these preferences as preferences over lotteries. We define a lottery as anything that makes our future wealth random. A literal lottery is one example. You reduce your current wealth by a dollar to get a very, very small chance at winning, say, $45 million.

An investment in a security is also a lottery, since you can't know for sure what your return will be into the future. An investment in a house is also a lottery. An investment in an education is a lottery. In fact, almost anything is a lottery.

So how do economists model your preferences over lotteries? The most popular way is according to the expected utility hypothesis of Von Neumann and Morgenstern.

The expected utility hypothesis says that a person's preferences over lotteries can be captured by the expected value of a carefully chosen indirect utility function. Let's see how this might work with a simple example.

Let's consider three consumption bundles: X_1, X_2, and X_3. Let's say if you had $10,000, you would buy X_1 out of all those choices you had available to you. And if you had $15,000, you would buy X_2. And if you had $17,000, you would buy X_3.

In terms of indirect utility functions, it might be the case that $u(\$17{,}000) > u(\$15{,}000) > u(\$10{,}000)$. In fact, that must be the case. Note that there are many such functions that capture your preferences over money. The following will work: $u(\$10{,}000) = 3$, $u(\$15{,}000) = 12$, $u(\$17{,}000) = 13$.

This works because the functions maintain order. You like more income to less. But this different function works just as well. Let's let $g(\$10{,}000) = 10$, $g(\$15{,}000) = 15$, $u(\$17{,}000) = 17$. Alright. More on this later.

Now, let's say you are facing the following two lotteries. Lottery 1 is a 50-50 chance at either $10,000 or $15,000. Lottery 2 is a 60% chance $10,000 or a 40% chance $17,000. Let's say you prefer lottery 2 to lottery 1.

According to the expected utility hypothesis, there exists an indirect utility function—maybe it's u, maybe it's g, or maybe it's something else entirely—that will capture your preferences if we take the expected value of the utilities that are possible.

Let's see if u above captures your preferences. If the u captures your preferences over lotteries, then the expected utility under lottery 1 should be smaller than the expected utility under lottery 2. The expected utility under lottery 1 is $0.5 \times 3 + 0.5 \times 12 = 7.5$. The expected utility under lottery 2 is going to be $0.6 \times 3 + 0.4 \times 13 = 7$. That is, u says that lottery 1 is better than lottery 2. So that function does not represent your preferences over lotteries.

What about g? The expected utility of the lottery is then going to be $0.5 \times 10 + 0.5 \times 15 = 12.5$. And under g, the expected utility of lottery 2 is going to be $0.6 \times 10 + 0.4 \times 17 = 12.8 > 12.5$. This indirect utility function does capture your preferences over lotteries—at least, over these two lotteries.

It may not work for other lotteries. And there are clearly other functions that will also work for your choice over those two lotteries. So, what we need, for each person, is to find a function that, for that person, captures their preferences over all possible lotteries. Once we have that, we can start to predict people's answers to the following questions. "How much would I be willing to pay to get rid of a risk that I face now?" Alternatively, "How much would I have to get paid to bear a risk I don't have now?"

To see this last point, let's say that we have an indirect utility function for Jane and one for Ichabod. Consider a plot of Jane's. Also consider the lottery 1 described previously. Let's say that Jane already faces this lottery. Say she is a really, really, really bad driver and she has a 50% chance of being in an accident once a month, and that's going to cost her \$5000 since she is uninsured. For simplicity, let's let the only kind of accident she has be one that costs \$5000 to fix. Without the accident, she makes \$15,000 a month and achieves an indirect utility of, say, 10. With the accident, she only has \$10,000 after she fixes the car. She only receives an indirect utility of, say, 3 in that case. Given the risk, her expected utility is going to be $0.5 \times u(10{,}000) + 0.5 \times u(15{,}000) = 0.5 \times 3 + 0.5 \times 10 = 6.5$.

Note that her expected income is \$12,500. Right now, she never really gets that outcome, right? Rather, she only gets its expectation by getting \$10,000 half the time and \$15,000 the other half the time. But, how would she feel if she were always to get \$12,500 every month? Would she be better off, or worse off, or indifferent?

Let's say that she is indifferent. If so, then it must be the case that the indirect utility function at \$12,500 equals 6.5. Because the expected utility of the 50-50 lottery is 6.5, too, Jane is indifferent between the two cases—the lottery and the sure amount. That is, she only cares about the expected income. The variance in the income is unimportant to her. In this case, we would say that she is risk-neutral. Note that there are three points on this indirect utility function, and we can say that this function is a straight line. If at \$10,000 we have 3 and at \$15,000 we have 12, then a straight line that goes through both those points goes through 6.5 at \$12,500. Thus, an indirect utility function that is linear in wealth is consistent with risk neutrality.

Now let's say that Jane actually prefers \$12,500 for sure to the 50-50 lottery over \$10,000 and \$15,000. In that case, we would say that she is risk-averse.

Also, it must be the case that the indirect utility function that captures her preferences is bowed like a bowl facing down. That is, the indirect utility function at \$12,500 must be greater than 6.5, let's say it's 8. If so, then the slope from \$10,000 to \$12,500 must be bigger than the slope from \$12,500 to \$15,000. Specifically, the change from \$10,000 to \$12,500 is $8 - 3 = 5$. And the change in utility from \$12,500 to \$15,000 is only 2. Thus, a function that goes up, it goes up at a decreasing rate. That is a function that is consistent with risk aversion.

To see why that captures risk aversion, think about how Jane would feel if she started out with \$12,500 a month for sure. And something happened to increase her risk such that half the time she only had \$10,000, while the other half the time she had \$15,000. Her expected income is still \$12,500. But what happens to her expected utility? It falls. On the down side, she loses 5 utils. On the up side, she only gains 2 utils. The expected change in happiness is thus $0.5 \times (-5) + 0.5 \times 2 = -1.5$. That is, her happiness falls. The drop on the down side is worse than the potential increase in utils on the up side. To think about this, what is the shape of Jane's indirect utility function if she were actually a risk lover? I'll let you think about that on your own.

In summary, the shape of the indirect utility function tells us something about people's aversion to variation in outcomes. So, how do we get indirect utility functions for people in the market? The answer is we don't. Rather, we typically just assume some function that has some nice features. The nice features we're typically looking for are things like they're easy to work with. And this is where financial economists are on thin ice. Many of the functions used in finance are such that only the expected value and only the variance matter.

There is much evidence to suggest that people care about other things other than just expected value and variance. For example, many people care about skewness. Skewness is the likelihood that there will be a big, big, big positive outcome. Lottery tickets have lots of skewness. In fact, many small stocks have lots of skewness. They either languish or fall from a fairly low price, or they skyrocket.

Why is this important? If we use utility functions that imply only mean and variance matter, then we will have missed some important features of investor's preferences. If we use such functions to build asset pricing models, then the model may imply something is not important when, in fact, it is. That means that when we use a model to tell us what is risk and what is the return you should get for that amount of risk, it may be completely misleading.

Later, when we develop various asset pricing models, I will point out when an asset pricing model has an implication that is based solely on mean/variance preferences.

Managing Risk in Portfolios

Lecture 15

In this lecture, you will learn about the value of diversification. In addition, you will learn how different combinations of individual securities create different portfolio return characteristics (in terms of risk and return) and the extent to which risk can be reduced without also reducing average return. You will also learn the benefits in terms of risk and return associated with diversity in the characteristics of the available securities and the types of information on individual securities needed in order to build an optimal portfolio.

Portfolios

- The return of a security from t to $t + 1$ is defined as $R_t = \frac{(P_{t+1} + D_{t+1}) - P_t}{P_t}$. For the purposes of this lecture, we are going to simply think of these returns as just random variables. It is important to always keep in mind that for any given period, the actual return on an individual security may be very different from its expected value.

- For a random variable, such as the return on a specific security, we might refer to the expected value and the realized value. The realized value is the value that actually occurs given a single draw from the distribution; the expected value is the probability-weighted sum of all of the possible values that might be realized.

- Portfolio theory considers how the return characteristics of individual securities affect the characteristics of the return on a portfolio of individual securities. In portfolio theory, a portfolio is defined as a set of weights $w = (w_1, w_2, w_3, \ldots, w_n, \ldots, w_N)$, where N is the total number of securities being considered, n is a generic index for a security (ranging from 1 to N), and w_n is the weight placed on the nth security.

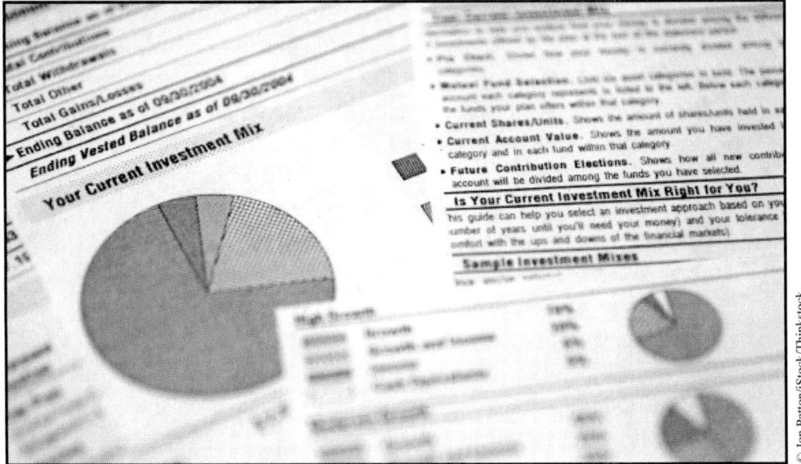

In order to build an optimal portfolio, you must understand the value of diversification.

- In general, the expected return on a portfolio is the weighted average of expected returns on the individual securities, where the weights used in the average are the portfolio weights for each individual security: $E(R_{port}) = (w_1(E(R_1))) + ((1 - w_1)(E(R_2)))$. With this expression, we can systematically vary the weights between the two securities and see how the expected return and standard deviation vary.

Variance (or Standard Deviation) Effects

- The variance of a portfolio return is more complicated than that of an individual security because we need to know how the return on one security is related to the return on the other.

- For example, consider the case in which when one security has a big positive return, then the other security typically has a big negative return, and when the first has a big negative return, the other has a big positive return. Let's say that these securities infrequently have small or medium negative or positive returns. Thus, both of these securities have high variances alone.

- Consider a portfolio with a 50-50 split between the two securities. In this case, the expected return on the portfolio return will clearly be close to zero. What about the variance in this case? When the first security has a positive return, then the typically negative return of the other pulls the portfolio return *down* to zero. Similarly, when the first security has a negative return, then the typically positive return on the other pulls the portfolio return *up* to zero.

- In this case, the variance of the portfolio return is low because regardless of what happens to either individual security, the portfolio return is close to its mean return of zero. This implies that the portfolio return has a small variance. Thus, even though both of the individual securities have high variance on their own, the portfolio variance is small.

- In contrast, consider the case in which when one security has a big positive return, so does the other usually, and when the first security has a big negative return, so does the other. Taken alone, they both have only large positive and negative returns and, as a result, have large individual variances.

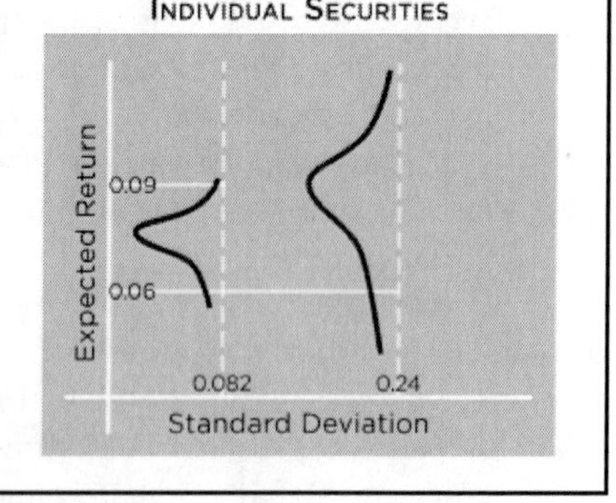

- In this case, the return on a 50-50 portfolio will either be big positive (when both are big positive) or big negative (when both are big negative). Because we don't know a priori which will occur, the average return for the portfolio will be close to zero (the average of a big positive and a big negative). But the variance will be large because the realized returns on the portfolio will either be big positive or big negative.

- Note that in both cases, the individual securities had large variance. However, in the first case, the variance of the portfolio return was small, whereas for the second case, the variance of the portfolio variance was large. This relationship can be captured using the concepts and formulas for correlation and covariance. Recall that the covariance of two random variables is the expected value of the product of one variable's deviation from its mean and the other variable's deviation from its mean.

- If the most likely outcomes are associated with one being above its mean while the other is also above its mean, then the covariance is positive. If the most likely outcomes are associated with one being above its mean while the other is below its mean, then the covariance is negative.

- The correlation ranges from 1 to −1, with the sign indicating whether the covariance is positive or negative and the magnitude of the correlation indicating the strength of the relationship. If the correlation is 1 or −1, then they are perfectly positively or negatively correlated, and knowing one tells you exactly what the other is. A correlation of zero says that there is no connection between the two.

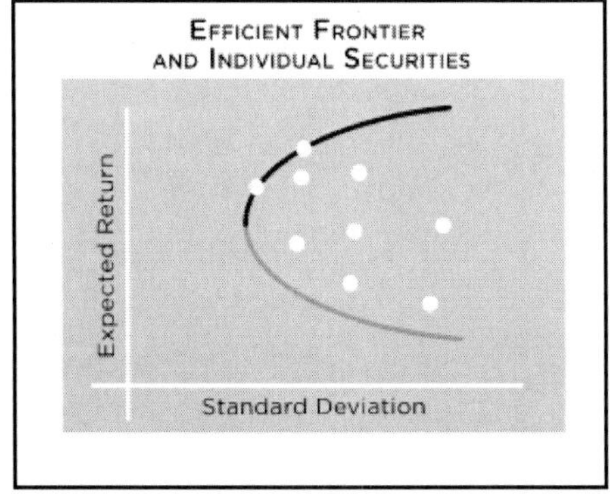

- Given the variances of two returns and the covariance between those two returns, there is an expression for the variance of a linear combination of random variables. We can use this expression for portfolios because the return on a portfolio is just a weighted average of the returns on the individual securities.

- For a two-security case, the variance of the return on the portfolio consists of three main parts. The first is the weight on the first security squared multiplied by the variance of the return on that security. The second is a similar expression but for the second security; it is the weight on the second security squared multiplied by the variance of that security. The third component utilizes the correlation between the two securities: It is 2 times the weight on the first security times the weight on the second security, with all of that multiplied by the covariance. The covariance is equal to the correlation between 1 and 2, times the standard deviation of 1, times the standard deviation of 2.

- Consider three special cases: when the correlation is positive, when there is no correlation, and when the correlation is negative. Of these three cases, positive correlation is the most likely for most securities. This is true because most securities move in the same direction: When there is good news in the market, that is typically good news for most securities, which will all likely have positive returns on that day. Similarly, most securities will have negative returns on a bad-news day.

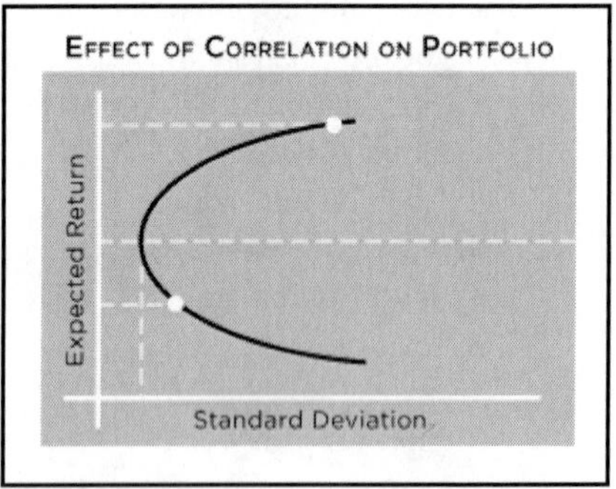

- In the case of perfect positive correlation, the standard deviation is $SDrp = w_1\sigma_1 + w_2\sigma_2$, where $w_1\sigma_1$ is the weight on security 1 times the standard deviation of return on security 1 and $w_2\sigma_2$ is the weight on security 2 times the standard deviation on security 2.

- Perfect negative correlations are rare for securities that represent the claims on actual cash flows from firms, like stock and bonds. This is true because it requires that when one firm is doing well, the other firm is doing poorly.

- In the case of perfect negative correlation, the standard deviation becomes $SDrp = w_1\sigma_1 - w_2\sigma_2$. That is, the standard deviation has the same two parts as with the perfect positive correlation case, but in this equation, $w_2\sigma_2$ is subtracted from $w_1\sigma_1$.

- In the perfect negative correlation case, because the two parts are subtracted, this means that we can create some really good combinations of expected return and standard deviation by picking the weights to place on each security.

- In fact, we can actually create a combination that has no standard deviation. To form such a portfolio, the weights are as follows.
    - $w_1 = \dfrac{\sigma_2}{(\sigma_1 + \sigma_2)}$

      $w_2 = 1 - w_1$

- With imperfect correlation, the result is essentially in between the perfect negative and perfect positive cases. In the case where there is no correlation, the standard deviation of the portfolio return is $SD_{rp} = \sqrt{w_1^2\sigma_1^2 + w_2^2\sigma_2^2}$. In this case, there will be a reduction in standard deviation possible.

Multiple Securities

- So far, we have considered just combining two securities together into a portfolio. If you combine many securities together, then you can get even bigger variance benefits. In fact, for any given level of expected return, a portfolio of the complete set of securities can be formed to produce the lowest possible standard deviation.

- To get the minimum variance portfolio for a particular mean return, simply search over all the different sets of weights (w_1, w_2, … , w_k) until you find the weights that are associated with the lowest variance.

- The set of combinations of expected return and lowest standard deviation is referred to as the minimum variance frontier. This frontier looks like a hyperbola. The portfolio that is associated with the lowest standard deviation is called the global minimum variance portfolio. This is the portfolio associated with the bottom of the "on-its-side U."

Efficient Frontier

- There are some points on the minimum variance frontier that are not particularly useful. For example, why would anyone want a portfolio on the lower part of the hyperbola? On the lower part of the hyperbola, the expected return is lower than that associated with the global minimum variance portfolio.

- For any possible level of portfolio risk, you can get a higher expected return by picking the portfolio on the upper branch associated with that level of standard deviation rather than the portfolio on the lower branch associated with that standard deviation.

- The efficient frontier is the minimum variance frontier with all of these useless portfolios thrown out. Note that you may be able to shift the frontier toward the *y*-axis (that is, toward less variance) by adding additional securities.

- This is especially true if you add securities that are either uncorrelated or negatively correlated with the current set of securities. Such a shift typically occurs when you add the securities of foreign markets. This is good in that for any given expected return, you will have less "risk" in the return on the portfolio.

Which Portfolio is Optimal?

- The efficient frontier only contains risky securities. These are either stocks or bonds that mature at times different than your holding period. The portfolio you want will contain both risky and risk-free securities. You will want to hold a fraction of your wealth in the risk-free investments and only one of the portfolios on the frontier.

- In an expected return standard deviation plot, consider a portfolio on the frontier. Because the risk-free return is not random, then any combination of wealth invested in the risk-free and that portfolio will create the set of expected return–standard deviation combinations along the line from R_f at zero risk through the point representing the risky portfolio.

- If you want to bear little risk, you invest less in the risky portfolio and more in the risk-free security. As you increase the amount of your wealth that you put at risk, you will slide up the line. The slope of this line is the Sharpe ratio for that risky portfolio.

- In general, the Sharpe ratio for any portfolio is defined as $S_p = \frac{E(R_p) - R_f}{\sigma_p}$. Intuitively, this measure tells you how much extra expected return you get per unit of standard deviation for a given portfolio.

- You want the portfolio on the efficient frontier that generates the highest Sharpe ratio. You then control the amount of risk by deciding how much of your wealth to put at risk. However, for each unit of risk, you will be getting more return above the risk-free rate than any other portfolio available on the frontier.

Suggested Reading

Bernstein, *Capital Ideas*.

Bodie, Kane, and Marcus, *Essentials of Investments*.

Markowitz, "Portfolio Selection."

Questions to Consider

1. Can you think of two or three securities that are negatively correlated with the market? What are they?

2. Consider two securities that have returns that are positively correlated with each other. If you take a short position in one and a long position in the other, will the returns on the short position be positively or negatively correlated with the returns on the long position?

Managing Risk in Portfolios

Lecture 15—Transcript

So far, we've examined some sources of risk for various securities. Mostly we have examined risky outcomes for an individual security in isolation. For example, we characterized how the return of a long-term bond might deviate from its yield to maturity over a short investment horizon.

But investors do not, and should not, just hold one security at a time. In this lecture, we'll examine how holding combinations of securities can alter the nature of the risk of each individual security. Once we understand how an investor's overall risk depends upon how securities are combined together, then we can see how to combine them purposefully to generate a sensible investment goal.

The material in this lecture will also be useful for understanding the subsequent lectures on asset pricing models, models that determine the amount an investor should get paid for bearing risk contained in an individual security.

In this lecture, we'll examine the following topics: the value of diversification, how different combinations of individual securities create different portfolio return characteristics, in terms of risk and return, and the extent to which risk can be reduced without also reducing average return as captured in something called the efficient frontier.

We'll also look at the benefits in terms of risk and return associated with diversifying the characteristics given available securities. We'll also look at the type of information on individual securities needed in order to build an optimal portfolio.

So let's start by considering an investor who has $100,000 to invest. Initially, we will just consider a situation in which the investor is trying to decide how much money to allocate across two risky securities. Think of this problem as one an investor trying to think about how to decide how much to invest in a domestic versus foreign security or how much to invest in stocks versus risky corporate debt.

We will characterize each one of these securities in two dimensions: its expected return and its return variance. We will consider another set of characteristics later when we discuss how the characteristics of the return of an individual security affects the characteristics of the return on the portfolio comprised of those individual securities.

As defined in earlier sections of the course, recall that the return on a security from t to $t + 1$ is defined as $Rt = [(Pt + 1 + Dt + 1) - Pt]/Pt$.

For the purposes of this lecture, we're going to simply ask you to think about the returns as just random variables. So, when I talk about the characteristics of an individual security, I will be referring only to that security's expected return and its return variance.

To see things visually, think about a plot of the characteristics of individual securities on a graph. On the horizontal axis, put the standard deviation and on the vertical axis put the expected return.

For example, let the expected return for Ford be 8.1%, with a standard deviation of 8.2%. Let IBM have an expected return of, say, 5% but a higher standard deviation at 17.3%. Finally, let Caterpillar have the highest expected return at 10% and the highest standard deviation at 24%.

Two quick asides: First, I should stress here that often the numbers used in the graphs or numerical examples are just for concreteness and may not be current or even realistic. When the magnitude of a variable is important, I will stress that you should take the number seriously. In the case of Ford, IBM, and Caterpillar now, both the levels and the numbers and their rankings, in terms of which is higher or lower, have been chosen just purely for illustration. Second, I will also slip back and forth between variance and standard deviation. Realize that both give you the same information. Knowing one tells you what the other one is. While I might refer to the variance of the return of a security or a portfolio, the figures you typically see in textbooks and on the web usually show the standard deviation.

There are two reasons for this. One, as we discussed before, standard deviation is easier to interpret for returns because it is in percent, rather than with variance, which is percent squared. Two, some of the relationships are linear (i.e., are straight lines) when plotted in expected return-standard deviation space. Some things, when plotted in expected return-variance space, are not linear. So, while I might refer to the variance of some security, the information contained in that variance might be depicted or expressed as a standard deviation in a figure or an equation.

Back to the characteristics of individual securities. It is important to always keep in mind that in any given period, the actual return of an individual security may be very different from its expected value. In order to keep this in your mind, I will always use some terminology routinely used in probability and statistics. For a random variable, such as the return on a specific security, we might refer to the expected value and the realized value. The realized value is the value that actually occurs given a single draw from the distribution. The expected value is the probability-weighted sum of all of the possible values that might be realized.

For example, consider the flip of a fair coin. Let's say that you get \$1 if it comes up heads, and you have to pay \$1 if it comes up tails. The expected value is $0.5 \times \$1 + 0.5 \times (-\$1) = \$0$. If a coin is flipped, and it comes up heads, we would say that \$1 was the realized value. If it comes up tails, then the realized value is $-\$1$. In this case, the expected value is \$0, and it is also not one of the two possible values on any one flip.

For securities, even though the expected return for Ford is lower than the expected return for Caterpillar, the return actually realized for Ford in one period may be actually higher than that realized for CAT.

In the next section of the lecture we will examine what is referred to as portfolio theory. Portfolio theory considers how the return characteristics of an individual security affect the characteristics of the return on a portfolio of individual securities.

In portfolio theory, a portfolio is defined as a set of weights: $w = (w_1, w_2,$ w_3, all the way up to a generic entry, w_n, all the way up to the final entry, $w_N)$. Here, N (i.e., cap N) is the total number of securities being considered.

The little n is the generic index for a generic security, ranging somewhere between 1 and N). w_n is the weight placed on this generic security.

At this point, don't worry about how we got to know about these N securities. Later, we will discuss which N securities might be good to know about and whether it makes any sense for you to spend time and/or money getting to know about additional securities.

To create intuition, let's first consider a simple portfolio consisting of only two securities. We will examine how the characteristics of the portfolio returns change as we systematically vary the weights from all on one and none on the other to none on the first to all on the other.

For example, consider the following simple portfolio: out of $100,000 to invest, invest $30,000 in Ford and $70,000 in IBM. In this case, the portfolio weights will be 30%, or $30,000 out of $100,000, in Ford and 70% in IBM, or $70,000 divided by $100,000. With this portfolio, the expected return on the portfolio is the weighted average of the expected returns on the individual securities, where the weights used in the average are the portfolio weights for each individual. So, $E(R_P) = 0.3 \times E(R_F) + 0.7 \times E(R_I) = 0.3 \times 0.081 + 0.7 \times 0.05 = 0.0716$, 7.16%. That's the expected return on the portfolio of 30% in Ford and 70% in IBM.

In general, we can write the expected return as the following formula: $E(R_{port}) = w_1 \times E(R_1) + (1 - w_1)E(R_2)$. With this expression, we can systematically vary the weights between the two securities and see how the expected return and the standard deviation vary.

Let's first examine what happens to the expected return. To see the relationship, let's start off with all our weight on Ford and examine what happens to the expected return on the portfolio if we take some of the weight away from Ford and give it to IBM. Such an exercise is equivalent to starting off with investing all of your $100,000 in Ford and then taking money away from Ford—say, $1000 at a time—to invest in IBM. If we start with a portfolio that has the whole $100,000 invested in Ford, then $w_{Ford} = 1.0$, $w_{IBM} = 1 - w_{Ford} = 0$, so the expected return on that portfolio is trivially just the expected return on Ford.

If we take away $1000 from Ford, we're reducing the weight on Ford by 0.01 (or $1000/$100,000) and we're increasing the weight on IBM by 0.01. Since the expected return on IBM is lower than Ford's expected return, the expected return on the portfolio gets pulled down by moving money to IBM.

Every time an extra 1% weight is taken away from the higher expected return on Ford and reallocated to the lower expected return on IBM, the expected return on the portfolio falls. It falls by 0.01 times the difference between the expected returns on Ford and IBM. In this example, the difference is 3.1%. Thus, if we take 50% of the weight away from the initial 100% allocation to Ford, the expected return on the portfolio will be the expected return on Ford minus $0.5 \times 3.1\%$, for a total portfolio expected return of $8.1\% - 0.5 \times 3.1\%$, or 6.55%.

If we take all of the initial weight away from Ford and give it to IBM, then the expected return on the new portfolio is simply 5%, the IBM expected return. Now, let's see what happens to the variance, or the standard deviation, as we take weight away from one and give it to another.

As discussed previously, the variance of the portfolio return is more complicated than that of an individual security because we need to know how the return on one security is related to the return on the other.

For example, consider the case in which one security has a big positive return, and the other security typically has a big negative return. And when the first has a big negative return, the other has a big positive. Let's say that these securities very infrequently have small or medium negative or positive returns. Thus, both of these securities are high variances when considered alone.

Now consider a portfolio with a 50-50 split between the two securities. In this case, the expected return on the portfolio return will clearly be close to zero. What about the variance in this case? When the first security has a positive return, then the typically negative return of the other security will pull down the portfolio return, and it'll pull it down to zero. Similarly, when the first security has a big negative return, then the typically positive return of the other pulls the portfolio return up to zero. In this case, the variance of the portfolio return is low, since regardless of what happens to either individual security, the portfolio return is close to the mean return of zero. This implies that the portfolio return has a small variance. Thus, even though both of the individual securities have high variance on their own, the portfolio variance is small.

In contrast, consider a case in which when one security has a big positive return, so does the other. And when the first security has a big negative return, the other one does as well. Taken alone, they both have only large positive and large negative returns and, as a result, they both have large individual variances.

In this case, the return on a 50-50 portfolio will either be big positive when both are big positive or big negative when both are big negative. Since we don't know a priori which will occur, the average return on the portfolio will be close to zero, the average of the big positive and the big negative. But the variance will be large because the realized returns on the portfolio will either be big positive or big negative.

Note that in both cases, the individual securities have a large variance. But, in the first case, the variance of the portfolio return was small, whereas in the second case, the variance of the portfolio variance was large.

This relationship can be captured by using the concepts and formulas for correlation and covariance discussed in an earlier lecture. Recall that the covariance of two random variables is the expected value of the product of one variable's deviation from its mean and the other variable's deviation from its mean.

If the most likely outcomes are associated with one being above its mean while the other is also above its mean, then the covariance is positive. If the most likely outcomes are associated with one being above its mean while the other is below its mean, then the covariance is negative. The correlation ranges from 1 to −1, with the sign indicating whether the covariance is positive or negative, and the magnitude of the correlation indicating the strength of the relationship. If the correlation is 1 or −1, then they are perfectly positively or negatively correlated, and knowing one tells you exactly what the other is. A correlation of zero says that there is no connection between the two at all.

Given the variances of the two returns and the covariance between these two returns, there is an expression for the variance of a linear combination of these random variables. We can use this expression for portfolios because the return on a portfolio is just a weighted average of the returns on the individual securities.

For a two-security case, the variance of the return on the portfolio consists of three main parts. The first is the weight on the first security squared multiplied by the variance of the return on that security. The second is a similar expression, but for the second security. It is the weight on the second security squared multiplied by the variance of that security. The third component utilizes the correlation between the two securities. It is two times the weight on the first security times the weight on the second security, all of that multiplied by the covariance. The covariance is equal to the correlation between 1 and 2, times the standard deviation of 1, times the standard deviation of 2.

Let's consider three special cases: (1) when the correlation is positive, (2) when there is no correlation, and (3) when the correlation is negative. Of these three cases, positive correlation is the most likely for securities. This is true since most securities move in the same direction. When there is good news in the market—say, the economy is recovering from a recession—then that is typically good news for most securities, which are also likely have very positive returns on that day. Similarly, most securities will have negative returns on a bad-news day.

Let's consider this positive correlation case next. To get some intuition for this case, let's consider the extreme case in which the positive correlation is very, very strong, with a correlation equal to 1.

When the correlation is 1, then a bit of algebra shows that the standard deviation of the portfolio return reduces to the following expression: $SDrp = w_1 \times \Sigma_I + w_2 \times \Sigma_2$. That is, just like the expected return, the standard deviation of the portfolio is just the weighted average of the standard deviations of each.

It is useful to see combinations of expected return and standard deviation that you can create for yourself with a portfolio with just two securities. For this, consider a plot of return characteristics that we discussed earlier. On this plot are two points for each security. Let's say security A has a low standard deviation but also a low expected return. Security B has a high expected return but also a high standard deviation.

If we start with all the weight on A, the portfolio return will have a low standard deviation and a low expected return. As we take weight away from A and reallocate it to B, both the expected return and the standard deviation will rise. In fact, as we take weight from A and move it to B, we plot out a straight line from the point that represents A to the point that represents B.

Let's next examine combinations we can create for ourselves if there is perfect negative correlation. This is rare for securities that represent the claims on actual cash flows from firms, like stocks and bonds. This is true because it requires that when one firm is doing well, the other firm is doing really poorly.

This requires something of a zero sum game. A zero sum game is one in which when one person wins, the other one loses. When you have firms that compete in the same products in the same markets, then there is some sense in which that's a zero sum game, when one takes some market share from the other. But that does not necessarily result in perfect negative correlation, because both are going to benefit when the market expands and both will also suffer when that market contracts.

However, we will see that there are derivative securities that are designed to be negatively correlated with other securities. What we'll show next shows why you might want to have such derivative securities. In the case of perfect negative correlation, the standard deviation of the portfolio becomes: $SDrp = w_1 \times \Sigma_1 - w_2 \times \Sigma_2$. That is, the standard deviation has the same two parts as in the perfect positive correlation case. Part 1 is the weight on the first security times the standard deviation on the return on that security. Part 2 is the weight on the second security times the standard deviation of that second security. With positive correlation, the two parts are added together. In contrast, with negative correlation, the second part is subtracted from the first.

If the perfect negative correlation case exists, since we have the two parts subtracted from one another, this means that we can actually create some really good combinations of expected return and standard deviation by picking the weights to place on each security.

In fact, we can actually create a combination that has no standard deviation at all. To form such a portfolio, the weights are $w_1 = \Sigma_2/(\Sigma_1 + \Sigma_2)$ and $w_2 = 1 - w_1$.

Why these weights? Consider what happens when the standard deviations are the same. In that case, a 50-50 portfolio has a return with no variance. When one is down one standard deviation, the other is up one standard deviation, which exactly cancels each other out. If the standard deviation of one is bigger than the other, then put more weight on the one with the smaller standard deviation. When that one goes down one standard deviation, the other will go up by more. But, because you have less weight on the one with the bigger standard deviation, it exactly cancels.

Consider the plot we discussed earlier. For two perfectly correlated securities, consider the return characteristics of portfolios you can form by moving weight from one to the other. The line is shaped like a V that's on its side, with the point of the V touching the vertical axis. This is the point where the standard deviation is zero. That is, this is the portfolio that has no variance.

So far, we've been looking at combinations of securities in which we have perfect positive or perfect negative correlation. We've been putting those into portfolios to look at what the expected return is and the standard deviation of that. What happens if we have imperfect correlation? The result is essentially in between the perfect negative and perfect positive cases. To see what happens exactly, let's consider the case in which there is no correlation. In that case, the standard deviation of the portfolio return is going to be equal to the following: $SDrp = \sqrt{(w_1^2 \times \Sigma_1^2 + w_2^2 \times \Sigma_2^2)}$. In this case, there will be a reduction in standard deviation that is, indeed, possible.

To see this, consider a simple example of two variables that have the same variance and are uncorrelated with each other. The two random variables are two independent flips of a coin. Let heads pays \$1 and tails pay −\$1. Now let's form a portfolio that is half of the payoff from one flip and half of the payoff from another flip. Which would you prefer? The payoff of one flip? Or would you prefer this portfolio?

In the one-flip case, you can only get \$1 or −\$1 for a standard deviation of \$1. What about in the half the two-flip case? Well, there are three distinct outcomes in terms of payoffs. You could get \$1. That only happens when both flips are heads. Thus, that only happens 25% of the time, or 0.5×0.5.

Also, you could lose \$1. That only happens when both flips are tails. And that, again, only happens 25% of the time. These two outcomes are the same as those associated with one flip of the coin. But, with the flip of just one coin, 1 and −1 are the only two possibilities, covering 100% of the probability. With half the two flips, we only have covered 50% of the total probability with 1 and −1.

The other cases with the other 50% of the probability are better. One outcome is first is heads and the second is tails. This occurs 25% of the time. The other outcome is the first is tails and the second is heads. This also occurs 25% of the time.

In these cases, which happen a total of 50% of the time, the payoff is zero, which equals the mean. Thus, the standard deviation of the portfolio of independent flips is lower than the standard deviation of any one flip.

What this implies with respect to the plots we've discussed before is that you can get a reduction in the standard deviation of the portfolio return relative to the standard deviations of each individual security. Rather than an "on-its-side V" for the perfect negative correlation case, what you get an "on-its-side U," where the bottom of the U corresponds to less standard deviation than either of the two individual securities.

So far, we've considered just combining two securities together into a portfolio. If you combine many securities together, then you can get an even bigger variance benefit. In fact, for any given level of expected return, a portfolio of a complete set of securities can be formed to produce the lowest possible standard deviation. To get the minimum variance portfolio for a particular mean return, simply search over all the different sets of weights—remember w_1, w_2, all the way up to w_k—until you find the weights that are associated with the lowest possible variance.

There exist formulas for the minimum variance portfolio weights for any given expected return, but it's very complicated and it's best calculated using something like a spreadsheet or a statistical package like Mathematica. There are some portfolio optimization tools that you can find online that will do this as well.

The set of combinations of the expected return and the lowest standard deviation is referred to as the minimum variance frontier. This frontier is actually a hyperbola. It's like this U that's sitting on its side. The portfolio that is associated with the lowest standard deviation is called the global minimum variance portfolio. This is the portfolio associated with the bottom of the on-its-side U, the point that is closest to the vertical axis.

Note that there are some points on the minimum variance frontier that are not particularly useful. For example, why would anyone want a portfolio on the lower part of the hyperbola—on the lower part of the U? On the lower part of the hyperbola, the expected return is lower than that associated with the global minimum variance portfolio. For any possible level of portfolio risk, you can get a higher expected return by picking the portfolio on the upper branch associated with that level of standard deviation, rather than the portfolio on the lower branch associated with that standard deviation.

The efficient frontier is the minimum variance frontier with all of those useless portfolios thrown out.

Note that you may be able to shift the frontier towards the *y*-axis—that is, towards less variance—by adding additional securities. This is especially true if you add securities that are either uncorrelated or are negatively correlated with the current set of securities that you have. Such a shift typically occurs when you add the securities of foreign markets, actually. This is good in that any given expected return you will have less risk in the portfolio.

Clearly, portfolios on the efficient frontier are better than any inside the frontier, because the efficient frontier gives you the highest expected return for the lowest variance. But of the portfolios on the frontier, which is the one that you actually want? There's many on the frontier. Which one do you want? Before we get to that, let's put this risky portfolio into a larger context. Specifically, note that the efficient frontier only contains risky securities. These are either stocks or bonds that mature at different times, different horizons, than your holding period.

The portfolio you want will contain both risky and risk-free securities. The risk-free securities will be investments like in treasury bills or money market accounts, say.

What kinds of trade-offs between risk and expected return can you create for yourself when you include risk-free investments? Basically, you will want to hold a fraction of your wealth in the risk-free investments and only one of the portfolios on the frontier. In an expected return standard deviation plot, consider a portfolio on the frontier. Because the risk-free return is not random, then any combination of wealth invested in the risk-free and that portfolio will create the set of expected return-standard deviation combinations along the line from that risk-free rate at zero risk through the point representing that risky portfolio. If you want to bear little risk, then you want to invest less in the risky portfolio and more in the risk-free security. As you increase the amount of your wealth that you put at risk, you slide up the line.

The slope of this line is called the Sharpe ratio for that risky portfolio. In general, the Sharpe ratio for any portfolio is defined as: $S_p = [E(R_p) - R_f] / \Sigma\text{P}$. Intuitively, this measure tells you how much extra expected return you get per standard of deviation for that given portfolio. For example, consider a risky portfolio with an expected return of 10%, which exceeds the risk-free rate of 3% by 7%. Let the standard deviation be 20%. Then the Sharpe ratio for this portfolio is going to be 0.07/0.20 = 0.35. Thus, with this portfolio, you'll get a 35% return per each percentage point of standard deviation.

So, which of the portfolios on the efficient frontier do you want? You want the portfolio that generates the highest Sharpe ratio. You then control the amount of risk you want by deciding how much of your wealth to actually put at risk. But, for each unit of risk, you'll be getting more return above the risk-free rate than any other portfolio per unit of risk.

In the next lecture, we'll examine a parsimonious way to get the parameters required to form an efficient portfolio. The set of techniques will also be useful for getting indications of mispricing that might suggest opportunities for excess returns. Before we get to such opportunities, however, we will explore an asset pricing model that will provide some useful benchmarks in terms of what is considered excess, but we're going to be using the tools that we've developed in this lecture in those subsequent lectures.

The Behavior of Stock Prices

Lecture 16

In this lecture, you will be introduced to a statistical model of returns that has some parameters that correspond to variables that have been discussed previously. You will then learn how to estimate these parameters using data on the past returns of securities—a technique known as regression analysis. With the estimates from regression analysis, you will be able to quantify the characteristics of a security. This will be useful for understanding the security's risk and perhaps the mispricing it might have relative to an asset pricing model. You will learn how to use these estimates to quantify the variance-covariance matrix, which is useful for forming optimal risky portfolios.

Data-Generating Process

- Let's develop a simple statistical model to describe security returns. With such a model, we will be able to build up to the variance-covariance matrix. It will be useful to think of the information we have as coming from what we call a data-generating process (DGP), which is just a mathematical description of how the observed data is generated.

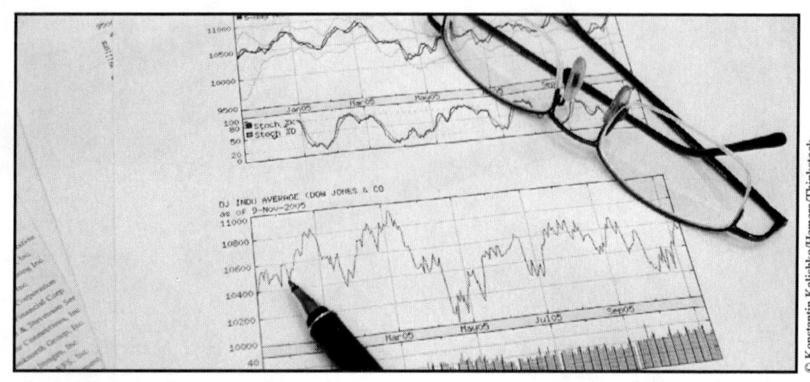

Regression analysis is a model that uses mathematical and statistical techniques to describe returns.

- The simplest DGP is the following: The return on a specific security in excess of the risk-free rate can be divided in to two independent sources, as follows.
    - The first source is common across all securities and is related to general features or happenings in the economy as a whole. These "features" include things like the level of interest rates; the amount of GNP growth; and the level of input prices, such as the price of natural gas and petroleum products, and so on.

    - The second source is specific to that particular firm; this source is "idiosyncratic" to that security rather than common across all securities. These things might include factors like the fact that the CEO is going through a divorce and is a bit more distracted than usual, or that the R & D team has made a technological advance that will make their products more reliable than the competition's.

- To keep the model simple, we aggregate all of the individual common factors down into one factor, which we will say is the market factor. Because it is difficult for us to have a good idea of how all of these individual common factors "aggregate" up, we will simply let the market tells us that and use some broad-based index of security prices as the market factor. For example, we could use the return on the S&P 500 to indicate all of the things that affect the market.

- If you think you have all of the common factors appropriately aggregated in the market factor r_M, then the idiosyncratic component of return is simply everything that is not "explained" by the common factor. We can summarize the DGP via the following mathematical expression.
    - $r_i - r_f = \alpha_i + (\beta_i(r_M - r_f)) + \varepsilon_i$

- In the expression, r_i is the return in the ith security and r_f is the risk-free rate, so $r_i - r_f$ is the return on security i in excess of the risk-free rate. The common factor is the return on the market (r_M) in excess of the risk-free rate (i.e., $r_M - r_f$).

Security #	1	2	3	4	5	6	7	8
1	0.02	0.016	0.026	0.009	0.008	0.014	0.016	0.018
2	0.016	0.0881	0.0416	0.0144	0.0128	0.0224	0.0256	0.0288
3	0.026	0.0416	0.1301	0.0234	0.0208	0.0364	0.0416	0.0468
4	0.009	0.0144	0.0234	0.023725	0.0072	0.0126	0.0144	0.0162
5	0.008	0.0128	0.0208	0.0072	0.0208	0.0112	0.0128	0.0144
6	0.014	0.0224	0.0364	0.0126	0.0112	0.0821	0.0224	0.0252
7	0.016	0.0256	0.0416	0.0144	0.0128	0.0224	0.128	0.0288
8	0.018	0.0288	0.0468	0.0162	0.0144	0.0252	0.0288	0.0724

Correlation	1	2	3	4	5	6	7	8
1	1	0.38116852	0.50970595	0.41316583	0.39223227	0.34549476	0.316227766	0.473029498
2		1	0.38856773	0.31497162	0.299013191	0.26338345	0.241072142	0.360607911
3			1	0.42118617	0.399846243	0.35220146	0.322366347	0.482211898
4				1	0.324113946	0.28549326	0.261309017	0.390879254
5					1	0.27102838	0.248069469	0.371074868
6						1	0.218510069	0.326858422
7							1	0.299170123
8								1

- This is called a single-factor model because there is a single factor that explains the returns of securities. In this case, the single factor is the return on the market. This single-factor model is also called the market model.

- Although every security is affected by the common factor $r_M - r_f$, the amount that it is affected by can vary by security according to β_i, the coefficient on the common factor in the expression. Thus, the amount the ith security is affected by the common factor is $\beta_i(r_M - r_f)$. You can think of the beta as summarizing how the return reacts to market conditions, as summarized by the market return.

- In the expression, there are two other parts. The α_i is a constant component. It says that the excess return for security i has a constant component that doesn't change when the market moves.

The second other part is everything else: the idiosyncratic part—all the stuff that is not explained by the market movement.

- With the single-factor model, we have two sources of variation in returns: the market and idiosyncratic returns. And we have three parameters that characterize the nature of the relationship between returns and these sources. The first parameter is the constant α_i. The seconds is the β_i. The third variable of interest is the variance of the idiosyncratic part.

- We need to be able to estimate the values of α_i, β_i, and Var(ε_i) for a bunch of securities. Numbers corresponding to the beta are readily available all over the Internet. But you need to be careful with these betas, because sometimes they don't make sense, depending on which site you look at.

Regression

- All of the parameters that characterize the security return can be estimated using a statistical technique called regression analysis, which is a process whereby you let data determine the best relationship for "fitting" the data.

- Data on the risk-free rate is difficult to find. Also, the return on "the market" is difficult to find, depending on how you want to define "the market." Kenneth French's personal website has a data library section that provides this data at a variety of different intervals, such as annually. The data is periodically updated to include the most recent periods.

- Regression analysis seeks to find the single straight line that fits the data the best. The word "best" refers to the notion that the average size of the errors about the line is the smallest. What is meant by "error"? In regression analysis, we divide the data into two categories: the dependent variable and explanatory variables.

- The dependent variable is what we are trying to explain. It is the variable that depends on the variables whose variation explains the variation in the dependent variable. In the single-factor model, we are trying to explain the return on an individual security given the return on the market.

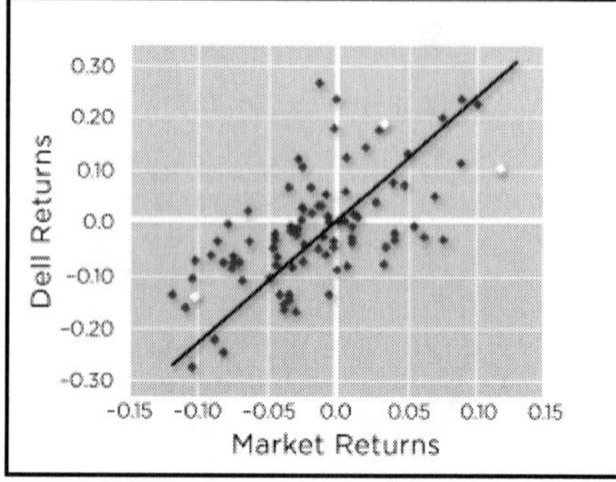

- The return on the individual security is the dependent variable; the return on the market is the explanatory variable. The "error" is the difference between what the explanatory variable "predicts" and what actually happened.

- Regression analysis is all about finding the best line. The criterion used to pick the best line is the sum of squared errors. This is equivalent to looking at the mean squared error, which in this case is simply the average squared error for the observations.

- Regression picks the single line that has the smallest sum of squared errors or the smallest mean squared error. That is, it picks the line that fits the data the best in the sense that the errors from the line are the smallest on average.

- You have to be careful with regression analysis if there are outliers, which are observations that are really out of the ordinary. If you had to pick a line that fits best in terms of mean squared error, you would have to pick a line that goes through the outlier. Because this outlier is very far away from the others, if you put the regression line through it, it will have a gigantic error.

- If you fit a line through that outlier, then the regression line will indicate a negative relationship between the return on the firm and the market. That is, the estimating regression will give you a negative beta.

- The outlier should be downplayed, if not completely ignored. If the regression is re-estimated without the outlier, the regression line will go through the normal cluster of data and will have an upward slope. This will be a much more accurate reflection of the actual relationship.

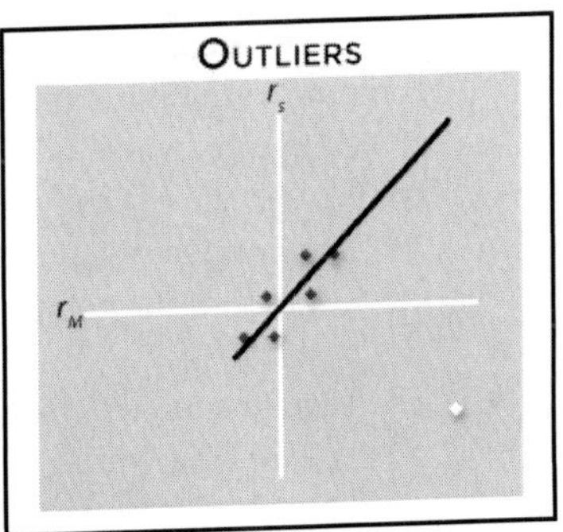

Idiosyncratic Variance

- Once we have the best alpha and beta from regression analysis, we can also get the variance of the idiosyncratic terms. The errors are just the difference between the line and the actual data. If the regression line is the relationship between the return on the security and the market, then the regression errors are the idiosyncratic terms. Thus, the mean square error from the regression is the variance of the idiosyncratic part.

- If you estimate a linear regression single-factor model for a set of securities, you have enough information to write down the variance-covariance matrix, which is simply a table of variances for each security and the covariances of each pair of securities. You could create such a table in a spreadsheet. You can also use the variance-covariance matrix to form efficient or minimum variance portfolios.

- To get the variance-covariance matrix, we need to calculate the variances. Then, we need to calculate the covariance. First, let's consider the variances. The return DGP for security i is $r_i - r_f = \alpha_i + (\beta_i(r_M - r_f)) + \varepsilon_i$.

- Based on this expression, we can calculate the variance of the return on this security. There are only two sources of variation for r_i. Alpha is a constant, so it doesn't vary (by definition). Because beta is a parameter, it presumably doesn't vary either.

- However, because r_M varies, the variance of the component due to common variation is $(\beta_i^2)(\mathrm{Var}(r_M))$. That is, recall that the variance is the expected value of the squared deviations. Because we want to get the variance of the deviation caused by the common factor and the common factor is multiplied by beta, we get beta squared times the variance of the common factor.

- The second source is from the idiosyncratic part. The idiosyncratic part is all the variation that cannot be explained by market movements. The variance of the idiosyncratic terms is then simply the average, or mean, of the squared errors.

- Let's simply denote this variance by $\sigma\varepsilon_i^2$. Then, for any asset *i*, we have the variance of the excess return on *i* equals $\mathrm{Var}(r_i - r_f) = (\beta_i^2(\mathrm{Var}(r_M - r_f))) + \sigma\varepsilon_i^2$.

- Thus, from the regression output, you can decompose the variance into two components: the part that is due to systematic or common factors, which is $\beta_i^2(\mathrm{Var}(r_M - r_f))$; and the part that is due to idiosyncratic factors, which is $\sigma\varepsilon_i^2$.

- If you are going to take an active position in a security that has a significant portion of its variance from the idiosyncratic component, then you should realize that if you take a large position in that security, you will be bearing idiosyncratic risk that would normally be diversified away if you simply held that security in a market-like portfolio.

- Next, let's get the covariances. To see how, line up the return expressions for any two securities.
    - $r_1 - r_f = \alpha_1 + (\beta_1(r_M - r_f)) + e_1$
    - $r_2 - r_f = \alpha_2 + (\beta_2(r_M - r_f)) + e_2$

- If you do this, you can see that they have only one element in common: the excess return on the market $(r_M - r_f)$. The constants α_1 and α_2 don't vary (by definition). Also, e_1 and e_2 don't covary because they are due to things that are unique to each firm or security. When e_1 is negative (e.g., the CEO was discovered committing fraud), that tells you nothing important about any other unique thing that might be happening at the second firm.

- Thus, the only source of covariance is $r_M - r_f$. Because one moves at a rate β_1 and the other at a rate β_2 given movements in the market, the covariance is simply $(\beta_1)(\beta_2)(\text{Var}(r_M))$. So, once you have a set of regression outputs, one for each security, you can form the variance-covariance matrix for a collection of securities using the output of the regressions.

Suggested Reading

Bodie, Kane, and Marcus, *Essentials of Investments*.

Taleb, *The Black Swan*.

Questions to Consider

1. Given your answer to question 1 for Lecture 15, can you confirm that those securities are indeed negatively correlated with the market using information from the Internet? What beta would they need to have to be negatively correlated with the market?

2. Which firms do you think will have higher amounts of idiosyncratic variance than others? Why?

3. Over time, the relative size of idiosyncratic volatility relative to volatility created by common factors has declined. Why do you think that might be true? Increasingly, markets have been more integrated and more wealth is contained in pension funds managed by professional managers. Why might that account for this trend?

The Behavior of Stock Prices

Lecture 16—Transcript

In this lecture, I'm going to show you about the kinds of data that you can get on individual securities from public websites and how you can use that data to get the inputs needed for some of the techniques that we've discussed so far.

In particular, we will start by considering a statistical model of returns. This model will have some parameters which correspond to variables we've discussed in the past. For example, these variables will allow us to calculate covariance. We will then discuss how to estimate these parameters using data on past returns for securities. This technique is known as regression analysis.

With the estimates from regression analysis, we will be able to quantify the characteristics of a security. This will be useful for understanding the security's risk and perhaps the mispricing it might have relative to an asset pricing model. In this lecture, I will show you how to use these estimates to quantify the variance/covariance matrix that is useful in forming optimal risky portfolios.

Versions of the output of this process that we develop in this lecture will be available on websites. While you could simply use these outputs, I want you to have an understanding of where these numbers come from. My hope is that once you see that, you'll have a healthy appreciation for what these numbers mean.

To start, let's develop a simple statistical model to describe the way security returns behave. With such a model, we will be able to build up the variance/covariance matrix. It will be useful to think of the information we have as coming from what is called a data generating process, or a DGP. A data generating process is just a mathematical description of how the observed data is generated. The simplest data generating process is the following: The return on a specific security in excess of the risk-free rate can be divided into two independent sources.

The first source is common across all securities and is related to general features or happenings in the economy as a whole. These features include things like the level of interest rates, the amount of GNP growth, and the level of input prices, like the price of natural gas and petroleum products, and so on.

The second source is specific to a particular firm. This source is idiosyncratic to that security, rather than common across all securities. These things might include things like the fact that the CEO is going through a divorce and she is a bit more distracted than usual, or that the team of R&D specialists has made a technological advance that will make their products more reliable than their competitor's.

To keep the model simple, we will aggregate all of the individual common factors down to one factor, which we will say is the market factor. Since it is hard for us to have a good idea how all these individual common factors aggregate up, we will simply let the market tell us that and use some broad-based index of security prices as the market factor. For example, we could use the return on the S&P 500 to indicate all of the things that affect the market.

There are a couple issues that you might be thinking about with respect to the S&P 500. First, if each of the securities in the S&P 500 has idiosyncratic factors, won't the index also have a bunch of idiosyncratic factors? But, even though the S&P 500 is comprised of individual securities, the idiosyncratic things won't really matter that much in the index, since all of those things are going to sort of average out.

Second, the S&P 500 may not be representative of a sample of the firms throughout the market as a whole. The S&P 500 firms are the largest firms in the economy, and large and small firms are likely to be different and face different challenges and be affected differently by various different economic challenges and conditions. Thus, the S&P 500 may not be a good aggregator of all the common factors. You could get more complicated and use a more broad-based index like the Morgan Stanley Capital International, or the MSCI all country index. Also, you could use some combination of NYSE, NASDAQ, and AMEX stocks, which represent essentially all of the securities available to be traded in the United States. Of course, if you look at the correlation between all of these indices, they're all very high, exceeding about 90 to 95%. For simplicity, I'm going to use r_{M} to denote the return on the market, where you can decide which data that you want to use. All of these data sources are readily available on the web for either the NYSE, NASDAQ, and AMEX, or for the MSCI.

Now that we have a common aggregator for all the common factors, how do we get the idiosyncratic factors for each individual security? That must be a monumental task. Well, if you think that you have all of the common factors appropriately aggregated in the market factor r_M, then it's actually very easy. The idiosyncratic component of return, by definition, is simply everything that is not explained by the common factor.

We can summarize the DGP via a mathematical expression as follows: $r_i - r_f = \alpha_i + \beta_i \times (r_M - r_f) + \varepsilon_i$. In the expression, r_i is the return in the individual security, and r_{f} is the risk-free rate. So, $r_i - r_f$ is the return on the security in excess of the risk-free rate. The common factor is the return on the market, R_m, in excess of the risk-free rate. So the common factor is $R_m - r_f$. For example, if the market return is 10% and the risk-free rate is 3%, then the excess return on the market is 7%. If the return on an individual security is 12%, then its excess return will be 12% − 3% = 9%. That would be the excess return on that individual security.

This model is called a "single factor model" because there is just one factor that explains the returns on the securities. In this case, the single factor is the return on the market. This single factor model is also called the "market model."

Although every security is affected by the common factor $R_m - r_f$, the amount that is affected by $R_m - r_f$ can vary by security according to the β_i, the coefficient on the common factor in the expression. Thus, the amount the ith security is affected by the common factor is going to be $\beta_i \times (R_m - r_f)$.

For example, SteveCo might have a β equal to 0.5. AlbiCo might have a β equal to 1.5. Some securities—for example, KathrynCo—might have a negative beta (β), for example, $\beta = -0.3$. Thus, if the excess return on the market was 7% in a given period, then the component of return for SteveCo will be 0.5 × 7% = 3.5%. For AlbiCo, it's going to be 1.5 × 7%, or 10.5%, and for KathrynCo, it will have an excess return of −0.3 × 7%, or −2.1%. That is, since the market went up, the return on KathrynCo will be negative.

By the way, what explains the variation in betas across securities? You can think of the beta as summarizing how the return reacts to market conditions, as summarized by the market return. For example, an airline firm is likely to have a very large beta. A significant fraction of profits from airlines derive from business travel. This kind of travel is not very price-sensitive. It is typically scheduled at later notice, and the prices then are not discounted. Thus, if the economy is booming, there is likely to be significant business travel, which raises profits. At the same time, the market will be up reflecting generally rising profits for everyone. Thus, given the higher profits to the airline, the return on the airline will be high when the return on the market is high.

But, the market also includes a bunch of firms that are not as sensitive to the boom or the bust cycles of the market as a whole. Thus, the market return will be the average sensitivity of all firms. The airline will have a greater-than-average sensitivity. Thus, the airline will be an amplification of the market, and it will have a beta that's greater than one.

Consider a grocery store. Its sells about the same amount of food when the economy is booming as when it is in a recession. However, it may sell more luxury items, those with larger profits margins built in, when the economy is booming versus when it is in a recession. Thus, the beta of a grocery store is likely to be positive, but not nearly as sensitive to the economy as, say, an airline. So, while the airline return will be an amplification of the market, the grocer will be a damped version of the market.

So SteveCo, in our example previously, is a grocer, while AlbiCo is an airline. By the way, since I like to cook, I let SteveCo be a grocer. Albi is my dog. He's a giant Bernese Mountain Dog, and he's fairly sedate, but he overreacts when anyone comes to the door. That's why I gave him a beta bigger than one.

What about KathrynCo? Well, Kathryn is my wife. Early in our relationship—this is 1000 years ago—she was in law school and worked as a lawyer for many years after we got married. While most law firms are partnerships and not publicly traded, I was able to effectively have—and I hesitate to use the word, but here goes—ownership in the security of a negative beta security.

She worked for a firm that represented plaintiffs in securities fraud cases. Most people don't sue when the market is up. They don't even look to see if there's anything wrong since they're making a lot of money. But, when the market price is down and the security price is down, that's when people tend to sue. And if the whole market is down, there's even more people who like to sue in that case.

So, when the market was down, her firm made more money. When the market was up, her firm made less money. And since her bonus was tied to firm performance, my return was low when the market was up and high when the market was down. That is, there was an inverse relationship. The beta in her data generating process is negative.

As we've seen, negative correlation is useful. It allows you to shift the efficient frontier farther to the left. It allows you to reduce the amount of variance for a given amount of expected return. And a negative beta indicates negative correlation. Since the returns on KathrynCo are negatively correlated with the market, I was able to shift my efficient frontier more to the left than most people who can't trade in securities law firms.

She, by the way, thinks to this day that I married her for love. By the way, I have yet to gaze into her eyes lovingly and say, "Darling, you have the most beautiful negative beta." This is going to be our secret.

Back to the math. In the expression, there are two other parts to the data generating process. The α_i is a constant component. It says that the excess return for the security has a constant component that doesn't change with the market as the market moves. We'll discuss later how to interpret the value of alpha (α). The second other part is everything else. The idiosyncratic part. All the stuff that is not explained by the market movement.

So, going back to the examples, let's say that SteveCo, that has an excess return of 9% (its raw return was 12% and the risk-free rate was 3%). Its beta is 0.5 and the excess return on the market was 7%, so the common component is 0.5 × 7%, or 3.5%. Let the alpha for SteveCo be 0. Thus, the idiosyncratic return must be the epsilon, such that $0.09 = 0 + 0.5 \times (0.07) + \varepsilon_i \rightarrow \varepsilon_i = 0.09 - 0.035 = 0.055$ or 5.5%.

Thus, given the beta of 0.5, it must have been the case that there was a lot of good idiosyncratic news on SteveCo. The market being up was good news for SteveCo. But there must have been some extra good news specific to SteveCo's business that boosted the return over 3.5% due to the market being up.

So, with the single factor model, we have two sources of variation in returns—the market and idiosyncratic returns. With the single factor model, we have three parameters that characterize the nature of the relationship between returns and these three sources.

The first parameter is α_i. The second is the beta. The third variable of interest is the variance of the idiosyncratic part. We need to be able to estimate values of α_i, β_i, and the variance of the idiosyncratic part for a bunch of securities. Numbers corresponding to the beta are readily available on the Internet. For example, if you go to Yahoo! Finance and type in the name of a company to get to their page, it will provide you information on the betas for those companies. There's a list on the left-hand side of the page that lists separate pages of information organized by type of information. Under the "Key Statistics" link, you will find the beta for a security.

You need to be a little careful when you look at these betas, as sometimes they don't make a lot of sense. Depending upon which site you look at, they estimate the betas differently. Many sites make ad hoc adjustments that produce kind of odd estimates. Once we see the basic technique for estimating a beta, I will revisit why the numbers on the web may seem a little bit odd.

All of the parameters that characterize the security return can be estimated using a statistical technique called regression analysis. Regression analysis is a process whereby you let the data determine the best relationship for fitting the data. To see exactly what that means, let's consider a bunch of data we have on a particular security. Think of a plot of the monthly return on, say, Dell Computer against the monthly return on the market.

To make this concrete, let's say that for every month I collected a pair of returns for Dell and the market. You can do this too. Yahoo! Finance and Google Finance both allow you to download data on the returns for many individual securities into a spreadsheet. Once downloaded, I'm going to subtract the risk-free rate that applies during that month from both the return on Dell and the return on the market. I used the T-bill rate for securities maturing in a month for the risk-free rate. Make sure that you if you download monthly data, the risk-free return is not annualized. Rather, it should be the effective monthly rate to correspond to the monthly return that you have on Dell and the market, for example.

Data on the risk-free rate is hard to find. Also, the return on the market is also a little bit hard to find, depending upon how you want to define the market. Kenneth French's personal website has a data library section that provides you data at a variety of different intervals, like annually. The data is periodically updated to include the most recent periods. All you have to do is Google "Ken French's website" and you'll find this data. As you will see later, this site also provides other data that are extremely useful for the types of analysis that we're going to be discussing in later lectures. I highly recommend Professor French's website.

Once the data is obtained, for each Dell market return pair, plot Dell's return on the vertical axis against the market return on the horizontal axis. Any spreadsheet program will have a routine that produces such a scatter plot. If you do this, you will get a scatter plot of points. It will look like a shotgun shot at a piece of paper—lots of dots all over the place. Hopefully, this scatter plot will have some trend to it.

Regression analysis seeks to find the single straight line that fits that scatter the best. What do I mean by best? By best, I mean that the average size of the errors about the line are the smallest. What do I mean by error? In regression analysis, we divide the data into two categories—the dependent variable and the explanatory variables.

The dependent variable is the thing we're trying to explain. It's the variable that depends upon the variables whose variation explains the variation in that variable. In the single factor model, we're trying to explain the return on an individual security given the common factor, which is the return on the market. The return on the individual security is then the dependent variable. The return on the market is the explanatory variable.

The error is the difference between what the explanatory variable predicts and what actually happened. Again, consider a plot of Dell against the market. Draw a line through the scatter. Then, for a particular observation of the market return, read up to the value of Dell that is on that line. This is the value predicted by the line that you drew. The error is the difference between the actual return for Dell for that observation and the predicted value for Dell that you got off the line.

For example, let's say that one observation for Dell and the market is 4% for Dell and 10% for the market. Let's say you drew a line such that the line predicts a 10% return for Dell. Since the actual return is 4%, the error is going to be 4% – 10%, or –6%. If you do this for every observation, you will have a series of errors for each observation. Regression is all about finding the best line. So, let's see what criterion this analysis uses for determining that best line.

The criterion used is to pick the best line in terms of the sum of squared errors. By the way, this is equivalent to looking at the mean squared error, which, in this case, is simply the average squared error divided by the number of observations.

Regressions pick the single line that has the smallest sum of squared errors, or the smallest mean squared error. That is, it picks the line that fits the data the best in the sense that the errors from the line are the smallest on average. Now, you have to be careful with regression analysis if there are things called outliers. Outliers are observations that are really sort of out of the ordinary. For example, an observation on the day of a market crash or a day where something extreme happened in the firm. If you're trying to predict the relationship that will occur during normal times, then you may get misleading answers by using the whole data if you don't recognize the fact that you have an excessive effect with an outlier.

To see this, consider again a scatter of the data that has an upward trend that is fairly clumped together. But, in addition to this main clump of data, there's a single outlier that is for a day in which the market soared but the firm fell very sharply. This might have been a day in which the CEO died in a plane crash, very bad news, but Ben Bernanke said that we would continue to keep money supply very loose. This is really good news for the market. This observation is very far away from the rest, and it's very unusual. It's hardly a normal circumstance.

If you had to pick a line that fits best in terms of mean squared error, you would have to pick a line that goes through the outlier. Because the outlier is very far away from the others, if you don't put the regression line through that outlier, the outlier is going to have a gigantic error. And when you square that error, you get gigantic squared, which I think is ginormous. If you fit a line through the outlier, then the regression line will indicate a negative relationship in this case between the return on the firm and the return on the market. That is, the estimated regression will indicate a negative beta. But remember, the data was upward-sloping. The real relationship is such that the scatter was upward-sloping.

All but one of the days of the data indicated there was a positive relationship between the return on that firm and the return on the market. The outlier should be completely downplayed, if not completely ignored. If the regression is re-estimated without the outlier, the regression line will go through the normal cluster of data and have an upward slope. This is a much more accurate reflection of the actual relationship.

I suggest looking at the data by plotting and looking for outliers. Similarly, when you get estimates of beta off the Internet, I suggest you look at the data to see if the estimates are from anything sort of sensible, or whether they're maybe subject to outliers, too.

Once you have the best alpha and the best beta from the regression analysis, we can also get the variance of the idiosyncratic terms. Recall that the errors are just the difference between the line and the actual data. If the regression line is the relationship between the return on the security and the return on the market, then the regression errors are simply those idiosyncratic terms.

Thus, the mean squared error from the regression is the variance of the idiosyncratic part. This number will be important later in the course when we discuss active versus passive management. If you estimate a linear regression single-factor model for a set of securities, now you're going to have enough information in order to write down the variance/covariance matrix.

Recall that the variance/covariance matrix is simply a table of variances for each security and the covariance of each pair of securities. Now, you could create such a table in a spreadsheet. You would list the securities across the top and down the side.

The first entry in the table would correspond to the first column, for the first security, and the first row, also for the first security. That entry would contain the covariance between security 1 and itself. This is simply the variance of the first security.

The next entry over to the right would correspond to the first security, from the first row, and the second security, from the second column. This entry is the covariance of the first security with the second security. Similarly, the entry in the second row and the first column is the covariance of the second security with the first security. By the way, this is just the same number as the covariance of the first security with the second security.

Thus, the matrix that we've built in this spreadsheet table is symmetric around the diagonal. The diagonal elements are the variances of each security. Above and below the diagonal are mirror images of each other since the covariance between, say, security I and J is equal to the covariance between J and I.

Also, recall that you can use the variance/covariance matrix to form efficient portfolios, or minimum variance portfolios. To get the variance/covariance matrix, you need to calculate the variances for each individual security. Then we need also to calculate the covariance.

First, let's consider the variance. Remember that the data generating process for the security is: $r_i - r_f = \alpha_i + \beta_i(R_m - r_f) + \varepsilon_i$. Based on this expression, we can calculate the variance of the return on this security. There are only two sources of variation in r_i. Alpha is a constant, by definition, so it doesn't vary. Since beta is a parameter, it presumably doesn't vary either. But, R_m does vary. The variance component that's due to the variation in the market return is going to be the $\beta_i^2 \times \mathrm{Var}(R_m)$. That is, recall that the variance is the expected value of squared deviations. Since we want to get the variance of the deviation caused by the common factor and the common factor is multiplied by the beta, we get a β^2 times the variance of the common factor.

The second source is from the idiosyncratic part. The idiosyncratic part is all of the variation that cannot be explained by the market movements. The variance of the idiosyncratic terms is then simply the average, or the mean, of the squared errors. Any regression output from any statistical package, say, from a spreadsheet program, will have this labeled as MSE, for mean squared error. Let's simply denote this variance by $\Sigma\varepsilon_i^{2.}$

Then, for any asset *i*, we have the variance of the excess return is equal to: $\mathrm{Var}(r_i - r_f) = \beta_i^2\,\mathrm{Var}(R_m - r_f) + \Sigma\varepsilon_i^2$. Thus, from the regression output, you can decompose the variance into two components: the part that is due to systematic or common factors [that's the $\beta_i^2\,\mathrm{Var}(R_m - r_f)$]. The second part is due to idiosyncratic factors, that's the $\Sigma\varepsilon_i^2$ that you get as MSE off the regression output.

If you're going to take an active position in a security that has a significant portion of its variance from the idiosyncratic component, then you should realize that you're going to take a large position in that security and you're going to be bearing idiosyncratic risk that you would normally diversify away if you simply held that security in a market-like portfolio. In a subsequent lecture, we'll examine exactly how you should use the information on the idiosyncratic variance when forming an optimal portfolio with active positions.

Next, let's get to the covariances. To see how to calculate the covariances, line up the return expressions for any two securities. If you do that, you can see that the only thing they have in common is the return on the market ($R_m - r_f$). The constants, $\alpha 1$ and $\alpha 2$, don't vary by definition. They're constant.

Also, ε_1 and ε_2 don't covary because they are due to things that are unique to each firm or security. When ε_1 is negative, say, for example, the CEO was discovered committing fraud, that tells you nothing about any of the other unique things that might be happening at the other firm. Thus, the only source of covariance is $R_m - r_f$. Since one moves at a rate β_1 and the other at a rate of β_2, given movements in the market, the covariance is simply $\beta_1 \times \beta_2 \times \text{Var}(R_m)$.

So, once you have a set of regression outputs, one for each security, you can form the variance/covariance matrix for a collection of securities using the output of these regressions. Note that a K-by-K matrix has K^2 entries. For 10 securities, that's 100 different entries. But, to get those entries, all you need to know is 10 betas and 10 idiosyncratic variances and one variance for the market—that's only 21 outputs from regression. If you have 100 securities, then you're going to need only 201 parameters from the regressions, and that will allow you to determine 100 × 100 different entries in the variance/covariance matrix. That's 10,000 different entries.

So, in addition to being able to characterize the variance and covariance of many securities, the regression output also provides estimates of alpha. As we will see in the next few lectures, asset pricing models have implications regarding what the value of alpha should be. We will also see that if alpha is not what it should be, then there may be a trade strategy that can generate some excess profits. In order to optimally exploit such trade strategies, the information on the variance component and the betas we obtain from the regression analysis will be very important. We will discuss how to use these estimates over the next few lectures.

The Capital Asset Pricing Model (CAPM)

Lecture 17

In this lecture, you will explore what an equilibrium asset pricing model is in general. As part of this exploration, you will learn what equilibrium is and why an equilibrium model is useful. In addition, you will learn about the most popular and well-known asset pricing model: the capital asset pricing model (CAPM). In the process, you will see why and how the implications of such a model depend on assumptions. Finally, you will address the intuition that CAPM generates. The outcome of this process is obtaining a way to measure risk in the context of a portfolio.

Equilibrium

- There are two types of analyses that economists (and financial economists) conduct: normative and positive. Normative analysis tells you how you should behave—that is, it gives you advice for optimally solving a problem that you as an individual face.

- The second type of analysis is positive. With this type of analysis, economists posit individual behavior and the mechanisms by which individuals interact. Then, they derive the implications of those behaviors and mechanisms. In economics and finance, most of the implications are on market prices.

- Scientists, including financial economists, are interested in understanding how the world works. Because there is no manual that describes how the world works, we instead posit certain relationships that generate implications so that we can test those implications. This is the scientific method. Financial economists are constantly making assumptions, deriving their implications, testing these implications, and eliminating those that are inconsistent with the data.

- While many people may only be interested in understanding how the world works for its own sake, another reason that we model investor behavior is to derive equilibrium implications, which might actually help us with normative analysis.

- A system is in equilibrium when it is at rest. The system is at rest when there are no internal tensions or forces that are creating change. Knowing about equilibrium allows us to make some predictions when we are out of equilibrium. But, more importantly, if we know where a stock price is going eventually, we can predict its average movement over time based on knowing the equilibrium value.

- In finance, we model investors' behavior so that we can make them interact with each other mathematically in order to predict where the equilibrium price will be once everyone is done making trades. This tells us where prices will end up. This then tells us the direction prices will move on average.

- Of course, one potential drawback of this approach is that the whole premise is wrong. The premise is that something happens, then things react, until they stop happening. Instead, what is more likely is that something happens, things react, and then something new happens. That is, we never have "until they stop happening."

- Most economists would say that equilibrium analysis is still useful, however, because it predicts what happens between stimuli: There is some structure to the reaction. Furthermore, perhaps we can get better predictions if we can build even bigger models to figure out the equilibrium behavior of the stimuli. Rather than give up on the notion of equilibrium, we just need more complex models with more complex equilibria.

CAPM

- The first normative result we get from the capital asset pricing model (CAPM) is a measure of risk for an individual security. Remember, the return variance of an individual security cannot be risk.

- The second normative result is a measure of the amount of extra return an investor should get for bearing the risk of an individual security. This is normative in the sense that it tells you the rate to use to discount future cash flows given the riskiness of those cash flows. It also tells you when a security is mispriced—which then suggests a trade opportunity.

- As is true with all equilibrium asset pricing models, CAPM is a model of the cross-section of returns—that is, CAPM tells us what explains or generates variation in average returns across the large set of securities available in the market. Whether you take the normative advice of CAPM depends on whether you believe that CAPM describes the world you live in.

- Equilibrium models all have the same elements. They all have individual demands as a function of prices. Then, they impose the condition that supply equals demand. When supply equals demand, we are in equilibrium. When supply equals demand, there is no need for prices to change.

- So, we need investor demands first. What are the demands used by CAPM? People have information on how the returns of all the securities are jointly distributed, and based on that information, they pick an optimal risky portfolio that maximizes the Sharpe ratio, which is the expected return on a portfolio minus the risk-free rate—the expected excess return—all divided by the standard deviation of the return on that portfolio. The Sharpe ratio is a measure of the extra return you get in excess of the risk-free rate per unit of standard deviation.

- By assuming that investors pick portfolios to maximize the Sharpe ratio, we assume that all investors have mean/variance utility functions—that they don't care about other things like skewness. However, it is clear that the model will capture something important because it is clear that investors do care about the mean and the variance of their returns.

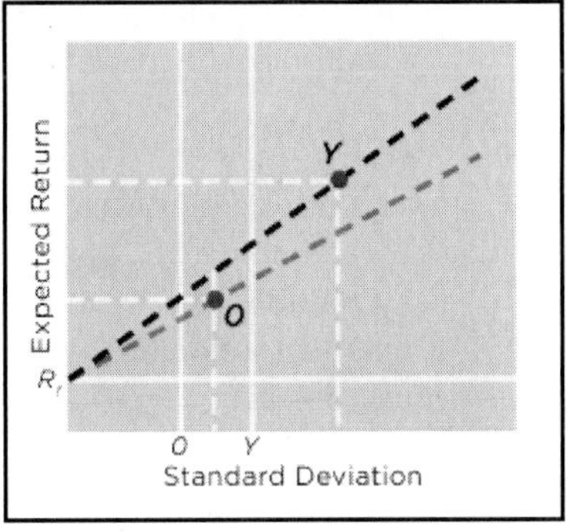

- The standard deviation of the return on an individual security is not a good measure of risk. However, from now on, the standard deviation of the best risky portfolio will be called "risk." If it is the best risky portfolio, then you want to hold it—and only it. If it is the only risky portfolio you hold, then all the variance you face in terms of your wealth comes from the returns on this portfolio. In that case, the standard deviation of the return on this portfolio is risk. So, standard deviations for individual securities are not risk; the standard deviation for the best risky portfolio is risk.

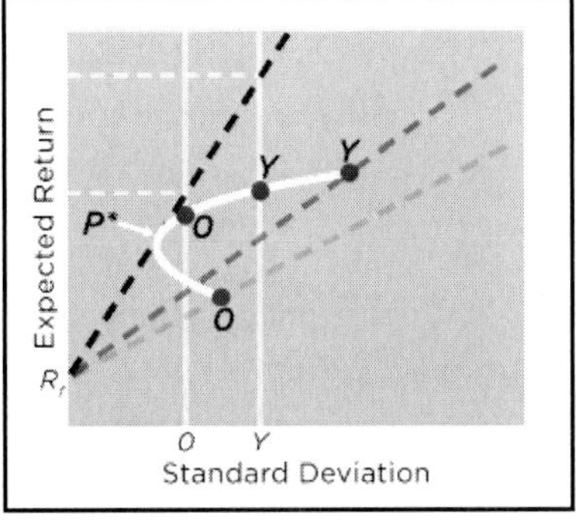

- What is the best risky portfolio? You want a portfolio with a high Sharpe ratio because, if you're going to take on some risk, you want to get paid as much as possible per unit of risk you take on. Also recall that you can control the total amount of risk by deciding how much money to invest in that risky portfolio and how much money to invest in risk-free securities (like savings accounts).

- This last step is key. It says that everyone wants a high Sharpe ratio. Some investors don't mind risk, while others do. Both types of people can control the total amount of risk in their overall portfolio—which includes the risky and riskless investments—by deciding how much to put in the best risky portfolio. They should not control risk by picking a different risky portfolio.

Market Clearing

- Everyone wants the same portfolio of risky securities. That portfolio must be one where supply equals demand. As such, that optimal risky portfolio that everyone wants must be the market portfolio. If not, then we don't have market clearing—we don't have supply equals demand.

- So, the prices of securities adjust until everyone wants the market portfolio. If the market portfolio is the optimal portfolio, then we can ask, what is the risk of an individual security in the context of the best portfolio you can hold? We will measure risk as the volatility or variance of the return on our risky investment portfolio. The risky investment portfolio is what generates variation in our wealth, which is risk.

- If our overall portfolio consists of risk-free assets and the optimal risky portfolio, then it is fairly clear that our only source of risk is the variance of the return on the risky portfolio. So, let's measure the risk of an individual security as the amount that security contributes to the variance of the return on the optimal risky portfolio.

- To do that, we just take a mathematical derivative, which is an analytical expression for the rate of change in something given a change in something else. In the case of the security, we ask, what is the rate of change in the market portfolio variance given that we change the weight on the ith security a little bit? That derivative is equal to something called the market beta, which is defined as $\beta_i = \dfrac{Cov(R_i, R_M)}{Var(R_M)}$.

- This is equivalent to the slope of a regression line of the excess return on security *i* on the excess market return. The beta of a security with respect to the market portfolio is the measure of risk for that security.

- We could ask how much a particular security contributes to the variance of any portfolio—for example, the one you currently hold (which may not be the market portfolio). Given what you hold, we could calculate the covariance of the return on security *i* with the return on your risky portfolio, divided by the variance of the return on your portfolio. That would be the amount of risk security *i* contributes to your portfolio. If we all held different portfolios, then we would all need to have different measures of risk.

- This is why CAPM is so popular. It says that there is only one measure of risk for a security that works for everyone. That measure is the beta of that security with the market only—because we are all supposed to be holding just that portfolio. This makes it easy. We can tell everyone the same thing.

- Market beta is risk. But, if you are not holding the market, the market beta may not be risk for you. However, unless you have a good reason not to, you should be holding the market as your risky portfolio.

The CAPM Pricing Equation

- For any individual risky security, we have the following.
  - $E(R_i) - \gamma\beta_i = R_f =$
  - $E(R_i) = R_f + \beta_i\,(E(R_M) - R_f)$

- This is the CAPM pricing equation. Intuitively, it says that the return on the ith security should be equal to the risk-free rate plus an amount extra to compensate you for holding the risk of that security, where the risk is measured by its market beta and the price per unit of risk is $E(R_M) - R_f$.

- If you have a security that has more units of risk—that is, its beta is high—then it should get a higher expected return. The more units of risk, the higher the expected return.

- CAPM is a single-factor model. It says that there is only one source of risk—the risk that the market will go up and down. Thus, whether a security is risky or not depends on how correlated it is with the market. A security that goes down when the market is down is risky. Just when you need a good payoff—when the market is down—so is the return on that security. Risk is correlation.

- CAPM is also a little judgmental. It says that you only get compensated for the risk of a security in the context of the market portfolio, even if you don't hold the market portfolio. Because everyone else only holds the market, then you should only get compensated for the amount of risk that security produces in that portfolio. If you want to hold some nonoptimal portfolio, go ahead. But the market will not compensate you for the extra variation a security produces in a suboptimal portfolio because no one forced you to do that.

- CAPM also tells us that idiosyncratic volatility—the variation not explained by systematic or market movements—does not matter. Such idiosyncratic variation is due to economic factors that are not common, or shared, across securities. If you hold a well-diversified portfolio, then all of the idiosyncratic volatility will get diversified away, and what is left is only variation created by common, or market, movements.

- Another way to interpret CAPM is that the market only pays you for risk that cannot be avoided. The movements that cannot be avoided are the movements caused by general market conditions that are common to all. Because you can eliminate idiosyncratic volatility, you should not be compensated for bearing it.

Suggested Reading

Bernstein, *Capital Ideas*.

Bodie, Kane, and Marcus, *Essentials of Investments*.

Clement, "Interview with Eugene Fama."

Fama and French, "The CAPM is Wanted, Dead or Alive."

Questions to Consider

1. The CAPM is based on assumptions about investors that imply that the "market portfolio" is the sole optimal risky portfolio that all investors should hold. Do you hold the market portfolio? If not, why not? Are you not holding it because you think the portfolio you are holding is better? Or are you not holding it because you haven't considered it?

2. The interior decorator fallacy says that different types of people who vary by risk aversion should control risk not by considering different sets of risky securities, but by altering the amount of money they put at risk in the first place. Do you think that you consider different sets of potential investments than other investors you feel have different tolerances for risk? If so, why? Do you think that the interior decorator fallacy is a fallacy?

The Capital Asset Pricing Model (CAPM)

Lecture 17—Transcript

In this lecture, we will explore an equilibrium asset pricing model called the Capital Asset Pricing Model, or CAPM for short. To put this model in context, let's review a bit. So far, we examined what causes security returns to fluctuate.

For example, we have examined how bond prices change given changes in expectations of future shifts in yield curves. We've also examined how stock prices change with the arrival of new information about future cash flows and growth opportunities. Given these fluctuations in security values, we have then examined how to combine securities together into a portfolio to control the amount of risk that you have to face in order to achieve a particular target expected return.

So far, we've examined the features of security returns so that you can optimally react. For example, we answered the following two important questions: (1) Given the features of returns, what is the optimal portfolio that minimizes the variance for a given target expected return? and (2) Given the whole efficient frontier, which risky portfolio on that frontier is best?

So far, we've taken the characteristics of returns as given and optimized with respect to some objective. An asset pricing model is very different. Rather than take the return characteristics as given, an asset pricing model answers the question "What should the distribution of security returns be?" That is, these models are less about what you should do and more about what the market should look like.

In this lecture, we will do three main things. First, we will explore what an equilibrium asset pricing model is in general. As part of this exploration, we will discuss what is meant by equilibrium. We will also discuss why an equilibrium model might be useful.

Second, we will build the most popular and well-known asset pricing model, the CAPM. As we build this model, you'll see why and how the implications of such a model depend upon the assumptions.

The third thing that we will do is stress the intuition that CAPM generates. The outcome of this process is that we will get a way to measure risk in the context of a portfolio. This is one of the most important ideas of the whole course.

Let's start. So, what's an equilibrium? And why might you care about one? As background, realize that there are two types of analyses that economists and financial economists typically conduct. One is normative, and the other is positive.

Normative analysis tells you how you should behave. That is, it gives you advice. So far, much of the course has been normative. It's clear why you might want normative analysis. It tells you how to do something optimally. It gives you advice for solving a problem that you as an individual would face.

The second type of analysis is positive. With this type of analysis, economists posit individual behavior and the mechanism by which individuals interact. They then derive the implications of those behaviors and mechanisms. In economics and finance, most of the implications are on market prices.

It is not clear why an individual should care about this kind of equilibrium model of behavior. Scientists, including financial economists, care because they're interested in understanding how the world works. Since there is really no manual that describes how the world works, we instead posit certain relationships that generate implications so that we can test those implications.

Sherlock Holmes stated that "When you have eliminated the impossible, whatever remains, however improbable, must be the truth." This is the scientific method. Financial economists are constantly making assumptions, deriving their implications, and testing these implications, and then eliminating those that are inconsistent with the data.

While many people may only be interested in understanding how the world works for its own sake, another reason we model investor behavior is to derive equilibrium implications, which might actually help us with some normative analysis.

So, let's turn to the notion of an equilibrium. What do I mean by equilibrium? We say that a system is in equilibrium when it is at rest. The system is at rest when there are no internal tensions or forces that are creating change.

Imagine a ping pong ball and a bowl. When I drop the ball from the top of one side, it rolls around and eventually comes to rest at the very bottom of the bowl. Unless something else happens to, say, jostle the bowl, it remains at the bottom. That is, it's at rest. It's in equilibrium.

Why do we care about equilibrium? We care because knowing it allows us to make some predictions when we are out of equilibrium. That is, if I drop the ball from the top again, you will likely predict that it's going to roll around. But, more importantly, you can predict some structure to the way it rolls around. For example, it seems to go down to the bottom and then back up the side and then down to the bottom and up the side, but each time it goes less far up the side, until it eventually comes to rest at the bottom. That is, we see that it swings less and less, and it always ends up at the bottom.

If the future price of a security is analogous to the future position of the ball, then you can see why we might want to do this type of equilibrium analysis and make equilibrium predictions as part of an investment strategy. If we know where the stock price is going, we could predict its average movement over time based on knowing this equilibrium value.

In finance, we model investors' behavior so that we can make them interact with each other mathematically in order to predict where the equilibrium price will be once everyone is done making trades. This tells us where prices will end up. This tells us the direction prices will move on average.

Of course, one potential drawback of this approach is that the whole premise is wrong. The premise is: (1) something happens (the ball is dropped), then (2) things react (the ball rolls around), and then (3) until they stop happening (the ball comes to rest at the bottom). Is that a process we have ever really observed?

Instead, what is more likely is that: (1) something happens, (2) things react, and (3) something new happens. That is, we never, ever get to the point where "until things stop happening" occurs.

Consider the movement of the ball if we were to keep, say, changing the position of the bowl. Most economists would say that the equilibrium analysis is still useful, however, because it still predicts what happens between stimuli. There is some structure to the reaction.

Furthermore, perhaps we can get better predictions if we can build even bigger models to figure out the equilibrium behavior of the stimuli. That is, maybe we need to model how I move the bowl in addition to modeling what happens inside the bowl. Rather than give up on the notion of equilibrium, we just need more complex models with more complex equilibrium. That is, the solution is not less science; the solution is actually more science. And I have to admit I'm sympathetic to this view.

Let's take a closer look at the equilibrium by building the capital asset pricing model. To give away a bit of the ending, let me highlight some of the normative results that we get from CAPM first. The first normative result is that there's a measure of risk for an individual security that comes out of CAPM. Remember, the return variance of an individual security cannot be risk. We'll see what it is in the CAPM.

The second normative result is a measure of the amount of extra return an investor should get for bearing the risk of an individual security. This is normative in the sense that it tells you the rate to use when discounting future cash flows, given the riskiness of those cash flows. It also tells you when a security is mispriced, which then suggests a trade opportunity. We will discuss how to exploit such mispricings in a subsequent lecture.

As is true with all equilibrium asset pricing models, CAPM is a model of the cross-section of returns. That is, CAPM tells us what explains or generates variation in the average returns across the large set of securities available in the market. It tells us why, for example, the return on a grocery store would be smaller, than, say, the average return on a pharmaceutical company. Whether you take the normative advice of CAPM depends upon whether you believe that CAPM describes the world we live in. So, it's really important for us to sort of derive what CAPM is so you can see whether you believe in it or not.

Equilibrium models all have the same elements. They all have individual demands as a function of prices. Then they impose the conditions that supply equals demand. When supply equals demand, we say that we are in equilibrium. When supply equals demand, there is no need for prices to change or adjust.

So, we need investor demands first. What are the demands used by CAPM? For this, we are going to use the ideas that we've developed earlier. People have information on how the returns of all securities are jointly distributed and, based on that information, they pick an optimal risky portfolio that maximizes the Sharpe ratio.

Recall that the Sharpe ratio for a portfolio is the expected return on that portfolio minus the risk-free rate—that is, the expected excess return—all of that divided by the standard deviation of the return on that portfolio. The Sharpe ratio is a measure of the extra return you get in excess of the risk-free rate per unit of standard deviation.

We just made a big assumption. Remember when we talked about investor behavior and the expected utility hypothesis? Recall that I said we mostly use utility functions that are easy to use. And many of these utility functions imply that people only care about expected return and variance in their wealth.

By assuming that investors pick portfolios to maximize the Sharpe ratio, we just assumed that all investors have mean/variance utility functions—that they don't care about other things like skewness. But, it is clear in the model that we'll capture something important, though, since it's clear that investors do care about mean and the variance.

So far, I've been very careful to not call standard deviation or variance "risk." That's because, as we've seen in previous lectures, you can combine securities with high standard deviations together in a portfolio to get a low portfolio standard deviation. So the standard deviation of the return on an individual security is not a good measure of risk.

From now on, however, I'm going to call the standard deviation of the best risky portfolio "risk." If it is the best risky portfolio, then that's the one that you want to hold, and it's the only one that you want to hold. If it's the only risky portfolio that you want to hold, then all the variance that you face in terms of the return on your wealth comes from that portfolio. In that case, the standard deviation, or the variance is risk. So, standard deviations for individual securities are not risk. The standard deviation for the best risky portfolio is risk.

What is the best risky portfolio? You want a portfolio with a high Sharpe ratio because, if you're going to be taking on some risk, you want to get paid as much as possible per unit of risk as you can.

Also recall that you can control the amount of risk by deciding how much money to invest in that risky portfolio and how much money you want to invest in risk-free securities (like savings accounts). This last step is key. It says that everyone wants a high Sharpe ratio. Some investors don't mind risk, while others do. But both types of people can control the total amount of risk in their overall portfolio, which includes both risky and riskless investments, by deciding how much to put in the best risky portfolio. They should not control risk by picking a different risky portfolio.

To see this last point more closely, let's consider a situation in which brokers show different types of clients different sets of securities. Specifically, let's say that there are two sets of risky securities—one set that's intended for, say, young clients, while there's another set that's intended for older clients. With the set intended with younger clients, let's say that you can create a portfolio. Let's call that portfolio Y. And with the set intended for older clients, you can create a portfolio. Let's call that one O.

Let's say that portfolio Y has a high standard deviation of 35%, and its expected return is also high at 28%. Let's say that O has a lower standard deviation of only 15% and also a lower expected return of 11. And let's let the risk-free rate be 2%.

Let's say that older people only feel comfortable with a level of risk in their wealth of 5%, a standard deviation of 5%. What will older people be able to achieve in terms of expected return if they are only shown the securities that generate portfolio O?

If older people use O as the risky portfolio, then to get a standard deviation of only 5%, they would put 5/15 of their money into portfolio O and the rest (10/15) into the risk-free investments. Five divided by 15 is the ratio of the target standard deviation and the standard deviation of portfolio O's return. The expected return of this overall risky plus risk-free portfolio is (5/15) × 0.11 + (10/15) × 0.02 = 0.05 (or 5%). The standard deviation of the return on this portfolio is, by design, 5%. One last thing. The Sharpe ratio for this portfolio is (0.05 − 0.02)/0.05 = 0.6.

Note that the Sharpe ratio for the portfolio O is also 0.6. That is, for every 1%age point of standard deviation, O generates 60% in excess returns over the risk-free rate. Since older people only want 5% standard deviation, they will only get 0.05 × 0.60 = 0.03 (or 3%) in excess of the risk-free rate with their overall portfolio with (5/15 at risk and 10/15 in the safe). Since the risk-free return is 2%, then they're going to get the 3% plus the 2%, they're going to get 5% in total, given a standard deviation for the overall portfolio of also 5%. So, 5% is the expected return.

Let's say that younger people feel comfortable with more standard deviation, say 25%. If the young only use portfolio Y and invest an amount such that the overall portfolio only has 25% standard deviation, then they will get an expected return of actually 20.6%. That is, they're going to invest 25/35 in portfolio Y and the rest in risk-free T-bills. The expected return on the overall portfolio is 20.6%, and the Sharpe ratio is going to be (0.206 − 0.02)/0.25 = 0.74.

Note that if older people had been shown the securities that form Y, they could have actually improved their expected return significantly, without increasing their risk. Specifically, with Y you get 0.743 extra return over the risk-free return per unit of standard deviation. They only wanted 5% standard deviation. Thus, with Y they can actually get an expected return equal to 0.05 × 0.743 = 0.037, or 3.7%. The total expected return using an investment in Y is then 3.7% + 2% = 5.7%. With O, they were only able to get 5%. So 70 basis points, by the way, is nothing to sneeze at. So it's a big difference.

Thus, the brokers should not show older and younger clients different sets of securities just on the basis of their standard deviation and their expected return. Even more to the point, if both old and young people had been shown all of the securities included in O and also in Y, they may have been able to actually form a portfolio out of O and Y that might generate an even better Sharpe ratio. If the returns on the two portfolios are uncorrelated, then we can generate a hyperbola that connects the two. A point on that hyperbola may produce an even better Sharpe ratio than 0.743, the Sharpe ratio suggested with Y.

In fact, everyone should consider the widest set of securities and pick the portfolio off the efficient frontier that has the highest Sharpe ratio. This portfolio will be the best risky portfolio. People will control the risk by putting a larger or smaller fraction of their wealth into this risky portfolio. But at least for the fraction that they are investing in this portfolio, they will be getting the highest extra return per unit of risk possible.

This analysis showed us that all people should demand the same risky portfolio. The next step in equilibrium analysis is to impose "market clearing." We just said that everyone wants the same portfolio of risky securities. What does that portfolio have to be? That portfolio must be where supply equals demand. As such, the optimal risky portfolio that everyone wants must be the market portfolio. If not, then we won't have market clearing—we don't have supply equals demand.

To see that, let's consider if it doesn't hold. For example, suppose that the optimal risky portfolio has no use for SleazeCo. Then, in that case, no one would hold SleazeCo. There's no demand for SleazeCo stock. But, I sold SleazeCo shares at an IPO (that is, I supplied the shares). So, if no one wants to hold SleazeCo because it isn't part of the portfolio that produces the highest Sharpe ratio, then what will happen to the price of SleazeCo? The price must fall until people want to buy some. When the price falls, the return on SleazeCo will increase until somebody wants it.

In fact, the price will keep on falling until everyone wants to hold SleazeCo in their optimal risky portfolio in proportion to the market value of SleazeCo relative to the total value of the market. If everyone wants to put a weight on SleazeCo that is less than the market weight of SleazeCo, the supply doesn't equal demand. So, the prices of securities are just going to adjust until the weights in everyone's market portfolio is exactly equal to the market weights.

What's next? If the market portfolio is the optimal portfolio, then we can ask "what is the risk of an individual security in the context of the best portfolio you can hold?" How are we going to measure risk? I suggest we measure it as the volatility or the variance of the return on your risky investment portfolio. The risky investment portfolio is what generates all of the variation in your wealth. That's risk.

If your overall portfolio consists of risk-free assets and the optimal risky portfolio, then it's fairly clear that our only source of risk is the variance of the return on the risky portfolio. So, let's measure the risk of an individual security as the amount that that security contributes to the variance of the return of that optimal risky portfolio. To do that, we just take a mathematical derivative. A derivative is an analytic expression for the rate of change in something given a change in something else.

In the case of a security, we can ask, "What is the rate of change in the market portfolio variance given a change in the weight in the ith security if we're just going to change it a little bit?" As it turns out, that derivative is equal to something called the "market beta." The market beta is defined as: $\beta_i = \text{Cov}(R_i, R_M)/\text{Var}(R_M)$. By the way, this is equivalent to the slope of a regression line in the excess return on security i against the excess return of market returns. We saw this in the previous lecture.

The beta of a security with respect to the market portfolio is the measure of risk for that security. By the way, this is where the importance of market clearing comes from in our story. We could ask how much a particular security contributes to the variance of any portfolio, say the one you hold currently (which may or may not be the market portfolio). Given what you hold, we would calculate the covariance of the return on security i with the return on the risky portfolio you hold, and then divide that by the variance of the return on the portfolio you hold. That would be the amount that that risky security i contributes to the risk in your portfolio.

But if we all held different portfolios, then we would all need to have a different measure of risk. And this is why CAPM is so popular. It says that there's only one measure of risk for a security that works for everyone. That measure is the beta of that security with respect to the market only, and that's because we're all supposed to be holding just that market portfolio. This makes it easy. We can tell everyone the same thing. Market beta is risk. But, if you're not holding the market portfolio, the market beta may not be risk for you. But, unless you have a good reason not to, you should be holding the market portfolio as your optimal risky portfolio.

So now we have optimal demands, we have market clearing, and now we have a measure of risk. We need one more thing. How much return should you get for each unit of risk? This is a question about what is the price of risk. The following argument is used by CAPM to pin this down. I'll warn you, this argument is a bit involved, so let me break it down into four steps.

Step 1: A feature of any optimal portfolio is that the marginal contribution to utility of each and every security must be the same. It's got to be the same across all those different securities. If not, then it's not an optimal portfolio. For example, if I'm putting a little bit more weight on SleazeCo, if doing that could increase my happiness by, say, 3 utils, but putting a little bit more weight on, say, Security Z produces only 2 utils, then I could make myself happier by reweighting. By taking weight away from Z, I give up 2 utils. But, once I take the weight away from Z, I have some money to spend and I can increase the weight on SleazeCo, which produces 3 utils. The net change is up 1 util. So, we should do it.

Now, once we've exhausted all of the types of opportunities from Step 1, then I will have an optimal portfolio. This is Step 2. At this optimal portfolio, the net benefit of each security will be the same across all securities. The benefit of a security is the contribution of that security to the mean return of the optimal portfolio.

The bad thing about a security is the risk that it produces in that optimal portfolio. That risk, as we have argued, is the covariance of the security return with the market return, divided by the variance of the market return. This is a "bad" in terms of variance, right? How much does this security contribute to the variance of your portfolio? Now, what we need to do is we need to translate that into an expected cost or cost in terms of expected returns.

Let's say that the cost of the risk in terms of expected returns is proportional to that risk. And let's let that proportionality be a constant. Let's call it gamma (γ). Think of gamma as the per-unit cost of risk. Gamma is called the "market price of risk."

The value of gamma will be increasing in the amount of risk aversion in the economy on average. That is, the cost is higher the more risk-averse investors are. The net benefit, or the benefit minus the cost, for all securities is the expected return for that security minus the price of risk (gamma) times the beta of that security. That is, the net benefit on any security in the portfolio is $E(R_i) - \gamma \times \beta_i$. So, it's the expected return on that individual security minus the gamma, which is constant across all securities, times the beta of that individual security. That's the net benefit for that individual security.

What's Step 3? We need to pin down the value of gamma. We can do that by recognizing that the net benefit of the risk-free security is simply the risk-free rate. This is true since the risk-free rate has a zero beta and its expected return equals its actual return, right? Because it's risk free.

Since the net benefit must be the same across all securities, then for all securities, that net benefit has to be equal to the risk-free rate. So: $E(R_i) - \gamma \times \beta_i = R_f$, the risk-free rate for all different individual securities—for all values of i. If this last expression holds for every security, it must hold for even efficiently priced portfolios, including the market portfolio itself.

Thus, for the market portfolio itself, $E(R_M) - \gamma \times \beta_M = R_f$. But look, the beta of the market portfolio is 1, so this is going to imply what? This implies that $E(R_M) - R_f = \gamma$ since $\beta_M = 1$. That is, the expected return on the market in excess of the risk-free rate is equal to gamma, the market price of risk.

So we've now pinned down what is the market price of risk. The expected return on the market in excess of the risk-free rate is also called the market risk premium.

What's the final step? This, then, given the market price of risk, implies that for an individual security we're going to have: $E(R_i) - \gamma \times \beta_i = R_f \rightarrow E(Ri) = Rf + \beta i(E(R_M) - R_f)$. This is the CAPM pricing equation.

Alright, let's look at what this means intuitively. Intuitively, it says that the return on the ith security should equal the risk-free rate plus an amount extra to compensate you for holding the risk of that security, where the risk is measured by its market beta and the price per unit of risk is the market risk premium. If you have a security that has more units of risk—that is, that it has a higher beta—then it should get a higher expected return. The more units of extra risk, the higher the expected return.

Here. Let's put some numbers on this. Let's say that the risk-free rate is 1%. Let's say that the market risk premium is 8%. So, if you have a security that has a beta of 1, the security should have an expected return of: $0.01 + 1(0.08) = 0.09$, or 9%. A security that has only a half a unit of market risk—that is, it has a beta of 0.5—should only get half a unit of market risk premium. That is, its expected return is going to be: $0.01 + 0.5 \times 0.08 = 0.05$ (5%). A really risky security with two units of market risk (say, a beta of 2) should have an average return on $0.01 + 2 \times 0.08 = 0.17$ (or 17%).

So CAPM is a single-factor model. Remember this from the last lecture we talked about. What it says is that there is only one source of risk—the risk that the market will go up or go down. Thus, whether a security is risky or not depends upon how correlated it is with the market. A security that goes down when the market goes down is very risky. Just when you need a good payoff, when the market is down, so is the return on that security. And that's risk. Risk is correlation.

So, by the way, CAPM is a little bit judgmental. CAPM says that you only get compensated for the risk of a security in the context of a market portfolio, even if you don't hold the market portfolio. Because everyone else holds the market portfolio—they're supposed to hold that optimally—then you should only get compensated for the amount of risk that that security produces in that portfolio. If you want to do something stupid and hold some non-optimal portfolio, go ahead, but the market will not compensate you for the extra variation that security produces in that sub-optimal portfolio, because no one is forcing you to do something stupid.

Also, CAPM tells you some things don't matter. For example, the idiosyncratic volatility does not matter. Why is this? Recall that idiosyncratic volatility is the variation not explained by systematic or market movements. Such idiosyncratic variation is due to economic factors that are not common or shared across securities. If you hold a well-diversified portfolio, then all of the idiosyncratic volatility will get diversified away. And what is left is only variation created by the common, or market, movements.

Another way to interpret CAPM is that the market only pays you for the risk that you cannot avoid. The movements that cannot be avoided are the movements caused by general market conditions that are common to all. Since you can eliminate idiosyncratic volatility in a well-diversified portfolio, you should not be compensated for bearing it.

We will discuss later whether CAPM does a good job at explaining the cross-section of returns. For now, let's just bask in the glory of the intuition that it provides. What CAPM says is that the cross-section of returns is driven by common risk that cannot be eliminated through diversification. It also says that the amount that you should get paid per unit of risk is linear in the amount of risk that you have, in its beta.

Thus, if a security has half a unit of market/undiversifiable risk, then its expected return, in excess of the risk-free rate, should be half of what you get with a whole unit of common/market risk. This makes perfect sense.

Over the following lecture, we will see how to use CAPM to identify and exploit mispricing. Later, we will also examine whether the implications of CAPM are borne out in the data.

How to Exploit Mispriced Securities

Lecture 18

In this lecture, you will learn how the equilibrium models developed in previous lectures can be used to determine if something is too expensive or cheap enough. First, you need to examine short selling in detail. The second step is to develop a framework in which you can take the implications of an asset pricing model and apply them to securities in the market to identify mispricing. The third step entails using information about a stock's alpha and its idiosyncratic volatility to form an optimal risky portfolio that exploits mispricing without taking on too much risk.

Step 1: Short Sales

- The overarching idea of this lecture is "everything is a good idea if it's cheap enough, and everything is a bad idea if it's too expensive." As it turns out, this statement is not completely accurate for investments because you also can make a gain if the price is too high. In order to do so, however, you have to be able to take a short position in a security.

- A short position is when you sell a security that you don't own. To do that, you have to borrow it; then, you sell it. At some point in the future, you have to return it, which you do by buying back at the market price then.

- Another famous saying is "buy low; sell high." A short position lets you make money by reversing the order: "sell high; buy low." So, even if something is too expensive, it may still be a "good idea"—if the idea is to short it. Of course, shorting might turn out badly.

- The way to think about a short sale is that it is—on average—borrowing money at the expected rate of return on the security you borrowed. So, you can use a short sale to either speculate on a drop in price or to borrow money.

- But when you sell short via an online broker, you need to have a margin account. In that case, you may be borrowing just to be able to borrow (by shorting). You might end up paying interest twice: If the stock price rises, then you will be paying interest with the run up in the stock price, and the broker will charge you interest on any money you might have to borrow to keep the margin current.

- In addition to these costs, you should also realize that there might be a limit to the amount you can short due to a lack of availability of shares to borrow. Also, sometimes after you have shorted, you may have to close out your short position before you want—before the price falls. Typically, when you short, you borrow shares from some other account at your broker's.

- In fact, when you open an account, you typically will agree to allow the shares you have to be lent to other customers of the broker. You will not care if they are lent out because if the stock pays a dividend while it is lent out, the short seller must pay you the dividend. And if you want to sell shares that have been lent, the broker will give your shares back and lend out shares from another account to the shorter. Thus, you really don't give anything up by lending shares.

- There are times when nobody is willing to lend shares anymore (because perhaps they want to sell). In that case, you will not be able to maintain your short position. Once your broker cannot find shares to borrow, you will have to close out your short position—and that might be at a loss. The other problem with a short position is that you can lose more than your initial position.

Step 2: Mispricing Relative to an Asset Pricing Model

- In general, an asset pricing model will tell you how to trade based on a deviation from the implications of that asset pricing model. We will stick with CAPM because it is a single-factor model, which simplifies things a bit and allows you to imagine the process more easily.

- Recall that CAPM says that the expected return for a particular security should exceed the risk-free rate exactly by the product of that security's beta with the market risk premium. Furthermore, CAPM says that this should hold for all securities.

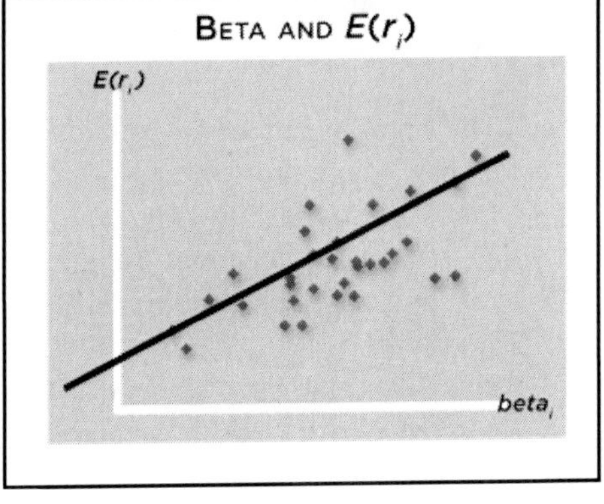

- If you form a scatter plot of the average return on the vertical axis against beta on the horizontal axis, according to CAPM, the data should have an intercept on the vertical axis at the risk-free rate; that is, a security with a beta of zero on the horizontal axis should, on average, return the risk-free rate.

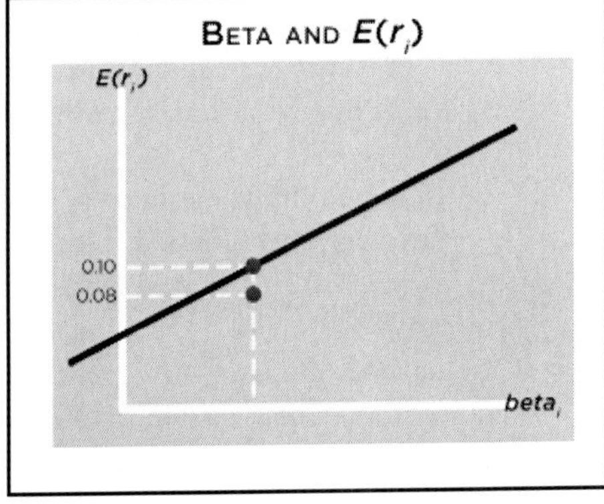

- Then, for beta larger than zero, the average return should increase at a constant rate. The constant rate should be the market risk premium (i.e., the expected return on the market minus the risk-free rate).

- Thus, according to CAPM, all of the data should land on a straight line. This line is called the security market line (SML). If there is any security that does not lie on the SML, then that security is mispriced.

- The CAPM model is consistent with the single-factor model, where the single factor is the market return. That is, the market return is a sufficient statistic for all of the risk in the economy. The single-factor model is $r_i = r_f + \alpha_i + \beta_i(r_M - r_f) + \varepsilon_i$. You want to take advantage of the nonzero alpha by forming a portfolio with a neutral beta.

- The hardest part of investing is finding securities with nonzero alphas. There are two approaches to finding nonzero alphas. The first is the result of the following process.
  1. Forecast cash flows. Either take analyst forecasts or make your own based on your knowledge of the firm and industry.

  2. Determine the riskiness of the cash flows. How sensitive are these cash flows to the market?

  3. Calculate the discounted value of the free cash flows to determine the firm's value. Subtract an estimate of the value of debt to get the value of the equity. Think of this as the future value that will occur once the market reaches equilibrium.

  4. Compare the value in step 3 with the current market price. If different, then guess at a horizon as to when your value from step 3 will be reflected in the market.

- The second approach is to run a regression of the return on the equity minus the risk-free rate on the returns of the market minus the risk-free rate. The constant in this regression is alpha. Use this alpha as your estimate of the return in excess of what CAPM implies it should be.

- Both methods have problems. With the first method, it is difficult to come up with good estimates of the firm's free cash flows. It is also difficult to come up with how these cash flows will be correlated with the market to determine the correct discount rate to apply.

- Typically, professionals look at the required rates of returns on the assets—not the equity—of other comparable firms. They do this because they want to value the free cash flows of the whole firm. When they do that, they typically calculate the weighted average cost of capital for the firm. They then estimate the value of the stock as the value of the whole firm minus the value of its debt.

- For the second method, you should realize that the alpha from a regression is an average value of mispricing. It may not be the alpha going forward. In fact, alphas from regressions are notoriously bad. They are noisy at the individual security level.

Step 3: Optimal Portfolios with Active Positions

- The Treynor–Black model for active portfolio management provides a framework for thinking about how much of your portfolio should be active and passive. In addition, it gives you some explicit expressions for the magnitudes of the positions you should take with securities that you think have nonzero alphas.

- This framework admits that you may be able to beat the market by finding mispriced securities. If you could not find mispriced securities, then you should just hold a passive market portfolio. However, if you can find mispriced securities, then you should not do what CAPM says, which is to just hold the market; rather, you should supplement a passive position in the market with an active portfolio that consists of securities that you have found to be mispriced.

- Within this context, there are two things you need to decide: What is the optimal active portfolio? And given an optimal active portfolio, what is the optimal portfolio of the passive and active portfolios?

- First, to form the optimal active portfolio, you need the alpha and the idiosyncratic variance of each mispriced security. For each security, take the ratio of the alpha to the idiosyncratic variance.

Note that some of these ratios might be negative because the alpha for an overvalued security might be negative.

- Add all of these ratios. The weight for the ith mispriced security in the active portfolio should be its ratio divided by the sum of all of the ratios. These weights seek to exploit nonzero alphas. However, at the same time, the weights reflect a concern about the idiosyncratic volatility of the security, which is a problem because there are typically too few securities in the active portfolio for the idiosyncratic components of returns to be diversified away.

- Thus, a big nonzero alpha is good. But a big idiosyncratic volatility is bad. A security with an alpha that is relatively large in magnitude but that has a small idiosyncratic variance should receive a larger weight in the active portfolio. Also note that, because some of the ratios might be negative, some portfolio weights might be negative. These are the securities you might need to short.

- Once you have the weights for the active portfolio, you will need to determine the active portfolio's beta, alpha, and the variance of idiosyncratic components. The beta is just the weighted average of the betas of the individual securities—and the same goes for the alpha. The variance of the idiosyncratic components is simply the weight on each individual security squared times the variance of the individual's idiosyncratic variance—added up for all of the mispriced securities in the active portfolio.

- The active portfolio alpha, beta, and idiosyncratic variance are all used to answer the following question: What is the right weight to put in this active portfolio versus the passive portfolio?

- A first step is to take the ratio of the active portfolio alpha to its idiosyncratic variance. Think of this ratio as the extra return (the alpha) per unit of idiosyncratic variance. If this ratio is not large, then the active portfolio will contribute little in terms of excess return but will contribute a lot in terms of idiosyncratic risk. If so, you want to put little of your money in the active portfolio.

- Let's call this ratio the expected return to variance ratio. You can also calculate a ratio like it for the market. Let this ratio be the expected return on the market divided by the variance of the market return.

- To see exactly how much to put in the active portfolio, you want to see how big the expected return to variance ratio is for the active portfolio relative to the ratio for the market. If this ratio of ratios is large, then you should put more in the active portfolio. If the ratio of ratios is small, put in less. In some cases, the ratio of ratios will be negative. This means that you should short the active portfolio you determined in the first step.

- The intuition is that in order to exploit mispricing, you necessarily must take an undiversified position in these mispriced securities. And when you do, you must bear the risk associated with idiosyncratic returns. The amount you want to put into the active portfolio should be bigger if the mispricing in these active securities is big relative to the amount of idiosyncratic risk these securities expose you to.

Suggested Reading

Bodie, Kane, and Marcus, *Essentials of Investments*.

Swensen, *Pioneering Portfolio Management*.

———, *Unconventional Success*.

Questions to Consider

1. If you had taken an active position in BP just prior to the Deepwater Horizon well blowout on April 20, 2010, you would have experienced a very large loss on that position. Can you think of other stocks that have experienced very bad idiosyncratic events that caused a huge drop in value like the Deepwater Horizon case? Do you think that these types of events are fairly common across all industries, or are they mostly concentrated in a few industries?

2. Rather than try to exploit mispriced securities by trading in individual securities, many professional investors look for portfolios of securities that seem to be mispriced. Why might this be a better strategy than seeking profits on individual securities?

How to Exploit Mispriced Securities
Lecture 18—Transcript

Everything is a good idea if it's cheap enough, and everything is a bad idea if it's too expensive. In this lecture, we'll examine how the equilibrium models that we developed previously can be used to determine if something is too expensive or too cheap. We'll explore how to do this in three steps.

First, we need to examine short selling in greater detail than we did earlier in the course. This first step is important because shorting allows an investor to exploit mispricing when a security is overvalued.

The second step is to develop a framework in which you can take the implications of an asset pricing model and apply it to securities in the market to identify mispricing. The result of this second step is to develop a measure of mispricing called "alpha."

The third step entails using information about a stock's alpha and its idiosyncratic volatility to form an optimal risky portfolio that exploits mispricing without taking on too much risk.

Let's get started. Step 1 is to examine how to short. The overriding idea of the lecture is "Everything is a good idea if it's cheap enough, and everything is a bad idea if it's too expensive." As it turns out, this statement is not completely accurate for investments, because, as we will discuss next, you can actually make a gain if the price is too high. In order to do so, however, you're going to have to be able to take a short position in a security.

A short position is when you sell a security that you don't own. How do you do that? Well, first you have to borrow it, then you sell it. At some point in the future, you have to return it, which you do by going back into the market and buying it back at whatever the market price is then. Another famous saying, of course, is "Buy low, sell high." A short position lets you make money by reversing the order. "Sell high, buy low."

Let's consider another SleazeCo example. You think SleazeCo is currently too high at $20 per share and expect it to fall over the next six months. If you currently owned SleazeCo, you could benefit from this knowledge just by selling it now to avoid the loss. But, if you didn't own it, you could make money by shorting it. Borrow 1000 shares from someone and sell them at \$20 per share to get \$20,000. With that money, you can invest it in something else in the meantime.

Let's say you invest in short-term T-bills and you get 1% per annum. And after six months, your \$20,000 will grow to \$20,100. During that six months, the true value of SleazeCo has become apparent to the market. It now trades at \$10 per share. You close out your short position by buying the 1000 shares back, for a cost of \$10,000. And you pocket the difference between the \$20,100 − \$10,000 = \$10,100.

So, even if something is too expensive, it may still be a good idea—if the idea is to short it. Of course, shorting might turn out badly. If the price of SleazeCo were to rise to \$30 per share, you would have to buy back those 1000 shares for \$30,000. In that case, you paid \$30,000 to have the use of \$20,000 for six months. That's not a good deal. Essentially, you paid an effective interest rate of 125% per annum. That is, you paid the rate r such that \$20,000 = \$30,000/(1 + r)(1/2), that's r = 125%.

The way to think about a short sale is that, on average, you are borrowing money at the expected return for that security that you borrowed. For example, if the expected return on SleazeCo was 8% per annum, then on average the price of SleazeCo would have risen at that rate for six months from, say, \$20 to \$20.00 × (1 + 0.08)(1/2) = \$20.78.

So, if you short 1,000 shares at \$20, you have the use of the \$20,000 for six months. When you close out your position, on average you will have to pay \$20.78 per share, for a total cost of \$20,780. Thus, you borrowed \$20,000 for six months and paid it back by paying back the original \$20,000 plus interest of \$780—that is, an 8% interest per annum.

So, you can use a short sale to either speculate on a drop in price or just to borrow money. But you need to realize that when you short sell via an online broker, you may need to use what is known as a margin account. In that case, you may be borrowing just to be able to borrow by shorting.

Let's work through an example. Let's say you have an account at a broker that has $20,000 in cash and $300,000 in securities. If you short 1000 shares at $20 per share, then they will put $20,000 in cash into your margin account. This is so that if the price rises you have no incentive to default and not return the shares.

If the price rises to $21, then the margin account must have $21,000. Since you only had $20,000 in cash, the broker will loan you $1000 to bring the margin up to $21,000. But, since the broker is lending you that $1000, they're also going to charge you some interest. Thus, you will be paying interest twice—once with the run-up in the stock price, and the second time on the amount that is needed to be put into the margin account that you may have to borrow.

In addition to these costs, you should also realize that there may be a limit on the amount that you can short due to a lack of availability of shares to borrow. Also, sometimes after you have shorted, you may have to close out your position before you want to, before the price actually falls. Typically, when you short, you borrow shares from some other account at your broker's.

In fact, when you open an account, you typically agree to allow the shares that you have to be lent to other customers of that broker. You will not care if they're lent out since if the stock pays, say, a dividend in the meantime while it's lent out, the short seller must pay you the dividend. And if you want to sell the shares that have been lent out already, the broker will give back your shares and lend the shares out from some other account to the shorter. Thus, you really don't care if your shares are lent out at any point in time.

There are times when no one is willing to lend shares anymore, since perhaps they all want to sell. In that case, you will not be able to maintain your short position. Once your broker cannot find shares to borrow, you will have to close out your short position, and that might be at a loss.

The other problem with a short position is that you can lose more than your initial position. If you borrow $20,000 to buy 1000 shares of SleazeCo and the price falls to zero, you have lost $20,000. But, if you short at $20 per share and the price goes to $100, you will owe 1000 × $100 = $100,000 for an $80,000 loss. So you can lose a lot by shorting.

Now that we've seen what it means to short, we can examine what it means for a security to be mispriced. This notion will lead us to what is known as alpha. In general, an asset pricing model will tell you how to trade based on a deviation from the implications of that asset pricing model. We will consider some alternative asset pricing models in subsequent lectures, but for this lecture we'll stick with CAPM since it is a single-factor model. The fact that it's a single-factor model actually simplifies things quite a bit and allows us to imagine this process a little bit more easily.

Recall that CAPM says that the expected return for a particular security should exceed the risk-free rate exactly by the product of that security's beta with the market risk premium. Further, CAPM says that this should hold for all securities. So let's consider if you formed a scatter plot of the average return on the vertical axis against the beta on the horizontal axis.

According to CAPM, the data should have an intercept at the vertical axis at the risk-free rate. That is, a security with a beta of zero on the horizontal axis should, on average, return the risk-free rate of return. So let's say that this risk-free rate is 2.8%.

Then, for beta larger than zero, the average return should increase at a constant rate. The constant rate should be the market risk premium (i.e., the expected return on the market minus the risk free rate). For concreteness, let's let this market risk premium be 6%.

Thus, according to CAPM, all of the data should land on a straight line. This line is called the security market line (or the SML for short). If there's any security that does not lie on the SML, then that security is mispriced relative to CAPM.

For example, consider SleazeCo. Let's say that the beta of SleazeCo is 1.2, and it has an expected return of 8%. According to the SML, a security with a beta of 1.2 should have an expected return of the risk-free rate of 2.8% plus the beta times the market risk premium. This second part is going to be 1.2 × 6%, or 7.2%. So the total is 2.8% plus 7.2%, or 10%.

Thus, with an expected return of only 8%, SleazeCo is below the SML. The difference between the expected return and that predicted by the asset pricing model (CAPM in this case) is the alpha. In this case, the alpha of SleazeCo is 8% − 10% = −2%.

A non-zero alpha implies that the price of the security is not what it should be according to the asset pricing model. That is, given the cash flows expected for SleazeCo and the riskiness of those cash flows, the price should be those cash flows discounted at 10%. But, the current price is discounted at 8%. It takes those cash flows and discounts them at 8%. Since the price would be lower if the cash flows were discounted at the appropriate 10%, the price of SleazeCo is too high with an expected return of 8%. Thus, SleazeCo might be a good candidate for shorting.

So, let's short it. If we just sell it short, then we will have what is referred to as a naked position. A naked position is one in which you don't have an offsetting hedged position in something else. If you just short, what might be the return?

Recall that CAPM is a model that is consistent with the single-factor model, where the single factor is the market return. That is, the market return is a sufficient statistic for all of the risk in the economy. The single-factor model is: $r_i = r_f + \alpha_i + \beta_i(r_M - r_f) + ei$. For SleazeCo, we have $\beta_i = 1.2$ and $\alpha = -0.02$. If we take a short position in SleazeCo, the realized return can be any value that's consistent with the single-factor market model. What happens if, for example, the market soars on good news? Also, what about the idiosyncratic component? For example, what if rM = 0.20 and ei = −.10. Then what's going to be the realized return on SleazeCo? It's going to be: E[ri] = 0.028 − 0.02 + 1.2 × (0.20 − 0.028) − 0.10 = 11.44%.

What would be your gains from or losses from shorting in this case? Let's say that you shorted SleazeCo at $20.00. If the return over the next six months turned out to be 11.44%, then price of SleazeCo will have risen to

$\$20.00(1.1144)^{.5} = \$21.11$. You would have lost \$1.11 per share on, say, the 1000 shares that you shorted. You lost \$1110.

Alright, so the problem here is that even though there was bad news about SleazeCo, the market went up by so much that it overcame the effect of the negative news for SleazeCo. The price rose and you lost on your short.

Is there any way for you to avoid this? The answer is yes. What you want to do is you want to take advantage of a non-zero alpha by forming a portfolio that has a neutral beta. How about if there was another security that has the same risk as SleazeCo, but that lies on the CAPM line—that lies on the security market line? Let's consider a company, let's call it PriceRight Inc. Let's let it lie on the line, and it's going to have the same beta as SleazeCo, but its expected return is going to be what's on the security market line. It's going to be 10%.

Let's form a portfolio of SleazeCo and PriceRight so that we can exploit SleazeCo's alpha but neutralize its beta. Since PriceRight will give us an average return of 10% but SleazeCo only 8%, then that portfolio should be long PriceRight and short SleazeCo. In fact, for every \$1 that we go long PriceRight, we will want to short \$1 worth of SleazeCo. That is, sell \$20,000 worth of SleazeCo short and then use the proceeds to go out and buy PriceRight.

What will we get? The return on PriceRight over the next six months will depend upon idiosyncratic returns and also the return on the market according to the single factor model. The return on PriceRight is going to be equal to: $r\text{PR} = 0.028 + 0 + 1.2 \times (r\text{M} - 0.028) + e\text{PR}$. As before, the realized return on SleazeCo is going to be: $r\text{S} = 0.028 - 0.02 + 1.2(r\text{M} - 0.028) + e\text{S}$.

If we go long PriceRight and we short SleazeCo, then the net return is the difference in these two returns. And so you just do a little bit of algebra, and what you see is that the difference is equal to: $0.02 + e\text{PR} - e\text{S}$. Thus, on average, since the idiosyncratic terms are, on average, zero, by market efficiency, you will get 2% returns. The negative of the alpha for the mispriced security, completely independent of whether the market goes up or down. This strategy neutralizes market risk that we faced when we were just shorting SleazeCo alone.

Now, there is some risk that remains here due to the idiosyncratic terms. Thus, the riskiness of this strategy depends upon the variance of these idiosyncratic terms. The greater this variance, the greater the possible deviation from 2% you will get over this horizon.

Now, what if we can't find a security that has the same beta as the mispriced SleazeCo? Well, then let's form a portfolio of other securities that does. For example, let's consider TruValue and LevMark. TruValue has a beta of 0.7 and LevMark has a beta of 1.5. If you put x% into TruValue and $(1 - x)$% into LevMark, what value of x will generate a portfolio with a beta of 1.2 (the beta for SleazeCo)?

The beta of a portfolio is simply the weighted average of the individual betas, where the weights correspond to the fraction of the money invested in each. Thus, the answer to our question is the value of x that solves: $x \times 0.7 + (1 - x) \times 1.5 = 1.2$. A little algebra implies that $x = (1.2 - 1.5)/(0.7 - 1.5) = 0.375$. So, put 37.5% in TruValue and 100 − 37.5% = 62.5% in LevMark.

Then what? Use this portfolio of TruValue and LevMark to fill in for PriceRight. The whole strategy is to short SleazeCo. For every dollar received from shorting, put 37.5% of the proceeds into TruValue and 62.5% of those proceeds into LevMark.

What do you get at the end of the year? What you get is $0.02 + [0.375e\text{T} + 0.625e\text{L} - e\text{S}]$. This is even a little bit better than what we had before, because the variance of the idiosyncratic stuff will be partially diversified. That is, there's less variance in the idiosyncratic term of $0.375e\text{T} + 0.625e\text{L} - e\text{S}$, because we formed a portfolio of the idiosyncratic part of TruValue and the idiosyncratic part from LevMark.

So we've just seen what you do when you have found a non-zero alpha. But how do you find securities with non-zero alphas? This is the hardest part of investing. There are two approaches to finding non-zero alphas. The first is the result of the following process:

Step 1: Forecast cash flows for a particular firm. Either take analyst forecasts or make you own based on your knowledge of the firm or the industry.

Step 2: Determine the riskiness of the cash flows. How sensitive are these cash flows to market movements?

Step 3: Calculate the discounted value of these free cash flows to determine the firm's value. Subtract off the estimate of the value of the debt to get the value of the equity. Think of this as the future value that will occur once the market reaches equilibrium. Think of it as where the ball ends up at the bottom of the bowl.

Step 4: Compare the value that you get in step 3 with the current market price. If it's different, then guess at a horizon when you think the value from step 3 will be reflected in the market. For example, if you think that it's worth $20 based upon a discount rate of 12% and the current value is $18 on a discount rate of 15%, then your alpha is going to be 15% − 12% = 3%. That's your alpha. So you're going to have to wait to see when the price is actually reflected, but over that period of time you're going to get an alpha of 3%.

The second approach is to run a regression of the return of the equity minus the risk-free return on the returns of the market minus the risk-free return. The constant in this regression is the alpha that we discussed last lecture. Use this alpha as your estimate of the returns in excess of what CAPM implies.

As it turns out, both methods have problems. With the first method, it's hard to come up with good estimates of the firm's free cash flows. It's also hard to come up with how these cash flows are correlated with the return on the market to determine the correct discount rate to apply.

Typically, what professionals do is they look at the required rates of return on the assets of other comparable firms. Note that I said that they look at the required rate of returns on the assets of comparable firms, not the equity. They do this because they want to value the free cash flows of the whole firm. When they do that, they typically calculate the weighted average cost of capital for that firm. The weighted average cost of capital was discussed in lectures 12 and 13. With this estimate, they can then figures out what the present value of the cash flows are, and then once they get that value, they're going to subtract off the value of the debt to get the value of the stock.

For the second method, you should realize that the alpha from a regression is the average value of mispricing. It may not be the alpha going forward. Let me explain further. The alpha is a return in excess of what CAPM implies. Thus, alpha is a degree of mispricing. In some periods, this mispricing may be big positive, but in other periods it may be small negative. The alpha that you get from a regression is an average of the mispricing over the sample used to estimate the market model. As an average over the past sample, it may not be the alpha for that security going forward.

In fact, alphas from regressions are notoriously bad. They are very noisy at the individual security level. Thus, both approaches are hard. So maybe this is why even professional fund managers can't beat their benchmarks on average.

We just examined how to find non-zero alphas. We also discussed basically how to exploit them. What we did not do was figure out what's the optimal way to hold them in an overall portfolio.

In this next section, we'll examine the Treynor-Black model for active portfolio management. I must warn you. This model is very, very involved. But, it does a couple of very important things. First, and most important, it provides a framework for thinking about how much your portfolio should be active and how much of it should be passive. Second, it gives you some explicit expressions for the magnitudes of the positions you should take with securities that you think have non-zero alphas.

Let's first consider the framework. The framework admits that you may be able to beat the market by finding mispriced securities. If you could not find mispriced securities, then you should just hold a passive market portfolio.

But, if you can find mispriced securities, then you should not do what CAPM says. You should not just hold the market. Rather, you should supplement a passive position in the market with an active portfolio that consists of securities that you have found to be mispriced.

Within this context, there are two things that you need to decide. The first is, "What is the optimal active portfolio?" That is, if you've done a bunch of analysis on, say, 10 securities and you have found 6 to be mispriced, what are the best weights to use in forming an optimal active portfolio on these six securities? We'll see the answer to this in a minute.

The second thing you need to decide is, "Given an optimal active portfolio, how much do I invest in that portfolio versus in the passive market portfolio?" The question is, what is the optimal portfolio of these two portfolios—active and passive? Let's consider the first question. What's the optimal active portfolio?

To form the optimal active portfolio, you need the alpha and the idiosyncratic variance for each mispriced security. For each security, take the ratio of the alpha to its idiosyncratic variance. Note that some of these ratios may be negative because the alpha for an overvalued security may be negative.

Take all these ratios and add them up. The weight for the ith mispriced security in the active portfolio should be its ratio divided by the sum of all the ratios. These weights seek to exploit the non-zero alphas. But, at the same time, the weights reflect concern about idiosyncratic volatility in that security. Idiosyncratic volatility is a problem because there are typically too few securities in the active portfolio for the idiosyncratic returns to be diversified away completely.

A big non-zero alpha is good, but a big idiosyncratic volatility is bad. A security with an alpha that is relatively large in magnitude but has a small idiosyncratic variance should receive a much larger weight in the active portfolio. This process we just described above creates such weights. Also notice that, since some of the ratios may be negative, some portfolio weights will be negative. These may be securities that you're going to need to short.

Once you have the weights for the active portfolio, you will need to determine the active portfolio beta, alpha, and the variance of the idiosyncratic components. The beta is just going to be the weighted average of the betas of the individual securities in this active portfolio.

The alpha is just going to be the weighted average of the individual alphas for these same securities. The variance of the idiosyncratic components is simply the weight on each individual security squared times the variance of the individual's idiosyncratic variance, and you add them up across all of the mispriced securities in the active portfolio. Remember that you can get the idiosyncratic volatility from the mean squared error in a regression for the specific security that is in the active portfolio.

The active portfolio alpha, the beta, and the idiosyncratic variance are all used to answer the following question: "What is the right weight to put on this active portfolio versus the weight to put on the passive portfolio?" In other words, what's the right portfolio of the two portfolios?

A first step in this process is to take the ratio of the active portfolio alpha—not the individual alphas, but the active portfolio alpha (the alpha for the whole active portfolio)—take the ratio of that to the idiosyncratic variance of the active portfolio. Think of this ratio as the extra return (the alpha) per unit of idiosyncratic variance. If this ratio is not large, then the active portfolio will contribute little in terms of excess return, but contribute a lot in terms of idiosyncratic risk. If so, you want to put little weight, or a little bit of money into that active portfolio.

Let's call this ratio the expected return to variance ratio. You can also calculate a ratio like that for the market. Let this ratio be the expected return on the market divided by the variance of the market return.

To see exactly how much to put into the active portfolio, you want to see how big the expected return-to-variance ratio is for the active portfolio relative to the ratio for the market. If this ratio of ratios is large, then you should put more in the active portfolio. If the ratio of ratios is small, then put in less.

In some cases, by the way, the ratio of ratios will be negative. This means that you are going to want to short the active portfolio. And every now and then you're going to have some negative weights in the active portfolio. If you're going to short the active portfolio, a negative of negative means that you're going to be taking on a long position in those securities.

The intuition is that in order to exploit mispricing you necessarily must take an undiversified position in securities that are mispriced. And when you do, you must bear the risk associated with those idiosyncratic returns. The amount that you want to put into the active portfolio should be bigger if the mispricing in these active securities is big relative to the amount of idiosyncratic risk these securities are going to expose you to.

In subsequent lectures, we will examine some well-known violations of CAPM. These violations may give you some ideas where to look for mispricing. And when you find it, you can use the techniques developed in this lecture to optimize your portfolio return.

Performance Evaluation

Lecture 19

In this lecture, you will examine ways in which to evaluate whether active investing is actually producing anything useful in terms of expected return or risk. That is, the methods discussed in this lecture evaluate the performance of a manager's stimulus-response process. You will look at the set of performance metrics used, and you will examine how to interpret what they mean. You will also see that you will want to use different metrics depending on your specific investment objectives.

Context Is Important

- What is a good benchmark for evaluating the performance of a professional manager? The answer to this question depends on the context of that manager or fund in your overall portfolio. Let's consider the situations of Jane and Ichabod.

- Jane is doing her own investing. For this, she has a portfolio that consists of individual securities as well as a few passive index funds. This portfolio also consists of cash and some investments in short-term risk-free investments like certificates of deposit, money market deposits, and treasury bills. If you exclude these securities and deposits, she has about $2 million in risky stocks, corporate bonds, and index funds. She only has $500,000 in short-term deposits that are essentially default-free.

- In contrast, Ichabod also has about $2 million in risky investments and $500,000 in risk-free deposits. However, he has allocated a significant portion of his investments to a couple of actively managed funds. In fact, about $1 million is evenly split between a global equity fund that invests in the equity of mid- to large-cap non-U.S.-based companies and a fund that invests in growth firms (those that are fairly early in their life cycle and are still expanding operations into new markets). The rest of the $1 million he manages by picking stocks he thinks could take off.

Jane's Problem

- Jane's problem is very similar to the typical investor's problem we analyzed when we looked at how to form an optimal risky portfolio in Lecture 15. Recall that a risky portfolio consists of just risky securities, such as the passive index funds and individual securities Jane holds.

- The idea is to form the best risky portfolio, where "best" is defined as that which generates the highest return per unit of risk. Then, given that optimal risky portfolio, the investor can control the amount of risk by deciding how much of the wealth to put in that risky portfolio and how much to keep in safe deposits or risk-free bonds.

- In Jane's case, she should pick a portfolio that maximizes the Sharpe ratio. Thus, the appropriate evaluation criterion for Jane's risky portfolio is the Sharpe ratio; she should compare the Sharpe ratio of her risky portfolio to that of the global benchmark.

- If the Sharpe ratio of her portfolio is less than that of the benchmark, then she could try to improve her risky portfolio by changing the amount allocated to the two passive funds and the individual stocks she owns.

- The material in Lecture 15 should guide her decisions in this regard. However, the bottom line is that because the risky portfolio she is forming is the only overall risky portfolio she will hold, she should evaluate the performance of that portfolio (and alternatives) according to the Sharpe ratio.

Ichabod's Problem

- Ichabod's situation is a bit more complicated than Jane's because he has a few actively managed funds. That is, he has delegated the management of a portion of his portfolio to what are supposed to be two actively managed funds.

- He wants to get the extra boost from active management, but he also wants to be sure that he is not overpaying for the extra performance these funds provide. So, he needs to be able to measure their performance.

- What would constitute good performance in this case? Should he look at the Sharpe ratio for each fund? These numbers are commonly provided by fund managers—but is that the right metric in this case? Is what the Sharpe ratio measures really what he wants conceptually?

- Recall that the Sharpe ratio is the expected return of the portfolio minus the risk-free rate divided by the standard deviation. The Sharpe ratio is really an ex ante measure. That is, at the time the portfolio is being formed, the investor is supposed to pick the weights that maximize the Sharpe ratio. It is ex ante in the sense that the expected return and the standard deviation are conceptually related to things the investor expects to hold in the future.

- The Sharpe ratios that are reported in the financial press and on websites are an ex post measure. With these measures, the expected return minus the risk-free rate is the average excess return for that portfolio over some past period of time (for example, 5 to 10 years). The standard deviation is calculated as the standard deviation of the returns that occurred in the past.

- Using Sharpe ratios calculated in this way, most investors would rank managers from highest (or best) to lowest (or worst). But note that this measure is backward looking. You need to look for persistence in the Sharpe ratios over time, so compare the Sharpe ratios for a given manager over many years.

- Is this even the correct measure of what Ichabod cares about? This measure is supposed to be what you want to maximize when finding the optimal portfolio of risky securities only. His overall portfolio (which includes both risky investments and risk-free deposits) will have the highest amount of return per unit of risk if the portfolio of risky securities has a large Sharpe ratio. Once he has such a risky portfolio defined, he can then determine, given the risk of that portfolio, how much he wants to put at risk and how much he wants to keep safe.

- Thus, there are two overall questions: What is the best risky portfolio? And what fraction of his wealth does he feel comfortable putting at risk given that best risky portfolio? If he were to evaluate each of the managed funds by looking at their Sharpe ratios, for each actively managed portfolio, he would learn how much expected return per unit of risk each portfolio generates—if that was the only risky portfolio that he held.

- Thus, the Sharpe ratio for a given portfolio is sensible only if it is the only portfolio held. If the portfolio you are evaluating is the only risky portfolio you will hold, then the standard deviation in the Sharpe ratio is the risk the investor holds. However, if the investor holds two actively managed portfolios, then the standard deviation of the overall portfolio will be some combination of the two individual standard deviations.

- The real question Ichabod wants answered is as follows: How much extra return does the actively managed fund contribute to his overall portfolio relative to the extra risk that portfolio contributes to his overall portfolio? That is not what the Sharpe ratio tells Ichabod. Note that because Jane only has one risky portfolio, the Sharpe ratio of that portfolio *does* tell her what her return per unit of risk is.

Three Measures of Risk

- There are a few measures that are used to get at what Ichabod wants to know. One such measure is the Treynor measure. Because the standard deviation of the portfolio's return does not measure risk in a portfolio context, the Treynor measure replaces the standard deviation by the beta of the portfolio: That is, the Treynor measure is the expected return on the portfolio minus the risk-free rate divided by the beta of that portfolio.

- Thus, the Treynor measure captures the extra excess return that portfolio provides given the risk of that portfolio as measured by the portfolio's beta. The beta of an individual security—or an individual portfolio—is the incremental contribution of that security to the risk of the portfolio. Thus, the beta of a portfolio Ichabod holds should be the extra risk that portfolio contributes to his overall risky portfolio.

- Another measure of the contribution of a managed portfolio to the overall performance of the risky portfolio that adjusts for that managed portfolio's risk is Jensen's alpha. Jensen's alpha is a measure of the extent to which that portfolio return exceeds that which it should be according to CAPM. Specifically, Jensen's alpha is the average return on the portfolio minus the average of the risk-adjusted expected return.

- In general, the risk-adjusted expected return is the expected return implied by a particular asset pricing model. If we use CAPM, then the risk-adjusted expected return on the portfolio is the risk-free rate plus the beta of that portfolio times the market return minus the risk-free rate.

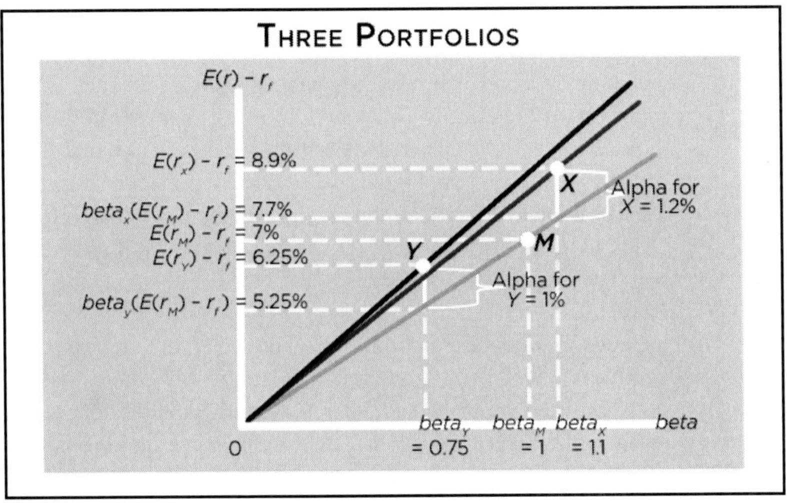

- For any period in the past, you can calculate the risk-adjusted expected return by taking the risk-free rate for that period and adding the beta of the portfolio multiplied by whatever the market return minus the risk-free rate was in that period. Think of this value as the value that the CAPM implies should have happened on average.

- For any given period, the difference between the realized return on the portfolio in that period and the risk-adjusted expected return in that period is the alpha for that period. Jensen's alpha is just the average of the alpha for all the past periods.

- There is another measure that is similar to the Treynor measure based on leverage called the M^2 measure (after Modigliani and Miller, two Nobel Prize winners in economics/finance). Their idea is to consider the amount of volatility in a passive market portfolio and lever up or down the managed portfolio until that position has the same volatility as the market.

- Once you have that position, you can compare the expected return on that position to that of the market. If the managed position dominates, invest in that—not the market.

The Information Ratio

- Why should Ichabod just hold one managed fund? In fact, most managed funds are actively managed knowing that investors will not hold them as their only risky portfolio. If they know that they are going to be held with other active funds in a portfolio of funds, what performance measure do they want to compete on? Each fund will want to in high demand as a component of an overall optimally formed portfolio of risky securities.

- When how to form the optimal risky portfolio on the basis of any active analysis was discussed, we noted that there was a trade-off between the alpha and the idiosyncratic volatility of active positions in the securities or portfolio. The information ratio is the ratio of the alpha to the idiosyncratic volatility. The reason this is the right metric is because of the following mathematical fact from portfolio math.

- $S_{new}^2 = S_{passive}^2 + \left(\frac{\alpha_A}{\sigma_A}\right)^2$

- The variable S_{new} is the Sharpe ratio for a "new" portfolio that optimally mixes in a position in active securities into a passive portfolio. Active securities are ones that have nonzero alphas. These are the securities that either you or a professional manager has spent time researching; they are the ones that appear to be under- or overvalued. S_{passive} is the Sharpe ratio for the passive market portfolio. The last term is the square of the ratio of the active portfolio's alpha to the standard deviation of its idiosyncratic terms.

- The expression says that an active portfolio will contribute to the overall trade-off between return and risk of the overall risky portfolio—as measured by the Sharpe ratio of the "new" portfolio.

- Recall that when we discussed the optimal mixture of active and passive positions, we divided the optimal risky portfolio into two parts: a passive part (consisting of as broad a portfolio as possible) and a portfolio of active investigated securities. By adding in the active portfolio, the Sharpe ratio will rise above what the purely passive part generates on its own.

- The amount the active portfolio adds to the Sharpe ratio of the passive portfolio is related to the alpha on that active portfolio divided by the idiosyncratic volatility of that active portfolio. This ratio is the information ratio. Thus, an actively managed fund with a high information ratio will increase your overall portfolio's Sharpe ratio significantly.

Suggested Reading

Bodie, Kane, and Marcus, *Essentials of Investments*.

Questions to Consider

1. If you have placed some of your wealth in an actively managed fund, what attracted you to that fund? Were you attracted by its past performance in terms of returns or by data on its Sharpe ratio or alpha? Did these measures correspond well with the purpose of the active fund in your portfolio?

2. What types of information do you react to? How do you know if this information is useful? How do you know if your reactions are profitable on average?

Performance Evaluation

Lecture 19—Transcript

So far, we've explored a number of very important issues. In my mind, the most important is risk. We've seen many ways to measure risk, and we've seen how these measures are related to average return.

In terms of the process of investing, I've argued that you should try to measure the risk of a security, examine its expected return, and then based on both, decide how much of that security you want to hold in an optimally formed portfolio.

This process has you collect information, analyze it, and then react. If you do not do this for yourself, then you will likely delegate the management of your wealth to a professional manager who will do a similar process.

If you or your professional does not undertake the types of scientific analysis that we've discussed throughout the course, opting instead to react intuitively to the information available in the market, the process still consists of a stimulus and a response.

There is a second most important issue, and that is to evaluate if a particular stimulus–response process produces any gains relative to a purely passive strategy. As we discussed earlier, one of your options is simply to adopt a purely passive strategy. For such a strategy, you'll need to decide on the set of securities you will hold and the amount of wealth you'll put into that risky, but well-diversified, portfolio. Do you want to bear the risk associated with the whole world or simply want to bear the risk associated with blue-chip stocks, say, in the United States?

I suggest that broader is better. While some international securities may be harder to own outright, increasingly there are ETFs and index funds that you can hold. To the extent that the various markets around the globe are not correlated with the United States markets, the more markets you hold, the better will be the risk–return trade-off that you have in your overall portfolio. So, a global portfolio like the MSCI all country index strikes me as a good passive benchmark portfolio.

But maybe you should be active, too. If your stimulus–response process is any good, then it must be the case that you can beat that benchmark. If not, then just do the passive strategy. By the way, if beyond the money that you make or lose, you also get satisfaction out of doing this investment analysis, then your enjoyment should enter into your calculus as well. Although we lose money on many hobbies, we still do them just for the fun of it, and the same should be true for investing.

In this lecture, we will examine the ways in which to evaluate whether an active investing strategy is actually producing anything useful in terms of expected return or risk. That is, the methods discussed in this lecture evaluate the performance of a manager's stimulus–response process.

We will look at the set of performance metrics used. We will examine how to interpret what they mean. We will also see that you will use different metrics depending upon your specific investment objectives. So, context is important.

Let's start by asking, "What is a good benchmark for evaluating the performance of a professional manager?" The answer to this question depends upon the context of that manager or fund in your overall portfolio. Let's consider a couple of different situations. Remember Jane and Ichabod? Jane is doing her own investing. For this, she has a portfolio that consists of individual securities as well as a few passive index funds. This portfolio also consists of cash and some investments in short-term risk-free investments like certificates of deposit, money market deposits, and treasury bills. If you exclude these securities and deposits, she has about $2 million in risky stocks, corporate bonds, and index funds. She only has $500,000 in short-term deposits that are essentially default-free.

In contrast, consider Ichabod's situation. Ichabod also has about $2 million in risky investments and $500,000 in risk-free deposits. Ichabod, however, has allocated a significant portion of his investments to a couple of actively managed funds. In fact, about a million is evenly split between a global equity fund that invests in equity of mid-cap to large-cap non-U.S.-based companies and a fund that invests in growth firms, those that are fairly early stages of the life cycle, and are still expanding operations into new markets.

The rest of his million dollars he manages by picking stocks that he thinks could really take off.

Both Jane and Ichabod want to evaluate what they have done. Let's consider Jane's problem. Jane's problem is very similar to the typical investor's problem we analyzed when we looked at how to form an optimal risky portfolio in Lecture 15. Recall that a risky portfolio consisted of just risky securities, such as the passive index fund and the individual securities that Jane holds.

The idea of Lecture 15 was to form the best risky portfolio, where best was defined as that which generated the highest return per unit of risk. Then, given that optimal risky portfolio, the investor could control the amount of risk by deciding how much of their wealth to put into that risky portfolio and how much to keep safe in deposits or risk-free bonds.

So, in Jane's case, she should pick the portfolio that maximizes the Sharpe ratio. Thus, the appropriate evaluation criterion for Jane's risky portfolio is the Sharpe ratio. She should compare the Sharpe ratio of her portfolio to that of the global benchmark. If the Sharpe ratio of her portfolio is less than that of the benchmark, then she could try to improve her risky portfolio by changing the amount allocated to the two passive funds and the individual stocks that she owns.

The material in Lecture 15 should guide her decisions in this regard. But the bottom line is that because the risky portfolio she is forming is the only overall risky portfolio she will hold, she should evaluate the performance of that portfolio, and any alternatives according to the Sharpe ratio. If she can't beat the benchmark, she should just invest in the benchmark.

Let's next consider Ichabod's case. I will show how the Sharpe ratio is calculated in practice in his case. Let's turn to his case now. Ichabod's situation is a bit more complicated than Jane's because he has a couple of actively managed funds. That is, he has delegated the management of a portion of his portfolio to what are supposed to be actively managed funds. He wants to get an extra boost from active management, but he also wants to be sure he's not overpaying for the extra performance these funds provide. He also needs to be able to measure their performance.

The first question that comes to mind, however, is what would constitute good performance in this case? Should he look at the Sharpe ratio for each fund? These numbers are commonly provided for fund managers, but is that the right metric in this case? Is what the Sharpe ratio measures really what he wants conceptually?

Let's recall what the Sharpe ratio is. The Sharpe ratio is the expected return on the portfolio minus the risk-free rate divided by the standard deviation of that portfolio. The Sharpe ratio is an ex-ante measure. That is, at the time the portfolio is being formed, the investors are supposed to pick the weights that maximize the Sharpe ratio. It's an ex-ante measure in the sense that the expected return and the standard deviation are conceptually related to things that the investor expects to hold in the future.

For example, the expected return is based upon your notion of the degree of mispricing getting corrected during the holding period horizon. The standard deviation is based upon your forecast of volatility. The Sharpe ratios that are reported in the financial press and on websites are ex-post measures. With these measures, the expected return minus the risk-free rate is the average excess return of that portfolio over some past period of time, say, the last five to 10 years. The standard deviation is calculated as the standard deviation of the returns that occurred in the past 10 to five years. Thus, if you have 10 years of data on a managed fund, the Sharpe ratio would be calculated based upon the average return of the portfolio in excess of the risk-free return and the sample standard deviation of those excess returns would be used in the denominator of the Sharpe ratio.

Using Sharpe ratios calculated in this way, most investors would rank managers from highest (or best) to lowest (or worst). But note that this measure is backward-looking. By looking at this ex-post ratio, you are implicitly saying that you think that a manager's past rank will be indicative of that manager's future ranking. That is, if a given fund had a higher Sharpe ratio based upon past returns than another fund, then you might want to pick that one because you think that the rankings are persistent. This is a pretty big leap. You need to look at the persistence in the Sharpe ratios over time for a particular manager. For a particular manager, look at their Sharpe ratios over many years.

Back to the main issue at hand. Is this even the correct measure of what Ichabod cares about? To see if this is the right measure, recall what it measures. It's supposed to be what you want to maximize when you're finding the optimal portfolio of risky securities only. His overall portfolio, which includes both risky investments and risk-free deposits, will have the highest amount of return per unit of risk if the portfolio of risky securities has a large Sharpe ratio. Once you have such a risky portfolio defined, he can then determine, given the risk of that portfolio, how much he wants to put at risk and how much he wants to keep safe.

Thus, there are two overall questions. What is the best risky portfolio, and what is the fraction of his wealth that he wants to put at risk in that portfolio? If he were to evaluate each of the managed funds by looking at their Sharpe ratios, then what would he learn? Well, for each actively managed fund, he would learn how much expected return per unit of risk each portfolio generates, if that was the only risky portfolio that he held.

Thus, the Sharpe ratio for a given portfolio is sensible only if that's the only portfolio to be held. If the portfolio you are evaluating is the only risky portfolio you want to hold, then the standard deviation in the Sharpe ratio is the risk that that investor bears.

But, if an investor holds two actively managed portfolios, then the standard deviation of the overall portfolio will be some combination of the two individual standard deviations.

The real question Ichabod wants answered is how much extra return does the actively managed fund contribute to his overall portfolio relative to the extra risk that that actively managed portfolio contributes to his overall portfolio? That is not what the Sharpe ratio tells Ichabod. Note that for Jane, since she has only one risky portfolio, the Sharpe ratio does exactly that for her. It tells her exactly what her return is per unit of risk.

So, what does Ichabod really want? Well, there are a couple of measures out there that will get to what Ichabod really wants to know. One such measure is called the Treynor measure. Since the standard deviation of the portfolio's return does not measure risk in a portfolio context, the Treynor measure actually replaces the standard deviation by the beta of the portfolio. That is, the Treynor measure is the expected return of the portfolio minus the risk-free rate divided by the beta of the portfolio—not the standard deviation of the portfolio.

Thus, the Treynor measure captures the extra excess return that portfolio provides given the risk of that portfolio as measured by that portfolio's beta. Recall that when we developed the CAPM I argued that the beta of an individual security or an individual portfolio was the incremental contribution of that security to the risk of the portfolio. Thus, the beta of a portfolio Ichabod holds will be the extra amount of risk that that portfolio contributes to his overall risky portfolio.

Another measure of the contribution of a managed portfolio to the overall performance of the risky portfolio that adjusts for risk in the managed portfolio is called Jensen's alpha. Jensen's alpha is a measure of the extent to which the portfolio's return exceeds what it should be according to, say, CAPM. Specifically, Jensen's alpha is the average return on the portfolio minus the average of the risk-adjusted expected return.

In general, the risk-adjusted expected return is the expected return implied by a particular asset pricing model. If we use CAPM, then the risk-adjusted expected return on the portfolio is the risk-free rate plus the beta of that portfolio times the market return minus the risk-free rate.

For any period in the past, you can calculate the risk-adjusted expected return by taking the risk-free rate for that period and adding the beta of the portfolio multiplied by whatever the market return minus the risk-free rate was in that period. Think of the value of this as the value that the CAPM implies should happen on average.

For any given period, the difference between the realized return on the portfolio in that period and this risk-adjusted expected return in that period is the alpha for that period. Jensen's alpha is just the average of the alphas for all the past periods.

By the way, if you want to use a different asset pricing model, then each year in the data calculate the expected return implied by that model and subtract that from the realized return on the portfolio being evaluated. Think of this as the alpha relative to that particular asset pricing model. Then you just average those to calculate Jensen's alpha for that asset pricing model.

Note that Jensen's alpha adjusts for risk by measuring the amount of return that should be paid given its risk. This is important to you because you should not give a manager credit for good performance if all that manager did was load up on risk. It's easy and likely to get high average returns if you just buy very risky securities. What is not easy is finding mispriced securities with real non-zero alphas. Thus, if the return on a portfolio being evaluated is high simply because the risk of that portfolio is high, then Jensen's alpha will be knocked down for that.

While Jensen's alpha does adjust for the risk in the managed portfolio, the measure does not capture the effect of that portfolio's extra risk on the overall risky portfolio. This is also true of the Treynor measure. Although they are similar, you should realize that you may get different answers when you look at portfolios and rank on the basis of the Jensen's alpha versus the Treynor measure.

To see the relationship between Jensen's alpha and the Treynor measure, let's consider a portfolio that has three different characteristics. Let's consider three different portfolios, say, that Ichabod needs to evaluate.

You might also imagine a plot of expected return minus the risk-free rate for each portfolio against its beta. Let zero denote the origin of this plot. Let one of the portfolios be the benchmark market portfolio. Let's call this one M. This portfolio, by definition, has a beta of one and has an average return equal to the average return on the market. So, M stands for the market. Let's say that the average return on the market in excess of the risk-free rate is 7%. So I can economize on words. I'm going to refer to the return in excess of the risk-free rate as the excess return. Thus, the expected excess return on the market is 7%.

On a plot, imagine a line emanating from the origin through portfolio M. Let's call this the 0M line. This line depicts the relationship between the average excess return and beta as implied by CAPM. Since the market has a beta of 1 by definition, the slope of the 0M line is the market risk premium, which in this case is 7%.

Let the other two portfolios be denoted by X and Y. These two portfolios are portfolios that Ichabod wants to evaluate so that he can decide whether he wants to buy or sell them. Let's say that Y has a beta of 0.75 and an expected excess return of 6.25%. X has a beta of 1.1 and has an expected excess return of 8.9%. Also imagine a line from the origin going through point Y. Call this the 0Y line. And also, imagine a line from the origin through point X portfolio. Call this the 0X line.

Now think about moving along the 0M line. As we move up and down the 0M line, the beta and the excess return rise and fall as implied by CAPM. We can use this line as a benchmark. We can pick any beta on the horizontal axis, then read up from that beta to the point that corresponds to that beta on the 0M line. Then, by reading over to the expected excess return on the vertical axis, the value on that axis is the expected excess return implied by the asset pricing model (CAPM in this case).

For example, for portfolio Y, which has a beta 0.75, the expected excess return on Y should be its beta times the market risk premium—that is, 0.75 × 0.07 = 0.0525, 5.25%. But note that the average excess return on Y is higher than that. It's expected to be 6.25%. The difference between its expected excess return of 6.25% and that predicted by CAPM on the 0M line of 5.25% is just Jensen's alpha. In this case, it's 1%.

Similarly, we can calculate Jensen's alpha for X. In this case, the Jensen's alpha for portfolio X is 1.2%. For a beta of 1.1, the 0M line predicts that the excess return on X should be 7.7%. But, because the excess return on X is expected to be 8.9%, the alpha is 1.2%.

Thus, if Ichabod were to simply pick a managed portfolio based upon Jensen's alpha, he would pick managed portfolio X, because it has a bigger Jensen's alpha. But, is this the right choice? Jensen's alpha only makes sense if Ichabod is not going to strategically pick the weights in his portfolio. By strategically picking the weights, Ichabod can implicitly lever up a portfolio.

For example, if he borrows by buying on margin, Ichabod can form a portfolio with Y and leverage a portfolio that has the same beta as X. Maybe that levered portfolio will have a larger alpha than X. To see this, consider a portfolio of Y and risk-free borrowing. Let w_Y be the weight in Y and w_B be the weight on borrowing. If Ichabod can lever, by, say, borrowing on margin, then each of the weights need not be less than 1. They do have to add to 1 but they don't have to be all less than 1. We will look at dollar amounts in a minute, after we look at the weights.

Recall that the beta of a portfolio, even a portfolio of portfolios, is simply the weighted average of the betas of the individual securities in that portfolio. Thus, what we want are values of w_y and w_B such that $w_Y \times$ betaY $+ w_B \times$ betaB = betaX. In this case, if we borrow on margin, then we're borrowing at the risk-free rate and the beta of borrowing is 0. Thus, we need to solve $w_y \times 0.75 + w\text{B} \times 0 = 1.1$. That is, $w_y = 1.46667$. And then in that case, $w_B = -0.47$.

That is, if Ichabod has \$100,000 of his own money to invest in Y, he uses that but borrows \$47,000 on margin to buy \$147,000 worth of Y. Let's let the risk-free rate be 2% in this case. What is the expected excess return on this levered portfolio that has exactly the same beta as X?

The portfolio excess is actually 1.47%. The excess return on this portfolio we just formed has an excess return, in excess of the risk-free rate of 1.47%. That is, this levered portfolio creates a position that has a beta of 1.1 and has an alpha of 1.47%. This levered portfolio alpha is bigger than the one associated with the managed portfolio X, which has an alpha of 1.2%. But, when we compared the Jensen's alpha between X and Y, X looked better.

This example points out the value of the Treynor measure over Jensen's alpha as a measure of performance. The Treynor measure is the slope of the line from the origin through the portfolio point. In our example plot, the slope of the 0Y line is steeper than that of the 0X line. So the Treynor measure of Y is bigger than that of X. Specifically, the slope of the 0Y line is 0.062/0.75 = 0.0833. The slope of the 0X line is only 0.089/1.1 = 0.0809. It's less.

If Ichabod is only going to pick one of these two managed portfolios and not lever up, then he should pick X, not Y. If he does that, he's going to get an expected excess return of 1.2% rather than 1%. But, if Ichabod is going to form a portfolio with one of these managed portfolios and perhaps lever up, he should use Y, not X. He can create for himself an alpha of 1.47% out of Y rather than an alpha of 1.2% with X.

There's another measure that is similar to the Treynor measure based upon leverage called the M2 measure, after Modigliani and Miller, two Nobel Prize winners in economics and finance. Their idea is to consider the amount of volatility in a passive market portfolio and lever up and down the managed portfolio until that position has the same volatility as the market. Once you have that position, you can compare the expected return on that position to that of the market. If the managed position dominates, invest in the managed portfolio. If not, invest in the market.

To see how to do this, let's see what would happen if the volatility of the market was, say, 20%. Remember that such a volatility corresponds to 0.20^2, which is a variance of 0.04.

Also, let's say that the managed portfolio is a portfolio Y from earlier. Let's say it has a volatility of 25%, or a variance of 0.0625. Again, let's form a position with the managed portfolio and borrowing or lending that will match the volatility of the market. That is, let's again pick w_Y and wB. This time let's pick them not so that we can match betas, but so that we can match the volatility with that of that in the market.

For a given value of w_Y and w_B, in general, the variance of that portfolio will be: $\text{Var}(r_p) = w\text{Y}^2 \times \text{Var}(r_Y) + wn^2 \times \text{Var}(r_B) + 2 \times w_Y \times w_B \times \text{Cov}(r_Y, r_B)$. But look, because the borrowing at rB is risk-free, the rate does not vary, and $\text{Var}(r_B) = 0$ and $\text{Cov}(r_Y, r_B) = 0$.

Thus, the variance of the portfolio Y and borrowing and lending simplifies to simply: $\text{Var}(r_p) = w_Y^2 \times \text{Var}(r_Y) = w_Y^2 \times 0.0625$. This implies that the volatility is equal to the square root of that, the standard deviation is $w_Y \times 0.25$. We want to pick w_Y such that this volatility is the same as the market's volatility of 20%. Thus, $w_Y = 0.2/0.25 = 0.8$, or 80%.

Thus, if Ichabod took his $100,000 and invested $80,000 in the active fund that is Fund Y and $20,000 in T-bills, then he would have a position that has 20% volatility. This 20% volatility is the same that he could achieve if he just put his $100,000 into the market.

But, how does the expected return compare? The expected return on the market is the risk-free rate plus the market risk premium of 7%, for a total of 9%. The expected return on the 80/20 portfolio of Y and T-bills is going to be equal to: $0.8 \times [0.02 + 0.75 \times (0.07) + 0.01] + 0.2 \times 0.02 = 0.09$; that's 9%, too.

Thus, even though the managed portfolio Y has a positive Jensen's alpha, if that's the only portfolio that Ichabod is going to hold, then extra performance in the alpha is going to be eaten up in its extra volatility. This is because the managed portfolio Y is designed to beat the market, not be the market. In order to beat the market, it has to have non-market weights on some of its various securities. If the active managers of this fund do that, then they're likely to be less diversified than if they had market weights.

In fact, in order to exploit deviations from equilibrium returns, the managers must take extreme positions. Recall that in the lecture on optimal active portfolios we discussed how the optimal positions necessarily entailed bearing some idiosyncratic volatility. Thus, it is likely that fund Y has greater volatility than the passive market because it does not have a diversified position that takes away all of the idiosyncratic volatility completely. What the M2 measure says is that if Ichabod is going to hold just one active portfolio, he should not hold Y. He should hold the market instead.

But why should Ichabod just hold one managed fund? In fact, most managed funds are actively managed knowing that the investors will not hold them as their only risky portfolio. If they know they are going to be held with other active funds in a portfolio of funds, what performance measure do they want to compete on? Each fund will want to be high in demand as a component of an overall optimally-formed portfolio of risky securities. So for example, at my university, the chief investment officer for the university manages the university's nearly $1 billion portfolio. He is not allowed to take positions in individual securities. He is only allowed to invest in the portfolios managed by others. Thus, rather than pick individual securities, he picks managers. How can he evaluate whether a manager is any good or not? This is essentially what Ichabod needs to do as well.

Well, given that what he is going to do is decide how to allocate his $1 billion dollars amongst a bunch of different risky portfolios that are actively managed, what he wants to do is look at how each individual managed portfolio contributes to the Sharpe ratio that can form out of the portfolio of all these actively managed portfolios. The university, by the way, only holds this one risky portfolio that he is creating. He's creating this out of a bunch of individual managed portfolios. So what should happen in this case is that the university should actually measure his performance on the basis of the Sharpe ratio. But how should he measure the performance of all the other people that he's buying actively-managed portfolios from?

The appropriate metric is called the information ratio. Recall that when we discussed how to form the optimal risky portfolio on the basis of any active analysis, we noted that there was a trade-off between the alpha and the idiosyncratic volatility of active positions in securities or portfolios.

The information ratio is the ratio of the alpha to the idiosyncratic volatility. The reason this is the right metric is because of the following mathematical fact from portfolio math: $S^2_{new} = S^2_{passive} + (\alpha_A/\sigma_A)^2$.

The variable S_{new} is the Sharpe ratio of the new portfolio that optimally mixes in a position in the active securities into a passive portfolio. What I mean by active securities are the ones that have non-zero alphas. These are the securities that you either find or a professional manager has spent time researching. These are the ones that appear to be under- or overvalued.

So, $S_{passive}$ is the Sharpe ratio for the passive, or the market portfolio in this expression. The last term is the square of the ratio of the active portfolio's alpha to the standard deviations of its idiosyncratic terms. What the above expression says is an active portfolio will contribute to the overall trade-off between return and risk in the overall risky portfolio as measured by the Sharpe ratio of this new portfolio. Recall that when we discussed the optimal mixture of active and passive positions, we divided the optimal risky portfolio into two parts—a passive part (consisting of a broad-based portfolio as a passively managed portfolio) and a portfolio of active investigated securities. By adding in an active portfolio, the Sharpe ratio will rise above that that is generated by the purely passive part by itself.

The amount the active portfolio adds to the Sharpe ratio of the passive portfolio is related to the alpha on that active portfolio divided by the idiosyncratic volatility of that active portfolio. This ratio is called the information ratio. Thus, an actively managed fund with a high information ratio will increase the overall portfolio's Sharpe ratio significantly.

In this lecture, we have seen a number of performance metrics—the Sharpe ratio, the Treynor measure, Jensen's alpha, and the M2 measure, and then finally the information ratio.

We have also seen that the measure you need to look at depends upon how you are using that portfolio that you're evaluating. If it is the only portfolio you will hold, use the Sharpe ratio. If you're going to mix that portfolio in with other actively managed portfolios, first identify good candidates with the Treynor measure, then use the information ratio. Since Jensen's alpha is often reported, you also need to be aware of how this measure works as well.

Market Making and Liquidity
Lecture 20

What is liquidity? And should you be willing to pay for it? If so, how much? In this lecture, you will explore these questions. First, you will examine exactly what financial economists mean by liquidity. Then, you will examine the things that determine whether the market for a particular security is liquid. Next, you will examine how to measure the liquidity of a security. Finally, you will learn how to think about whether you should be willing to pay the market price for liquidity.

Liquidity

- Liquidity is typically defined in two dimensions: the time and the price dimension. A liquid security is one that can be turned into cash (i.e., liquidated) very quickly and without having the price fall significantly. If, keeping the price fixed, it takes a long time to find a buyer at that price, that security is not very liquid. And, if, keeping the time over which you must liquidate fixed, you have to drop the price by a lot to get a buyer, then that security is not very liquid.

- Over time, the liquidity of most securities has increased. In fact, for many stocks traded on organized exchanges, you can sell a stock in seconds while only pushing the average transaction price down by a penny.

- In exchanges, there are two forms of transactions costs: the bid-ask spread and brokerage fees. The brokerage fee is what you pay for a broker to execute your trade. Brokerage fees are small, and they are getting smaller.

- The second cost is the bid-ask spread. At any point in time, there are two prices for any security. If you, as an investor, want to buy, you will pay the ask price. If you, as an investor, want to sell, you will sell at the bid price.

- The ask price you pay when buying is always above the bid price you get when selling. The difference between the bid and the ask is the bid-ask spread. At any given time, the bid and the ask prices bracket the market's best guess at the fundamental value of the security. Thus, if you buy at the ask, you have to pay above the fundamental value, and if you sell at the bid, you get less than the fundamental value.

- At any point in time, there are many prices being offered or bid at in the market for any security. These prices are from limit orders, which are price-contingent orders that specify the price at which the person who submitted the order is willing to trade. There are limit orders to sell and limit orders to buy.

- The set of limit sells are the current set of ask, or offer, prices. These are the prices at which someone, mostly securities dealers, is willing to sell the security. That is, they are the prices the dealers are asking buyers to pay. They are also called offer prices because they are the prices at which they are offering to sell.

- The unfilled limit buy orders that remain constitute the set of bid prices, the prices at which various dealers are willing to buy the security. They are called bid prices because they are the prices the dealers are bidding.

- Among the set of bid and ask prices there is a best ask, which is the lowest ask price. It is "best" from the perspective of someone wanting to buy. The lower the ask, the lower the price the buyer has to pay the dealer who is posting that ask. Similarly, at any point in time, there is also a best—i.e., highest—bid price. The difference between the best ask and the best bid is the bid-ask spread.

- Limit orders are typically placed by dealers trying to take advantage of a temporary lack of either supply or demand at a specific point in time. Many dealers place limit orders on both sides of the market.

- An alternative to a limit order is a market order. Such orders are submitted by investors either wanting to invest in a security or wanting to liquidate an existing position in a security. Such an order simply says that you are willing to transact—either buy or sell—at the going price. That is, it is not an order that specifies a particular price contingency as with a limit order. If you place a market order, your order is filled at the highest available bid if you are selling and at the lowest available ask if you are buying.

- So, with a market order, the good news is that if you are selling, you get to sell at the highest available bid, and if you are buying, you only have to pay the lowest available ask. However, with a market order, the bad news is that the highest bid is below the lowest ask. Therefore, when you buy, you have to pay more than you would get if you were selling.

- With a limit order, the person who submitted the order specifies the amount they are willing to trade at the specified price (or better). Thus, because the best bid and the best ask are limit orders, there are a number of shares or units of the security that the dealers are willing to trade at each of these price points. The total number of shares at each price is called the depth at that price.

- Note that that depth can be comprised of a single bid or offer from a single dealer or multiple bids or offers from multiple dealers. For most trades, the number of units of the security people want to buy or sell is smaller than the depth at the highest bid or the lowest ask.

- In that case, if you submit a market order, your whole order will get transacted at that highest bid or lowest ask. However, if you want to trade quantities bigger than those being offered at the highest bid or the lowest ask, then your order will get filled at multiple prices.

Bid-Ask Spreads and Liquidity

- In this context, liquidity is immediacy. If you want to buy now, you will place a market order. And you will have to pay what the limit order sellers are willing to take—and that is above the fundamental value of the security. If you want to sell now, you have to sell it for what the limit order buyers are willing to pay—and that's below the fundamental value.

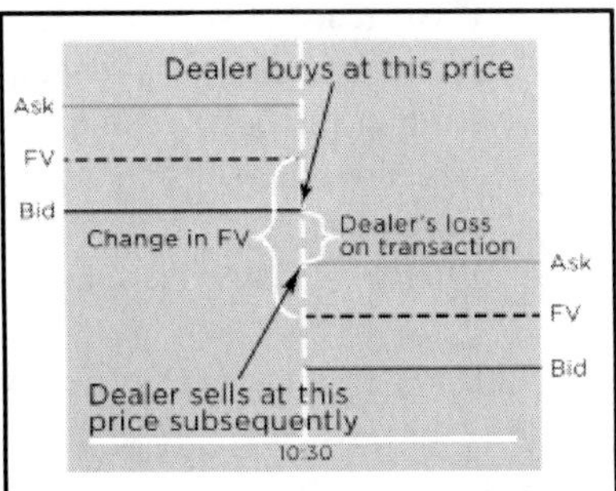

- A good way to think about the difference between the bids and asks is that it compensates the dealers who are placing limits for providing liquidity. They are allowing people to get immediacy. And they get paid to provide immediacy by being able to sell above the fundamental value and buy below the fundamental value.

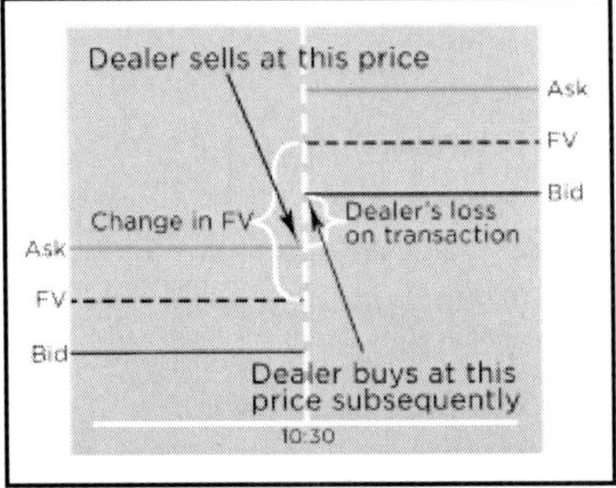

- From the perspective of someone demanding immediacy, the more they have to pay above the fundamental value, the less liquid the security, and the farther below the fundamental value they get when they sell, the less liquid.

- Again from the perspective of someone demanding immediacy, the liquidity cost is the size of the difference between the transaction price and the fundamental value. It is half of the effective bid-ask spread, which is, for a given quantity, the difference between what you would pay to get that quantity versus what you could sell that quantity for.

- If there were not much depth below the best bid, then a larger market sell order would transact at an average price below the best bid. Similarly, a larger market buy order would pay an average price above the best ask. The less depth, the worse the execution is.

- The spread between the best bid and best ask is not a true indication of the liquidity cost for larger orders, unless there is significant depth at the best bid and best ask. Thus, a liquid market is where there are many dealers willing to buy at the highest bid and many dealers willing to sell at the lowest ask—and there is only a small difference between that bid and ask.

- There can be fairly large variation in the liquidity of various securities. Large household names, such as Procter & Gamble and Microsoft, have very small bid-ask spreads, while other securities that are less frequently traded can have little depth and fairly large bid-ask spreads.

- Because there are multiple dealers that compete with each other, the spread can be thought of as the competitive price of liquidity. Competition should drive the price of liquidity down to the cost of supplying it.

Figure 20.1 Bid-Ask Spread

	Cap delta			
p	1	2	3	4
0.4	−0.8	−1.0	−1.2	−1.4
0.5	−0.6	−0.6	−0.6	−0.6
0.6	−0.4	−0.2	0.0	0.2
0.7	−0.2	0.2	0.6	1.0
0.8	0.0	0.6	1.2	1.8
0.9	0.2	1.0	1.8	2.6
1.0	0.4	1.4	2.4	3.4

Fundamental Risk and Adverse Selection

- Financial economists have divided the spread into two main logical components based on the source of the cost to dealer of supplying liquidity. There are two types of costs: fundamental risk and adverse selection.

- Fundamental risk is the risk that the fundamental value of the security will change significantly at any moment in time. This represents a risk to a dealer because dealers make money by buying low (at the bid) and selling high (at the ask).

- Adverse selection is the risk faced by a dealer that the traders will systematically select trades that are adverse to the dealer. Adverse selection occurs when traders have superior information about the value of the security.

- Again, fundamental risk and adverse selection are the two costs. The bigger any of these costs are, the bigger the competitive spreads must be. Thus, securities with more fundamental risk have wider spreads. Securities with lots of adverse selection have wider spreads. The securities with the most adverse selection and the widest spreads are securities that are not traded by many uninformed investors. The stocks of small companies are like this.

Measuring Liquidity

- The liquidity cost of a security cannot be measured solely by the difference in the best bid and best ask. Of course, if that spread is wide, that security is not liquid. However, at any moment in time, this spread may be narrow, but there may be little depth at these quotes. In this case, a sizable market order to sell will push the price way down, and a sizable market order to buy can push the price way up.

- A measure developed by Yakov Amihud, referred to as the Amihud measure, is a measure of the liquidity of an individual security that incorporates depth. The Amihud measure is the average of the absolute value of the daily price change divided by the dollar volume in that day. Note that this is really an illiquidity measure, because higher values of this measure indicate an illiquid market, or one in which the prices change by a lot for a given amount of trade volume.

- This measure is calculated as follows: For every trade day in a month, take the absolute value of the price change that day divided by the dollar amount of trade in that security for that day. Then, take these values and average them over the 20 or so trading days in the month. That is the Amihud measure for that month.

- Academic research has shown that the Amihud measure varies significantly across securities. It also shows that the less liquid a security is, the higher its return is on average. This makes sense in that liquidity costs will erode your return. Thus, investors appear to be willing to pay less for less liquid securities than more liquid securities. This lowering of the price generates a higher return.

- You can think of the effect that liquidity costs have on the return as being the amount the average person needs to be compensated in extra return in order to compensate for the average amount of liquidity costs they incur given the average length of time they intend to hold that security. If you intend to hold the security for longer than the average investor, then the return per period is more than enough to compensate you for the liquidity costs you will incur. But if you intend to hold it for a shorter period of time, the extra return will likely be insufficient.

Suggested Reading

Acharya and Pedersen, "Asset Pricing with Liquidity Risk."

Amihud, "Illiquidity and Stock Returns."

Amihud and Mendelson, "Asset Pricing and the Bid-Ask Spread."

———, "The Effect of Beta, Bid-Ask Spread, Residual Risk and Size on Stock Returns."

Harris, *Trading and Exchanges*.

Patterson, *Dark Pools*.

Teall, *Financial Trading and Investing*.

Questions to Consider

1. Do you think that you need to trade more frequently than most private investors? Do you think that you do trade more frequently than most investors?

2. Can you think of a few securities that are likely to have a significant amount of adverse selection? In most countries, it is illegal for corporate insiders to trade the securities of the firms they manage based on the private information they possess due to their position in the firm. If such trading is allowed, what would you predict would happen to the liquidity of markets?

Market Making and Liquidity
Lecture 20—Transcript

What is liquidity? And should you be willing to pay for it? And if so, how much? In this lecture, we'll explore these questions. We'll do this in four steps.

First, we'll examine exactly what financial economists mean by liquidity. Second, we'll examine the things that determine whether or not the market for a particular security is liquid or not. Third, we'll examine how to measure the liquidity of a security. And then fourth, we'll discuss how you should think about whether you should be willing to pay the market price for liquidity.

Let's start by defining liquidity. Liquidity is typically defined in two dimensions—the time dimension and the price dimension. A liquid security is one that can be turned into cash (i.e., liquidated) very quickly and without having the price fall significantly.

If keeping the price fixed, it takes a long time to find a buyer at that price, that security is not very liquid, and, if, keeping the time over which you must liquidate fixed, you have to drop the price by a lot to get a buyer, then the security is also not very liquid.

Housing is very illiquid. Shares of Procter & Gamble are very liquid. For most individual investors, the market for corporate bonds is not liquid. It is difficult to find active prices for bonds. This is also true for many foreign securities in the United States. Yet, these securities are potentially the types of securities that you would actually want to invest in because they allow you to earn a very good rate of return, given that the prices are so discounted in the market.

Over time, the liquidity of most securities has increased. In fact, for many stocks traded on organized exchanges, you can sell a stock in seconds while only pushing the average transaction price down a penny.

So, why might you care about liquidity? For one, many less well-known stocks may be less liquid. But, because they are less well-known, they are more likely to be mispriced, thus presenting potential trade opportunities for you. So let's say that you want to buy such a stock as a short-term investment, because you think it is mispriced. You do think that the price will get to the appropriate level fairly soon, however. So, you buy it anticipating that you will be able to sell it in the future for a gain.

You need to recognize that your gain will depend heavily on the stock's liquidity. To see this, let's consider two stocks that you think are equally undervalued. Specifically, you expect that both will go from \$100 to, say, \$110 in a month. While both securities have the same values, let security A, a fairly well-known firm, have a 0.5% liquidity cost, and let security B, a more obscure firm, have a 1% liquidity cost.

Now, what do I mean by liquidity cost? What I mean by a liquidity cost is the amount your trade pushes the price up or down. We will see exactly how this happens later, and we will also look at why such a cost might be high or low for certain securities. For now, let's just take the liquidity costs as given for these two firms.

With a liquidity cost of 0.5%, if you want to buy A, you will have to pay half a percent over its current value when you buy. And when you go to sell A, you'll have to sell it at half a percent below its value at that point in time. More specifically, you will go to buy A, and you'll have to pay $\$100 \times (1 + 0.005) = \$100.50$. And then when you go to sell A in a month or so, after its fundamental value has been recognized and it's risen to \$110, you're only going to be able to get $\$110 \times (1 - 0.005) = \$109.45$. So your effective return in this case is going to be: $(\$109.45 - \$100.50)/\$100.50 = 0.089$ or 8.9% return.

Now, if you were to trade B instead, then what would you pay? $\$100 \times (1.01) = \$101.00$ and you would sell it for $\$110 \times (1 - 0.01) = \$108.90$, for a return of only 7.8%.

An alternative way to think about what just happened here is that to get the same return as you got for security A, then it would have to be the case that the value of B has to rise in terms of its fundamental value 11.1%. Thus, if you trade in illiquid stocks, you're going to have to work harder to find bigger mispricings. If you churn your investments, the greater the liquidity cost, the smaller your realized return will be.

Now let's turn to how liquidity costs manifest themselves in the market. In exchanges, there are two forms of transactions costs. One is the bid-ask spread and the other one is brokerage fees.

The brokerage fee is what you pay a broker to execute your trade. Brokerage fees are small and are getting smaller. Most any online broker will charge about $10 per transaction, while many are competing to be charging only $5 to $6. If you have a trade that's for 100 shares of a $50 stock, that's on the order of one- to two-tenths of a percent in terms of the brokerage cost.

The second cost is the bid-ask spread. Let's see what a bid-ask spread is. At any point in time, there are two prices for any security. If you, as the investor, want to buy, you will pay the ask price. If you, as the investor, want to sell, you will have to sell at the bid price. The ask price you pay when buying is always above the bid price you get when selling. The difference between the bid and the ask is the bid-ask spread. At any given time, the bid and the ask prices bracket the market's best guess at the fundamental value of that security. Thus, if you buy at the ask, you have to pay above the fundamental value. And if you sell at the bid, you'll get less than that fundamental value.

Who determines the bid-ask spread? At any point in time, there are actually lots of prices being offered or bid at in the market for any particular security. These prices come from limit orders. A limit order is a price-contingent order that specifies the price at which the person who submitted the order is willing to trade. There are limit orders to sell and limit orders to buy.

Let's see how this works by imagining that you are submitting a limit order. By the way, you can easily submit limits order via online trade platforms. Let's say that you are also a buyer. If you're a buyer, you want to pay a low price. Thus, if you were to submit a limit order to buy at $20 per share, then your order will only get filled if the price is $20 or less. In contrast, if you place a limit order to sell at $20, your order is filled only if someone is willing to pay you $20 or more.

In addition to the price contingency, you also have to specify the number of shares that you are willing to trade. At any point in time, there will be a set of limit orders that have contingencies that no one is willing to satisfy. For example, someone may have placed a limit order to buy at two cents for a stock that typically trades around $100. Of course, this person is willing to buy at two cents or less.

But as we will see, this type of order is not going to get filled. In fact, most limit orders actually trade very close to what I would say is the fundamental value of the security. So something like this two-cent order, these are referred to as stub orders, and they're kind of just sort of silly, actually.

This set of unfilled orders at any point in time determines what is referred to as the limit order book. To see what this book might look like, consider four possible limit orders, each placed by a different dealer, say. By the way, dealers place these limit orders in order to provide liquidity. We'll return to this shortly.

So let's say that dealer A placed a limit order to buy at $20 for 100 shares, and then dealer B placed a limit order to buy 100 shares at $10—dealer B wants to get a really good deal. Let's say dealer Y placed a limit order to sell 100 shares at $19 and dealer Z placed a limit order to sell 100 at $25.

Now, since dealer A is willing to buy for $20 or less and dealer Y is willing to sell for $19 or more, there's a deal. Let's just say that they split the difference and the trade is at $19.50. They're both happy. Now, since these orders get filled, they are no longer present in the market.

What remains is a limit order to buy from dealer B for $10 and a limit order to sell from dealer Z for $25. Dealer B will buy at prices $10 or below, but dealer Z will only sell if the price is $25 or higher. There is no deal between these two dealers.

Now, these orders will remain on the book unfilled until, perhaps, new orders come. So, once all of the mutually beneficial trades have been cleared out of the book, the limit order book, what remains is a set of limit buys and limit sells.

The set of limit sells are the current set of ask or offer prices. These are the prices at which someone, mostly securities dealers, are willing to sell the security. That is, they are the prices the dealers are asking buyers to pay. They're also called offer prices, as these are the prices at which they are offering to sell.

The unfilled buy orders that remain constitute the set of bid prices. These are the prices at which various dealers are willing to buy the security. They are bid prices because these are the prices the dealers are bidding. Among the set of bid and ask prices, there is a best ask, which is the lowest possible ask. It is the best from the perspective of someone wanting to buy. The lower the ask price, the lower the price the buyer has to pay the dealer who is posting that ask.

Similarly, at any point in time, there is also a best (i.e., highest) bid price. The difference between the best ask and the best bid is the bid-ask spread. Recall that the highest bid and the lowest ask will bracket the market's best guess at the fundamental value of the security at that time.

Limit orders are typically placed by dealers trying to take advantage of a temporary lack of either supply or demand at a specific point in time. For example, if there is little supply but an investor wants to buy, then a dealer who placed a limit order to sell with a very high price will likely get to sell to the buyer at that high price. Similarly, if there is little demand and an investor wants to sell, then a low limit order to buy will allow a dealer to get a good deal on that transaction. Many dealers place limit orders on both sides of the market, by the way.

Now, an alternative to a limit order is called a market order. Such orders are submitted by investors either wanting to invest in a security or wanting to liquidate an existing position in the security. Such an order simply says that they are willing to transact—either buy or sell—at whatever the going price is. That is, it is not an order that specifies a particular price contingency as does with a limit order. If you place a market order, your order is filled at the highest available bid if you are selling and at the lowest available ask if you are buying.

So, with a market order, the good news is that when you're selling, you get to sell at the highest available bid. If you are buying, you only have to pay the lowest available ask. But, with a market order, the bad news is that the highest bid is below the lowest ask, so when you buy, you have to pay more than you would get if you were selling.

Recall that, with a limit order, the person who submitted the order specifies the amount that they are willing to trade at that specific price. Thus, since the best bid and the best ask are limit orders, there are a number of shares or units of the security that the dealers are willing to trade at each of those price points. The total number of shares at each price point is called the depth at that price.

Note that the depth can be comprised of a single bid or offer from a single dealer or multiple bids or offers from multiple dealers. For most trades, the number of units of the security people want to buy or sell is smaller than the depth at the highest bid and the lowest ask. In these cases, if you submit a market order, your whole order will get transacted at the highest bid or the lowest ask, depending on whether you're buying or selling.

But, if you want to trade quantities bigger than those being offered at the highest bid and the lowest ask, then your order will get filled at multiple prices. For example, let's say you want to buy 20,000 shares of SleazeCo. The two lowest ask prices are $20.00 and $20.10. Whoever is willing to sell at $20.00 is only willing to sell 15,000 shares. The person willing to sell at $20.10 is willing to sell 30,000 shares.

Of your 20,000 shares, you will have to pay $20.00 for 15,000 shares, which wipes out the lowest ask, and $20.10 for the remaining 5000 shares, which reduces the shares offered at $20.10 from 30,000 to 25,000 shares. So therefore, on average, what you're going to be paying per share is going to be: $(15/20) \times 20.00 + (5/20) \times 20.10 =$ \$20.025, or 2.5 cents.

Given this context, what is liquidity? Liquidity is immediacy. If you want to buy now, you'll place a market order, and you will have to pay what the limit order sellers are willing to take, and that is going to be above the fundamental value of the security. And if you want to sell now, you have to sell it for what the limit order buyers are willing to pay, and that's below the fundamental value.

A good way to think about the difference between the bids and the asks is that it compensates the dealers who are placing limits for providing liquidity. They are allowing people to get immediacy. They get paid to provide immediacy by being able to sell above the fundamental value and buy below the fundamental value.

From the perspective of someone demanding immediacy, the more they have to pay above the fundamental value, the less liquid the security, and the farther below the fundamental value they get to sell it for, also the less liquidity for that security.

Again, from the perspective of somebody demanding immediacy, the liquidity cost is the size of the difference between the transaction price and the fundamental value. It is half the effective bid-ask spread. The effective bid-ask spread is, for a given quantity, the difference between what you would pay to get that quantity versus what you could sell that quantity for.

Going back to the SleazeCo example, recall that if you wanted to buy 20,000 shares, you would pay $20.025 per share on average, that's 15,000 units at $20.00 and 5000 at the ask price of $20.10. Now, if the highest bid in the market for SleazeCo was $19.75 for 40,000 shares, then the effective spread for SleazeCo would be the price that you would pay to buy 20,000 shares, that's $20.025 minus the price that you could sell 20,000 shares for, that's $19.75. So, the effective spread is essentially 25.25 cents.

If there was not much depth below the best bid, then a larger market sell order would transact at an average price below the best bid. Similarly, a larger market buy order would pay an average price above the best ask. The less depth, the worse the execution. The main point is that the spread between the best bid and the best ask is not a true indication of the liquidity cost for larger orders, unless there is significant depth at the best bid and the best ask. If there is not significant depth there, then each of those types of orders, a buy or a sell order, is going to push the price up through the limit order book.

Thus, a liquid market is where there are lots of dealers willing to buy at the highest bid and lots of dealers willing to sell at the lowest ask, and there is only a small difference between those two bids and asks. So that makes that a very liquid market. You can trade large quantities without moving the price around much.

Now let's see what determines whether the spread is wide or narrow—whether it's liquid or illiquid. There can be a fairly large variation, by the way, in liquidity over a variety of different securities. Large household names like Procter & Gamble and Microsoft have very small bid-ask spreads, while other securities that are less frequently traded have little depth and have a fairly large bid-ask spread. So what explains the difference in these cases?

Since there are multiple dealers that compete with each other, the spread can be thought of as the competitive price of liquidity. Competition should drive the price of liquidity down to the cost of supplying it. Financial economists have divided the spread into two main logical components based upon the source of the cost to dealers supplying liquidity.

These two types of cost are the following: One is fundamental risk; the second one is adverse selection. So let's look at each in turn.

Fundamental risk is the risk that the fundamental value of the security will change significantly at any moment in time. This represents a risk to the dealer because they made money by buying low, at the bid, and selling high, at the ask.

To see how changes in fundamental value would affect the profits that they make, to see this consider what happens if the fundamental value first doesn't change much, and then we'll compare that to a situation in which the fundamental value does change significantly.

If the fundamental value does not change frequently, then the dealer will be able to buy many shares at the lower bid and sell many shares at the higher ask, making the spread on each pair of shares sold and bought. For example, let's say that a sell order for 100 shares arrives now. The dealer buys 100 shares at his bid. But, a few minutes later a new market order to buy 100 shares arrives. The dealer will then sell the 100 shares he just bought at the higher ask price, making the spread on those 100 shares.

And this happens over and over and over again. If buy-and-sell market orders arrive at the same rate over time and there's no revision in the value of the security, then the dealer will just continue to make the spread for each pair of shares traded. In this case, the costs are low and we would expect that the spreads, which compensate the dealers, would also be very low.

Now, consider what happens if the fundamental value changes frequently. In that case, the dealer has a significant probability of losing money on any one transaction. So let's revisit the previous example. The initial sell order for 100 shares comes in at, say, 10:29 a.m. in the morning, and the dealer fills that order by buying the shares at the bid. But, before the next order can arrive, news that the firm is being sued for selling products that harm customers comes out at, say, 10:30 a.m.

The fundamental value of the firm is going to fall. And, most of the orders are sell, sell, sell. The new competitive ask price will be much lower than the prior bid the dealer just paid when filling the previous sell order. Thus, the dealer loses money on this transaction.

Now, notice that the dealer also faces risk if there is really good news that comes out. If the initial order had been to buy, the dealer would have just had to finance a short position and then face the risk that good news would come out about the firms, thus raising the competitive ask price above the prior bid price, generating a loss for him on that short position. So it's completely symmetric, whether it's good news or bad news. Changes in fundamental value can end up eating into a dealer's profit.

The greater the volatility of the underlying security's value, the greater is the chance that the dealer will have a market move against him and he will ose money. So, the greater the volatility of the underlying security's value, he greater the risk to the dealer, and the greater the spread has to be to compensate the dealer for bearing that risk.

Next, let's move on to adverse selection. Adverse selection is the risk faced by a dealer that the traders will systematically select trades that are adverse to the dealer. Adverse selection occurs when traders have superior information about the value of the security.

To see how adverse selection works with securities and how it affects liquidity, consider what would happen to a dealer if the only traders active in the market were those that had superior information about that security's value. How much would the dealer make by providing liquidity and quoting bid-ask prices?

Well, to see this, put yourself into the dealer's position. What bid-ask spread would you quote? Let's say you think that the fundamental value is $20. And you, the only dealer present in the market, set a bid-ask spread for $19 and $21—that, by the way, is a huge spread. If the only traders that are present in the market are those that have superior information, then what's going to happen in this case? Well, in this case, at best you're not going to make any money, but alternatively you could end up losing a lot, even though your spread is very large. So why is that?

There are two possible logical cases here. The first case is when the traders with the superior information think that the fundamental value is between your bid and ask. While you think it's $20, they might think it's $20.50 or $19.50. Either way, they will not trade with you. Your spread is too wide.

The second case is when the trader with superior information thinks that the fundamental value is outside your bid ask. While you think the fundamental value is $20, they might think it's $22 or $18. For both of those values, they will want to trade with you. If they know the value is $18, they will want to sell to you at your $19 bid, and what's going to happen? You're going to lose $1. And if they think it is worth $22, they will buy from you at your $21 ask. Again, you're going to lose $1.

So, you might respond by widening the spread, say, to $15 for the bid and $25 for the ask. This is a gigantic spread. This lowers the chance of you losing. If the probability that an informed investor knows that the true price is greater than $21 or less than $19 is, say, 10%, then the probability that the true value is above $25 or below $15 will be even less. So, by widening the spread, the dealer reduces the amount of losses from adverse selection.

But, informed traders are not the only traders present in the market. There are also traders that do not have special information—people who just want to buy the security to get a return for bearing the risk, but sometimes they maybe want to sell some shares in order to buy a new car. So, to contrast those traders with informed traders, I will simply call them uninformed traders. They are uninformed only in the sense that they do not impose any adverse selection on the liquidity providers.

If the dealer widens the spread to control adverse selection, then these uninformed traders are likely not to buy the shares in the first place. And if they don't buy shares in the first place, the dealer will not have any uninformed traders to provide liquidity to. And this is how the dealers make the money—by providing liquidity to uninformed traders.

So, dealers have a balancing act. They cannot set the spread so wide as to eliminate adverse selection, since if they did they would also eliminate uninformed trades, which is why they're there in the first place.

So, dealers set the spread so as to balance the benefit of reducing adverse selection against the cost of lost uninformed trade volume. If there's lots of uninformed volume for a security, then the dealer can make more off the uninformed trades to compensate themselves for the possibility of adverse selection. With there being much more volume, they can make the spread more frequently on many more people. Thus, if there's lots of uninformed volume, the spreads can be narrower, and if the spreads are narrower, there's going to be lots of uninformed volume, because this is a very liquid security. So there's some sense in which liquidity begets more liquidity.

In summary, we have two costs—fundamental risk and adverse selection. The bigger any of these costs are, the bigger the competitive spreads must be. Thus, securities with more fundamental risk have wider spreads. Securities with lots of adverse selection have a wider spread. The securities with most adverse selection and the widest spreads are those securities that are not traded by many uninformed investors. The stocks of small companies are just like this.

So now, as argued earlier, the liquidity cost of a security cannot be measured solely by the difference between the best bid and the best ask. Of course, if the spread is really wide, that security is not liquid. But, at any moment in time, this spread may be narrow, but there may be very little depth at these quotes. In this case, a sizable market order to sell will push the price way down and a sizable market order to buy will push the price way up.

What we need is a measure of liquidity of an individual security that incorporates this issue of depth. A measure developed by Yakov Amihud, referred to as the Amihud measure, does just that. The Amihud measure is the average of the absolute value of the daily price changes divided by the dollar volume in that day. Note that this is really an illiquidity measure, since the higher value of this measure indicates an illiquid market, or one in which the prices change a lot for a given amount of trade volume.

This measure is calculated as follows: (1) For every trade day in a month, take the absolute value of the price change that day divided by the dollar amount of trade in that security for that day. Then, (2) take these values and average them over the 20 or so trading days in the month. So what you get is a monthly Amihud measure for that month.

Now, what academic research has shown is that the Amihud measure varies significantly across securities. It also shows that the less liquid a security is, the higher its return on average. Now, this makes sense in that, as we discussed before, liquidity costs will erode your return. Thus, investors appear to be willing to pay less for less liquid securities than more liquid securities. This lowering of the price for less liquid securities generates a higher return.

You can think of this effect that liquidity costs have on the return as being the amount the average person needs to be compensated in extra return in order to compensate for the average amount of liquidity costs they incur given the average length of time they intend to hold the security.

Let's think about it for you for a second. If you intend to hold the security for longer than the average investor, then the return per period is more than enough to compensate you for the liquidity costs that you will incur. But if you intend to hold for a shorter period of time, the extra return will likely be insufficient.

So, in this lecture we've explored liquidity. We have seen how to measure liquidity, and we have noted that studies show that there is a significant variation in liquidity across the various securities in the market, as captured by the Amihud measure.

We've seen that the liquidity of a security depends upon the amount of fundamental risk and the amount of adverse selection and the volume of uninformed trade.

We've also seen there is a cost to liquidity for less liquid securities. They pay a premium. Thus, if you only transacted in liquid securities, holding everything else, like beta, constant, you will have a lower return on average. This is true because less liquid securities compensate you for their illiquidity with a return premium, while liquid securities do not.

Whether you are willing to pay the liquidity cost associated with lower returns on liquid securities depends upon how frequently you intend to trade. If you rely on a steady stream of cash flow from periodic liquidations, then it is probably worth the cost to hold liquid securities.

Understanding Derivatives
Lecture 21

In this lecture on derivative securities, you will begin by learning what a derivative security is. You will then examine two prevalent examples: puts and calls. You will also learn when it is optimal to exercise an option. In addition, you will be introduced to payoff and profit diagrams to understand how the profit on an option depends on the future value of the underlying. Finally, you will examine how a lack of transparency in over-the-counter CDS transactions contributed to the instability during the financial crisis of 2008.

Derivative Securities

- Derivative securities come in many forms. For example, there are futures, options, swaps, and swaptions (options on swaps). At the most basic level, a derivative security is a contract that specifies payouts contingent on—or derived from—the values of other securities or goods. The types of other securities can be equity, fixed income (or bonds), commodities (like gold or soy beans), and currency (like the Japanese yen).

- One type of derivative security is an option. Once you understand options, you can understand the basics of almost all of the other derivative securities that exist. There are two basic types of option contracts: put options and call options (or, simply, puts and calls).

- As with any financial contract, with puts and calls, there are always two parties involved: the buyer and the seller. The seller is sometimes referred to as the "writer" of the contract. When one sells a put or a call, they write the contract.

- When a buyer buys a contract, he or she pays for the option to require the seller to do a particular thing (as specified in the contract) at some future date. The buyer has an option in the sense that he or she does not have to require the seller to do that particular thing; rather, the buyer has the option to ignore the contract and rip it up if he or she wants to.

- In contrast, the seller of the option is obligated to satisfy the buyer if the buyer chooses to exercise his or her option in the future. That is, the seller must honor whatever the buyer wants—even if the buyer wants to ignore the contract. Thus, options have one-sided commitment.

- With options, there are many different words or phrases used to describe or denote the same thing. Options professionals often refer to the buyer as being "long" or "having a long position," while a seller is "short" or "has a short position." That is, because the seller is obligated to make good on the promise in the future, the seller is short that obligation. Also, the buyer is sometimes referred to as the "holder" of the option.

- The difference between a put option and a call option is with respect to the specific action the buyer has the option to take in the future. A call contract gives the buyer of the call the "option"—not the obligation—to buy a prespecified security in the future for a prespecified price. The call option gives its owner the right to "call in"—or buy—some security in the future. The owner of the option doesn't have to if they don't want to, but they can if they do. Either way, the seller must honor the wishes of the holder.

Calls

- There are three important items a call contract must specify: Which security can be called in the future? At what price can it be bought for? When can it be called in? To answer the first question, the call contract specifies the security that the option is written on, which is also referred to as the underlying asset—that is, the asset whose value the option is derived from.

- Underlying assets can be equity (such as IBM), bonds (such as treasury bonds), currency (such as yen), commodities (such as live cattle), indexes (such as the S&P 500), and other derivate contracts (such as futures).

- To answer the second question, the call contract specifies the exercise price, which is the price that the holder of the call has to pay for the security (for example, IBM) if he or she chooses to exercise the option. The exercise price is also called the strike price.

- Finally, to answer the third question, the contract specifies the expiration date for the option. In this regard, there are multiple types of options: "European" options are those that can be exercised only on the expiration date, while "American" options can be exercised any time on or before the expiration date.

- It is often useful to depict the payoffs on an option as a function of the strike price and the price of the underlying asset at expiration. A payoff diagram depicts the payoff per share of the underlying that a person receives at the expiration date as a function of the price of the underlying on the expiration date.

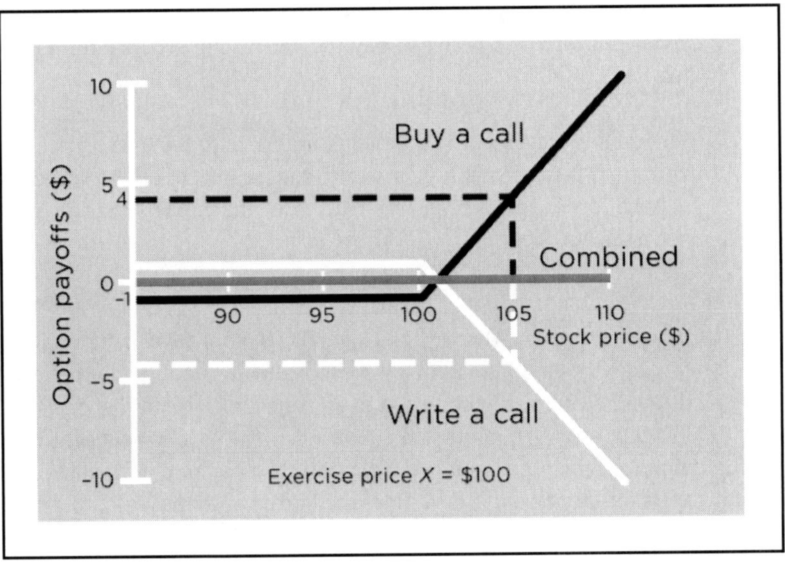

- A payoff diagram does not consider what was paid for the option initially. A profit diagram considers the initial cost of the option by shifting down the graphs by the amount of this cost. While it is traditional to do this, realize that it is not quite accurate because the cost is incurred at a time prior to expiration. Thus, a traditional profit diagram ignores the time value of money.

- Options are what economists call a zero-sum game. The amount one person gains is the amount the other person losses. Furthermore, rather than actually transacting in the underlying security, most options are cash settled.

Puts

- Rather than giving the holder the option to buy, a put gives the holder the option to sell a specific security at a specific price on or before a specific date. As with a call, the put also has a strike price and an expiration date. In addition, puts can be either American or European.

- Unlike with calls, the holder of a put benefits when the value of the underlying security falls below the strike price. That is, the put holder can force the writer to buy the underlying security for more than it's worth.

- If the underlying security's value is higher than the strike price at expiration, then the put holder would choose not to sell the security for that lower strike price. In that case, the holder lets the put expire unexercised.

Mortgages

- Options are everywhere. For example, if you have a mortgage, you actually have two options: a prepayment option and a default option. The prepayment option is an American option that lets the borrower swap the promised stream of monthly payments for the amount of the remaining principle, the present value of the amount that is left to be paid. This allows the borrower to move.

- It also allows the borrower to act strategically and refinance to his or her benefit. If interest rates fall, then the borrower can borrow the remaining principle by making smaller monthly payments. So, he or she would do that and use the borrowed money to exercise his or her prepayment option and repay the current loan. If interest rates rise, he or she won't refinance (and will continue to enjoy the low rate on the current mortgage).

- A mortgage borrower also has a default option: If the value of the home drops below the remaining principle owned, the borrower has the option to "put" the house for the amount owed. That is, the borrower can get out from under the mortgage contract simply by giving the house to the lender. This is just like a put option where the borrower forces the lender to buy the house for a strike price equal to the remaining principle.

- Options are valuable; people just don't hand them out for free. So, because the mortgage borrower receives two options with his or her loan, the price of the loan—the interest rate charged—reflects the cost of the lender of providing the borrower with these two options.

- Thus, mortgage rates would be lower if the law did not give borrowers the option to prepay and to default. Of course, this is only a problem if, given the choice, borrowers would voluntarily give up these options in order to get lower rates.

- Leading up to the financial crisis of 2008, many new mortgages were originated in which the borrowers put very little (if any) money down. In these cases, the loan-to-value ratios—the ratio of the amount borrowed to the value of the property—were close to one.

- So, for many mortgages, the principle was very close to the value of the home purchased. As a result, in many cases, it took only a small decline in the value of the home to make the default option "in the money."

- Another feature of options relevant to the financial crisis is the difference between exchange-traded options and those traded "over the counter." Standardized option contracts are traded at exchanges. Non-standardized options are negotiated and traded among people in what is referred to as the over-the-counter market.

- Over-the-counter markets are not transparent and were not regulated. While the exchanges have procedures that guard against the seller of the options reneging on their obligation, no such safeguards existed in the over-the-counter market. Rather, the over-the-counter market relies on relationships and trust built over repeated transactions.

- Moreover, there was no central clearinghouse that kept track of the size of the positions individuals or institutions have. Without this knowledge, there is something called counter-party risk, which is the risk that the trading party with the obligation (i.e., the option writer) will not be able to fulfill their obligations.

CDOs and CDSs

- Options were also thought to be a big contributor to the financial crisis of 2008. Aside from the default options that mortgage borrowers exercised, there were other derivative securities called credit default swaps (CDSs) that were written on another kind of derivative security called collateralized debt obligations (CDOs), which are bonds that are backed by the payments on bonds.

- Many CDOs were backed by the payments on mortgage loans. CDOs would take the payments from a pool of mortgages. They would then use the mortgages as collateral to sell bonds. Some of the bonds sold would be short term in nature. So, most of the cash coming from the mortgages would be used to pay those bonds off first. Other bonds were longer term in nature. These different bonds are called tranches.

- CDOs are complex because whether a longer-term tranche gets any payments depends on the defaults in the pool of the underlying collateral—mortgages, for example. And the defaults on the mortgages depend on the strike prices on the default options in the mortgages in the pool, which in turn depend on the loan-to-value ratio.

- A credit default swap (CDS) is an option to swap a defaulted bond for its face value. This is a put option. It allows the buyer of the option to insure against default. The buyer of the instrument acquires protection from the seller against a default by a particular company or country (the reference entity). The premium is known as the credit default spread. It is paid for the life of the contract or until default. If there is a default, the buyer has the right to sell bonds for its face value.

- Prior to the financial crisis, many mortgages where bundled together to create CDOs. Then, those institutions (many banks and pension funds) that bought CDOs also bought credit protection in the form of CDSs.

- However, because CDSs were not transparent, there was a surprise when AIG, who sold sizable amounts of CDSs, experienced such significant losses that it would have failed had it not been bailed out by the U.S. government. When the company that insures you against default defaults, you have no insurance. In order to prevent systemic failure, the United States bailed out the insurer—so that others would be insured.

Suggested Reading

Bodie, Kane, and Marcus, *Essentials of Investments*.

Hull, *Options, Futures, and Other Derivatives*.

Questions to Consider

1. There is a saying that options are valuable; this is certainly true with financial options because you will only exercise them if you get a better payoff than if you were to let them expire unexercised. Can you think of nonfinancial situations in which having more options might be detrimental? How are these situations different from the situation with a financial option?

2. In earlier lectures, we discussed "plain vanilla" bonds, which are securities that promise you a set of fixed payments. But there exist some non-plain-vanilla bonds that have option-like features. For example, there are convertible bonds and callable bonds. With a convertible bond, the owner of the bond (the investor) can, during some prespecified period of time during the life of the bond, convert a bond into a prespecified number of shares of equity in the firm. With a callable bond, the firm that sold the bond has the option to buy back the bond for a prespecified price (e.g., the face value of the bond) during a specified period. If everything else about the bond is the same, will callable bonds be more or less expensive than a similar plain vanilla bond? Will the yield to maturity be higher or lower? Also, what about the price and yield to maturity on a convertible bond relative to a similar plain vanilla bond?

Understanding Derivatives

Lecture 21—Transcript

This lecture starts our examination of derivative securities. First, we'll answer the question "What are they?" To do this, we'll look at two main types of derivatives—option contracts called "puts" and "calls." In subsequent lectures, we'll examine two other issues. What can you do with them? That is, how you can use them as part of a successful investment strategy?

We'll also look at pricing. What's a good price? For pricing, we'll look at two techniques for pricing—the Binomial Model and the famous Black–Scholes Formula. Let's start with what are they? Many have claimed they're evil. For example, Warren Buffet once described them as "weapons of mass financial destruction." And Frank Partnoy, Director of the University of San Diego's Center for Corporate and Securities Law, referring to the financial crisis of 2008, stated "The mania, panic, and crash had many causes. But if you're looking for a single word to use in laying blame for the recent financial catastrophe, there's only one choice. Derivatives."

Before we begin to examine derivatives in detail, I should mention that I personally don't think that derivatives are evil or good. As is true with most things in our nuanced and complex world, derivatives have both good and bad aspects.

Furthermore, similar to the saying that "guns don't kill people—people kill people, using guns," derivatives are not intrinsically bad, but they do have some features that can be dangerous if they're not well-understood. We'll examine some of these features.

In addition, options, a kind of derivative security, are everywhere. You really need to know what they are, how others use them, and how you can use them to your advantage, either as an investor or just as somebody active in modern society.

So, let's turn back to the question of what are they? Derivative securities come in many forms. For example, there are futures, there are options.

There are things called swaps, and there are even options on swaps called swaptions.

At the most basic level, a derivative security is a contract that specifies payouts contingent on or derived from the values of other securities or goods. That is the sense in which they are derivative securities. The types of other securities can be equity, fixed income, or bonds, commodities, like gold or soybeans, and currency, like the Japanese yen.

To give you a clear idea how derivatives work, we're going to focus on one type of derivative security called an option. Once you understand options, you can understand the basics of most other derivative securities that exist. Futures become actually particularly very easy to understand once you understand options.

There are two types of option contracts—put options and call options, or simply puts and calls. As with any financial contract, with puts and calls there are always two parties involved. One party is the buyer, while the other is the seller. The seller is sometimes referred to as the writer of the contract. The one who sells a put or a call, they write the contract.

When a buyer buys a contract, he or she pays for the option to require the seller to do a particular thing as specified in the contract at some future date. The buyer has an option in the sense that he or she does not have to require the seller to do that particular thing. Rather, the buyer has the option to ignore the contract and rip it up and throw it away if he or she wants to.

In contrast, the seller of the option is obligated to satisfy the buyer if the buyer chooses to exercise their option in the future. That is, the seller must honor whatever the buyer wants, even if the buyer wants to ignore the contract. Thus, the options are one-sided commitment.

With options, there are many different words or phrases used to describe or denote the same thing. Options professionals often refer to the buyer as "being long" or "having a long position," while a seller is "short" or "has a short position." That is, since the seller is obligated to make good on a promise in the future, the seller is short that obligation. Also, sometimes we refer to the buyer as the holder of the option.

The difference between a put option and a call option is with respect to the specific action the buyer has the option to take in the future. To make this less abstract, let's look at the details of a call. Once you get the idea of the call, you'll naturally get the put.

A call contract gives the buyer of the call option the option—not the obligation—to buy a pre-specified security in the future for a pre-specified price. That is, the future action in this case is buy security *x* for price *y* at date *z*.

The call option gives its owner the right to call in, or buy, some security in the future. The owner of the option doesn't have to if they don't want to, but they can if they do. But, the seller must honor the wishes of the holder of the option.

There are three important items call contracts must specify: (1) Which security can be called in the future? (2) At what price can it be bought for? And then (3) When can it be called in?

The answer to the question "Which security can be called in in the future?" the contract specifies the security that the option is written on. For example, a call option can be written on stock in IBM. The security that the option is written on is also referred to as the underlying security or the underlying asset. That is, the asset whose value the option is derived from.

Underlying assets can be things like equity, like IBM; bonds, like a treasury bond; currency, like the yen; commodities, like live cattle; indexes, such as the S&P 500; and other derivative contracts, such as futures. I will denote the value or the price of the underlying at time t by S_t. Although S_t is typically used to indicate the stock price, always remember that the option may be written on other things, other than stocks.

To answer the question "At what price can the security be bought for?" the call contract specifies something called the "exercise price." This is the price that the holder of the call has to pay for the security, say, IBM, if he or she chooses to exercise the option. The exercise price is also sometimes called the "strike price." Sometimes I will denote the strike price or the exercise price by an X.

Finally, to answer the question "When can it be called in?" the contract specifies the expiration date for the option. In this regard, there are multiple types of options. European options are those that can be exercised only on the expiration date. American options can be exercised any time before or on the expiration date.

Since the island of Bermuda is close to America, but has European influences, Bermudan options specify a sub-set of discrete dates when the option can be exercised prior to expiration. That is, Bermudan options, like Bermuda, are somewhere between an American and a European option.

You can see the variety of options and future contracts by going to the website for the CME Group, the publically traded firm that resulted from the merger of the Chicago Mercantile Exchange (the CME) and the Chicago Board of Trade (the CBOT) in 2007, resulting in the world's largest exchange for futures and options. Just click on the "Products and Trading" tab on the main page at CMEGroup.com to see the exchange-traded contracts. This link will also tell you all of the details of each of the option contracts.

Now let's work through some specific examples for a call. For concreteness, let's say that you are the buyer of the call that I wrote. Let the call be written on common stock, say, in McDonald's. Right now the price of a common share of McDonald's is about $100. Just to keep the numbers easy, let's say it's exactly $100.

Currently, there are standardized contracts with strike prices ranging from $75 to $115. Let's say the exercise price on the call you and I have transacted in is $100. When the exercise price is the same as the current price of the underlying security, the option is said to be "at the money."

The set of standardized contracts also vary by expiration date. Expiration dates are usually on the third Friday of every month ranging from one month out to many years out. Let's say that the expiration date for the call that you bought from me is for three months from now. Let's say that that's June 21st. So, I wrote—and you bought—a call on McDonald's with an exercise price of $100 and an expiration date three months, on June 21st.

Note that there are two transactions involved in this case—the transaction of the option and the possible future transaction on McDonald's stock. The price of the possible transaction in McDonald's stock is pinned down by the contract at $100. The price of the option, however, is determined by supply and demand—not for the stock, but for the option. So, even though the current price of McDonald's is $100 and the exercise price of the call is $100, the market price of the call option is probably around $1. Again, just to keep things simple, let's say it's exactly $1. Finally, let's say that the call is a European call. So, if you want to exercise it, you're going to have to wait until June 21st.

Now let's turn the clock ahead. It's now three months hence and the price of McDonald's has gone up to $105. Since you hold the option to call, and now is the expiration date, you have the option to buy McDonald's from me for a strike price of $100. Do you want to? Yes. If you exercise, you will get to pay $100 for something that's worth $105 in the market. So, you should exercise, pay $100, get a share of McDonald's, and then turn around and sell that share in the market for $105, and pocket the $5 difference between the exercise price and the market price of McDonald's at expiration. This is a case where the option is in the money, because the price of McDonald's is above the strike price.

Since you paid $1 for the option initially, your profit is going to be $4. Well, what happens if the price of McDonald's stock falls to $95 at expiration? What would you do then? If you exercise, you would have to pay $100 for something worth only $95. Why would you do that? Recall that you have the option to buy at $100, not the obligation. If you don't want to buy, you don't have to. In this case, you would simply let your option expire unexercised. You would just rip it up and throw it away. In this case, the option is out of the money.

It is often useful to depict the payoffs of the option as a function of the strike price, x, and the price of the underlying, S_T at the expiration date, T. As will be obvious in a minute, these diagrams are often referred to as hockey stick diagrams.

A payoff diagram depicts the payoff per share of the underlying that a person receives at the expiration date as a function of the price of the underlying on that expiration date. For example, a call option with a strike price of $100, what we would see here would be a plot of the payoff of the price if the price of the underlying turns out to be $90, $95, $100, $105. So what we would see here is we would have essentially a graph that along the horizontal axis are all the different prices that could occur in the market at the expiration date.

On the vertical axis, we're going to have how much money the holder of the option is going to get in the event that they have the security. Notice that if the strike price is $100 and the price falls below $100, then the person is not going to exercise their option, and so the payoff is essentially going to be completely flat at zero in that case. But if the price turns out to be above $100 on the expiration date, then the person is going to exercise their call option and they're going to start to make money. For every dollar the price is above the strike price, they're going to make a dollar in payoff. So what this plot looks like, essentially, it looks like a hockey stick. When the price is low, less than $100, it's completely flat. When the price is higher, above $100, we have a line that emanates from $100 up with a slope of 1.

By the way, the payoff diagram does not consider what you paid for the option initially. A profit diagram does consider the initial cost of the option by shifting down the graphs by the amount of the initial cost. While it is traditional to do this, I want you to realize that it's not quite accurate in that the cost was incurred at the time that you bought it, which is much prior to expiration. Thus, the traditional profit diagram ignores the time value of money of the cost associated with buying the option in the first place.

Let's go back to the previous example. What happens to me, the writer of the call? If the price of McDonald's at expiration is $105, then you will exercise. I will have to sell you something worth $105 for $100. I lose $5. Given the initial price at the option, on net, you gained $4 and I lost $4. That is, your gain is my loss.

We just went through the payoff diagram and the profit diagram for a long position in a call. What about the payoff diagram for a short position? In this case, it is simply the mirror image of the payoff on the long position.

Again, from my perspective, what if the price of McDonald's had fallen to $95 instead? You don't exercise, and I don't have to do anything. You're out the $1 from buying the call, and I get to keep the $1 from the sale. In this case, my gain is your loss. This is an important feature of options. They are what economists call a zero-sum game.

In fact, you can see by superimposing the profit diagram for a long position on a profit diagram for a short position, if you just add these things up, because they're mirror images, what you end up getting by adding them vertically is a complete flat line at zero. What that means is, whatever the person that has a long position gets, the person that has the short position loses. And whoever has the short position, if they get anything, the person with the long position would lose. So, in total, everyone will get nothing.

By the way, is there really any reason for us to actually transact in the shares? If I didn't have a share of McDonald's to sell you, I would have to go into the market to buy a share for $105, just to turn around and sell it to you for $100, and then you would probably go back into the market and sell that just so you could get the $5 gain. So, why don't we just skip all this buying and selling of the shares, and at expiration, I just give you the $5. This is called cash settlement. Most options are cash settled.

Before moving on to puts, let's review the set of concepts we have discussed so far. Call options allow the holder to call in, or buy, a specific security, the security the option is written on or the underlying asset, for a specific price, the exercise price, on or before a specific date, the expiration date. For every option transaction, one person is long the option, while the other person, the seller, is short the obligation to do whatever the option holder wants to do.

Call options are a zero-sum game. The amount one person gains is the amount that the other person loses. And then, rather than actually transact in the underlying security, most options are cash settled.

Now that we know something about calls, let's turn to puts. Rather than giving the holder of the option the option to buy, a put gives the holder of the option the option to sell a specific security at a specific price on or before a specific date.

As with a call, the put also has a strike price and an expiration date. And puts can be either American or European. Unlike with calls, the holder of a put benefits when the value of the underlying security falls below the strike price. That is, the put holder can force the writer to buy the underlying security for more than it's actually worth. If the underlying security value is higher than the strike price at expiration, then the put holder would choose not to sell the security for that lower strike price. In that case, the holder lets the put expire unexercised.

As I stated earlier, options are everywhere. For example, if you have a mortgage, you actually have two options—a prepayment option and a default option. The prepayment option is an American option that lets the borrower swap the promised stream of monthly payments for the amount of the remaining principle, the present value of the amount that is left to be paid. This allows the borrower to move, say, because they get a new job someplace or they want to relocate to a better house. It also allows the borrower to act strategically and refinance if that's to their benefit. If interest rates fall, then the borrower can borrow the remaining principle by making smaller monthly payments. So, what they would do is they would borrow that money and use the borrowed money to exercise their prepayment option. If interest rates rise, you're not going to refinance and you will continue to have the low rate that you locked in initially with the current mortgage.

A mortgage borrower also has a default option. If the value of the house drops below the remaining principle owed, then the borrower has the option to put the house for the amount that is owed. That is, the borrower can get out from under the mortgage contract simply by giving the house to the lender.

his is just like a put option where the borrower forces the lender to buy ie house for the strike price equal to the remaining principle. As we will uantify in subsequent lectures, options are valuable. People just don't hand iem out for free. So, since the mortgage borrower receives two options with ieir loan, the price of the loan—the interest rate charged—reflects the cost f the lender providing the borrower with these two options.

hus, mortgage rates would be lower if the law did not give borrowers the ption to prepay or to default. Of course, this is only a problem if, given the hoice, borrowers would voluntarily give up these options in order to get ower rates.

lso, leading up to the financial crisis of 2008, many new mortgages were riginated in which the borrowers put very little, if any, money down. In iese cases, the loan-to-value ratios, the ratio of the amount borrowed to the alue of the property, were very close to one. So, for many mortgages, the rinciple was very close to the value of the house purchased. As a result, in iany cases, it only took a small decline in the value of the home to make the efault option be in the money.

nother feature of options relevant to the financial crisis is the difference etween exchange-traded options and those traded over the counter. tandardized option contracts are traded at exchanges like the CME. Non-tandardized options are negotiated and traded amongst people in what is eferred to as the over-the-counter market.

he over-the-counter markets are not as transparent as those that are traded n the exchanges. While the exchanges have procedures to guard against the eller of the options reneging on their obligation, there are no such safeguards hat exist in the over-the-counter markets. Rather, the over-the-counter narkets rely on relationships and trust built over repeated transactions.

Ioreover, there was no central clearing that kept track of the size of positions ndividuals or institutions had. Without this knowledge, there is something alled counter-party risk. This is the risk that the trading parties that have a ertain obligation will not make good on that obligation.

Options were also thought to be a big contributor to the financial crisis in 2008. Aside from the default options that mortgage borrowers exercised, there were other derivative securities called credit default swaps, or CDS, written on another kind of derivative security called a Collateralized Debt Obligation, or CDO. CDOs would take the payments from a pool of mortgages. They would then use the mortgages as collateral to sell bonds. Some of the bonds sold would be very short-term in nature, so, most of the cash coming from the mortgage payments would be used to pay those bonds off first.

Other bonds were much longer-term in nature. By the way, these different types of bonds that are sold that are backed by the payments from mortgages, these are called tranches.

CDOs are fairly complex because whether a longer-term tranche gets any payments or not depends completely on what the default experience is on the pool of the underlying collateral—in this case, mortgages. And the defaults on mortgages depend upon the strike prices on the default options in the mortgages that are in the pool, and that, in turn, depends upon the loan-to-value ratio.

By the way, the complexity of CDOs prompted Nobel Lauriat Paul Krugman, in a July 2nd, 2007 *New York Times* article titled "Just Say AAA," to offer the following: "What do you get when you cross a mafia don with a bond salesman? A dealer in collateralized debt obligations (CDOs)—someone that makes you an offer you don't understand."

A credit default swap, or CDS is an option to swap a defaulted bond for its face value. This is a put option. It allows the buyer of the option to ensure against default. So how does a credit default swap work? The buyer of the instrument acquires protection from the seller against a default by a particular company or a particular bond. We'll call that the reference entity. For example, a buyer of CDS pays a premium given the amount of the value of the bond. That premium is typically a number of basis points. For example, you might pay 90 basis points for $100 million for five-year protection against a default on a bond issued by, say, company X.

The premium, by the way, is referred to as the credit default spread. It's paid for life of contract or up until there is a default. If there is a default, the buyer has the right to sell the bond for its face value, so the owner of the credit default swap has the right to put into the seller of the credit default's hands a bond that has defaulted to get its face value. So, remember, what happens when there's a default? We look back before, and what happens when there is a default? You end up getting the recovery rate. The recovery rate ends up being a fraction of its face value, so, in the event of a default, the bond is worth less than its face value. And if you have a credit default swap as protection, as an owner of that credit default swap, what you want to do is you want to exercise your put option and put the defaulted bond into the hands of the person that sold you that credit default swap for a strike price of the face value.

Prior to the financial crisis, many mortgages were bundled together to create CDOs. Then what would happen is those institutions, many banks and pension funds, they would buy the CDOs, and they would also buy credit protection in the form of CDS (credit default swaps). Because CDS was not transparent, there was a surprise when it turns out that AIG, who had sold sizable amounts of credit default swaps, experienced such significant losses that if they were to have failed there was no way they would have been able to pay off on all of the credit default swaps that they sold. In that case, what ends up happening is people have bought a lot of credit protection in the form of credit default swaps from AIG, but if AIG had actually paid off on all of these credit default swaps, essentially insurance against default, then AIG would have failed.

So what happens when you get insurance for a company that essentially fails? You really don't have any insurance. If it weren't for the U.S. government bailing out AIG, then it would have been the case that most of the people that owned credit default swaps that they bought from AIG, they also would have gone under as well. Because what they were trying to do was protect themselves against losses. Those losses would have hurt them significantly without that insurance. When the company that insures you against default defaults, you have no insurance. In order to prevent a systematic failure, the U.S. government bailed out the insurer in this case so that others would essentially stay insured.

In this lecture, we have looked at what a derivative security is. We've examined two prevalent examples—puts and calls. We've also talked about how you would optimally exercise a put or a call. If you own a call and the price ends up at expiration above its strike price, then you exercise it and you get the difference between the price in the market at that time for the underlying and the strike price. If the price of the underlying at that time at expiration is below the strike price, then you do not exercise it. You let it go away. You just let it disappear unexercised.

In contrast, for a put option, what happens if the price at expiration is above the strike price? Then there is no reason for you to sell something for the strike price that's worth more than that. So, if you own the put, you let it expire unexercised. But if the price is below the strike price at expiration, then what you're going to do is you're going to exercise it. You're going to sell something worth less than the strike price for the strike price and make that difference.

The other thing that we've done in this lecture is we've looked at what a payoff or a profit diagram would look like. We've also understood that this is a zero-sum game. By looking at what long positions plus short positions look like, we're going to end up getting zero payoffs. We've also examined how the lack of transparency in over-the-counter credit default transactions contributed to instability during the financial crisis of 2008.

In subsequent lectures, we're going to see how to use these as part of an investment strategy. We're also going to figure out how to price them.

Using Derivatives
Lecture 22

The previous lecture described the elements of options and the nature of their payoffs and profits. In this lecture, you will learn how you can use options as part of your investment strategy. In particular, you will examine two ways that you can use them. You can use them to speculate, exploiting the fact that options are like highly levered positions in the underlying asset. You can also use options to control risk, or hedge.

Speculation

- Speculation can be very risky. A person is speculating when he or she is betting on the security moving in a particular direction. For example, suppose that you are reading the paper and find out that the fees for the disposal of used oil from deep fryers is likely to fall in the near future. If so, then the values of U.S. fast food companies, including McDonald's, are likely to rise, reflecting higher future profits.

- If you currently owned stock in McDonald's, then you would be happy. But if you didn't own any stock in McDonald's, you could do two things: You could either go buy some stock or you could speculate with options. By speculating with options, you can amplify your gains—and your losses, too.

- If you really know which way the price of the underlying is going to move, then you may want to use options. If you think prices will rise, buy a call. If you think prices will fall, you could either short or buy a put. The analysis of these cases is exactly analogous to the "buy" or "buy a call" analysis with a price rise. Speculating with options is very similar to speculating with borrowed money (or leverage).

- Buying a call is very similar to an extremely levered position in the underlying. Your returns are very sensitive to the return on the underlying. The same is true with the purchase of a put.

- You can also speculate by selling puts and calls. Rather than speculate that the price will rise by buying a call or speculate the price will fall by buying a put, you might sell a call to speculate that the price will stand still or fall, or you might sell a put to speculate that the price will stand still or rise. With this kind of speculation, you are just selling options to get the money—betting that the prices won't move in such a direction that the buyer will want to exercise them.

- When AIG sold credit default swaps, they were selling put options on bonds. One view is that they just wanted to make the money by selling the protection; they never thought that the puts they sold would be exercised. But they were wrong.

- Another type of speculative strategy is a kind where you bet on volatility. Consider the following strategy, where you combine puts and calls: Buy a call with strike X for \$$c$; buy a put with strike X for \$$p$. This strategy is called a straddle. What will you get as a function of the price of the underlying at expiration?

- To figure out what you get, draw a profit diagram for each position. Recall that the profit diagram plots the profit on the vertical axis as a function of the price of the underlying at expiration. Once you plot the profit for each, then you add each line vertically.

- The profit on the call will be a flat line from \$0 to the strike at \$$X$. Because you will have paid \$$c$, this flat line is drawn at a height of −\$$c$ on the vertical axis. Then, for every dollar the price at expiration is above the strike, the profit will rise \$1. Thus, at the point on the profit line at the strike price, the profit line slopes up \$1 for every \$1 above the strike.

- The profit diagram for the call looks like a hockey stick with its handle up in the air to the right. For the put, it's also a hockey stick—but with its handle up in the air to the left. The level of the flat part is at −$p.

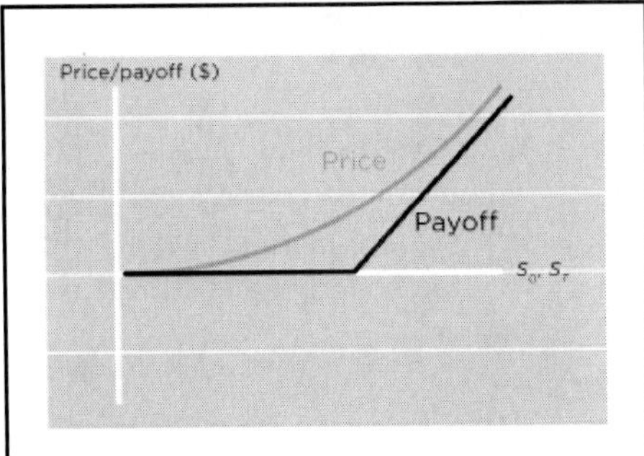

- Next, let's add them. The best way to do this is to simply start at the strike and add the two levels of the profits. If the price of the underlying at expiration is *X*, then you will not exercise either the put or the call, and your "profit" will be −($*c* + $*p*).

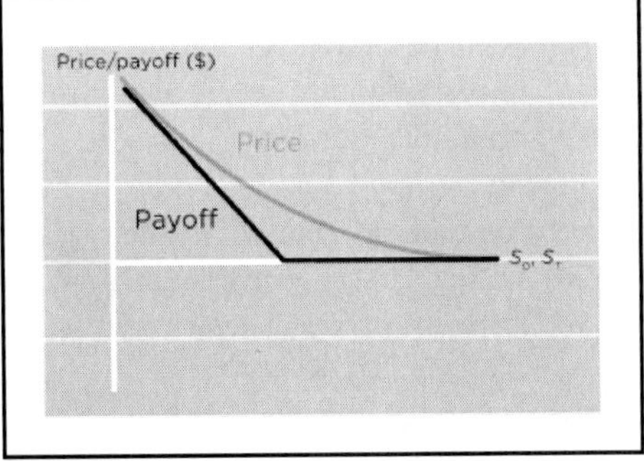

- What if the price is $1 lower than the strike *X*? Then, the call will be worth what it was at *X*—but the put will be worth $1 more than it was at *X*. Thus, the profit line rises $1 from what it was at *X*. For every dollar the price falls below the strike, the profit line rises $1. Thus, to the left of the strike, the profit line rises $1 for $1.

- Next, consider what the profit line looks like when the price of the underlying is above the strike at expiration. At *X*, it is at −($*c* + $*p*). As we move to the right, the call starts to pay off $1 for $1. The put is now worthless. So, combined, for every $1 above *X*, the line rises $1. What you get is a combined profit that is a V shape, with the bottom of the V at a profit of −($*c* + $*p*), the cost of the put and call.

- Note that if the price of the underlying ends up far away from *X*, then you will make positive profits. However, if the price of the underlying ends up close to the strike, you lose. Typically, speculators would do this with "at the money" puts and calls. This strategy is designed to speculate on lots of volatility in the underlying.

- With "just-call" or "just-put" strategies, we speculate that the price will move in one direction: up for calls; down for puts. The straddle strategy is used to speculate when you don't have any idea which way the underlying will move—you just think it's going to move a lot.

- However, realize that the prices of both puts and calls increase with the market's belief about volatility. If you think volatility is high, the market may think so, too. And if the prices of puts and calls rise, the bottom of the V falls. And the distance the price of the underlying must travel away from *X* before your straddle becomes profitable increases. Thus, you are less likely to make money.

- Another speculative strategy is called a butterfly spread. This strategy has you combine long and short positions in calls with different strikes. There are put versions, too.

Hedging

- In addition to speculating, another type of strategy you can do with options is hedging. A hedge is something you do to soften the blow from something bad. This is in contrast to speculation, which amplifies your returns.

- When you use options to hedge, you must already have some exposure to some risks that affect the value of the option's underlying security. A very common and effective hedging strategy is the protective put strategy. The best way to think about this strategy is that it is a side bet that pays off when things go bad for you.

- The protective put acts as insurance. In fact, it is just like insurance against an accident. As with insurance, the policy only pays off when you have an accident. And if you don't have an accident, you still have to pay the premium. Thus, with the protective put, the premium is the price of the put.

- You can wait until expiration to exercise a put, but you don't have to wait. With this approach, you take a position in an option such that when a bad thing happens to you, the price of the option rises. And when a good thing happens to you, the price of the option falls. The delta is the amount the option price changes (prior to expiration) given a change in the value of the underlying. The magnitude of option deltas is less than 1 prior to expiration.

- The intuition is as follows: The value of the option is related to the likelihood it will be in the money at expiration and, conditional on it being in the money, how far it will be in the money at expiration.

- Thus, for a call, as the value of the underlying rises, both the likelihood it will be in the money and the amount it will be in the money increase. This is true because it is either closer to being in the money or it is farther in the money already. As a result, the value of the call rises. Conversely, as the value of the underlying falls, the value of the call falls.

- A similar argument can be made for puts. For a put, as the value of the underlying rises, both the likelihood it will be in the money and the amount it will be in the money decrease. It is either farther away from being in the money or it is less in the money already. This results in the value of the put falling. Conversely, as the value of the underlying falls, the value of the put rises.

- But how much does the option price change given a change in the value of the underlying? Because it is not for certain going to be in the money at expiration, the option price does not change dollar for dollar with the underlying. However, the magnitude of delta gets closer to 1 the closer is it to being in the money and the farther it is in the money. The magnitude of the delta is smaller the farther it is out of the money.

Suggested Reading

Bodie, Kane, and Marcus, *Essentials of Investments*.

Hull, *Options, Futures, and Other Derivatives*.

Lowenstein, *When Genius Failed.*

Questions to Consider

1. Consider the following combination of options, called a butterfly spread: Consider call options written on the same underlying security, but with 3 different strike prices (e.g., \$95, \$100, and \$105); buy 1 call with the strike of \$95, buy 1 call with the strike of \$105, and short 2 calls with the strike of \$100. What is the payoff on this set of positions as a function of the price of the underlying at expiration? If you were to use this strategy to speculate, what would you be speculating will happen?

2. Consider two call options, one that is way in the money and the other that is way out of the money. Which one will have a larger delta? What about for way-in-the-money and way-out-of-the-money puts?

Using Derivatives

Lecture 22—Transcript

In the previous lecture, we described the elements of options and the nature of their payoffs and profits. In this session, we will discuss how you can use them as part of an investment strategy. In particular, we'll examine two ways you can use them. You can use them to speculate, exploiting the fact that options are like highly levered positions in the underlying asset. We will also examine how you can use options to control risk, or hedge.

Because speculation can be very risky, we're going to spend most of our time on hedging. But let's start with speculation. First, what do I mean by speculation? What I have in mind is that a person is speculating when he or she is betting on a security moving in a particular direction. For example, suppose you're reading the paper and you find out that the fees for the disposal of used oil from deep fryers is likely to fall in the near future. If so, then the values of U.S. fast food companies—say, for example McDonald's—they're likely to rise, reflecting higher future profits.

If you currently own stock in McDonald's, you would be happy. But what if you didn't own any stock in McDonald's? Well, you could do two things. You could either go buy some stock or you could speculate with options.

Let's compare these two strategies through a specific example. Let's say you have \$1000 to spend speculating. Let's say that the current price of McDonald's is \$100. So, with your \$1000, you can buy 10 shares. If, after three months, it's clear that the fee will fall, the McDonald's price, say, rises to \$105. So, your 10 shares will be worth 10 × \$105, or \$1050. Your three-month return is going to be r such that \$1000 = \$1050/(1 + r). That is, a return of \$50/\$1000 = 5%. Not bad. If you could get a 5% return every three months, after compounding, that's 21% per year.

Instead, if you choose to speculate with options, what kind of options could you use? And how many of these options could you get with \$1000? You want an option that pays off when the price of the underlying rises. So you're going to want a call option. With call options, if the price of McDonald's rises above the strike price at expiration, then you can call in McDonald's stock for that strike price. Or, according to cash settlement, you could also just get the difference between the price of McDonald's at expiration and that strike price. Thus, if prices rise, that's good for a call.

With a put option, if the price of McDonald's rises above the strike price at expiration, then your put is worthless. So, speculation on rising prices, puts are bad.

So, you want to buy calls. Now, you actually have many calls you could buy. For example, there are going to be calls with a strike price around $90. There are going to be calls with a strike price around $100, and calls with a strike price at, say, $110. Let's say the calls with a strike price of $90 cost $12, and the calls with the strike price at $100 cost $1, and the calls with the strike price at $110, let's say they cost 50 cents.

Let's consider the call with the strike at $100. That is the at the money option. It seems better than the other two. So why is that? The option with a strike at $90 is "in the money" now, but it's kind of expensive. It's expensive because if you could exercise it now, it would pay off $10. But, if the price of McDonald's doesn't go up by expiration, you would be out $2.

The one with the strike priced at $110 is out of the money. It's cheap, but the price will have to climb a lot before it gets into the money at expiration. The at-the-money call is a good compromise on cost and the likelihood of it being in the money at expiration.

So, with your $1000, you buy 1000 at-the-money calls. By the way, the standardized contracts for cash settlement are based on 100 shares. Thus, when you buy one option contract, you're really buying 100 individual options on one share. Although the contracts are for 100 shares, the prices are always quoted on a per-share basis. So, when you buy 1000 calls, you're actually buying 10 call option contracts.

So let's see what you get by buying 1000 calls. When the price of McDonald's rises to $105 in three months, you will exercise your calls and get $5 per call. So now, what is your return? Once you subtract the $1 you paid to get the call, you're going to have $4 in profit per call. On 1000 calls, that's $4000.

That's a net gain on your initial investment of $1000. It's equal to $4000. That's a 400% return over three months. So, the options are much better than just buying the stock. By speculating in the stock, you make 4% on your money. By speculating with the options, you make 400%.

But what happens if it turns out that the used oil fee is not lowered? Well, that would be bad news for McDonald's and the stock price would probably drop, say to $98. If you purchased 10 shares of McDonald's, at the end of three months you would still have the 10 shares. Each would be worth $98, for a total of $980. So you lost $20 out of your initial investment of $1000. That's a 2% loss. So that's not good, but it's not really all that bad either.

But what happens if you had speculated with those calls? If the price of McDonald's turns out to be $98 at expiration, you will not exercise your calls. They are out of the money. They're worthless. In this case, you get nothing. You have spent $1000 to buy 1000 calls, and you have nothing left. Your return is −100%. That's not bad. That's really, really, really bad.

So, by speculating with options, you can amplify your gains and your losses, too. If you really know which way the price is going to go for the underlying, then you may want to use options. If you think prices are going to rise, buy a call. If you think prices are going to fall, then what you want to do is you want to either short or you want to buy a put. By the way, the analysis of these cases is exactly analogous to the buy or the buy a call analysis that we just conducted with the McDonald's example.

Now, speculating with options is very similar to speculating with borrowed money, or leverage. To see this, consider speculation in which you again only have $1000 but borrow in order to leverage your returns. If we borrowed $79,000, we could combine that with our own $1000 and get 800 shares of McDonald's. Now, that's a leverage ratio of 79 to 1. Just to keep things simple, let's say that the interest on this loan is zero. The lender has no idea that you're speculating.

If the price of McDonald's rises to $105 per share as predicted, then you're going to get $105 × 800 = $84,000. And then once you pay back the $79,000 you borrowed, you're going to have $5000. Since you put up only $1000 and you get $5000, then your return is again 400%—the same as with the call option. So, the call option is like being levered 79 to 1.

What happens if the price falls to $98? In that case, your 800 shares are worth only $78,400. And after you pay back as much as you can, you have nothing left. Your $1000 is gone. Again, a −100% return. Buying a call is very similar to an extremely levered position in the underlying. Your returns are very sensitive to the return on that underlying. And, by the way, the same is true with the purchase of a put.

You can also speculate by selling puts and calls. Rather than speculate that the price will rise by buying a call or speculate the price will fall by buying a put, you might want to sell a call to speculate that the price will stand still or fall, or you might want to sell a put to speculate that the price will stand still or rise.

With this kind of speculation, you are just selling the options to get the money, betting that the prices won't move in such a direction that the buyer will want to exercise them.

When AIG sold credit default swaps, they were selling put options on bonds. One view is that they just wanted to make the money by selling the protection. They never thought that the puts would actually be exercised. And they were wrong, and they lost a tremendous amount.

There is one more type of speculative strategy I want to discuss. This kind of speculative strategy is where you bet on volatility. Consider the following strategy, where you combine puts and calls. Buy a call with a strike of X, say, for $\$c$. Buy a put with a strike of X, the same X, for $\$p$. This strategy is called a straddle, by the way. What will you get as a function of the price of the underlying at expiration?

To figure that out, I want you to draw a profit diagram for each position separately. Recall that the profit diagram plots the profit on the vertical axis as a function of the price of the underlying at expiration on the horizontal axis. Once you plot the profit for each, then I want you to do this: I want you to add them up vertically. The profit on the call will be a flat line from $0 to whatever the strike price is at $\$x$. Since you just paid $\$c$ to get it, the flat line is drawn at a height of $-\$c$ on the vertical axis.

Then, for every dollar the price at expiration is above the strike, the profit will rise by \$1. Thus, at the point on the profit line at the strike price, the profit line slopes up \$1 for every \$1 above the strike. So, it's a hockey stick with its handle up in the air to the right.

Let's think about the put. For the put, it's a hockey stick as well, but this time the handle is up in the air to the left. The level of the flat part is at $-\$p$. Next thing we need to do is we need to add them all up. The best way to do this is to simply start at a strike price and then add the two levels of the two profits. If the price of the underlying at expiration is the strike price, x, then you will not exercise either the put or the call, and your profit will be ($\$c + \$p$). You're going to have a negative profit in this case, so the profit is going to be negative of the combination of the price of the call plus the price of the put.

What if the price is \$1 lower than the strike price? Then the call will be worth what it was at x, but the put will be worth \$1 more than it was at x. Thus, the profit line rises \$1 from what it was at x. For every dollar the price falls below the strike, the profit line rises \$1. Thus, to the left of the strike, the profit line rises \$1 for every \$1.

Next, consider what the profit line looks like when the price of the underlying is above the strike price. At x again, it's -($\$c + \$p$). As we move to the right, the call starts to pay off \$1 for \$1 in the underlying. The put is worthless now. So, combined, for every \$1 above x, the profit line is going to rise \$1, pulled up by the profits on the call. What you get is a combined profit line that has a V shape, with the bottom of the V at the profit of -($\$c + \$p$), the cost of the put and call.

Note that if the price of the underlying ends up far away from x, then, only then, will you will make a positive profit. But, if the price of the underlying ends up close to where the strike price is, you're going to lose. Typically, speculators would do this strategy with the at-the-money puts and calls if they believe that volatility is going to be very high. This strategy is designed to speculate on lots of volatility in that underlying.

So with the previously discussed just-call or just-put strategies, we were speculating that the price would move in one direction for calls—up—and for puts—down. The straddle strategy that we just talked about is when you have really no idea which things are going to move. All you think is that they're going to move a lot. But, you should realize that, as we will see in the next lecture, the prices of both puts and calls increase with the market's belief about volatility. If you think volatility is high, the market may also think that it's high. And if the prices of puts and calls rise, then the bottom of the V is going to fall, and the distance the price has to move away from the strike price has to be even bigger in order for your straddle strategy to become profitable.

Another speculative strategy is called a butterfly spread. This strategy has you combine long and short positions in calls with different strike prices. There are also put versions. Let's consider an example. Let there be three different strikes—a strike at $90, $100, $110. Consider the following strategy: Buy a call with a strike at $90, buy a call with a strike at $110. So, buy two calls, one with a low strike price, the other one with a really high strike price. And then what I want you to do is I want you to sell, or write, two calls with the middle strike price at $x = \$100$. See if you can figure out what that looks like on a profit diagram. Also, what so you think that you are speculating on when you adopt this strategy? As a hint, it's sort of the opposite of a straddle.

So we've been looking at a few speculative strategies. Let's consider the second type of strategy that you can implement with options. You can hedge with an option. Okay, so now what do I mean by hedge? A hedge is something you do to soften the blow of something bad. This is in contrast to speculation, which amplifies your returns.

When you use options to hedge, you must already have some exposure to some risks that affect the value of the option's underlying security. A very common and effective hedging strategy is called the protective put strategy. The best way to think about the protective put strategy is that it is a side bet that pays off when things go bad for you.

grew up in Los Angeles, and because of that, I'm a huge fan of the Los Angeles Lakers basketball team. I was a huge fan, by the way, of the so-called showtime fast-break Lakers that had Magic Johnson and Kareem Abdul Jabbar.

Now that I live in the Eastern time zone, every year at playoff time, I literally and figuratively lose sleep over the Lakers. I literally lose sleep because their games are on late in the east, and I figuratively lose sleep because, while they fairly often get into the playoffs and win, they also often lose, and I am heartbroken.

Once I learned about hedging though, I made a bet with a friend against the Lakers in the playoffs. And when they lost, I was heartbroken. But I would console myself with a fabulous steak dinner with the winnings from my side bet. I hedged. And when the Lakers won, I was happy they won, but I had to give someone else a steak dinner. I was hedged. The side bet dampened my overall happiness.

I could have used options, actually, to much better effect. If my bets were put options, I could have gotten a steak dinner when they lost and not had to give someone else a steak dinner when they won. I would be consoled when the lost, but get all of the upside when they won.

So let's return to our McDonald's example from earlier. But now, let's say you are the owner of a McDonald's franchise. Thus, you face some risk associated with changes in, say, the used oil fees. If fees rise, the profitability of your franchise will fall, along with McDonald's stock. If fees fall, your profitability and the price of McDonald's will rise. So, in this case, you have an underlying exposure to risk—the risk that the oil fees will change. Also, the McDonald's corporation has an exposure also to these oil fees. Thus, you both have an exposure to the same risk. You cannot buy options written on your franchise, but you can buy options on McDonald's. Let's see how you can use this to your advantage.

Let's say you've done some analysis and have determined that for every dollar increase in the fee, the value of your franchise will drop $150,000. This is just the present value of the extra costs that you faced. Similarly, for every dollar drop in the fee, your franchise is going to increase $150,000. Also, when the fee changes by $1, the price of McDonald's common stock is expected to change by $5 per share.

In the parlance of hedging, we would say that your "hedge ratio" is $150,000 to $5, or $30,000 to $1. That is, for every $1 increase in McDonald's stock, there is an increase in your franchise value of $30,000.

So how can you protect yourself against a change in the used oil fee? By using a protective put. With this strategy, you will buy puts written on McDonald's common stock to go with what you have in your exposure in your McDonald's franchise. If the fee is increased, the value of your franchise falls, but your put options pay off big as the value of McDonald's stock will fall below the strike price of those puts. If the fee is reduced, the value of your franchise will rise and you won't need the protection from the put, which you let expire out of the money.

That is, the protective put acts as insurance. In fact, it's just like insurance against an accident—where the accident in this case is that the used oil fees are raised and your franchise's value falls (i.e., it crashes). As with insurance, the policy only pays off when you have an accident. And if you don't have an accident, you still have to pay the premium.

Thus, with the protective put, the premium is the price of the put. If there is no accident and the fee stays the same or falls, then you are out the cost of the put option, or the premium. But if there is an accident and the fees rise, your franchise is damaged, but the profit from the puts offsets that damage.

Now, how many puts should you buy in this case? Since your hedge ratio is 30,000 to 1, you want to make $30,000 every time the value of McDonald's stock falls by $1. Let's consider using, say, an at-the-money put option. Recall that the current price of McDonald's is $100, so let's consider a put with a strike of $100.

With this strike, for every dollar the price falls from $100, the put payoff will increase by $1 at expiration. Let's call the change in the payoff of the option per $1 change in the underlying that option's delta. In this case, ıe put delta is −$1 since, as the price falls, the put payoff goes up. It's a .egative relationship.

Iow many puts should you buy? Since your hedge ratio is 30,000 to 1, you vant to make $30,000 every time the McDonald's stock price falls by $1. Since the magnitude of the put delta is 1, you want to buy 30,000/1 puts, or 300 100-share put contracts.

Note that if the delta had been 0.5 for every $1 drop in McDonald's stock, then the put payoff would only go up by $0.5. In that case, you would need 30,000/0.5 = 60,000 puts to hedge your franchise's exposure to these oil fees. By the way, we will see why a delta may be less than one a little bit later.

But the magnitude here is one. So, let's go back to a magnitude of the delta being one. So let's go back to the example. If the fee goes up $1, and the price of McDonald's falls $5 to $95, you will make $5 at expiration on each one of your puts, for a total of 30,000 × $5 = $150,000. That gain of $150,000 exactly offsets your loss in the franchise value of $150,000 associated with that increase in the used oil fee.

Note that the insurance in this case cost you $30,000. And if the fee had stayed the same or dropped, you would still have had to pay the $30,000 for what turns out to be worthless puts. But, this is always true for insurance. You have to pay your premium whether or not you have an accident.

In the previous example, we waited until expiration to exercise the put. But, by the way, you don't have to actually wait. In that case, what you could do is you just have to use the delta that you get by considering what happens to the price change in the put.

With this approach, what you do is you take a position in an option such that when the bad thing happens to you, the price of the option rises. And when a good thing happens to you, then the price of the option is going to fall.

The delta is the amount the option price changes, prior to expiration, given a change in the value of the underlying. The magnitude of option deltas are always less than one prior to expiration.

I will make this much more precise when we develop the pricing models for options in the next lecture. The intuition, however, is as follows: The value of the option is related to the likelihood it will be in the money at expiration. And conditional on it being in the money, how far it's going to be in the money at expiration.

Thus, for a call, as the value of the underlying rises, both the likelihood it will be in the money and the amount it is likely to be in the money if it's in the money increases. This is true because it is either closer to being at the money or it's farther in the money already.

As a result, the value of the call will rise as the underlying rises. Conversely, as the value of the underlying falls, the value of the call is going to fall. A similar argument can be made for puts. For a put, as the value of the underlying rises, both the likelihood it will be in the money and the amount that it will be in the money actually decrease. It's either farther away from being in the money or it's less in the money already. This results in the value of the put falling as the underlying increases. Conversely, if the value of the underlying falls, the value of the put is going to rise.

But how much does the value of the option change given a change of the value of the underlying? Since it's not a sure thing that it's going to be in the money at expiration, the option price does not change dollar for dollar with the underlying value. So, what that means is the delta is not equal to one. The magnitude of delta, however, gets closer to one the closer is it to being in the money and the farther it is already in the money. The magnitude of the delta is smaller the farther it is out of the money.

In the next lecture on pricing, we will see how you can get an explicit expression for the delta. Once you have the delta, you can use that as we did use the delta in the McDonald's franchise example of hedging before.

In this lecture, we've seen how we can use options to speculate. We have seen how you can also make bets on the direction of movements of the underlying securities. But we've also seen how you can make bets on underlying volatility. By the way, I recommend that you're very careful with this speculation because speculating can be very risky. What you need to do when you're thinking about speculating is figure out why you think that the price is going to go in a particular direction or not, and if you're speculating on volatility, why you think volatility is going to be really large.

Now, one of the things that you have to realize is that the prices reflect the market's view on this, and so if you think that the volatility is going to be really large, you need to take into consideration the fact that that might already be reflected in the prices. So, you need to ask yourself if you think that the volatility is going to be large, what makes you think that the market also doesn't think that volatility is going to be very large, too. If you can give yourself a good reason why you would have superior information relative to the information in the market, then yes, you can speculate on volatility using the strategy we've talked about. But if you cannot come up with a really good reason, then I don't recommend doing it at all.

We have also seen that you can use options to hedge. We have seen that there are very important variables to figure out in order to come up with the right hedge strategy. What you need to figure out is what the hedge ratio is, and you also need to figure out what the option delta is. So, the option delta tells you how much the option value changes when there is a change in the underlying. This is telling you something about how sensitive the option value is to the underlying exposure that you have with that option.

If you have a hedge ratio, the hedge ratio tells you how much of the thing that you have changes with the underlying. Using both the hedge ratio as well as the option delta, you can put together a strategy that allows you to compensate yourself when a bad thing occurs but not give away any of the upside when good news occurs.

In the next lecture, we will discuss how to price options. This lecture will allow you to see the cost of insurance and see if it's too expensive. To give you a little insight into this, what we're going to do is we're actually going to price the options according to a replicating portfolio strategy. We're going to try to come up with a way in which we can replicate the payoffs on options using the underlying security and also the difference between borrowing and lending. By doing this strategy, what we're able to do is come up with a price for the option, but recognize with this strategy the option is essentially completely redundant to something that you can do for yourself. So you either want to get the insurance through the option, or you can actually build the replicating strategy for yourself. The price of the option that we get in the next lecture is something that is based upon this no arbitrage argument or based upon the notion that these two things will give you essentially the same payoffs. We will see how to do this in the next lecture.

Pricing Derivatives

Lecture 23

This lecture will examine two models used to price options: the binomial method and the Black–Scholes method. Both are based on risk-neutral pricing, which is based on being able to perfectly replicate the option payoffs with the underlying and risk-free bonds. Recent developments have noted that in some cases, you cannot fully replicate the payoffs. As a result, people may pay a premium over these risk-neutral valuation prices in order to achieve the sure downside protection from a put. However, the Black–Scholes and binomial methods serve as a good benchmark. Furthermore, both are used extensively.

Pricing

- Let's compare two calls that are identical except that one has a higher strike price than the other. The one with the higher strike price is less valuable: It is less likely to end up in the money, and if it does, the one with the lower strike will be more in the money than the one with the higher strike.

- Next, let's compare two calls or puts that are identical except that they expire at different times: The one with the longer time to expiration will be worth more than the one with the shorter time to expiration. The one that is alive for longer has a greater chance of meandering around until it ends up in the money.

- Finally, let's compare the value of a put or call when the volatility is low to the value when the volatility is high. As with the time to expiration, the greater the volatility, the more likely it is that the underlying will end up at an extreme point—which half the time will be in the money.

- Thus, the greater the volatility, the greater the value of the option. This holds for both puts and calls because volatility increases the chance of both big drops and big increases. A natural question to ask is how much bigger the price of the option should be for a given increase in volatility.

- Also, what is an appropriate price period? Say you want to buy protection from downside risk by buying a put (recall the protective put strategy). What is a fair price to pay for that protection? This is exactly the same question you'd ask when buying car insurance—so why not ask it with respect to options?

- So, how do you price an option? The pricing techniques discussed in this lecture price options relative to other securities traded in the market. The key insight of these pricing models is that you can build structures out of existing securities that behave just like the option.

- If that is true, then it must be the case that the option value is exactly the same as the cost of the so-called replicating strategy. If the values of the option and its replicating strategy are not the same, then there is an arbitrage opportunity, which is when two things that are the same have different prices or values. To exploit, buy the cheap one and sell the expensive one.

- For options, you will learn how to form a portfolio of the underlying asset and risk-free bonds that replicates the payoffs on the option. Thus, the cost of the replicating portfolio must equal the price of the option.

The Binomial Model

- With the binomial, we need to make what will initially appear to be a very tenuous assumption. However, although seemingly crazy, it really is not that bad. And it is a very powerful assumption, because it lets us price options in many situations.

- The big assumption is that at any point in time, over the next interval of time, the price of the underlying can only take on two values. This is why it is called the binomial model—"bi," meaning "two," refers to the number of possible outcomes after a period has elapsed.

- Given only two possible outcomes, we can match the payoffs on the option exactly. That's because we have two levers (the underlying and the risk-free bond) that we can pull to match the two possible outcomes.

- However, there are many more than just two possible outcomes for the underlying value, especially for options that are on very volatile assets, that expire many periods in the future. So, isn't this method very limited? The answer is no, because we are going to imbed this simple model in a multi-period model that will make what appears to be ridiculous very reasonable.

- At any point in time, the price will change over the next period by only one of two factors: one for "the price goes up" and the other for "the price goes down." Let the "up" factor be 1 + *u* (so, *u* is the percent return if the underlying goes up). Let the down factor be 1 − *d* (so, *d* is the percent return).

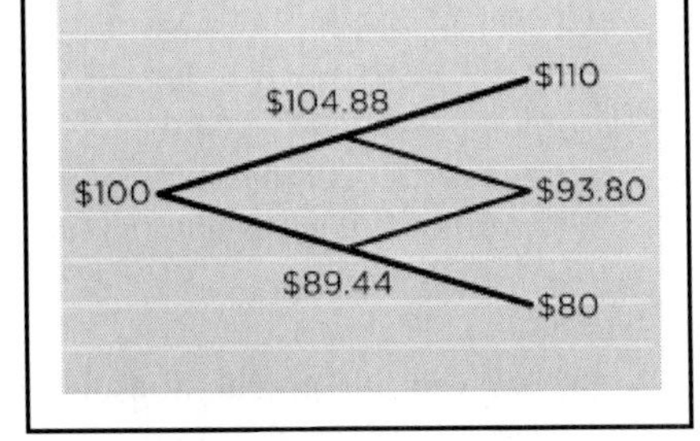

- For example, if $u = 0.10$ and $d = 0.20$ and the current price is $100, then over the next period—for example, 1 year—the price will be either $100(1 + 0.1) = $110 or $100(1 − 0.20) = $80.

- Let's say that the likelihood of up (denoted P_u) and down (denoted P_d) is such that a person investing in the underlying will get a positive return—or else they would not invest in the first place. For example, if $P_u = 0.80$ and $P_d = 0.20$, then the expected future value of the underlying is 0.80(110) + 0.20(80) = \$104. Thus, if we buy at the current price of \$100, the expected, or average, return over a year will be 4%.

- If the probability of up is 0.8 each day, then the likelihood of being at the top is $0.8^{252} = 3.8^{-25}$ (252 is the number of trading days the market is open). Similarly, the probability of the bottom-most down is $0.2^{252} = 7.23^{-177}$. This is much smaller because the probability of up is greater than the probability of down.

- When we replicate the payoff of the option, if the replicating portfolio and the option generate the same payoffs, then they must have the same price.

The Black–Scholes Model

- There is an alternative (but equivalent) way to price the option: risk-neutral valuation. The Black–Scholes formula is also based on risk-neutral valuation.

- The risk-neutral valuation argument is as follows: Risk and risk aversion have nothing to do with the pricing of the option. That's because there is no risk—in the option. We could replicate its payoff exactly. Thus, the option is a redundant security. Thus, the option is priced according to a "lack of arbitrage." That is, the price of the option must be the same as the cost of the replicating portfolio. If there is any risk in the economy, it will be in the price of the underlying.

- If we can find probabilities that explain the prices of the securities used to replicate the option, then we can just use those probabilities to price the option. These probabilities don't have to be actual probability. They can be "pseudo" probabilities that explain the price of the underlying under risk neutrality. All the probabilities have to do is consistently price one set of securities relative to one another. Risk-neutral valuation prices the option as the expected value of the final payoffs, using risk-neutral probabilities.

- We will follow a series of steps.
  1. Pretend that investors are risk neutral.

  2. Calculate the probabilities of up and down (P_u and P_d) that would make a risk-neutral investor indifferent between holding the stock and investing in the risk-free bond.

  3. Using these "risk-neutral" probabilities, calculate the expected payoff on the option.

  4. Discount the expected payoff to the current period.

- The price of an option is the expected value of its payoffs using risk-neutral probabilities inferred from the prices of the underlying security. The prices that result rely on the option being redundant. That is, they rely on someone being able to replicate the payoff on an option using a strategy that uses the underlying and risk-free borrowing and lending.

- In a multi-period setup, the replicating strategy is more complicated. What a replicator has to do is pick a portfolio of the underlying and risk-free bond that will replicate the value of the option over the next period. If it does, then the replicator can afford to buy a portfolio that replicates the prices of the option over the next period—and so on, until the end. Thus, in a multi-period setting, the replication strategy is a dynamic trade strategy.

- The Black–Scholes formula is based on two assumptions related to the dynamic strategy: that prices move continuously (this is the binomial with the interval size dropped to infinitely small) and that the replicator can continuously trade to form the replicating portfolio.

- Clearly, this is not a world with transactions costs. If it were, then the replicating portfolio would not work well. The costs would eat up its value. Thus, the Black–Scholes, like the binomial, is an approximation. It is the most popular option pricing formula, though.

- The Black–Scholes formula revolutionized modern finance. While there were antecedents by others, the Black–Scholes formula took pricing options to the mainstream, which led to the explosion in the use of options in all facets of the financial market.

- The formula looks quite complex, but it is fairly straightforward to use. Prior to their formula, people used something very similar. The advance of the Black–Scholes formula was to provide a solid theoretical foundation upon which it is based.

- Like the binomial method, the formula is based on risk-neutral valuation. That is, the value of the option is the present value of the expected payoffs on the option under the set of pseudo-risk-neutral probabilities.

- There are many places on the web where you can get a Black–Scholes calculator.

- The formula for a call is as follows.
    - $c = S_0 N(d_1) - Xe^{-r_f T} N(d_2)$, where

      $$d_1 = \frac{\ln \frac{S_0}{X} + \left(r_f + .5\sigma^2\right)T}{\sigma\sqrt{T}} \text{ and } d_2 = d_1 - \sigma\sqrt{T}$$

- $N(x)$ is the probability that a normally distributed variable with a mean of zero and a standard deviation of 1 is less than x. To calculate it, you can use an Excel spreadsheet function. Specifically, use +NORMSDIST(put your number here).

- You can think of the formula as follows: call price = present value of the expected payoff conditional on the call being in the money minus present value of the strike price times the probability of the call being in the money.

Suggested Reading

Bernstein, *Capital Ideas*.

Bodie, Kane, and Marcus, *Essentials of Investments*.

Hull, *Options, Futures, and Other Derivatives*.

Questions to Consider

1. All but one of the characteristics of the option and the securities that affect the price of an option are public information (e.g., the current market price of the underlying security, the risk-free rate, the strike price, and the expiration date). The volatility of the underlying, however, is not observable. Rather, investors must estimate volatility on their own. Implied volatility is the value of volatility that generates the current market price using a particular option pricing formula (e.g., Black–Scholes). If the price of a call option increases, will its implied volatility rise or fall? What about for a put?

2. The replicating strategies discussed in this lecture will not work well if there are relatively high transactions costs. In these cases, an investor who wants to hedge against a drop in the value of a security will want to buy a put option rather than creating a put-protected position by trading according to a replicating strategy. What this means is that put prices will likely be higher than those indicated by the replicating portfolio. If this is true, then will the implied volatilities on puts and calls be higher or lower than the volatilities people really expect?

Pricing Derivatives

Lecture 23—Transcript

Once again, everything can be a good idea if it's cheap enough, and everything can be a bad idea if it's too expensive. This is true whenever you want to buy anything.

It is also true for other strategies. For example, in the last lecture, we discussed a way to speculate on volatility. But, whether that strategy is profitable or not depends upon the prices of the options. As it turns out, it depends critically on whether the market prices reflect a better estimate of volatility than your estimate of volatility.

We also saw that you might want to hedge using options. One of the critical parts of the hedging strategy is the option delta, the amount the price of the option changes given a change in the value of the underlying. Again, price is important.

In this lecture, we're going to examine two ways to price options. The first way is called the binomial method. The second way is the famous Black–Scholes method.

Why two methods? There are two reasons. One reason is pedagogical. It is much easier for you to understand the Black–Scholes formula if you understand the binomial first. The second reason is that the binomial is actually more flexible than the Black–Scholes formula in many situations. These situations are complex and sort of beyond the scope of this course. However, once you see how the binomial works in this lecture, you'll be able to do some reading on your own to understand these other more complex cases. By the way, I recommend any of the books by John Hull. John Hull has a series of books, and they all have derivatives in the title. They're all basically very similar in terms of what they cover. Some are harder than others, but I highly recommend them. He also has a website that you can go to, just Google "John Hull's website" and he has a lot of lecture notes on options on his own personal website.

Now, before getting to the formulas, let's just get a sense of when an option will be expensive or cheap, or how the price of an option might change given a change in market conditions.

Let's compare two calls that are identical, except that one has a higher strike price than the other. The one with the higher strike price is less valuable. It's less likely to end up in the money. And if it does, the one with the lower strike will be more in the money than the one with the higher strike.

Let's compare two puts and calls that are identical except that they expire at different times. In this case, we're going to consider both puts and calls. The one with the longer time to expiration will be worth more than the one with the shorter time to expiration. This is true, again, for both puts and calls. The one that is alive longer has a greater chance of meandering around until it ends up in the money.

Finally, let's compare the value of a put or call when volatility is low versus the volatility being very high. As with the time to expiration, the greater the volatility, the more likely it is that the underlying will end up at some extreme point, which half the time puts it in the money, which makes it more valuable. Thus, greater volatility means a higher value for the option. This is true for both puts and calls. An increase in volatility increases the chances of both big drops, which improves the value of the put, but also big increases, which improves the value of the call. By the way, a natural question to ask is "How much bigger should the price of the option be given increase in volatility?"

Also, what's an appropriate price period? Say you want to buy protection from some down-side risk by buying a put. Recall the protective put strategy. What is a fair price to pay for that protection? This is exactly the same question that you would ask when buying car insurance. Why not ask it with respect to options as well?

So how do you price an option? The pricing techniques we will discuss here price options relative to other securities in the market. The key insight of these pricing models is that you can build structures out of existing securities that behave just like options. If that's true, then it must be the case that the option value is exactly the same as the cost of the so-called replicating strategy.

If the values of the option and its replicating strategy are not the same, then there's an arbitrage opportunity. Now, recall that an arbitrage opportunity is when two things that are the same have a different price or different values in the market. To exploit an arbitrage opportunity, you buy the cheap one and you sell the expensive one. And by doing that, you make the two prices come together.

This is just like if I had in my garage a bunch of spare parts. And let's say I was trying to build a 5-series BMW in my garage. What I would do then in this case is I would make a homemade BMW, and then I would see what that exactly cost. If that costs a different amount than the actual price of the BMW, then there's an arbitrage opportunity. If I could build, say, for example, a 5-series BMW for $40,000 in my garage, but BMW sold them for $60,000, then I would build them in my garage and sell them for $60,000. The opposite is also true. If BMW sold 5-series BMWs for $30,000, then I would buy one, tear it apart and sell it for the parts, which are worth $40,000. So, again, this arbitrage notion is that the price has to be just right. It can't be too high or too low. Either way, there's an arbitrage strategy that exploits it.

For options, not BMWs, I will show you how to form a portfolio of the underlying asset and risk-free bonds that replicates the payoff on the option. Thus, the cost of the replicating portfolio must equal the price of the option. Or, put differently, the price of the option has to be exactly equal to the price of that replicating portfolio.

You must be thinking, "I've got to see this. How on earth can he replicate the payoff on an option with just an underlying asset and bonds?" I'm going to show you this using the binomial model. With the binomial, I need what is going to appear to be kind of a really weird, tenuous assumption. But I'm going to argue that, although it seems crazy, it's really not all that bad. And it's a very powerful assumption, because it lets us price the options in many situations. After the binomial, we'll go through the Black–Scholes formula.

So what's the big assumption? The big assumption in the binomial is that at any point in time, over the next interval in time, the price of the underlying can only take on two values. This is why it's called the binomial model—bi, meaning two, refers to the number of possible outcomes after a period of time has elapsed. Given only two possible outcomes, we can match the payoffs on the option exactly. That's because we have two levers, the underlying and the risk-free bond, that we can pull to match the two possible outcomes on the option.

But, aren't there many more than just two possible outcomes for the underlying value, especially for options that are very volatile and expire many periods in the future? Well, of course there are. So, isn't this method very limited? The answer is no, because we're going to embed this simple model in a multiperiod model that will make essentially this kind of seemingly ridiculous assumption of only two values actually kind of go away. I'll show you this in a second.

Let's see exactly how this is going to work. At any point in time, the price will change over the next period by only one of two factors, one for the price goes up and the other for the price goes down. Let the up factor be $1 + u$, so, u is the percentage return in the underlying when it goes up. Let the down factor be $1 - d$, so d is the percent return when the underlying goes down.

Now, by the way, where do you get these *u*s and *d*s? In a second, we're going to go through an example in which I give you the *u*s and *d*s, but this is the method you would use to essentially figure out what the *u*s and *d*s are to use if you want to do this for yourself. You essentially have to calibrate u and d to the amount of volatility for the underlying security. So how do you get the volatility of the underlying security? Well, you could use a single factor model. Remember that the single factor model is a model that relates the return on an individual security to the return on the market and also idiosyncratic returns. But realize that the regression results that you get give you volatility from the past.

If you're trying to price an option going forward, you want to know what the volatility is into the future. So how would you get that? Well, you can actually get an estimate of market volatility by looking at something called the VIX. The VIX is actually a derivative contract that you can trade that's based upon the level of volatility as implied from the prices of options written on the S&P 500 future index.

So, let's hold on to this for a second. What does this say? We have the VIX, which is actually an implied volatility that we figure out from the prices of S&P 500 futures options. We look at the option prices, and then we say, "What must the market be thinking is the volatility for the S&P 500?" The VIX is essentially the level of that index. It tells you something about the market's view of what they think going forward will be the volatility in the S&P 500 over the next year. It's an annualized index, so it's annual volatility.

So the level of the VIX is actually the standard deviation of the return on the S&P 500 as implied from these option prices. Now, by the way, at the peak of the financial crisis in 2008, the VIX was close to 80%. So a more typical value for the VIX is closer to 15 to 20%, somewhere around 17%. So, 80%, that was unheard of. It was one of the highest values the VIX had ever achieved.

Once you have these volatilities, you can actually pick the u and d. Once you have the volatility of the market from, say, the VIX index, then you can use the single-factor model to figure out what the variance of the underlying security is by taking the beta of that security, squaring it, multiplying it by the VIX index (the VIX is a standard deviation, so you're going to have to square that), and then you can take probably the in-sample estimate of the variance of the idiosyncratic term and add that on. That will give you an estimate of what the volatility of the underlying security is that you're trying to price the option on.

Now, as soon as you get that underlying volatility, let's call that Σ, what you want to do is you want to calculate u as $\text{EXP}^{\Sigma\Delta T}$, take all of that minus 1. What's ΔT? ΔT is the length of the interval. So if you're talking about monthly ups and downs, ΔT would be 1/12. If you're talking about an annual up and down, ΔT would be 1. So we're counting time in years. The ΔT stands for what's the change in the amount of time over an interval that you're considering. That gives you a sense of how long the volatility will go ver, and so you scale up the volatility up or down by the amount of time ıat's going to elapse over the interval.

lright, so we have u = EXP$^{-\Sigma\Delta T}$. Subtract that from 1. That gives you the up actor. The down factor, d, is equal to 1 – EXP$^{-\Sigma\Delta T}$.

So, now once you get those, you now have the u and the d. That's how you vould get those. Given those us and ds, let's figure out how we would go bout pricing the option based upon the binomial formula.

For example, if u = 0.10, or 10%, and d = 0.20, or 20%. By the way, I'm just going to use these numbers. I sort of arbitrarily picked them so that the values would work out. They actually don't come from a particular volatility estimate. Now, let's let the current price be $100, and let's say that over the next year, what are going to be the prices for an underlying security? You take $100 × (1 + 0.1) = $110. Or, in the down case, we're going to take $100 × (1 – 0.20) = $80. So that's how you'd use the u and the d.

Just for now, let's say that the likelihood of up, let's call that Pu, and the likelihood of down, denoted Pd, is such that the person investing in the underlying will get a positive return. Else they wouldn't invest it in the first place.

For example, if Pu = 0.80 and Pd = 0.20, then the expected future value of the underlying is going to be 0.80 × (110) + 0.20 × 80 = $104. Thus, if you buy it at the current price of $100, the expected—or average—return over the year is going to be 4%.

Sometimes it's useful to depict this in a tree diagram. With the tree diagram, what you do is you would start over into the left margin with the current price of $100. And then you draw a line upward sloping that tells you where the price is going to go if the price goes up, and have that land on $110. Then draw a branch down that falls down to what the price is going to be in the down state. Let's call that 80.

By the way, this $100, $110, $80, this is clearly not realistic. To make it more realistic, we might want to divide the interval of time in half. In that case, what would we get? Well, you take $(1.1)^{0.5} - 1 = 4.88\%$. Let that be the up factor, and then the down factor is essentially going to be something like $0.8^{0.5} - 1 = -10.6\%$. Then what's going to happen if you do that is you have the tree start at $100. It goes up or it goes down, and then if it goes up, from there it can either go up again or it can go down. Alternatively, if it goes down, it goes down the tree branch, and from that point it can either go up or go down. So what ends up happening is you build a tree that has many more branches. Thus, the two-period problem has a tree with three final end points. By the way, each of the points that has two branches growing out of it is called a node.

The tree starts with one node at $100. After a period, it has two nodes, one at $104.55 and one at $89.44. Then there are three final nodes. If the option lives on past this final period, the tree would continue to branch.

Note that if we can solve a problem with only one interval and two outcomes, then we can solve a two-period, three-outcome problem. The two-period, three-outcome problem is just a bunch of separate one-period, two-outcome problems. And if we can solve the two-period, three-outcome case, then we can do many, many, many outcomes by the end of the year.

This is simply a tree with a bunch of branching nodes after every short interval of time. The tree, by the way, is often called a lattice. With such a tree, there are many outcomes possible at the end of the year. In general, there is a probability distribution associated with the end points. The likelihood of the extreme values is less than in the middle. That is, there's only one way to get to the very top on the final spot, right? The underlying has to go up and up and up every period.

If the probability of going up is 0.8 in this case, say, for each day, then the likelihood of it being at the top is going to be $0.8^{252} = 3.8e^{-25}$ (that's 24 zeros after the decimal point before we get to the three. So e^{-25}. Scientific notation. Now why did I raise it to the 252nd power? That's the number of trading days there are in a year. Similarly, the probability of the bottom node is going to be $0.2^{252} = 7.23e^{-177}$. This is a much smaller probability than the probability of the top node, because the probability of up is greater than the probability of down.

here are many more ways to get to the middle. You could have 126 up and 26 down. You could have 1 up, 1 down, 1 up, 1 down, do this over and over gain 126 times. So the probability in the middle bunch of possibilities is the higher than on the ends. Note that the peak of the distribution on the end need not be in the middle of the lattice. This is, again, because the probability of up and down are not the same.

If we let the number of periods grow by shrinking the interval between time periods, then the probability of each possible outcome actually becomes a normal distribution.

So the point here is that even though we start off with sort of a hokey assumption about it can only go up and it can only go down, we can actually use this over and over and over and over again to get solutions to the price of an option when there are many, many possible values at the end. We do this by essentially embedding this one-period to two-outcome problem into this much larger problem where we're solving that problem over and over and over and over again.

So now that we see that what we need to do is solve a one-period, two-outcome case, let's see how to do that. Let's consider a specific example. Let's consider a call option. Let the exercise price be $55. Let the risk free rate be 2% over the period before expiration. So this is going to be a periodic rate, not an annualized rate. One period, let's call it a month, before expiration, let's say the stock price is $55. At expiration, say, in a month, the stock price might either rise 33.3% to $73.33 or fall 25% to $41.25. So, the up factor is $u = 0.333$ and the down factor, $d = 0.25$.

Recall that the exercise price on this option is, let's say, $55. Thus, at expiration, the option is going to be worth $18.33 = Max($73.33 − $55,0) if the price goes up. But if the price goes down to $41.25, it's out of the money. It's worth nothing.

What we need to do is form the replicating portfolio. Let's let x denote the number of shares of the underlying stock we buy and let B denote the amount of the risk-free bond we buy. By the way, if B is a negative number, that means we're borrowing. So negative means you're short.

So what we're going to need to do here is we need to pick x and B to solve two equations simultaneously. The first equation is: $\$73.33x + (1.02)B = \$18.33$. So, in other words, if we have x shares of the stock and the price turns out to be \$73.33, and we have B units of the bond, that B units of the bond is going to grow in 2% from \$1 to \$1.02. That portfolio will be worth \$18.33, but only in the event that the stock price goes up to \$73.33.

The second equation that we need to solve is $\$41.25x + (1.02)B = 0$. That means we're replicating the payoff on the option when the stock price falls. A little algebra shows that the solution to this is x is equal to 0.57144, and B is equal to −23.11. That is, you should buy 0.57144 shares of a stock (so that's about 57% of the shares of the stock) and borrow \$23.11 at the risk-free rate. Recall that the option delta is defined as the change in the option price divided by the change in the stock price.

In this case, the delta is equal to what? It's equal to \$18.33, because that's the change in the option value at expiration. It's either worth \$18.33 or it's worth zero. Let's divide that by what is the change that's possible in the stock price. The stock price is either going to be \$73.33 or it's going to be \$41.25. So in this case, when I take \$18.33 and divide by the difference between \$73.33 and \$41.25, what do I get? I get 0.57144. That's what the delta is. The delta is the amount that you need to put in the underlying.

If we only buy 0.57144 of the stock, then what's going to happen to our values if the price goes up or it goes down? If we only take a stock position, what are we going to get? If the price goes up to \$73.33, then that 57% of the share is going to be worth \$41.90. But if the price goes down to \$41.25, then that 57% of the share is going to be worth \$23.57. So note that this difference between the \$23.57 and the \$41.90 is \$18.33, which is exactly the difference in the payoff on the option.

But we haven't really replicated the payoff on the option yet because the option goes from zero to \$18.33. What we have here is something that starts off at a different level and moves up \$18.33. So what we need to do is borrow an amount, B, so that we owe exactly, in this case, \$23.57. That way, we have \$23.57 worth of the stock if the stock price goes down, and then we owe \$23.57. When the stock price goes down, we end up having a value of ur portfolio, the replicating portfolio, is equal to zero, which is exactly the alue of the option in the event the stock price does drop. That is, what we eed to borrow one period before is the \$23.57 discounted back one period t the 2%, the interest rate. That's \$23.11.

Note that this B also works if the price of the underlying rises. If the stock price rises to \$73.33, then our stock position is worth $0.57144 \times 73.33 =$ \$41.90. And if we owe \$23.57 at that point, then our net is going to be exactly equal to \$18.33, and this is the payoff on the option when the stock price goes up.

So, what just happened? We replicated the payoff of the option, just using the underlying and the T-bills. We just built a BMW out of parts in my garage.

If the replicating portfolio and the option generate the same payoffs, then it must be the case that they have exactly the same price. In this case, what's the cost of the replicating portfolio? Well, we went out and we bought 57.144% of a share. The current price of the share was \$55, and we borrowed a B of \$23.11, so that was a negative number for B, so we take $0.57144 \times \$55 - \$23.11 = \$8.32$. This is the price of the option. This is what the option price should be according to a no-arbitrage strategy, or a strategy in which the replicating portfolio and the value of the option, which generate the same payoffs, have exactly the same value.

There is an alternative way that's equivalent, and this is called risk-neutral valuation. The Black–Scholes formula is also based upon risk-neutral valuation. The risk-neutral valuation argument is as follows:

Risk and risk aversion had nothing to do with the pricing of the option, and that's because there was really no risk in the option. We could replicate its payoff exactly. Thus, the option is considered a redundant security. So, if that's true, then we're going to price it according to a lack of arbitrage. That is, the price of the option must be the same as the cost of the replicating portfolio. If there is any risk in the economy, it's going to be in the price of the underlying. If we can find probabilities that explain the prices of the securities used to replicate the option, then we can just use those probabilities to price the option. And by the way, those probabilities don't have to be actual probabilities. They can be sort of pseudo probabilities that explain the price of the underlying under risk neutrality. All the probabilities have to do is be consistently able to price both the underlying security and the risk-free bond. Once we can figure out what those prices are based upon in terms of probabilities, we can use that probability to price the redundant security, the option.

Risk-neutral valuation prices the option as the expected value of the final payoffs, using these risk-neutral probabilities. Okay, so let's see if this works. Once we work through the example, you'll see exactly how it works. It can be a little bit mind-blowing at first, but we'll get through it. We're going to go through this in a couple of steps.

Step 1: Pretend that investors are risk-neutral. This is the fictional part of the story.

Step 2: Calculate the probabilities of up and down, *Pu* and *Pd*, that would make a risk-neutral investor indifferent between holding the stock and investing in the risk-free bond. So, we have *Pu* and *Pd*. $Pd = (1 - Pu)$. It must be the case that $Pu \times 1.3333 + (1 - Pu) \times 0.75 = 1.02 \rightarrow Pu = 46\%$, or 0.46. What's the next step?

Step 3: Using the risk-neutral probabilities, calculate the expected payoff on the option. So what are the two possible values the option could be at expiration? Either \$18.33 or zero. Take the probability of up, multiply it by the value in the up state, take the probability of down, multiply it by the value in the down state. $0.46 \times \$18.33 + (1 - 0.46) \times \$0 = \$8.48$.

Step 4: Because that's in the future, we need to discount it back to the current period. So take $\$8.4857/(1.02) = \$8.32$. This is exactly the price that we got using the replicating portfolio approach. So, risk-neutral valuation essentially works in this case.

We've just shown that the price of an option is the expected value of its payoffs using risk-neutral probabilities that are inferred from the prices of the underlying securities. The prices that result rely on options being redundant.

What we're going to do is, we're going to do the same thing for the Black–Scholes. So let's see what the Black–Scholes looks like.

The Black–Scholes, by the way, was completely revolutionary. It was very influential because it essentially gave a theoretical justification for techniques that were used prior to that. And with the development of the Black–Scholes, essentially what this did was this gave everyone permission to use it and it just sort of pervaded much of modern finance thereafter.

Let's go through the formula for Black–Scholes. This is what the formula looks like. It says that the price of a call is equal to the current stock price times something that we'll say is $N(d_1)$. In a second I'll tell you what $d1$ is, and I'll also tell you what $N(d_1)$ is.

The formula for a call is $c = S_0 N(d_1) - Xe^{-r_f T} N(d_2)$, where $d_1 = [\ln(S_0/X) + (r_f + 0.5\sigma^2)T]/(\sigma\sqrt{T})$ and $d_2 = d_1 - \sigma\sqrt{T}$.

$N(d_1)$ is the probability that a normally distributed variable with a mean of zero and a standard deviation of 1 is less than d_1. To calculate it, you would use your Excel spreadsheet function. Specifically, you can use the function +NORMSDIST(put your number here). That will spit out $N(d_1)$.

So, by the way, you can think of this formula as telling you the following: call price equals present value of the expected payoff conditional on the call being in the money minus the present value of the strike price. So the Black–Scholes formula is essentially just what is the expected payoff on the call using this risk-neutral valuation technique.

In this session, we've examined the two most-used models to price options. Both are based upon risk-neutral pricing, which is based on being able to perfectly replicate the option payoffs using the underlying and risk-free bonds.

More recent developments have noted that in some cases you cannot fully replicate those payoffs. As a result, people may pay a premium over those risk-neutral valuation prices in order to achieve the sure downside protection that you can get from a put.

But, the Black–Scholes and the binomial methods serve as a good benchmark. Furthermore, both are used extensively. Thus, it's important for you to know what they are and what they're based upon. And, by the way, there are numerous online calculators that will allow you to plug in all the different parameters and get a price based upon the Black–Scholes value.

Trade Opportunities or Risk?

Lecture 24

This lecture begins by discussing whether the capital asset pricing model works. It is a beautiful theoretical construct, but it turns out that it doesn't work very well. Therefore, you will learn about alternatives to CAPM that are based on the intuition that CAPM provides. You will also learn about a few anomalies—systematic phenomena that have been documented empirically that are at odds with the models. These phenomena might give you some good ideas on where to look for profitable excess returns.

Does CAPM Work?

- CAPM has three main implications.
  - Everyone should hold the market portfolio.
  - Because everyone holds the market portfolio, the risk of an individual security is measured solely by its market beta. Think of the beta as the number of units of risk the security has.
  - Because beta is the sole measure of the risk, the average return of an asset should exceed the risk-free rate by the number of units of risk that security has (i.e., its beta) times the market price of risk (which is the average return on the market in excess of the risk-free rate).
- If we apply these three implications to the data, what do they imply that we should see? Consider a scatter plot of the returns on a security against its beta. If we were to fit a regression line through this scatter plot, then we would get an intercept on the vertical axis where the beta equals zero. We would also get a slope to the relationship. This slope would indicate how much the returns go up on average for an increase in the betas in the sample.

- CAPM implies that with this empirical plot, the regression line should be such that the intercept is the risk-free rate on average and that the slope is the market risk premium (the average return on the market in excess of the risk-free rate). That is, the scatter plot should be consistent with the CAPM equation for expected return.

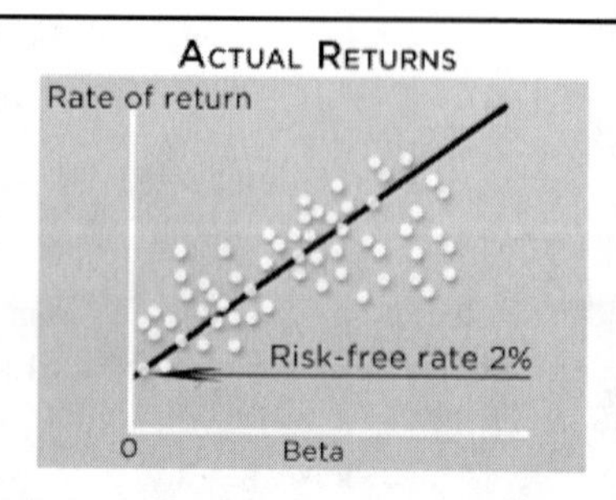

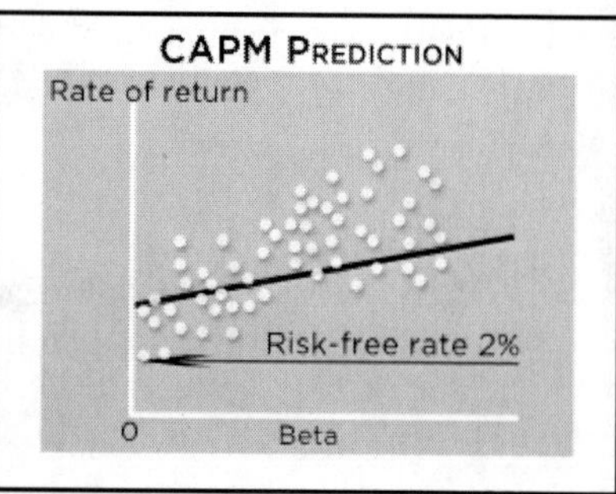

- What do we get when we do this? First, the intercept is too high—it's well above the average risk-free rate. Second, the slope is too flat—it's less than the market risk premium. Third, the fit is terrible. There is so much variation in average returns that is not explained by beta. The conclusion is that beta is no good. CAPM is no good.

- There are two possible explanations.
  - The market is not efficient. CAPM is right; the market is wrong. This means that you should be able to make money by trading on deviations from CAPM—but only if CAPM eventually holds, only if these "out of equilibrium" prices move toward their equilibrium values.

  - CAPM is wrong, and the market is right. These average returns are correct, but beta is not a good measure of risk. Investors know what risk is, and they know it is not beta. So, if you trade based on deviations from CAPM, all you will be doing is getting extra return because you are bearing more risk.

- So, which is more likely? It doesn't seem that people are getting rich trading on violations of CAPM. We know that even professional fund managers do not beat their benchmarks on average. So, let's consider that CAPM is wrong.

Alternatives to CAPM

- How can CAPM be wrong? First, it assumes that everyone should hold the market portfolio. While we should all be diversified and hold broad-based funds, it is clear that only a small percentage of the world actually does that.

- Let's look more closely at the CAPM notion of risk. The reason that market beta is risk is because everyone holds the market portfolio in the CAPM model. The key intuition is that if everyone holds the market and only the market, then the only variation in people's wealth comes from variation in the return on that market portfolio. As a result, the risk of an individual security is the covariance of that security's return to the market return (where the market return is the only thing all people care about).

- This is a good idea. The idea is that risk is correlation or covariance with something you care about. Something is risky if something bad happens to it at the same time that something bad happens to the thing that you care about. The reason this is risk is because you cannot buy that thing to soften the blow of something bad happening to the thing you care about. With securities, if a security return is down when the market is down, it's letting you down when you need it most. That's risk.

- This idea leads to alternatives to CAPM. These alternatives are called multi-factor models. The idea of a multi-factor model is that we should find some other factors that create risk in people's lives. Then, a security would be risky if its return is correlated with that factor. In fact, if there are many factors, then a single security might be correlated with more than one. Thus, an individual security may have multiple risks in it.

- The most popular alternative to the CAPM is the Fama–French three-factor model augmented with the momentum factor. This model uses four portfolios to capture the important risks investors face. The portfolios are as follows.
  - The market.

  - HML: This is a portfolio formed by sorting firms according to their book-to-market ratios. The book value of a company is based on accounting and is supposed to measure the replacement cost of the firm. The "market" is the market value of the firm as priced in the market. So, a high book-to-market firm is one with a small market price relative to its replacement cost. This is a firm with few growth opportunities. A low book-to-market firm is one with a high market value relative to its replacement cost. The "H" in "HML" stands for "high" book to market; the "L" in "HML" stands for "low" book to market. The portfolio is a long position in high book-to-market firms and an offsetting short position in low book-to-market firms. (The "M" in "HML" stands for "minus".)

  - SMB: This is a portfolio that is long small firms (for "S") and short big firms (for "B").

  - MOM: This is the momentum portfolio that is long past winners and short past losers.

- As it turns out, this model does really well. It explains a significant amount of the variation on average returns. Again, the idea is that each of these portfolios contains some risks that are important to investors.

Anomalies

- There is a debate in finance and investments concerning whether models like Fama–French (with MOM) are really capturing hard-to-identify risks or whether there are identifying excessive profit opportunities.

- The debate continues—and likely will always continue. As with any debate, it is not going to be easy to decide the truth. If it were easy, we would have decided on an answer already and we wouldn't still be debating.

- There are a few other phenomena that have been documented in the investment literature that are not explained by any models (so far). First, idiosyncratic volatility is related to average returns. CAPM says that idiosyncratic volatility is not risk. Thus, an investor should not get any extra expected return for holding a security that has more idiosyncratic volatility than others.

- However, empirically, when you form portfolios on securities that have high idiosyncratic volatility, you get average returns that are too low relative to our models (including the Fama–French MOM four-factor model).

- If this is mispricing, then you might want to short a portfolio of high idiosyncratic volatility stocks. Alternatively, it might just be that high idiosyncratic volatility stocks have less of some hard-to-find risk. As a result, they will have lower average returns to reflect that.

- A second phenomenon is that skewness is related to average returns. Similarly, stocks that have lottery-like payoffs (which have a small probability of paying off big but a big probability of losing a little) also tend to have average returns that are too small.

- Penny stocks are like this. The fact that such stocks have lower returns than they should (on the basis of CAPM and the Fama–French three- and four-factor models) indicates that their prices are too high.

- Stocks other than penny stocks can also have lottery-like payoffs. In fact, it has been shown that, on average, after a stock has had a big jump in the past month, the average return is too low going forward.

- It appears as if people see a jump and think another one is possible. Given that, they buy the stock and bid up its price too high. When it returns to its efficient level, it generates a low return.

Suggested Reading

Ang, Hodrick, Xing, and Zhang, "The Cross-Section of Volatility and Expected Returns."

———, "High Idiosyncratic Volatility and Low Returns."

Bernstein, *The Investor's Manifesto*.

Burmeister, Roll, Ross, Elton, and Gruber, *A Practitioner's Guide to Factor Models*.

Fama and French, "The Cross-Section of Expected Stock Returns."

———, "Multifactor Explanations of Asset Pricing Anomalies."

Fama and MacBeth, "Risk, Return and Equilibrium."

Jegadeesh and Titman, "Profitability of Momentum Strategies."

———, "Returns to Buying Winners and Selling Losers."

Lesmond, Schill, and Zhou, "The Illusory Nature of Momentum Profits."

Swensen, *Pioneering Portfolio Management*.

———, *Unconventional Success*.

Questions to Consider

1. Do you think that the returns associated with the momentum portfolio are due to mispricing or due to that portfolio having an additional hard-to-identify risk not captured by other risk factors?

2. According to the intuition of CAPM, securities that have returns that are positively correlated with your wealth are riskier than those that are uncorrelated or negatively correlated. A part of your overall portfolio is your human capital, the personal asset that allows (or did allow) you

to get returns by supplying your labor. Thus, if you work in an industry that prospers or languishes with the market, then you have a greater exposure to market risk than many other investors. How might you alter your portfolio of traded securities to reduce this extra exposure? Is it easier to alter your security portfolio or your human capital?

Trade Opportunities or Risk?

Lecture 24—Transcript

In this lecture I want to do four different things. First, I want to discuss whether the Capital Asset Pricing Model works. It's a beautiful theoretical construct, but is it predictive? Does it explain variation in average return? Is the market beta a good measure of risk?

As it turns out, it doesn't work very well. So why did I tell you about it? For one, it seems like everything in finance revolves around CAPM. There is so much information provided that is relevant because of the context provided by CAPM. You cannot be an investor and consume financial information without knowing what CAPM is.

The second reason I told you about CAPM is that it provides an intuition that is extremely useful for thinking about investing. While CAPM might not work that well, its intuition does beautifully.

That leads to the second thing I want to talk to you about in this lecture. I want to discuss alternatives to CAPM. These alternatives to CAPM are based upon the intuition that CAPM provides. In this section of the lecture, I will stress the intuition of CAPM and show you how it applies to these alternative asset pricing models, the models that do work much better.

The third thing that I want to do is to tell you about a few anomalies. These anomalies are systematic phenomena that have been documented empirically that are at odds with the predictions of our models. The reason I want to discuss these with you is because these phenomena might give you some ideas as to where to look for profitable excess profit opportunities.

The fourth thing I want to do is to discuss with you how to put all of this in perspective. We have covered a bunch of difficult material throughout the course, and I want to look back and put it into this broader context.

Let's begin. First, let's see if CAPM works. In a previous lecture, we explained the implications of CAPM. CAPM has three main implications: (1) Everyone should hold the market portfolio. (2) Since everyone holds the arket portfolio, the risk of an individual security is measured solely by its arket beta. Think of the beta as the number of units of risk that security as. (3) Since beta is the sole measure of risk, the average return of an sset should exceed the risk-free rate by the number of units of risk in that ecurity, its beta, times the market price of risk, which is the average return n the market in excess of the risk-free rate.

f we take these three implications to the data, what do they imply we should ee? So consider a scatter plot of the returns of a security against its beta. By he way, we typically do these on portfolios rather than individual securities ecause the estimates of beta are more precise with portfolios. Also, the diosyncratic terms are diversified in portfolios.

With this scatter, if we were to fit a regression line through the scatter plot, then we would get an intercept on the vertical axis where the beta equals zero. We would also get a slope to the relationship. This slope would indicate how much of the return goes up on average for an increase in the beta in the sample.

CAPM implies that with this empirical plot, the regression line should be such that the intercept is the risk-free rate on average and that the slope is the market risk premium (i.e., the average return on the market in excess of the risk free rate). That is, the scatter plot should be consistent with the CAPM equation for expected return.

So what do we get when we do this? First, the intercept is too high. It's well above the average risk-free rate. Second, the slope is too flat. It's less than the market risk premium. Third, the fit is terrible. There is so much variation in average returns that is not explained by beta.

So what can we conclude about CAPM? Is it any good? Well, there are two possible explanations. One explanation is the market is not efficient. CAPM is right—the market is wrong. This means that you should be able to make money by trading on deviations from CAPM, but only if CAPM eventually holds. Only if these out-of-equilibrium prices move toward their equilibrium values, and only if the people in the market start voting for who they actually believe is beautiful rather than vote for those people they think that other people will vote for.

The second explanation is CAPM is wrong and the market is right. These average returns are correct, but beta is no good at measuring risk. Investors know what risk is, and they know it's not beta. So, if you trade based upon deviations from CAPM, all you will get is you will be getting a bigger return, but because you're bearing more risk.

So, which is more likely of these two explanations? It doesn't seem that there are people getting too rich by trading on violations of CAPM. We know that even professional fund managers do not beat their benchmarks on average. So, I'm a little bit sympathetic to the explanation that it may just be pricing of risk, not mispricing.

Let's consider that CAPM is wrong. This leads to the second part of the lecture—alternatives to CAPM. How can CAPM be wrong? Let me count the ways. First, as I pointed out before, it assumes that everyone should hold the market portfolio. While I agree that we should all be diversified and hold broad-based funds, it's clear that only a small percentage of the world actually does that.

Let's look a little bit more closely at the CAPM notion of risk. The reason that the market beta is risk is because everyone holds the market portfolio in the CAPM model, not in the real world, but in the CAPM model. The key intuition is that if everyone holds the market—and only the market—then the only variation in people's wealth comes from variation in the return on the market portfolio. As a result, the risk of an individual security is the covariance of that security's return to the market return, where the market return is the only thing all people care about.

So, by the way, this notion, this is a good idea. The idea is that risk is correlation or covariance with something that you care about. That's a deep insight. Something is risky if something bad happens to it at the same time that something bad happens to something that you care about. The reason this is risk is because you cannot buy that thing to soften the blow of the something bad happening to the thing you care about. With securities, if a curity return is down when the market is down, it's letting you down when ou need it the most. That's risk.

his leads to the alternatives to CAPM. These alternatives are called multi-actor models. The idea of a multi-factor model is that we should find some ther factors that create risk in people's lives. Then a security would be risky f its return is correlated with that factor. In fact, if there are lots of factors, hen a single security might be correlated with more than one factor. Thus, n individual security may have multiple risks in it.

So what's the implication of that fact? Well, before we talk about the factors hat might work empirically, let's think more abstractly for one more minute. Let's say that there are 10 such factors that create risk. An individual security might be exposed to all 10. As a result, the security's return will be correlated with all 10.

The extent to which the return is correlated is called a factor loading. A security will have a factor loading for each factor. For the first factor, the second factor, and so on. These factor loadings are all like the market beta. Just like the market beta measures the sensitivity of the security's return to the market, the factor loadings measure the sensitivity of the security's return to the factor. And just like the beta is the number of units of market risk that security has, each factor loading for a particular factor is the number of units of risk for that factor that security has.

So, recall the intuition from CAPM. If a security had beta units of market risk, then it should pay, in expected return terms, beta units of the market price of risk, the risk premium.

Let's apply this to the multi-factor model. Given a set of factor loadings for a given security, the average return on the security should exceed the risk-free rate by the number of units of factor-1 risk times the market price of factor-1 risk plus the number of units of factor-2 risk times the market price of factor-2 risk, and so on, up to the last factor.

In order to do this, we're going to need factors and the market price of each one of those factors. What are the factors? And what are the market prices of risk for each of these factors? Well, we don't actually know, but we keep looking. Actually, what I should say is that we don't know exactly. This is a little like dark matter in physics. Now, I'm not a physicist, but my understanding is that they can't see dark matter itself. They can only see behavior that is consistent with its existence.

This is the same thing with multi-factor models in finance. We can't see a factor, but we can see a portfolio that behaves as if it has a bunch of some important factor in it. Let's call this portfolio a factor portfolio. If we have such a portfolio, then we can measure the risk of an individual security according to how correlated the return on that security is to the return on that factor portfolio.

So, a natural question is "What portfolios work? What portfolios capture factors that are really important?" The most important alternative to the Capital Asset Pricing Model is the Fama–French three-factor model that's also been augmented with the momentum factor. This model uses four portfolios to capture important risks that investors face. Let's go through each one of the four portfolios.

The first portfolio is the market portfolio, one that we've talked about all along. The second portfolio is called HML. This is a portfolio formed by sorting firms according to their book-to-market ratios. The book value of a company is based upon accounting and is supposed to measure the replacement cost of a firm. So, if you were to completely replace the firm and start it all over, you'd pay the book value. The market value is the market value of the firm as priced in the market. So, a high book-to-market firm is one with a small market price relative to its replacement cost. This is a firm with few growth opportunities. A low book-to-market firm is one with a high market value relative to its replacement cost. The H in HML stands for high book-to-market, and the L stands for low. The HML portfolio is a long position in the high book-to-market firms and an off-setting short position in the low book-to-market firms. So the M in HML stand for minus. High minus low.

SMB is the third portfolio. This is a portfolio that is long firms that are small, small for S, and short firms that are big, B for big. So SMB is small minus big.

The fourth portfolio is the momentum portfolio that we discussed earlier in the course. It's a portfolio that is long past winners and short past losers. This portfolio is typically identified just simply by calling it MOM. As it turns out, this model works really well. It explains a significant amount of the variation in average returns.

Again, the idea is that each of these portfolios contains some risks that are important to investors. Can we come up with a story that explains why that's true? For example, the SMB portfolio contains some risk that small firms have a lot of, but large firms do not have a lot of. Although we can't see the risk, we can kind of guess at what that risk might be. For example, it might be recession risk. Small firms are hit harder by recessions than large firms. The risk is that they will go out of business during a recession. Large firms, however, can weather the storm more easily. If you only used the market return as in CAPM, then you might not see this differential between large and small firms, and to the extent that many people are employed by small firms, this recession risk is a very important risk to them.

If this is true, then you can characterize the risk of an individual security not by just the market beta, but also its beta with respect to SMB, and also its beta with respect to HML. Those securities that move with SMB return have a lot of SMB risk, whatever that is—maybe it's recession risk, and, as a result, should have a higher expected return because it's riskier. Similarly, those securities that move with the HML portfolio return have more HML risk and should, as a result, have higher returns on average because of that.

So what about MOM? MOM was actually added later, after the Fama–French model was introduced. There was the Fama–French three-factor model, and they augmented it with MOM. Recall that the momentum strategy has you go long winners and short losers. Also recall that when we first discussed momentum profits in the lecture on market efficiency, I wanted to leave it as an open question as to whether it was return for risk or whether it was actually trade opportunity.

To see if it's risk, researchers looked to see if the Fama–French model could explain the returns on the momentum portfolio—on MOM—and they found that it did not explain those returns. So, there are two possible things that you can conclude. You can either conclude that it is a trade opportunity—that the extra return above and beyond what Fama–French says it should be is just gravy. Come and get it. Alternatively, you could say you found another portfolio that obviously contains an important risk that the other Fama–French portfolios do not contain. If so, let's just add that to the model. Right? If we found another portfolio that explains variation, that has risk in it, we'd better use that as a measure of risk. And that's exactly what the finance profession did.

This leads to the third section—anomalies. The key thing that I want you to see from this section is that there is a debate in finance and investments concerning the fundamental issues alluded to just a second ago. The debate is whether models like Fama–French, with momentum, are really capturing hard-to-identify risks, or whether they're identifying excessive profit opportunities.

To see this debate more clearly, let's consider first the case of HML. The it's risk explanation might go something like this. High book-to-market firms have a greater exposure to some important risk that low book-to-market firms don't have. Since high-book to market firms have low market values, they have few growth opportunities. Recall that the growth opportunity, or the stock value, is equal to the no-growth price plus the present value of growth opportunities. Thus, a low-priced stock is one with few present value of growth opportunities—like Kodak before it was in bankruptcy. Perhaps the Hs, the highs in the HML, have lots of bankruptcy risk because of that. In contrast, low book-to-market firms have high present value of growth opportunities and little, if any, bankruptcy risk. Thus HML captures bankruptcy risk that investors care about.

But there is a compelling case for the it's mispricing explanation as well. What it says is CAPM is fine. A high book-to-market firm is one with a low price. It's too low given its risk. It's actually mispriced. A low book-to-market firm is one with a high price. It's too high given its risk. It's also mispriced.

o why does HML have a positive return in excess of what CAPM says? ecause the prices will go where they're supposed to go eventually. Prices iat are too low, like with the Hs, will move up, generating positive returns. eing long Hs is good.

'rices that are too high, like with the Ls, will go down, generating negative eturns. Being short Ls, as in HML, is good. Thus, the portfolio HML enerates positive excessive returns relative to CAPM—not because of risk, ut because of mispricing.

'ust like you can come up with two explanations for HML, you can also do that for momentum and SMB. For MOM, the mispricing story is that there is under-reaction to information. That which goes up continues to go up, and that which goes down continues to go down. The it's risk story is, again, it's just a hard-to-find, hard-to-identify risk. But it exists heavily in the MOM portfolio.

For the SMB, the mispricing story is that small firms are small because their prices are low and big firms are big because their prices are high. When prices are too low, they eventually rebound, and when prices are too high, they eventually correct—the it's-risk story we discussed earlier.

So, what's the conclusion? My conclusion is that the debate continues and will likely continue. As with any debate, it is not going to be easy to decide what the truth is. If it were easy, we would have decided that already and we wouldn't still be debating.

In this section of the lecture, I also want to point out a couple of other phenomena that have been documented in the investment literature that are not explained by any of our models so far. The first one is that idiosyncratic volatility is related to average returns. CAPM says that idiosyncratic volatility is not risk. Thus, any investor should not get any extra expected return for holding a security that has more idiosyncratic volatility than some other. But, empirically, when you form portfolios on securities that have high idiosyncratic volatility, you get average returns that are too low relative to what our models say, including the Fama–French Momentum four-factor model. If this is mispricing, then you might want to short a portfolio of high idiosyncratic volatility stocks.

Alternatively, it might just be that high idiosyncratic volatility stocks have less of some hard-to-find risk. As a result, they will have lower average returns to reflect that.

The second phenomenon is the fact that skewness seems to also be related to average returns. Stocks that have lottery-like payoffs also tend to have average returns that are too small relative to our models. So what do I mean by a lottery-like payoff? What I mean by this is that they have a small probability of paying off really big, but a big probability of losing a little. Penny stocks are like this. If you buy 1000 shares of something that costs 10 cents a share, it's like you're buying 100 $1 lottery tickets. What's the most you can lose? $100. But what's the most you could gain? The sky is the limit. If the company takes off, it could rise to $20, and you would have $20,000.

The fact that such stocks have lower returns than they should, on the basis of CAPM and the Fama–French three-factor and four-factor models, indicates that their prices are too high. That is, rather than have a price of 10 cents maybe they should only have a price of 5 cents. By the way, stocks other than penny stocks can also have lottery-like payoffs. In fact, it has been shown that on average after a stock has had a big jump in the past month, the average return the next month is too low going forward. So, regardless of the size of the firm, if it had a really big jump, it appears that people see that jump and think that it's going to lead to more jumps down the road. Given that, they buy the stock, bid the price up too high, and when it returns to its efficient level, it generates a low return.

So far, in this lecture, we have seen that there is a debate about what constitutes a profitable trade opportunity and what constitutes just the pricing of risk. Throughout this course, I have shown you how to quantify variability in returns. The lectures on fixed income and bond pricing developed a way to quantify interest rate risk. Recall the duration measure. The lectures on stock prices as present values of future cash flows showed that the arrival of information about future prospects creates volatility. We examined how to control the volatility by forming portfolios. We also examined how you can antify volatility from market movements and idiosyncratic returns using e market model.

hen we examined risk. The main point was that risk can only be measured the context of a portfolio. That is, the volatility of your wealth is risk. The olatility of the return on an individual security is not risk. The risk of an dividual security is the correlation of that security's return with the wealth your portfolio.

Ve also discussed how to form a portfolio that consists of both passive nvestments and a portfolio of active investments. There, the important rade-off was the difference between diversification and idiosyncratic risk hat you must bear if you're going to be taking on active positions.

All of these parts of the course support a desire you might have to either be actively managing your investments or to have a passive portfolio. Recall the framework that I developed for the student managers for the student-run fund. This framework allows you to decide how active or passive you want to be.

On this, I have two final sets of comments. My first set of comments concerns if you decide to have an active management approach to your investments. This may be right for some, maybe not for others. I clearly think that active management is appropriate for some people. Otherwise, I wouldn't have told you all the things that I told you about in this course.

But, before you are active, or you let someone else be active with your money, realize that with active management you'll be making some bets. When you invest in one stock rather than an industry ETF in that stock's industry, then you're betting that that one stock will do better than the ETF. When you sell one ETF to buy another ETF, you are betting that the one industry or sector will do better than the other. Once you realize that you're making bets, that realization should focus you on the kinds of analysis that you do.

The first kind that you should do is to understand a sector or an industry. What allows some firms to make higher profits than others? Is that sustainable or contestable? If something is going to change in the future, what makes on firm better than another at adjusting to these changing conditions? And if th market is going to change in some way in the future, what changes favor on firm over another?

For example, I recall a time when I was discussing with the student managers airlines. There are two basic business models for the industry. One is hub-and-spoke, in which the airline has a fleet of large planes and a handful of large hubs that everyone must go through. Alternatively, you don't have to have any hubs, but you have a large fleet of smaller planes that travel from point to point.

This discussion was whether one strategy would be more profitable if the economy came back strong with a significant increase in business travel. Or which one would do relatively better if, because of advances in technology, there was less need for business travel, with the increased prevalence of remote conferencing and virtual teams. If the fund was going to sell off some of its transportation ETF to buy a single airline with the hub-and-spoke strategy, then we were clearly making a bet on business travel increasing. And, by the way, in the end, we decided not to make that bet. But at least we knew we were thinking about making that bet.

I also want you to think about what are the things that might go wrong. Does the company you're looking at have an advantage now? How typical is it for such advantages to be short-lived—that other firms can leapfrog over them in terms of, say, technology? Is there a risk that something big may fail? For example, with the explosion of the Deepwater Horizon well, BP stock experienced a loss of half its value. That one event had a huge impact on the firm and its stock. How common is such an event?

Basically, I want you to think about what would make a particular firm experience a significant loss. If you cannot think of such a loss, then that's good. But if you can, then ask yourself why you would just buy that single firm when you could own many such firms in an ETF. The chance of all of them having a catastrophic failure is much lower than any one of them having a failure by themselves. If you can think of any sources for such ilure, or that such failures are common, then you better be sure about your et paying off in order for you to expose yourself to such a bad outcome.

nce you have a clear picture of what you're betting on, then the second ning you have to do is ask yourself whether or not the market already knows nd reflects what you know. A company that is run better than another is not ecessarily a better investment. It's only a better investment if its superiority s not already valued by the market.

The third thing you have to do once you have convinced yourself that it is not reflected by the market is to ask yourself what other things that you may not have thought of may be reflected in the market price.

And then, finally, I want you to always remember my favorite saying: "Part of knowing is knowing when you know and knowing when you don't know." If you don't know if you know about an active position, then it's better to be passive.

The second thing that I want to stress is even though much of the material in the course is difficult, you should not shy away from investing passively. The other day, in a university course I teach, we were discussing time-value of money. As we did in an earlier lecture in this class, we were looking at how much money you'd need to save for retirement. I asked someone in the class how long that they were going to work, how long did they think they would live past retirement, and how much money did they want per month after retirement.

A very young student responded that he was going to work for about 50 years, and then live 25 years past retirement, and that he wanted—get this—$85,000 a month in retirement—in current dollars, not inflated. I just thought this was a huge number. But we ran the numbers anyway. If he can get an average annual return by investing in the passive market portfolio of just 8%, then he just needs to save around $1400 a month. That's not that much. And, by the way, this 8%, this is less than the market risk premium we've had in the last 100 years.

But if he is worried about the market and keeps his investments in risk-free accounts, earning only 2%, he would have to save almost $19,000 a month That's beyond reach.

The point is that you should not be scared by the market. Remember when we talked about you should be less risk-averse? You can be as risk-averse as you want to. But, my point with the retirement example is that you will give up a lot if you don't access the market.

My team of student managers did some analysis that is germane to this issue. We looked at what the fund would have grown to over the past 50 years under different allocations to low-risk versus market investments. We considered a 100% allocation to the market versus a 30%-safe/70%-risky allocation. While there would have been a bit more variation in the annual return in any given year under the 100% market allocation than under the 30/70 split, the 100% allocation soared to a much higher level. Thus, even though there were some years with larger losses under the 100% allocation, the drop was always from a much higher level.

So, the market is really not that risky over the long run. Of course, if you are in retirement, then one down year can be tough. So you'll probably not even want the 70% allocation of the market, let alone a 100% allocation. But my point is that you should not be afraid of the market. You should dive in and start building a smart portfolio—whether it's active or passive.

Glossary

abnormal return: A return that is larger than the fair return an investor should get given the risk the investor bears; the amount by which a security's average return deviates from the expected return implied by an asset pricing model.

active management: The practice of engaging in analysis designed to identify mispriced securities and then adopting investment strategies in which securities are actively traded in order to outperform the market.

alpha: See **Jensen's alpha**.

American option: An option contract that allows the holder to exercise the option on or before the expiration date of the option.

annuity: A security that pays a fixed payment every period (e.g., every six months) for a prespecified number of future periods.

arbitrage opportunity: An arbitrage opportunity exists when two securities or portfolios have identical characteristics (in terms of payoffs as a function of the state of the economy) but have different values in the market. With such a situation, an investor can make an abnormal return without bearing any risk; arbitrage is often referred to as a "free lunch." The arbitrage opportunity is exploited by taking a short position in the security with the high value and using the proceeds to purchase the security with the low value.

arbitrage pricing theory (APT): An asset pricing model in which there are multiple factors that generate risk. Each individual risk has a risk premium, which is the average amount an investor can expect to receive in excess of the risk-free rate for bearing one unit of that risk; the size of the risk premium for a particular risk is the same across all securities. However, each individual security has a set of factor loadings, one loading for each risk; the factor loading for a particular risk for an individual security measures the number of units of that risk possessed by that individual security. The product of the factor loading for a particular risk for that individual security and the factor risk premium for that risk is the premium—or extra return—on that security in excess of the risk-free rate to compensate the investor for bearing the amount of that type of risk in that security. Thus, under APT, the expected return of an individual security exceeds the risk-free rate by the sum of the premiums for that security for each of the types of risk.

asset-liability management: A set of techniques designed to manage the variability of a firm's equity value due to changes in the market values of the assets owned by the firm and the liabilities issued by the firm.

asset pricing model: A theoretical model that implies a specific relationship between the characteristics of a security's returns and that security's expected return.

autocorrelation: The correlation between the value of a variable in one period and the value of that variable during a prior period. That is, it is the correlation of the variable with itself, but at different points in time. Autocorrelation is typically used to quantify if there is a predictable pattern in returns over time. If the autocorrelation of the return on a security is positive (negative), then the return on that security will more likely than not be positive (negative) the next trading day after a positive (negative) return.

balance sheet risk: The risk of changes in the value of equity associated with revisions in the values of assets and/or liabilities on the firm's balance sheet.

basis point: One one-hundredth of a percentage point; 100 basis points equals one percentage point.

binomial model: An option pricing model that prices the option based on a no-arbitrage argument. The model determines the price of the option as the value of a replicating trade strategy that uses risk-free borrowing/lending and the underlying security of the option to replicate the payoff on the option. The model assumes that, at any point in time, the price of the underlying security in the next period can only go up by a fixed "up" percentage or down by a fixed "down" percentage.

lack–Scholes option pricing model: A model for pricing options based a no-arbitrage argument. The model determines the price of the option s the value of a replicating trade strategy that uses risk-free borrowing/ nding and the underlying security of the option to replicate the payoff on e option. The model assumes continuous trading and that the underlying ecurity value also evolves continuously over time.

udget constraint: The set of consumption bundles that can be consumed vith a given level of income or wealth.

all option: A financial contract that gives the holder of the option the ight to buy an underlying security for the strike (or exercise) price on a respecified date (or set of dates).

capital asset pricing model (CAPM): An asset pricing models that states that the expected return on an individual security should exceed the risk-free rate by the product of the security's market beta (the measure of risk in CAPM) and the market risk premium. Variation in expected returns across different securities is due solely to variation in the market betas of the securities.

compounding: The practice of charging interest on interest not paid in the past.

consumption bundle: A specification of the number of units of the complete set of goods and/or services a person might consume; a specific consumption bundle corresponds to a specific set of quantities for the goods and/or services available.

correlation or **correlation coefficient**: Correlation is a unit-less measure (ranging from −1 to 1) that translates covariance into a measure of the direction and the strength of the relationship between two variables. The correlation between two variables is defined as the covariance between the two variables divided by the product of the standard deviations of the two variables. The sign of the correlation coefficient indicates whether the two variables typically move in the same direction (positive correlation) or in the opposite direction (negative correlation). If the correlation is zero, there is no relationship between the movements of the two variables. As the correlation rises above zero, the strength of the positive relationship goes from none (at zero) to weak (e.g., at 0.2 or 0.3), to fair (e.g., at 0.6), all the way up to perfect (at 1). If the correlation is 1, then the deviation of one of the variables from its expected value is always (i.e., in all possible random outcomes) a constant multiple of the deviation of the other variable from its expected value. Thus, when the correlation is 1, the two variables move perfectly together. Similarly, as the correlation falls from zero, the negative relationship goes from none (at zero) to weak (e.g., at −0.1 or −0.2), to fair (e.g., at −0.5), to strong (e.g., at −0.8) to perfect (at −1).

cost of capital: The amount of return investors demand in order to invest in the securities of the firm. This is the cost the firm pays in order to finance the purchase of the firm's capital assets.

coupon rate: The percentage of a bond's face value that is paid as an annual coupon. Most bonds pay this total coupon in two equal installments (one every six months). Thus, the semiannual coupon payment is the product of half the coupon rate and the face value of the bond.

covariance: A measure of the degree to which two variables move in similar or opposite directions relative to their expected values. Each variable has a set of possible deviations from its expected value. Consider the product of the deviation of one variable from its expected value and the deviation of the other variable from its expected value. The covariance is the expected value of all of these possible paired deviation products. A positive covariance implies that, probabilistically, when one of the variables is above (below) its expected value, then more often than not the other variable will also be above (below) its expected value. A negative covariance implies that, probabilistically, when one of the variables is above (below) its expected value, then more often than not the other variable will be below (above) its expected value. If the covariance is zero, then if one of the variables is above (below) its expected value, then it is equally likely that the other variable will be above its expected value as below its expected value. For returns, the covariance between the returns on two securities is in percent squared.

edit default swap: A swap contract that allows a person to swap a bond at has experienced a credit event (e.g., a default, a downgrade in credit ting) for a prespecified payment (typically the face value of the bond). A edit default swap essentially provides insurance against a credit event.

redit rating: A rating assigned to a fixed-income security by a rating agency at gives a general indication of the likelihood that those who invested in at security will receive all of the payments promised by the issuing firm.

redit risk: Default risk.

lata-generating process (DGP): A statistical description of how observed lata is generated.

lefault intensity: See **hazard rate**.

default risk: The risk that a firm that issues a fixed-income security will not make all of the promised payments.

default spread: The difference in the yield to maturity on a bond that has default risk and the yield to maturity on an equivalent bond (in terms of payment size and timing) without any default risk.

derivative security: A security that derives its value from the values of other securities or commodities. Such a security specifies its cash flow or payoff as a function of the value of some other security (or set of securities) under prespecified conditions (e.g., a price on a specific date). Options and futures are examples of derivative securities.

discount rate: The rate r such that the present value of a future cash flow equals the value the market is willing to pay in the current period to receive that future cash flow; the interest rate charged to depository institutions (e.g., banks and savings and loans) by a central bank to borrow at its discount window.

duration: A measure of interest rate risk for either an individual fixed income security or a portfolio of fixed-income securities. The duration is the elasticity of the value of the security/portfolio with respect to a change in the yield to maturity.

duration mismatch: There exists a duration mismatch when the durations of a firm's assets and liabilities are different; a duration mismatch creates balance sheet risk.

duration gap: The difference in the duration of a firm's assets and liabilities.

effective annual rate: The annualized effective cost of borrowing, given the number of times per year interest is compounded. For example, if the monthly rate is 1% and the rate is compounded monthly, then a person who borrows money for 1 month would be paying an effective annual rate of $(1.01)^{12} - 1 = 0.126825$ (or 12.6825%) per annum over that month.

efficient market hypothesis (EMH): A hypothesis that stipulates that the market prices of securities accurately and quickly reflect available information regarding the future value of the securities or the cash flows from the securities. There are three forms, which vary in terms of the types of information that are reflected in prices. See **weak form**, **semi-strong form**, and **strong form market efficiency**.

elasticity: A measure of how sensitive the value of a given variable is to changes in other variables thought to influence that variable. Specifically, the elasticity of variable X with respect to variable Y is defined as the percentage change in quantity of variable X that results, given a percentage change in the quantity of variable Y.

equally weighted portfolio: A portfolio formed by holding equal dollar amounts in each security included in a set of securities.

equilibrium: A condition in positive analysis in which the posited system is at rest, whereby there are no forces internal to the posited system that might cause some variable or variables to change.

uity: A claim to the residual cash flows of a firm that remain after the firm tisfies all of its payment obligations (including payments of interest and incipile to the debt holders of the firm). Shares of stock are equity claims.

uropean option: An option contract that allows the holder to exercise the ption only on the expiration date of the option.

xercise price: The price at which the holder of an option has the right o transact.

xpectations hypothesis: The hypothesis that the forward rates calculated rom a yield curve are equal to the market's expectation of future short-term pot rates.

expected return: The weighted average of the possible returns that may occur in the future, with weights equal to the probability of each possible outcome. An expected return can be thought of as the average return that would occur with a large number of repeated samplings.

expected utility hypothesis: The hypothesis maintained by most asset pricing models that an individual's preferences over different frequency distributions of wealth (resulting from different investment strategies) can be ordered (most preferred to least preferred) according to the expected value of a set of suitably chosen utility values associated with each possible random wealth outcome. The hypothesis states that there exists a set of values for a person's indirect utility of wealth (one value for each possible random wealth outcome) that can represent a person's ranking over lotteries according to the expected value of the indirect utility values, where the probabilities used in the expected value correspond to the probabilities associated with the wealth outcomes under that lottery.

expiration date: The date after which the holder of an option contract cannot exercise the option.

face value: A fixed amount due at maturity on a bond. The face value is often thought of as the principle on a loan (i.e., the amount initially borrowed) that must be paid back at the end of the loan. In addition to this principle amount, borrowers have to make coupon payments on a bond; such coupon payments can be thought of as the interest that is paid beyond the principle to compensate the lender for making the loan. For zero coupon bonds, the face value on the bond represents both the initial amount borrowed and the interest (accumulated into the single final payment).

factor model: A statistical model that decomposes the return of an individual security in excess of the risk-free rate into three categories: a fixed or constant component, components due to variation in one or a set of common factors that (to varying degrees) affect all securities, and a component that is purely idiosyncratic to the security. For a specific individual security, the component due to variation in a specific common factor equals a coefficient that is specific to that individual security times the return on a portfolio that captures that common factor.

fixed-income security: Any security in which the issuer commits to make prespecified payments in the future (that is, future payments that are fixed). For example, a bond is a fixed-income security; the issuer is contractually obligated to make a series of coupon payments of a prespecified size at prespecified periods and a final payment of principle at maturity. A stock is not a fixed-income security because the issuing firm has discretion regarding the size and timing of dividend payments to the holder of the stock.

forward rate: A rate that specifies a breakeven interest rate for future short-term bond investments that would make an investor indifferent between making a series of short-term bond investments versus investing in a longer-term bond. For example, consider an investor who can either invest in a one-year bond and, at maturity on that bond, invest in a one-year bond next year or invest in a two-year bond. The forward rate is the rate for the one-year bond next year that would make the investor indifferent between these two strategies.

frequency distribution: A mathematical description of the probability associated with each possible value of a random variable. All the probabilities must sum to 1 because the frequency distribution provides a probability for every possible value of the random variable.

ndamental value: The value of a security based solely on its future cash ›ws and risk.

ıtures: A derivative security in which two parties agree to a future ansaction price on an underlying security or commodity.

azard rate: The probability of a default in a given year after issue, given ıat a default on that bond has not occurred up to that point in time.

olding period yield: The discount rate that, when used to discount the tream of payments an investor receives during the time in which that nvestor held (i.e., owned) the security (including the price received for the ecurity when sold), results in a present value equal to the value the investor nitially paid for the security. The holding period yield is the internal rate of eturn (IRR), given the cash flows received from a security during the period n which that security was held (i.e., during the "holding period").

human capital: The value of the personal skills, knowledge, and attributes that allows a person to generate future cash flows by supplying that person's labor.

idiosyncratic volatility: The variation in returns on an individual security of a firm that is due solely to changing conditions that affect only that firm. This volatility contrasts with systematic volatility that results from changes in common factors that affect (to varying degrees) all firms.

incremental: A generic term indicating the extra amount of one variable given an increase in some other variable that affects the first variable.

indirect utility of wealth function: Given a person's utility function defined on consumption bundles, the indirect utility of wealth function specifies the maximal level of utility a person can achieve as a function of wealth (i.e., the utility associated with the best consumption bundle that is affordable given that wealth level).

information ratio: The ratio of Jensen's alpha to the idiosyncratic volatility of a security or portfolio.

interest rate: The extra amount paid on a loan in excess of the initial amount borrowed as a percentage of the amount borrowed. Interest rates are typically quoted as the extra amount owed per year.

interest rate risk: The risk that changes in interest rates cause the return received by an investor to vary randomly.

internal rate of return (IRR): The internal rate of return is the single discount rate that, when applied to the projected future cash flows on an investment, makes the present value of these cash flows equal to the initial cost of the investment.

inverted yield curve: A yield curve that is downward sloping (i.e., the yields to maturity are lower for longer times to maturity).

Jensen's alpha: The difference between the expected return on a security and the return that is implied by an asset pricing model (typically CAPM).

Keynes's "animal spirits": A phrase used by John Maynard Keynes to describe how he thought investors behaved in stock markets. Keynes stated that investors' animal spirits—rather than unemotional deliberate thought—created changes in stock values.

Keynes's beauty contest: A fictitious game defined by John Maynard Keynes to describe stock markets. In the game, contestants are asked to identify (out of a set of photographs of people) who they think is the most beautiful. However, contestants only have a chance of winning if they pick the photograph that the other contestants picked most frequently. Thus, rather than picking the photograph of the person the contestant actually thinks is most beautiful, the contestant may pick the photograph of the person who that contestant thinks the most other people will pick as the photograph that the most others will pick.

ttice: The set of all possible paths the underlying security can take over ultiple periods in a binomial option pricing model.

verage: Using borrowed money to make investments.

verage-adjusted duration gap: The difference between the duration of a rm's assets and the product of the duration of the firm's liabilities and the tio of its liability value to total firm value. If the leverage-adjusted duration ap is zero, then the value of equity for the firm is insensitive to changes in iterest rate (or shifts in yield curves).

iabilities: Any promise to make a future payment that the firm sells in order o raise money for its activities. For example, a bond sold by a firm is a iability; an insurance policy that promises to make a specific payment when specific event (e.g., the death of a prespecified person) occurs for which the nsurance company receives a premium payment is also a liability.

liquidity: How quickly and cheaply a security can be exchanged for cash. A security is liquid if it can be sold quickly without having to lower the price. A less liquid security is one in which you either have to wait to find a buyer at a high price or you have to lower the price in order to induce someone to buy quickly.

long or **long position**: An investor is long or has a long position in a specific security if he or she owns that security.

lottery: Any situation in which the future value of wealth for an investor is random. The lottery is characterized by the set of possible wealth values and the probabilities associated with each. That is, a lottery is characterized by the frequency distribution over possible wealth values.

marginal: See **incremental**.

marginal utility of wealth: The extra amount of utility achieved given an increase in wealth. Mathematically, it is the derivative of the indirect utility of wealth function with respect to wealth.

market beta: A measure of risk for an individual security under the capital asset pricing model (CAPM). The market beta of an individual security is the ratio of the covariance of the return on the individual security and the return on the market portfolio to the variance of the return on the market portfolio.

market capitalization: The value of the outstanding shares of equity for a firm; equal to the price per share times the number of shares.

market clearing: A condition in a market whereby the price is such that the quantity supplied at that price equals the quantity demanded at that price.

market model: A single-factor model in which the single factor is the return on the market portfolio in excess of the risk-free rate.

market portfolio: The return on a value-weighted portfolio of all the traded securities in the market.

market price of risk: The return per unit of risk (as measured by the market beta) that investors in an economy receive.

momentum: A market is said to have momentum if a portfolio that is long past "winners" and short past "losers" generates a positive return on average, where "winners" are defined as securities that had relatively high returns (for example, in the top 10% of returns) and "losers" are defined as securities that had relatively low returns (for example, in the bottom 10% of returns).

mortality rate: The probability that a default on a bond will occur within a number of years since that bond's initial issue.

multi-factor model: A factor model in which there are multiple common factors. The arbitrage pricing theory is based on multi-factor models. An example of a multi-factor model is the Fama–French three-factor model, where the factors are the return in the market portfolio in excess of the risk-free rate, the return on a portfolio that is long high book-to-market firms and short low book-to-market firms (i.e., the so-called HML portfolio), and the return on a portfolio that is long small firms and short big firms (i.e., the so-called SMB portfolio).

t present value: The difference between the present value of the future sh flows of an investment or project and the cost required in the present riod to fund that investment/project. The net present value is the present lue of the value added from making that investment.

ormative analysis: A type of analysis in which the results are intended to ovide advice on how to optimally achieve a given goal or objective.

pportunity cost of capital: A measure of the cost associated with making n investment in a specific security or project rather than investing in vailable alternative securities or projects. The opportunity cost of capital is he return an investor (an individual or a firm) could obtain by investing in ecurities with characteristics (e.g., in terms of risk and liquidity) similar to hose of the specific security or project being considered.

ption: A financial contract between two parties in which one of the parties (the holder, or the owner of the option) has the right to do something specified by the contract. The holder has the option in the sense that the holder is not obligated to carry out the terms of the contract. Rather, if the holder does not want to do what is allowed by the contract, the holder can simply let the contract expire unexercised. The other party to the contract (the seller, or the writer of the contract), however, is obligated to honor the wishes of the holder.

passive management: The practice of adopting passive investment policies that entail holding well-diversified portfolios of securities that are not intended to outperform the market.

periodic rate: The effective rate for a period of a given length. If the periodic rate is 0.01 and the period is 1 month, then the monthly periodic rate is 0.01 (1%) and the 2-month periodic rate is $(1.01)^2 - 1 = 0.0201$ (2.01%).

perpetuity: A security that pays a fixed payment at even intervals into the infinite future.

positive analysis: A type of analysis in which a set of relationships between variables is posited and the implications of these posited relationships with respect to other variables of interest are derived.

present value: The equivalent value in the current (or present) period of a value or payment to be received in the future. If a person can earn an interest rate of r per period between the current and the future period, the present value (PV) of a future value (FV) t periods in the future is $PV = FV/(1 + r)^t$.

present value of growth opportunities: The present value of the stream of net present values associated with a firm's management making good investment decisions in the future.

price risk: The risk that when an investor sells a bond prior to maturity, the yields in the market at the time the bond is sold are such that the investor does not receive the bond's initial yield to maturity.

probability density function: Frequency distribution.

portfolio: A collection of securities, including those that can be traded quickly (e.g., stocks and bonds) and those that trade infrequently (e.g., housing and human capital). A portfolio is defined by both the set of securities in the portfolio and the relative amounts of money invested in each security.

put option: A financial contract that gives the holder of the option the right to sell an underlying security for the strike (or exercise) price on a prespecified date (or set of dates).

random variable: Any variable for which the outcome is uncertain.

random walk: A variable is said to follow a random walk if the changes in the variable from one period to the next are unpredictable, given the series of past changes in the variable. With a random walk, the expected value of the variable at the next period is equal to the current value (because the expected change in the variable is zero).

covery rate: The fraction of a bond's face value that is the price of that ›nd when a default has been announced. For example, if after a default is nounced the bond sells at $800 per $1000 in face value, the recovery rate 0.8 (or 80%).

einvestment risk: The risk that interest rates will fall by the time an ivestor needs to make an investment, causing future returns to be smaller ian expected.

egression: A statistical method for determining how a variable of nterest (the dependent variable) varies with a set of other variables (the ndependent variables).

equired rate of return: The minimum return an investor requires on an nvestment before that investor is willing to make that investment. The equired rate of return is equal to the opportunity cost of capital.

risk aversion: An aversion to random variation in wealth levels.

risk-free rate: The return on default-free bonds (e.g., U.S. Treasury securities) that mature at the end of an investor's short-term investment horizon.

risk neutrality: A person is risk neutral or has risk neutrality if he or she is indifferent between random distributions of wealth that have the same expected value but different variances.

risk-neutral probabilities: A set of probabilities that is consistent with a set of security prices under the assumption that the equilibrium is that which occurs when all market participants are risk neutral.

semi-strong-form market efficiency: A form of the efficient market hypothesis that stipulates that any information from past prices or returns and public announcements regarding the economy or the firm that can be used to predict the future values or cash flows of securities is reflected in the current price of the security. This implies that an investor cannot make excessive profits from trading based solely on public announcements; excessive profits are those in excess of what an investor should earn simply by bearing risk by investing. The semi-strong form is stronger (i.e., harder to satisfy) because it includes information stipulated to be reflected under the weak form plus public information. Also, because the hypotheses are nested, a rejection of the weak form is a rejection of the semi-strong form. However, a rejection of the semi-strong form (i.e., that some public information is not reflected in current prices) is not necessarily a rejection of the weak form (e.g., past returns and price information may be fully reflected).

Sharpe ratio or **measure**: A measure of the efficacy of a portfolio as the single risky portfolio for an investor to hold. It is calculated as the difference between the expected return on the portfolio and the risk-free rate divided by the standard deviation of the return on that portfolio. Thus, the Sharpe ratio for a portfolio is the extra return (in excess of the risk-free rate) per unit of risk (as measured by the return standard deviation) for that portfolio.

short or **short position**: An investor is short or has a short position in a specific security if he or she has borrowed the security and sold it.

short sale: A short sale is when a security is borrowed and then sold. The borrower/seller must return the borrowed security at some point in the future. If the price of the security rises, then the borrower must buy the security back at a higher price than he or she received when the security was sold, producing a loss; alternatively, by borrowing the security and selling it short, the borrower is borrowing money, with the borrowing cost per dollar borrowed equal to the return on the security borrowed. If the price of the security falls, then the borrower will be able to buy the security back (to return to the lender) at a lower price, thus generating a gain.

short-term investment horizon: The interval of time in which an investor is expected to maintain positions in most of the securities held in that investor's portfolio. At the end of this interval, the investor is likely to rebalance or alter the composition of his or her portfolio in response to new information.

gle-factor model: A factor model in which there is only one common ctor. The market model is an example of a single-factor model; the single mmon factor in the market model is the return on the market portfolio in cess of the risk-free rate.

ot rate: The rate or yield to maturity of a bond traded in the current market r delivery now.

tandard deviation: A measure of the variability of a random variable equal the square root of the random variable's variance.

tated annual rate: The periodic rate times the number of periods per year. 'or example, if the periodic rate is 0.01 and the period is 1 month, the stated nnual rate is $12 \times 0.01 = 0.12$ (or 12%). Note that if interest is compounded nonthly, then the effective annual rate is $(1.01)^{12} - 1 = 0.126825$ (or 2.6825%), which is greater than the stated rate. Also note that if a person vere to borrow $1 at a stated rate of 12% compounded monthly, then the periodic rate is $0.12/12 = 0.01$ and, after borrowing that dollar for a whole year, that person would have to pay back $(1 + (0.12/12))^{12} = \$1.126825$, for an effective annual interest cost of $0.126825 (or 12.6825% of the borrow dollar), which is the effective annual rate (not the stated rate).

strike price: See **exercise price**.

strong form market efficiency: A form of the efficient market hypothesis that stipulates that, in addition to the information stipulated to be reflected under the weak and semi-strong forms, any private information also can be reflected in current prices. This implies that even a corporate officer with inside information cannot make excessive profits by trading on this private information.

swap: A derivative security that specifies conditions under which one party can swap one security for another (including cash).

systematic volatility: The variation in the return on an individual security that is due to changing economy-wide conditions that affect all firms (to varying degrees).

term structure of interest rates: The relationships between the yields in a yield curve.

Treynor–Black model: A model in which an investor divides his or her portfolio into an active portfolio (comprised of securities that the investor thinks will generate abnormal returns) and a passive portfolio (consisting of a well-diversified portfolio).

Treynor measure: A measure of the return per unit of risk, where (rather than using the standard deviation of the portfolio as in the Sharpe ratio) the risk of the portfolio is measured by its market beta.

underlying security: The security (or commodity) that an option holder has the right to buy (for a call) or sell (for a put).

utility function: A mathematical description of the level of satisfaction a person achieves for a given consumption bundle. The numerical value of the utility function is said to represent a person's preferences over possible consumption bundles if, for every possible pair of consumption bundles, the numerical value of the utility function for the preferred bundle is larger than the numerical value of the utility function for the less preferred bundle. The utility function will produce equal numerical values when the person is indifferent between the two bundles.

value-weighted portfolio: A portfolio formed by holding a specific set of securities in proportion to the value of their market capitalizations.

weighted average cost of capital (WACC): The weighted average of the returns on each of the securities issued by a firm to finance its activities. The weighted average cost of capital is a measure of the firm's cost of capital; it is the return that an investor would receive if he or she were to hold all of the securities sold by a firm (e.g., stocks and bonds) in proportion to the securities market value relative to the firm value.

weak form market efficiency: A form of the efficient market hypothesis that stipulates that any information from past prices or returns that can be used to predict the future values or cash flows of securities is reflected in e current price of the security. This implies that an investor cannot make cessive profits from trading rules based solely on predictable patterns in turns or prices; excessive profits are those in excess of what an investor ould earn simply by bearing risk by investing.

ield to maturity: A measure of the return from holding a bond until aturity. The yield to maturity is the value of the discount rate that, when pplied to the cash flows from a bond, generate a present value equal to the urrent price of that bond.

ield curve: A plot of the yield to maturity (on the vertical axis) against the me to maturity (on the horizontal axis). This plot shows how the yields to aturity at a particular point in time vary by time to maturity.

ero coupon bond: A bond that has a coupon rate of zero; such a bond pays o coupons, paying only its face value at maturity.

variance: A measure of the uncertainty or unpredictability of a variable. The variance is the expected value of the squared deviations of the possible values of the variable from that variable's expected value.

volatility: The standard deviation of the return on a security.

Bibliography

Acharya, V. V., and L. H. Pedersen. "Asset Pricing with Liquidity Risk." *Journal of Financial Economics* 77 (2005): 375–410.

Amihud, Y. "Illiquidity and Stock Returns: Cross-Section and Time-Series Effects." *Journal of Financial Markets* 5 (2002): 31–56.

Amihud, Y., and H. Mendelson. "Asset Pricing and the Bid-Ask Spread." *Journal of Financial Economics* 15 (1986): 223–249.

———. "The Effect of Beta, Bid-Ask Spread, Residual Risk and Size on Stock Returns." *Journal of Finance* 44 (1989): 479–486.

Ang, A., R. Hodrick, Y. Xing, and X. Zhang. "The Cross-Section of Volatility and Expected Returns." *Journal of Finance* 61 (2006): 259–299.

———. "High Idiosyncratic Volatility and Low Returns: International and Further U.S. Evidence." *Journal of Financial Economics* 91, no. 1 (2009): 1–23.

Ariely, Dan. *Predictably Irrational, Revised and Expanded Edition: The Hidden Forces That Shape Our Decisions*. New York: Harper Perennial, 2010.

Barber, B., and T. Odean. "Trading Is Hazardous to Your Wealth: The Common Stock Investment Performance of Individual Investors." *Journal of Finance* 55 (2000): 773–806.

Bernstein, Peter L. *Capital Ideas: The Improbable Origins of Modern Wall Street*. New York: JohnWiley & Sons, 2005.

Bernstein, William J. *The Investor's Manifesto: Preparing for Prosperity, Armageddon, and Everything in Between*. Hoboken, NJ: Wiley, 2010.

attacharya, Utpal, Benjamin Loos, Steffen Meyer, Andreas Hackethal, d Simon Kaesler. "The Dark Side of ETFs and Index Funds." Working per, University of Indiana, Kelley School of Business.

odie, Zvi, Alex Kane, and Alan Marcus. *Essentials of Investments*. Boston: cGraw-Hill/Irwin, 2010.

ogle, John C. *Common Sense on Mutual Funds: Fully Updated 10th nniversary Edition*. Hoboken, NJ: Wiley, 2010.

———. *The Little Book of Common Sense Investing: The Only Way to Guarantee Your Fair Share of Stock Market Returns*. Hoboken, NJ: John Viley & Sons, 2007.

Brealey, Richard A., Stewart C. Myers, and Franklin Allen. *Principles of Corporate Finance*. Boston: McGraw-Hill/Irwin, 2008.

Burmeister, Edwin, Richard Roll, Stephen A. Ross, Edwin J. Elton, and Martin J. Gruber. *A Practitioner's Guide to Factor Models*. Charlottesville, VA: Research Foundation of the Institute of Chartered Financial Analysts, 1994.

Clement, Douglas. "Interview with Eugene Fama." *The Region*, December 1, 2007. http://www.minneapolisfed.org/publications_papers/pub_display.cfm?id=1134.

Conrad, J., and G. Kaul. "An Anatomy of Trading Strategies." *Review of Financial Studies* 11 (1998): 489–519.

Daniel, Kent, Mark Grinblatt, Sheridan Titman, and Russ Wermers. "Measuring Mutual Fund Performance with Characteristic-Based Benchmarks." *Journal of Finance* 52 (1997): 1035–1058.

Fabozzi, Frank. *Fixed Income Mathematics, 4E: Analytical & Statistical Techniques*. New York: McGraw-Hill, 2006.

Fama, Eugene F., and Kenneth R. French. "The CAPM is Wanted, Dead or Alive." *The Journal of Finance* 51, no. 5 (Dec. 1996): 1947–1958.

———. "The Cross-Section of Expected Stock Returns." *Journal of Finance* 48 (1992): 427–465.

———. "Multifactor Explanations of Asset Pricing Anomalies." *Journal of Finance* 51 (1996): 55–84.

Fama, E., and J. MacBeth. "Risk, Return and Equilibrium: Empirical Tests." *Journal of Political Economy* 81 (1973): 607–636.

Fox, Justin. *The Myth of the Rational Market: A History of Risk, Reward, and Delusion on Wall Street*. New York: Harper Collins, 2006.

Harris, Larry. *Trading and Exchanges: Market Microstructure for Practitioners*. Oxford: Oxford University Press, 2003. (Especially chapters 2 and 4 and part IV.)

Holt, Charles A., and Susan K. Laury. "Risk Aversion and Incentive Effects." *American Economic Review* 92, no. 5 (Dec. 2002): 1644–1655.

Hull, John C. *Options, Futures, and Other Derivatives*. 8th ed. Boston: Prentice Hall, 2011.

Jegadeesh, N., and S. Titman. "Profitability of Momentum Strategies: An Evaluation of Alternative Explanations." *Journal of Finance* 56 (2001): 699–720.

———. "Returns to Buying Winners and Selling Losers: Implications for Stock Market Efficiency." *Journal of Finance* 48 (1993): 65–91.

Jha, Siddhartha. *Interest Rate Markets: A Practical Approach to Fixed Income*. Hoboken, NJ: John Wiley, 2011.

ıhneman, Daniel. *Thinking, Fast and Slow*. 2011. New York: Farrar, Straus d Giroux, 2013.

reps, David M. *A Course in Microeconomic Theory*. Princeton, NJ: inceton University Press, 1990.

esmond, D. A., M. J. Schill, and C. Zhou. "The Illusory Nature of omentum Profits." *Journal of Financial Economics* 71 (2004): 349–380.

owenstein, Roger. *When Genius Failed: The Rise and Fall of Long-Term apital Management*. New York: Random House Trade Paperbacks, 2001.

Ialkiel, Burton G. *A Random Walk Down Wall Street: The Time-Tested trategy for Successful Investing*. 10th ed. New York: W. W. Norton & ompany, 2012.

Markowitz, H.M. "Portfolio Selection." *Journal of Finance* 7 (1952): 77–91.

McGrayne, Sharon Bertsch. *The Theory That Would Not Die: How Bayes' Rule Cracked the Enigma Code, Hunted Down Russian Submarines, and Emerged Triumphant from Two Centuries of Controversy*. New Haven, CT: Yale University Press, 2011.

Patterson, Scott. *Dark Pools: The Rise of the Machine Traders and the Rigging of the U.S. Stock Market*. New York: Crown Business, 2012.

Ross, Stephan A., Randolph W. Westerfield, Jeffrey F. Jaffe, and Bradford D. Jordan. *Corporate Finance: Core Principles and Applications*. New York: McGraw-Hill/ Irwin, 2011.

Sharpe, William F. "The Arithmetic of Active Management." *The Financial Analysts' Journal* 47, no. 1 (January/February 1991).

Smith, Donald. *Bond Math: The Theory behind the Formulas*. Hoboken, NJ: Wiley Finance, 2011.

Swensen, David F. *Pioneering Portfolio Management: An Unconventiona Approach to Institutional Investment*. New York: Free Press, 2009.

———. *Unconventional Success: A Fundamental Approach to Persona Investment*. New York: Free Press, 2005.

Taleb, Nassim Nicholas. *The Black Swan: The Impact of the Highly Improbable* [with a new section: *On Robustness and Fragility*]. New York: Random House, 2010.

Teall, John L. *Financial Trading and Investing*. Amsterdam: Academic Press, 2013.

Tuckman, Bruce, and Angel Serrat. *Fixed Income Securities: Tools for Today's Markets*. 3rd ed. Hoboken, NJ: Wiley Finance, 2012.

von Neumann, J., and O. Morgenstern. *Theory of Games and Economic Behavior*. 2nd ed. Princeton: Princeton University Press, 1947.

Notes

Notes